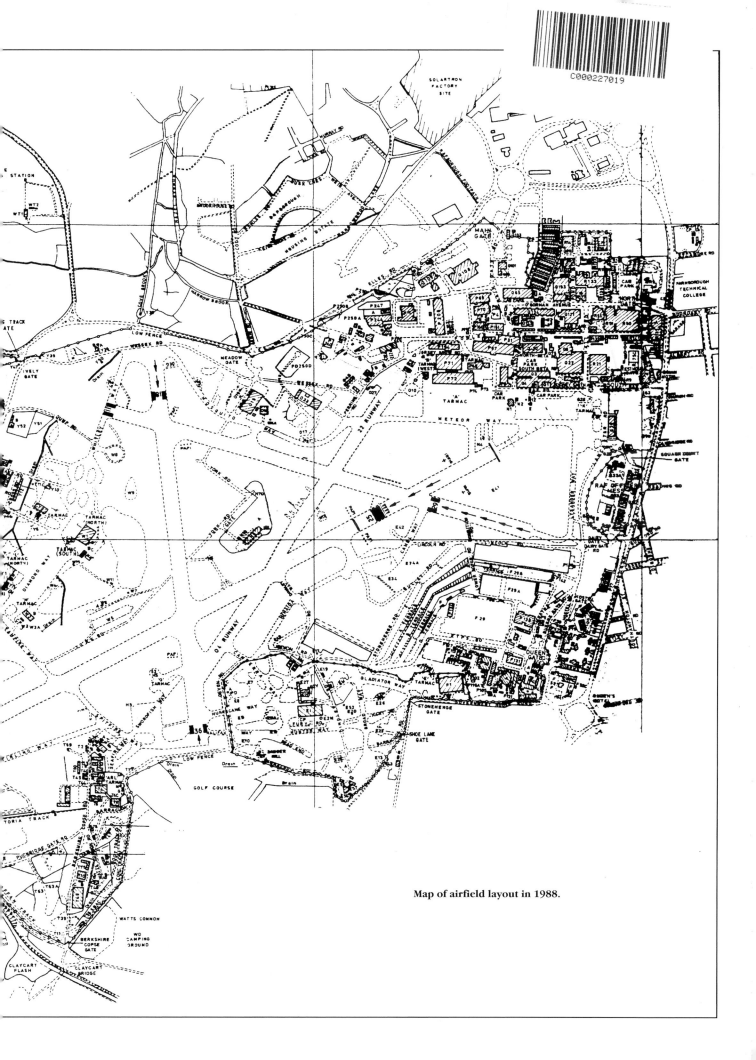

Map of airfield layout in 1988.

Farnborough

100 Years of British Aviation

Farnborough: 100 Years of British Aviation
© Peter J Cooper, 2006

ISBN (10) 1 85780 239 X
ISBN (13) 978 1 85780 239 9

Published by Midland Publishing
4 Watling Drive, Hinckley, LE10 3EY, England
Tel: 01455 254 490 Fax: 01455 254 495
E-mail: midlandbooks@compuserve.com

Midland Publishing is an imprint of
Ian Allan Publishing Ltd

Worldwide distribution (except North America):
Midland Counties Publications
4 Watling Drive, Hinckley, LE10 3EY, England
Tel: 01455 254 450 Fax: 01455 233 737
E-mail: midlandbooks@compuserve.com
www.midlandcountiessuperstore.com

North America trade distribution:
Specialty Press Publishers & Wholesalers Inc
39966 Grand Avenue
North Branch, MN 55056, USA
Tel: 651 277 1400 Fax: 651 277 1203
Toll free telephone: 800 895 4585
www.specialtypress.com

Design and concept
© 2006 Midland Publishing
Layout by Sue Bushell

Printed in England
by Ian Allan Printing Ltd
Riverdene Business Park, Molesey Road
Hersham, Surrey, KT12 4RG

Visit the Ian Allan Publishing website at:
www.ianallanpublishing.com

Farnborough

100 Years of British Aviation

Peter J Cooper

MIDLAND
An imprint of
Ian Allan Publishing

CONTENTS

GERALD HOWARTH MP
SHADOW DEFENCE MINISTER

HOUSE OF COMMONS

LONDON SW1A 0AA

Direct Line: 020 7219 5650
Fax: 020 7219 1198

Foreword

Farnborough: 100 Years of British Aviation

It is almost 10 years since Peter Cooper produced *Forever Farnborough* in which he recorded in great detail the history of Farnborough's development, richly illustrated with over 300 photographs.

At that time, in 1996, there was great uncertainty about the future of Farnborough aerodrome as the Ministry of Defence had declared it no longer needed it. All test flying had ceased in 1994 under the Defence Research Agency and in 1996 the re-named Defence Evaluation & Research Agency (DERA) was on the point of moving out of its historic buildings to a new, purpose-built site at the North-West end of the airfield. The future of the famous Air Show was also in doubt.

Since then, Farnborough has developed in a way few of us thought possible. TAG Aviation have in a very short space of time transformed the flying side into Europe's most prestigious executive aviation centre. Elegant new hangars and terminal building have been complemented by an award winning control tower. Slough Estates have built a superb business park and, thanks in part to the determined efforts of a band of volunteers in FAST, are investing £20 million in the preservation of the historic buildings. DERA has become QinetiQ, spreading its research wings across the Atlantic, and the Air Show continues.

As we approach the centenary of Samuel Cody's first flight from Farnborough's Laffan's Plain we are all indebted to Peter Cooper for his work. Not only has he produced a painstaking account of Farnborough's history, but he has also compiled a chronological, detailed account of the part played by Farnborough in the centenary of aviation, the iconic symbol of the 20th Century. He has provided all of us who love aviation with a truly valuable record.

Gerald Howarth MP
Member of Parliament for Aldershot & Shadow Defence Minister
1st March 2006

FROM THE COCKPIT

On first impressions, you could be forgiven for thinking that Farnborough is just like any other small British town. On deeper inspection, however, its true position in aviation heritage will be revealed for it was this humble Hampshire hamlet that gave birth to the entire British aircraft industry as we know it today. To the majority, the airfield will be famous for its SBAC displays that have gained a global aeronautical reputation. To others, it will be forever synonymous with the Royal Aircraft Establishment (RAE) that can lay claim to the development of aerial accomplishment to the highest order.

My family (the Coopers and Deans), have achieved 160-man-years at RAE between the years of 1914 and 1975, so it was hardly surprising that working at the RAE was considered the 'done thing'. I duly commenced a five-year Craft Apprenticeship in 1963 in the famous Apprentice Training Shop, this branching out into aircraft engineering after the first year, and eventually worked within 32 Department, (Experimental Aircraft Servicing); but it was long before this that my aviation interests began. Born in Farley House, the then-local hospital maternity wing off Church Road East and practically under the approach to Runway 25, aviation was a constant influence from a very early age. It seemed perfectly normal to look skyward as aircraft passed overhead when living along the Farnborough Road under the approach to Runway 29. Blame it on my father who used to point out all the different aircraft types, even when I was a mere toddler. This is exactly what happened with my son who is now the Editor of *Combat Aircraft* and Deputy Editor of *Aircraft Illustrated*, both leading Ian Allan Publishing magazine titles. Aircraft at Farnborough have been my lifetime passion and, with the majority of my life having been in the town, it has led to considerable knowledge being acquired since the mid-1950s.

My previous book *Forever Farnborough*, which covered flying from Farnborough between the years of 1904 and 1996 has sold out, but this, its sequel, covers the aviation achievements from this famous airfield in a chronological order covering its 10 decades of excellence.

Forever Farnborough contained 353 photographs, mainly from the vast and precious RAE/DERA photographic archives. However, during the research for this book, it became apparent that a number of photographic images have been destroyed over the years, having been unceremoniously declared no longer worth keeping. Indeed it is reported that some of the priceless glass plate negatives were smashed in the 1970s and used as part infill on airfield groundwork! Other images were similarly treated many years ago and particularly many of those from the 1920s/1930s were destroyed by those who thought they knew best at the time, resulting in large gaps in this era. Strange as it may seem, some of the well-known RAE aircraft, particularly of the 1950s right through to the 1970s, do not seem to have been photographed, or at least there is no record of them now. As a consequence, some images in this book have been sought from sources other than that of the previous RAE collection.

Many of the surviving glass photographic plates now show their age. The ravages of

The author, seen in the cockpit of his ex-RAE Canberra nose, B(I)6 WT309, at the FAST Museum. *Richard Cooper*

time have resulted in the emulsion on some older examples wearing away and others have been cracked or broken, requiring a digital repair. Another problem, of course, is that there are no longer any actual photographic printing services available within QinetiQ (or other outside processors for that matter) that can accommodate the glass plates – some as large as 12in x 10in, and very delicate. Consequently most of the images contained here have come from existing photographic prints, or from direct professional scans. Colour photographic work did not start being used until the 1960s and even then not much was taken in colour as all the reports issued by RAE contained black and white images. But colour there was and, although not everything was covered, we should be thankful for what is available and the collection gives a fine record of what was achieved and undertaken at Farnborough over the past 100 years. Due credit must go to the numerous photographers who covered the various topics, whether it be a retirement presentation, a fatigue failure in a piece of metal, or a then-secret installation deep inside an aircraft. Even with their large and cumbersome plate cameras, we would be poorly off without them today.

During research for this second Farnborough book, it became apparent that there were indeed many more interesting images available in the archives than I had previously seen. Some of these had been either erroneously recorded, or placed under what can only be described as obscure subjects, albeit subjects that would have undoubtedly made more sense to the photographers and 'boffins' of the time.

At this point during 2000, I (along with others) had made appropriate suggestions within DERA, and later QinetiQ, to lay the basis of the Farnborough Air Sciences Trust (FAST) obtaining the majority of these images for posterity. DERA were duty bound to involve both the MoD and the Public Records Office (PRO) in these negotiations. There then followed further discussions and official meetings where it was decided that a review and necessary culling of this vast collection was required. The PRO appointed the Imperial War Museum (IWM) to manage the collection's future retention policy and a team of appointed experts from FAST, myself included, reviewed the entire archive collection in 2002 where those negatives not required were culled and the remainder retained. Eventually some 30,000 of the earliest negatives were selected by the IWM and were transferred to its London headquarters, whilst the remaining 300,000 negatives were to be retained and managed by FAST and were removed from Pyestock's 415 building in 2002 and put into temporary storage. The images taken by the PRO/IWM would also be for public consumption, but retained as part of the Museum's National Archive.

The images retained by FAST, from the RAE/DERA negative archive, are now being catalogued for future use and these will be available for public access in due course. This is a demanding task that will take some time to complete. However, in the fullness of time, FAST will have a comprehensive record of what is available, as a unique photographic history of RAE Farnborough.

Needless to say the majority of images contained within this book are from the said archive, and credited to the FAST Collection as custodians of this vital piece of aviation history. Material for this book has been collected throughout the last 10 years and, where possible, I have endeavoured to show different images from those used in *Forever Farnborough*. It was, however, inevitable that some duplication would exist – particularly of those early years, where very little survives in terms of variety.

Information has come from many sources, including many of my own notes over the years, and also various reports, diary notes and issues of RAE News. Perhaps the most useful sources were the RAE Flight Books that recorded the experimental flying, at least up to the early 1950s, which served to prove in some cases that dates of aircraft movements have been incorrectly recorded elsewhere. There has been considerable checking and cross-referencing but sometimes accuracy cannot be substantiated, so please forgive me if any fellow aviation historians differ from what I have written. The recordings in this book have been done to the best of my knowledge, and others, at the time. Research for this project has been an immense task and I have not attempted to cover everything as this would probably result in at least four volumes! Therefore if you, the readers, were involved in a specific aircraft-related project that is not covered, then I would like to hear from you and will endeavour to include them in another book, yet to come, as I intend to cover more of the RAE aircraft, research and development in the future.

For now, I trust the content of *Farnborough – 100 years of Aviation* will appeal to you all in respect of its content and coverage and give an insight into what has been accomplished at Farnborough throughout the past 100 years. An airfield that is, without doubt, 'Nulli Secundus – Second to None'.

Enjoy!

Peter J Cooper

ACKNOWLEDGEMENTS

Compiling this book has been a long and sometimes difficult task. This has resulted in many hours of dedicated research, let along word-processing, and I wish to acknowledge the assistance and support my family have given me. Therefore sincere and heartfelt thanks go to my wife Dawne, Richard/Natalie, Clare/James, Lisa/Luke, for putting up with so much over the past two years, and having papers, books and photographs strewn throughout the house, notwithstanding some lack of attention to my two grandchildren Lily and Abe. There are other notable persons who have helped, especially my father Geoffrey Cooper for his memories of RAE and assistance over detail, my son Richard for his encouragement and editorial skills – it's sometimes not easy to listen to a son's point of view (but his expertise was essential), Patricia Norman for her endless late night and weekend word-processing sessions (to get the text into a readable format), Nigel Soane for his assistance in research for details and photographs, Maurice Shakespeare for his general assistance and encouragement, Jean Roberts for her intimate knowledge of the Cody era, Brian Kervell – the last curator of the RAE Museum – for his tireless accounts of historical interest and knowledge.

Others to who I am grateful for their assistance include: David Allen; Ann Bartaby; Les Batty; Tony Best; Paul Cooper; Paul Drane; Mike Draper; Tony Dudley; Gerry Allen; Eddie Fuller; Richard Gardner; Fin Gordon; Sid Hawkins; Gerald Howarth MP; Chris Kelleher; Tony Knight; Steven Lord; Neil McGow; Roger Marson; Ken Odgers; Helen Rawlings; Len Rayment; Lawrence Peskett; Dave Sherlock; Mike Slade; Richard Snell; Mark Taylor; Tony Thomas; Roger Walker; Simon Woodger; and all the airfield and engineering staff of TAG Aviation.

There are others I have probably missed, you know who you are, but many thanks for your help however little the information may have been.

May God bless you all.

Peter J Cooper

IN THE BEGINNING

Wilbur and Orville Wright accomplished man's ultimate goal near Kill Devil Hills at Kitty Hawk, NC, on 17th December 1903. Orville flew a distance of 852ft and became recognised as the first to experience powered flight. Man's quest to feel air beneath him had, however, been evident for many years before that landmark day.

In the late 1800s, balloons were becoming prevalent in Great Britain, where the Royal Engineers began experimenting with them at Woolwich, London, and later at Aldershot, Hampshire. The War Office directed Capt J L B Templer in 1878 to build a balloon for service use, the first ascent being made on 23rd August of that year. This then set the scene for the future, as the first School of Ballooning was established at Woolwich. What has this got to do with Farnborough you may ask? Well, it was in these humble beginnings that the Balloon Factory and its multi-titled successors have their roots.

Taking Flight
By this time a variety of balloons had been constructed and, in 1882, the school was moved to Chatham, Kent, where further development took place under Captain Templer, who later rose to the rank of Major and became an Instructor in Ballooning. The Balloon School built several successful balloons and it was the British Army military manoeuvres of 1889-1890 in Aldershot that gave the military hierarchy the thoughts of establishing a Balloon Section and moving the Balloon School to the Hampshire town, as this is where most of the balloons would be operated. So in 1892 the Balloon School moved to Aldershot, under the command of Major Templer, and took up residence in the Stanhope Lines within the Royal Engineers base that had been established at South Camp. This was located on the southern bank of the Basingstoke Canal near what is now the Airborne Forces Museum. A large (for the period) balloon shed was constructed in 1892 for the production and

housing of the balloons (and it was this shed that would be later moved to Farnborough).

Meanwhile, nearby Pirbright Common had been the location of experiments for man-lifting kites by Capt B F S Baden-Powell in 1894. Further experiments with these were undertaken at the Balloon School, with the incorporation of a man-lifting kite section, and additional flight trials followed on nearby Laffan's Plain where kites were used to good effect by the Army during manoeuvres.

With many more different types of balloons being built, it was decided to rename the school as the Balloon Factory, this occurring on 1st April 1897, with Lt Col Templer, as he now was, naturally being appointed the Superintendent.

Templer had been dispatched to the Boer War in South Africa, holding the rank of Colonel, and returned to Aldershot in 1901 to continue as Superintendent of the Balloon Factory. Having gained experience where balloons had been successfully employed in a war scenario, his attention was now turned to dirigibles. He gained permission from the War Office to commence non-rigid airship experiments and the con-

Army balloon, seen at Aldershot circa 1900, with the Balloon shed in the background. It was this shed that was transferred with the Balloon Factory to Farnborough in 1905.
Drachen Foundation via Jean Roberts

struction of an envelope of some 50,000ft³ was begun. However, due to construction problems and a lack of funds, the project was shelved. The Balloon Factory was ordered to maintain balloon activities and cease from peripheral operations, although airships and man-lifting kites were deemed acceptable.

Due to cramped conditions, the Balloon Factory was relocated to new premises in 1904 at what became known as Balloon Square, still in Aldershot. Here more space was available for the construction and testing of balloons, and possibly, eventually, airships. The search for a new and permanent venue continued, as conditions at Balloon Square were still not ideal for further expansion and, after lengthy deliberations on various possible locations throughout southern England, it was decided to move the Balloon School to a new site at South Farnborough, just off the main Farnham to Bagshot Road (now the A325), on the eastern edge of what was then known as Farnborough Common.

A little earlier, the year 1890 had become possibly one of the most important for British aviation as that was the year that a certain Samuel F Cody arrived on these shores. An American native born in Davenport, Iowa, in 1867 as Franklin Cowdery, this early entrepreneur had been building kites since 1900 and had succeeded in persuading the War Office that such contraptions had a future for aerial reconnaissance activities. Successful demonstrations were given to the Royal Navy in 1903. Cody came to Aldershot on 6th June 1904 and during that month undertook some very successful kite demonstrations with the Royal Engineers on Laffan's Plain. Cody's work later continued, with Cody as Instructor of Kiting, from April 1906, at the Balloon School after it was relocated to Farnborough, and further kite experiments were undertaken. Cody would later turn his attention to powered flight in a heavier-than-air aeroplane and the rest, as they say, is history.

Flying Foundation
So it was that, during the cold winter of 1904/05, the Balloon School had moved in to its new site and the balloon shed, gasholder and hydrogen production plant,

were all moved to this new location, which became fully functional in 1906. It is this historic milestone that eventually led to Farnborough becoming the centre of aviation in the United Kingdom for the next 90 years, in respect of experimental and research flying and associated activities. This indeed continues today within QinetiQ, at its Farnborough Headquarters, in respect of its prominent research and development activities throughout the aviation and space technological fields on behalf of the UK government and private companies alike.

Things have since moved on – no longer are weird and wonderful jets, turboprops, piston aircraft and helicopters pounding the airfield circuit, as research flying ceased in 1994. There is a new style to this, the oldest aerodrome in the United Kingdom, with massive changes having taken place since 2000. It has been transformed into a modern high-tech, state-of-the-art, business aviation centre, with the MoD assigning a 99-year lease to TAG Aviation, Europe's largest and leading business jet company.

So Farnborough has seen much through those 100 years of excellence – changes in technology, design, build, research and experimentation, the likes of which will never be seen in the UK again. Naturally, change comes at a price. The demise of the Royal Aircraft Establishment as the world

knew it and the downsizing in aircraft, laboratories and facilities took its toll, so much so that the old RAE Factory site was no longer needed and much of this was demolished in 2000-2001 to make way for a new high-tech Business Park, which continues under construction and development today by Slough Estates International.

Notwithstanding the work being undertaken on the old Factory Site, the 90ft-high, 24ft wind tunnel and clock tower (a Farnborough landmark since 1935) is still extant and, along with other significant buildings, is Grade I listed for preservation. This is where the Farnborough Air Sciences Trust (FAST) came into play 13 years ago, to promote the history of this important site and endeavour to safeguard many of the old buildings and artefacts from those formative days of yesteryear. The goal is to retain them for future generations to learn about the activities at Farnborough – from the early balloon and airship flying, through the birth of powered flight in the UK, to the technological excellence of today. Thus, the cradle of British military aviation and its legacy of research and development has resulted in Farnborough being recognised throughout the world as a centre of excellence and a place of historic significance in the global sphere of aviation… a hundred years in the making.

Man-lifting kite with a party of Royal Engineers on Laffan's Plain, during manoeuvres circa 1904. *FAST collection*

Man-lifting kite ascending from Balloon Square in Aldershot in 1904. *FAST collection*

1905 to 1914

From Balloons to Aeroplanes

Up to 1905 the site of Farnborough Common was just that, common land leading westward from the area of what is now the A325 road and The Swan public house to Laffan's Plain a mile and a half away. This was all about to change as Farnborough made the first steps in becoming a household name that would remain forever synonymous with aviation. This decade saw the first military airship produced at Farnborough, followed by the first

sustained powered flight in Britain, and ended in the midst of World War One with aircraft production for the Royal Flying Corps and experimentation moving on apace.

1905

Towards the end of 1904 and throughout the winter of 1905, the Balloon Factory moved from nearby Aldershot to its new site at South Farnborough, on Farnborough Common,

into what is now the northeastern edge of the present airfield. The balloon shed, gasholder and hydrogen production plant were dismantled and moved to the site, with the re-erection of same being completed by 1906. Work continued on the new site with design and construction of balloons and airships.

The eccentric Samuel Franklin Cody, an American born in Davenport, Iowa, in 1867 as Franklin Cowdery, had firmly become part of the local scene. He had been busy building kites in England since the turn of the century and in 1903 had succeeded in interesting the War Office in his kites for use as aerial reconnaissance platforms. One of these entrepreneurial designs included the biplane glider kite, which Cody had flown at Long Valley in 1905 whilst lying in the forward (prone) position on the lower wing. During the previous year (1904), Cody had conducted a series of kite experiments at Aldershot for Col J E Capper RE, which resulted in the recommendation to the Royal Engineers that Cody's kites be introduced into service.

The first building to be constructed at the new Farnborough site in 1904/1905 was a large airship shed (160ft long, 82ft wide and 72ft high), which was followed by an access road and then the re-erection of the buildings removed from Aldershot. The original balloon shed, with a workshop and stores, was re-erected alongside the main airship shed.

1906

By now the Balloon Factory had become fully operational and S F Cody was appointed 'Chief Instructor of Kiting' to the Balloon School and his man-lifting kite experiments continued on nearby Laffan's Plain. Work now re-commenced on a non-rigid airship and Cody, along with Col Capper, now Superintendent of the Balloon Factory and Commandant of the Balloon School, started

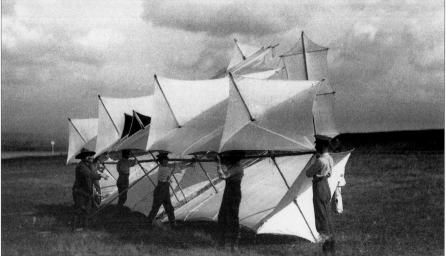

A party of Royal Engineers are preparing to inflate an Army balloon at the Balloon Factory, Farnborough during 1905. Note the protective screen beyond, sheltering them from the wind. *FAST collection*

S F Cody, seen instructing the Royal Engineers on assembly of a glider kite on Farnborough Common in 1905. *Drachen Foundation via Jean Roberts*

During 1907, construction of Army Aeroplane No 1 was started in the Balloon Factory Beta shed. Here S F Cody, seen holding the undercarriage at right, inspects the progress, whilst female workers at the factory sew together the fabric covering. *FAST collection*

its design and construction. The Balloon Factory was given authority to purchase an Antoinette V-8 engine of 50hp for the new airship, which was to be known as the *Nulli Secundus* (Second to None). The original envelope of the airship consisted of hemispherical ends that were previously made at the Aldershot site in 1904, but shelved.

The first Farnborough wind tunnel was built within the Airship Shed, being completed on 14th December 1906. This was a basic wooden framework covered in canvas, which had wallpaper pasted onto it to make it airtight, the section being 6ft 6in square and about 50ft long. The first experiments conducted were the resistances of various struts and fairings for airships and the early aeroplanes. Although this was a very primitive form of wind-tunnel aerodynamics (compared to today's standards) with only basic results being achieved, it remained in use for the next 10 years or so and paved the way for Farnborough's future aerodynamic research in various tunnels, its legacy continuing to this day with the QinetiQ 5-metre tunnel on the other side of the airfield.

1907

Construction work continued on Britain's first military airship and 10th September 1907 saw the first flight of the *Nulli Secundus*, powered by an Antoinette 50hp engine. Col Capper, Samuel Cody and Capt W A de C King, the latter being the Chief Instructor in Ballooning, were on board but this inaugural flight was cut short by engine problems. Further flights also occurred and, on 5th October, *Nulli Secundus* took off for a flight over London, which included Buckingham Palace, Whitehall, The Strand and St Paul's Cathedral. A freshening wind prevented its return to Farnborough and, after 3hr 20min flying time and covering 50 miles, the airship landed at Crystal Palace, thus terminating the already record-breaking flight. Unfortunately on 10th October, while still at Crystal Palace, the envelope was being battered in deteriorating weather conditions and was intentionally slit to prevent the airship breaking free from its moor-

ings. It eventually returned to Farnborough by road where a rebuild was commenced in the factory, this time with a semi-rigid structure, and the rejuvenated airship was to be called *Nulli Secundus II*.

King Edward VII was the first monarch to visit the Balloon Factory, which may have been at the time of the naming of *Nulli Secundus*, as this name was shared with one of the King's favourite racehorses.

Meanwhile, Lt J W Dunne had arrived at the factory in 1906 and had built his own experimental glider, known as the D1, which underwent secret tests at Glen Tilt near Blair Atholl in Scotland. Following a crash, the glider was converted to a powered glider, now known as the D1B, although it was further damaged and did not fly again.

By now Farnborough had become a renowned centre for balloon and airship production and experimentation, and was firmly rooted in the earliest forms of aerodynamics. Cody continued to show his spirit. Determined to make a powered flight, he had actually commenced the building of his own 'Army Aeroplane No 1' within the Balloon Factory airship shed. The man had also succeeded in producing a powered kite with a Buchet 12hp, three-cylinder engine, which was flown along a long wire supported between two poles, one a ship's mast acquired from Portsmouth, erected 300 yards apart outside of the airship shed on Farnborough Common. It is reputed that a free flight was also made, but this has never been substantiated.

Making her first flight after rebuild on 24th July 1908, *Nulli Secundus II* is seen here on Farnborough Common with a huge crowd of onlookers, which actually made launch of the airship rather difficult. After her third flight on 15th August, she was dismantled and no further flying was undertaken. *via Jean Roberts*

1908

On 1st April, in recognition of its various achievements and status, the Balloon Factory was renamed His Majesty's Balloon Factory, thus commencing the Royal association with Farnborough that lasted until 1991, although Royal was not used in the name until 1912.

Nulli Secundus II undertook its maiden flight on 24th July 1908, but the rebuilt airship was considered unstable and, after two further flights on 14th and 15th August, it was dismantled with no further flying undertaken.

Cody had now completed his aeroplane and short hops were made during September, which led to his becoming very enthu-siastic and yearning to make a 'proper' flight. Some modifications were made to the aeroplane before it was rolled out again on 14th October.

Then came arguably the most significant happening of the UK's foray into the heav-ens, as it was this year that Samuel F Cody successfully completed the first 'heavier than air' powered flight in the British Isles. So it was that, on 16th October 1908, Cody took off from Farnborough Common in his 'Army Aeroplane No 1', powered by an Antoinette 50hp engine. The flight started from the Swan Inn plateau, close to where the No 1 RFC (later RAF) Mess was built in 1914, and headed in a northwest direction. He achieved a distance of some 1,390ft before he crashed on Farnborough Com-mon when the tip of his port wing struck the ground whilst trying to avoid a clump of trees. Cody was uninjured and parts of the aircraft were used in the construction of the next aeroplane. Undeterred by his crash, Cody bounced back with further flights in 1909, (by January his aircraft had been rebuilt as the Cody Aeroplane 1B), and he had become the first test pilot at Farnbor-ough – his monumental achievement heralding him as the father of powered flight in the UK.

It is worthy of mention here that A V Roe had also developed a biplane, known as the 'Roe 1'. On 8th June he succeeded in rising from the ground at Brooklands, but it was not considered to be of enough distance to constitute a free flight.

Little would Cody have realised at the time – neither would the Wright brothers with their Wright Flyer those five years ear-lier – the far-reaching consequences of what would be accomplished in the years follow-

S F Cody is seen here, airborne, at the start of the first sustained powered flight in Great Britain in his Army Aeroplane No 1 on 16th October 1908. A distance of 1,390ft (423.7m) was covered before a crash-landing when his port wingtip struck the ground whilst trying to avoid a clump of trees. *FAST collection*

Army Aeroplane No 1 looks a sorry sight after its accident. The aircraft was returned to the Balloon Factory and rebuilt as the Cody Aeroplane 1B. *FAST collection*

The path of Cody's epic first flight is overlaid on this view of the Royal Aircraft Establishment at the eastern end of the aerodrome, taken during the summer of 1954. *FAST collection*

ing their epic achievements. The aeroplane has evolved in leaps and bounds from the humble beginnings of, at least as far as the UK is concerned, 'Army Aeroplane No 1'.

1909

Despite the success of powered flight, the UK War Office decreed that aircraft production and development should cease at Farnborough and in March the employment of Cody and Dunne was terminated. A short-sighted decision this, as Cody was given permission by His Majesty's Principal Secretary of State for the War Department on 21st October 1910, to erect a shed on Laffan's Plain (75ft x 42ft, and 800ft to the north of Eelmoor Flash on the nearby Basingstoke Canal), where he conducted further experiments and constructed additional aircraft. These would prove to be a great success over the next few years.

Cody's completed land leasing document was sent by Maj A Bannerman, The Commandant Air Battalion RE, and dated 7th September 1911. A clause within the Licence Agreement document states 'The Licensee (ie Cody) shall pay to the Secretary of State in respect of the land which he is by this licence permitted to enclose the rent or sum of £8 (eight pounds) per annum on the 1st day of January in every year during the continuance of this agreement etc'. Dunne, meanwhile, had formed his own company at Eastchurch, where further successful aircraft were produced.

Flight trials of 'Cody Aeroplane 1B' continued and many more successful flights were accomplished. Long streamers had been attached to the inter-plane struts, to gain airflow pattern experience. The Cody 1C Cathedral was the next aeroplane built and flew in August 1909 and Col Capper became the first passenger in a heavier-than-air machine on 14th August 1909. That date saw a flurry of activity at Laffan's Plain as Lela, Cody's wife, became the first woman passenger in the UK when she flew with her husband in the Cathedral on the same day.

The War Office stated in April of this year that all aeroplane experiments by His Majesty's Balloon Factory were officially ended, as there was no future for them. Thankfully, this proved short-lived – it only took a year before the decision was reversed.

Donated by Hon C S Rolls, this Wright biplane was the first aeroplane taken on charge by the War Office. It is seen here outside the Balloon shed in January 1910, but it did not fly at Farnborough.
FAST collection

The Balloon School now acquired its first aeroplane – a Wright Biplane that was donated by Hon C S Rolls, a co-founder of the Rolls-Royce company. This was in fact the very first military aeroplane taken on strength by the War Office. It appears that this aircraft did not fly at Farnborough and eventually went to Hounslow Barracks. The Balloon School also ordered Farman and Paulhan aircraft, of French origin, which were duly delivered in 1911.

Work on airships and balloons continued in His Majesty's Balloon Factory with the construction of Dirigible No 3, which was sized at 21,000ft³. Later named *Baby,* this effort was constructed of streamlined gold beaters' skin and was first flown on 4th May 1909, powered by two Buchet 12hp engines. These were later replaced with a single REP engine of 25hp and further modifications saw a lengthening of the envelope and the installation of a 35hp Green engine. In this

guise *Baby* was renamed *Beta* and made its first flight as such on 26th May 1910.

October saw Mervyn O'Gorman appointed as Superintendent of His Majesty's Balloon Factory, he being the first civilian to take this post. Up to this time the workforce of the Balloon Factory consisted of some 50 personnel and included a small machine shop, one large shed for the manufacture of balloons, one airship shed, a workshop and fabric shop, drawing office, stores, accounts and administration departments. Much reorganisation of the facilities took place under O'Gorman and design, construction and flying of airships for the Army continued.

Q27 Building, as it was latterly known, was built during this year for the Balloon Factory but by the time it was added to and completed in 1912 it was already being used

for Airship gondola construction and the production of aeroplanes.

1910

The airship *Gamma* of 75,000ft³ was powered by an 80hp Green engine that drove two counter-rotating propellers and first flew on 10th December 1910. The airship was later damaged and was rebuilt in 1912 as *Gamma II*, with two Iris 45hp engines, and made its first flight after rebuild on 10th September 1912. A French-built airship, the *Lebaudy* weighing in at the much larger size of 350,000ft³, arrived at Farnborough on 26th October 1910 for demonstrations to the Balloon Factory. After arrival, the ground handlers tried to place it in the large airship shed but the envelope snagged on the structure and was torn, thus it collapsed from the escaping hydro-

gen and fell on the handling party. *Lebaudy* was rebuilt and flew again only to be damaged beyond repair during 1911. Meanwhile construction of the fourth Farnborough airship, known as the *Delta*, was started. This was to be powered by two White & Poppe 110hp engines. *Beta* (of 35,000ft³) first flew on 26th May 1910 initially powered by a 35hp Green engine, only to be later rebuilt in 1912.

Elsewhere, a certain Geoffrey de Havilland flew for the first time on 10th September in what was in fact the second of his self-designed aeroplanes. The flight, in the 45hp Iris-powered de Havilland Biplane No 2, took place at Seven Barrows near Newbury. The first design (the de Havilland Biplane No 1) suffered a structural failure that resulted in a crash during take-off in December 1909. The successful machine was purchased by the Balloon Factory for £400 in December and became the first Farnborough aeroplane, becoming known as the F.E.1 (Farman Experimental No 1). At this time Geoffrey de Havilland joined the Factory as designer and test pilot.

Queen Mary visited the Factory during this year, accompanied by Lord Kitchener, and was shown the various projects under way, perfectly illustrating the importance of the work that was now being undertaken.

During October the War Office announced that His Majesty's Balloon Factory should be enlarged to repair and maintain the Balloon School aeroplanes. The Balloon School had also been instructed to develop training aircraft and dirigibles. A Henri Farman was purchased by the War Office and was handed over in France on 26th November for arrival at Farnborough in December.

In order to assist in the growing concerns over the scientific methods of aircraft design and construction, F M Green was drafted in; he also assisted in development of the R.A.F. series of engines.

Another particularly notable success of the time was the Cody IIA Flyer, which was finished in June 1910 and flew with a 60hp Green engine. This aeroplane was modified

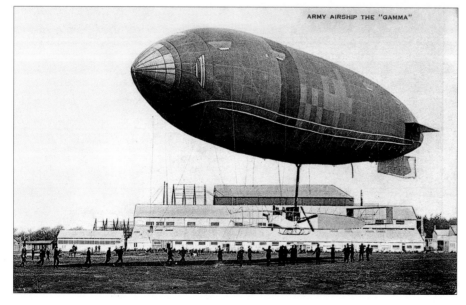

Geoffrey de Havilland flew his second aeroplane for the first time on 10th September 1910. It came to the Balloon Factory and became the first Farnborough aeroplane, known as the F.E.1. It is seen here on Farnborough Common during 1910. *FAST collection*

into a IIB and then a IIC variant by Cody and it was in this latter guise that he won the prestigious British Empire Michelin Cup on 31st December 1910. Cody sustained flight in his IIC aeroplane from Farnborough for 4hr 47min, covering a distance of 189.2 miles. He was thus awarded the Michelin Cup and a cash prize of £500 for the longest distance flown within a closed circuit before the year had ended. Further trophies and successes would follow over the next two years.

G1 Building (which is today the Headquarters of the Farnborough Air Sciences Trust and Museum) was built for the Royal Engineers Balloon School during this time, the School having been separated from the Factory in 1908. This building is the oldest

surviving aeronautical structure in the United Kingdom and is now Grade II* listed.

An early form of apprenticeship was commenced by the Balloon Factory, which served to teach young lads the basis of aeronautical skills. In 1916 evening classes were commenced to broaden their knowledge, but it was not until 1918 that this scheme was put on a properly organised basis.

1911

Capt Burke took to the air in Farnborough's Farman on 7th January but it also crashed later this day (its second flight) when the right wing impacted the ground heavily. It was rebuilt as a 'new' machine and flew again on 6th March with Geoffrey de Havilland at the controls. It also suffered further damage and was repaired again before

CODY'S TREE

In those early days, legend has it that Cody had tied his aeroplane to a tree in order to measure the thrust of the engine and to secure it in high winds. Indeed, a plaque placed on the tree after World War One read 'This tree was used as a picket for the Aeroplanes belonging to Colonel Cody. A pioneer in Aviation. During the year 1911' and this plaque lasted until c1950. The tree had finally died around 1940, probably due to oil spillage or ingress, even though railings had been erected around it in the mid-1930s. Positioned off Lysander Way in front of the 'Black Sheds' (G29 building), the original Royal Flying Corps hangars, this tree became famous as an icon of Farnborough and moves were put in place to preserve its posterity even at this early stage. Due to the eventual rotting of the tree's wood, it was decided in 1949 that a concrete plinth was to be cast around it and more substantial railings put in place. The feasibility of impregnating the tree with resin was considered and then sanctioned, and it was dismantled in 1953 to be filled with resin and put back together again by use of steel rods and coach bolts. It was accordingly re-erected on the site during mid-1953 and surrounded by a further high fence. The surface of the tree was treated with seaplane varnish. However this was not to last for too long, as it was further decided to produce a metal facsimile, which was undertaken by the RAE Foundry in 1959. The resultant re-erection looked much as it had done previously, but it would now be able to withstand all the elements, without rotting or requiring any further impregnation. It remained on the spot until it was moved to the

This 1953 view shows the reinstalled Cody's Tree, surrounded by a high fence, with the RAE buildings and control tower beyond. *FAST collection*

new Defence Evaluation Research Agency (DERA) Headquarters site on 23rd July 1996 and is displayed outside the main entrance to the now-QinetiQ Headquarters 'Cody Building', located within the aptly named Cody Technology Park. A concrete embossed image of the tree, and commemorative plaque, lies on the original site today, adjacent to the black sheds and Lysander Way, which reads: 'S F Cody measured the thrust of his first aeroplane in 1908-9 by tying it to a tree which stood here. Nearby he made his first tests with his powered aeroplane on 16th May 1908 and his first flight of 1,390ft on 16th October 1908 – the first sustained aeroplane flight in Great Britain.'

The plaques on Cody's tree today read 'S F Cody measured the thrust of his first aeroplane in 1908-9, by tying it to a tree. His first tests with his powered aeroplane were made on 16th May 1908. His flight of 1,390ft on 16th October 1908 was the first sustained aeroplane flight in Great Britain. A plaque marks the original position of the tree'. Furthermore, 'This plaque was unveiled on 26th November 1996 by Cllr Maurice Banner, Mayor of Rushmoor, to mark the relocation of Cody's Tree'.

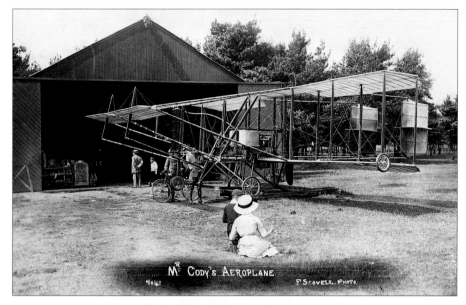

Mr. CODY'S AEROPLANE

Cody III Circuit of Britain aeroplane, seen outside Cody's shed on Laffan's Plain during 1911. The aircraft eventually crashed and was written off on 3rd July 1912. *FAST collection*

The B.E.1, known as the 'silent Army aeroplane', first flew on 4th December 1911 and is seen here on Farnborough Common. The B.E.1 went on to serve with the Royal Flying Corps. *FAST collection*

The airship *Beta* had continued operations with the Balloon School but had been damaged and was later rebuilt as *Beta I*, with a 50hp Clerget engine, and made its first flight as such on 12th September 1912 before being handed over to the Royal Naval Air Service on 1st January 1914 as HM Airship No 17. The *Lebaudy* airship experienced difficulties during landing on 4th May 1911 and, when control was lost, it was driven by the prevailing wind across Farnborough Common, over the road running from Farnborough to Farnham (now the A325), then collapsed upon Woodlands Cottage, still with the engines running, after the trailing mooring ropes had snagged in the trees. The airship was totally wrecked and was not repaired. This airship had also been known as the *Morning Post* as it had been purchased from France with funds raised by the readers of this newspaper of the time. As for Woodlands Cottage, it was demolished in the late-1960s to make way for the new Farnborough telephone exchange.

Around this time early radio equipment trials were undertaken by the *Beta* airship for transmission and receiving of radio signals from a ground station located at the Factory.

Geoffrey de Havilland had established himself as quite a proficient test pilot for His Majesty's Balloon Factory, literally learning as he went. Lt Theodore John Ridge, the factory's Assistant Superintendent, learnt to fly on the F.E.1, but the aircraft suffered an accident on 15th August 1911 and was not repaired. Parts were supposedly used for the build of the F.E.2 but this had already been completed at the time of the demise of the F.E.1. Thus the first F.E.2 (No 604), made its initial flight on 16th August 1911, powered by a 50hp Gnome rotary engine, with de Havilland as pilot. On 14th April 1912 the F.E.2 was flown to nearby Fleet Pond, landed on the bank, and was fitted with floats. Trials of this 'Hydro-Aeroplane' were conducted on the pond where a number of water take-offs and landings were made, with further waterborne flights on 27th and 29th April. It was returned to standard undercarriage configuration and was later fitted with a .303 machine gun in the nose. A second F.E.2 (later also to become No 604) was built in the factory workshops during 1913, being a slightly different

being transferred to Larkhill. A single Paulhan was purchased in France from the factory at Buc and was handed over to the War Office on 11th January, for arrival at Farnborough on 25th February. It first flew in the UK on 1st May, though crashed on 5th May due to a sideslip that resulted in a crumpled wing from a heavy ground impact. It too was repaired and flew again on 7th July 1911.

During the first few months of 1911, Cody himself had managed to modify the IIC Flyer into a IID version and continued to fly passengers from Laffan's Plain. The IID was re-engined with a 120hp Austro-Daimler, becoming the Cody Omnibus IIE, but this crashed in April 1912 and was not rebuilt. The next machine to emerge from Cody's shed was the Cody III Circuit of Britain aeroplane, which first flew on 13th July 1911 and was entered into the Daily Mail Circuit of Great Britain Race that was staged between 22nd July and 5th August. Cody actually finished fourth and 10 days behind the winner! This aeroplane was also entered into the Michelin Trophy and flew 377 miles on 11th September and 261.5 miles (closed circuit) on 29th October.

Aeroplane construction had now commenced at the Balloon Factory, this leading to many prototype designs, some of which led to full-scale production whilst others never left the drawing board. However at this stage the factory had not been given official permission to allow the design and production of its own types.

The first day of April saw the Royal Engineers Balloon Section become known as No 1 (Airship) Company Air Battalion Royal Engineers, which was later to become No 1 Squadron RFC in 1912. On 26th April the factory was renamed as His Majesty's Aircraft Factory but was generally referred to as the Army Aircraft Factory, as originated by Mervyn O'Gorman. The emergence of the Army Aircraft Factory presented its own huge challenges in that there was no aircraft industry outside of what was going on at Farnborough and the learning curve was indeed steep. Little was known about aerodynamics or even the general flight envelope, but the factory designers, engineers and pilots forged ahead, learning as they went, sometimes literally 'by the seat of their pants'.

design, and was fitted with a 70hp Renault V-8 engine but the aircraft crashed on 23rd February 1914 and was not rebuilt.

Completed during October, the B.E.1 No 201, which was a total remanufacture of a Voisin biplane, made its first flight on 4th December with Geoffrey de Havilland at the controls. This aeroplane was used for much development work and also served with the RFC until at least 1916.

A damaged Bleriot XII arrived at the Balloon Factory for a repair in late 1910, and authority had been given to reconstruct it during 1911, which resulted in the S.E.1 – the factory's first design. It bore little resemblance to its original design, although the same 60hp ENV engine as used in the Bleriot powered it. The S.E.1 was first flown on 8th June 1911, but required some modification. On 18th August, Lt Ridge took the aircraft up for the first time, but during a slide-slip and sharp turn, it crashed on Farnborough Common, unfortunately killing Ridge. A plaque to commemorate Ridge and his achievements was originally placed in Queens Road Baptist Church at Farnborough, where he had previously been a lay preacher, but since 1984 it has been in the possession of the British Balloon Museum. The plaque reads: 'To the glory of God and in memory of Theodore John Ridge, who served as a Private in the 34th Company (Middlesex) I.Y. in South Africa, 1900; and who was later a Lt in the London Balloon Corps. He lost his life on 18th August 1911, in the 36th year of his age, on Farnborough Common, in an accident to an aeroplane of the Royal Army. This tablet is erected by comrades of the 34th'.

1912

Aircraft production was now really accelerating within the Army Aircraft Factory, as well as the continuation of reconstruction work. The B.E.2 (No 601) made its first flight on 1st February, with Geoffrey de Havilland as pilot, and on 1st May it was fitted with floats and wheels but this proved unsatisfactory and consequent modifications were incorporated before the aircraft was taken to nearby Fleet Pond on 11th May where waterborne trials were conducted (though these were also not very successful). It was returned to standard wheel configuration and no further amphibian trials were undertaken. The B.E.2 also undertook wireless experiments in March with communications equipment made at Farnborough.

The B.E.1 (No B7, later to become No 201) was handed over to the Air Battalion Royal Engineers on 11th March and

The prototype Royal Aircraft Factory B.E.2 is seen here on Farnborough Common, with Mr Winfield-Smith in the cockpit. The B.E.2, in its various derivatives, went on to become a successful design. *FAST collection*

given its acceptance certificate, as the first Certificate of Airworthiness issued and certified by the factory. The B.E.3 (No 203) was the next from the factory, being a reconstruction of a Paulhan Biplane (No F2) but actually no parts were used except for the 50hp Gnome engine. It first flew on 3rd May, this being the only example built, and went on to serve with the RFC. It was followed by the B.E.4 (No 204), allegedly a reconstruction of a Box Kite No F9, which first flew on 24th June and, after various trials, was handed over to the RFC but crashed on 11th March 1914. The B.E.5 (No 205) that was reconstructed from a Howard Wright biplane, first flew on 27th June and was passed to the RFC for service, but crashed in 1913 and was not repaired. The B.E.6 (No 206) was rebuilt from the S.E.1, undertook its maiden flight on 5th September and went into service with the RFC.

The balloon shed was extended this year by a further 75ft in length and the internal workshops were involved in the covering and doping of aeroplane wings. In 1915 this work moved to a new building, which became known as Q65. By World War One the balloon shed, or house as it was known, had become the main stores of the factory. The balloon shed became Q3 building in the spring of 1947, and was, until its demolition in August 1987, the oldest aeronautical building in the UK.

Following a government White Paper dated 11th April 1912 a significant name change occurred, as the Army Aircraft Factory became known as the Royal Aircraft Factory, which was then tasked by the War Office to perform the following duties:
- Train mechanics for the Royal Flying Corps
- Undertake repair and construction of aeroplanes on behalf of the Royal Flying Corps
- Test British and foreign aeroplanes and engines
- Undertake experimental work
- Maintain airships, balloons and kites and the manufacture of hydrogen
- The continuation of general maintenance duties

The Royal Flying Corps (RFC) was formed during April of this year at Farnborough, with its Headquarters established in the Balloon School/Royal Engineers Air Battalion building, by Lord Trenchard. The first RFC Squadrons, No 1 and No 2, were formed at Farnborough on 13th May, with No 4 Squadron following during August. This building, known as G1 and built about 1910, is externally still of the same basic appearance today, as it was at this time. The main meeting room of the Farnborough Air Sciences Trust is known as the Trenchard Room to honour the 'Father of the Royal Air Force', who had his offices and administration department in this building.

On the airship front, the *Beta II* airship was also used in Army manoeuvres and to train Naval personnel in the art of handling airships. *Gamma II* was used for wireless experiments during September and *Delta,* of $173,000\text{ft}^3$, made its first flight on 7th September 1912 and took part in Army manoeuvres and wireless transmissions. Both *Gamma II* and *Delta* were transferred to the Royal Naval Air Service on 1st January 1914.

Early structural tests were being accomplished in the Royal Aircraft Factory, with bags of sand or lead shot piled on the wings, (with the aircraft inverted), simulating normal flight loads, thus the early concept of load safety factors was begun for stress calculations.

As would be expected given the nature of its pioneering position in aircraft production and development, Farnborough had started to become involved in various research experiments. These tentative eval-

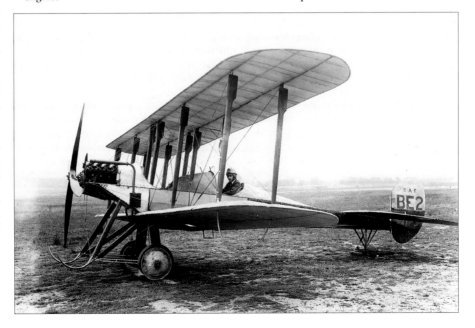

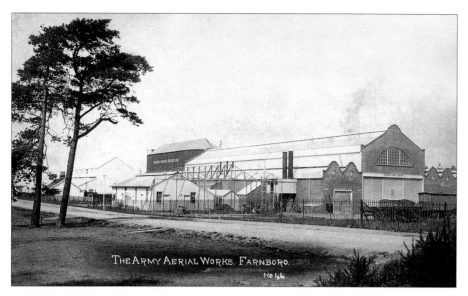

THE ARMY AERIAL WORKS, FARNBORO.
No 144

View of the Army Aircraft Factory, showing the Aeroplane shop to the right (which became Q27 Building), with the Beta shed (Q29 building) seen beyond, and the Balloon shed (became Q3 building) at left. This 1911/12 view is taken from the approximate position where the RAE main (south) gate entrance was built.
FAST collection

uations covered full flight trials, including stability and control, effects of vibration, testing of propellers, fabric strength tests, material tests and establishing new ways of aircraft construction, to name but a few of the tasks being undertaken.

Early aero engines suffered from inadequate performance and a competition was held at Farnborough during this year to enhance development and design of British engines. The winner was the 60hp Green engine, but the six participants were considered generally unsatisfactory and the Royal Aircraft Factory was required to build its own engine, although at first, in its own inimitable way, the War Office had refused such a request.

The Cody IV, a monoplane, was built on Laffan's Plain, being completed in June and powered by a 120hp Austro-Daimler engine. This aircraft was wrecked when it collided with a cow on 4th July 1912 – just another of the hazards that Cody had to contend with at the time! In July there then followed the emergence of the Cody VA Military Trials Biplane No 1. This aeroplane was entered in the War Office military trials at Larkhill in August and resulted in Cody's 'Military Trials Machine' (allocated No 32) winning the event. The Royal Flying Corps purchased the aircraft and gave it the serial number 301, being delivered to the RFC at South Farnborough on 27th November 1912. However its service was short lived as it crashed on 28th April 1913 with the loss of the RFC pilot. In all, 30 aeroplanes competed in this trial, but it was a B.E.2 from Farnborough flown by Geoffrey de Havilland (although not allowed to compete) that convinced the delegates that this should be the type for RFC usage and consequently the War Office chose the B.E.2 over the Cody machine, probably much to Cody's disgust. Whilst at Larkhill, de Havilland flew the B.E.2 with Maj F H Sykes (Officer Commanding the RFC) as his passenger

and managed to gain the British altitude record for a flight with a passenger, topping out at a height of 10,560ft, which was reached in 45 minutes.

The Cody VC, a 'Michelin Biplane' powered by a 100hp Green engine (basically a re-engined VA type) won the Michelin Trophy on 12th October 1912, completing a cross-country circuit of 220 miles.

By now at Eastchurch and undeterred by his dismissal from Farnborough, Dunne had developed an inherently stable aeroplane known as the D8, with a 50hp engine. This was ordered by Col Capper and delivered to Farnborough in March 1914 for tests, becoming No 366.

During this year, King George V made an official visit to the Royal Aircraft Factory, taking interest in these early aircraft under development and production and keeping the important Royal links alive.

1913

The whirling arm was built during this year to test propellers. It remained in use until 1917 and was dismantled in the 1920s. However its concrete base remains on site today, just outside the site developer's perimeter fence behind The Swan public house.

The R.E.1, No 607, two-seat tractor biplane of all-metal fuselage structure first flew during May and it remained at Farnborough for trials throughout its life. A second example, No 608, was produced in September and incorporated means of inherent stability, designed by E T Busk and went on to serve with the RFC. The R.E.2, No 17, completed its maiden flight on 1st July and was converted into a 'Hydro-Aeroplane' fitted with floats, and a larger rudder, and was known as the H.R.E.2 (Hydro Reconnaissance Experimental). It underwent trials on Fleet Pond and on Southampton Water at Hamble, but it was damaged when it failed to take off from the water and

ran into a bank. It was repaired by the factory and converted back to conventional undercarriage before being handed over to Sub Lt Wilson of the Royal Navy Air Service on 6th September 1914.

The B.E.7 prototype, No 438, first flew on 28th February in the hands of Geoffrey de Havilland and entered RFC service the same year, this being the sole example produced. The B.E.8 prototype, No 416, made its first flight on 20th August and others followed, being built by industry and serving with the RFC. The B.S.1, a Scout fighter prototype, first flew on 13th March, but suffered an accident on 27th March and was rebuilt into the S.E.2, No 609, which first flew during October. After further tests it too passed to the RFC for service use.

The *Eta* airship of 118,000ft^3 and powered by two 80hp Canton Unne engines was completed and flown on 18th August 1913. It was handed over to the RFC on 20th September and then to the Royal Naval Air Service on 1st January 1914. Wireless telegraphy experiments led to successful transmission between two airships, the *Delta* and the *Eta*, during October.

The portable airship shed was constructed during this time and remained in use until 1915-16. It was then dismantled and the structures eventually used in the building of the fabric shop (Q65 building, lower structure) and the forge and foundry (R51 building, upper structure) on the RAE Factory site. These girders were recovered from these two buildings during late 2004/early 2005. The framework of the portable airship shed has been cleaned, inspected and re-protected and re-erection commenced in April 2006 on the new Slough Estates development as a commemoration of those pioneering years.

The War Office granted the Royal Aircraft Factory authority to build its own engines This resulted in the R.A.F.1 air-cooled V-8, based on an earlier Renault design and subsequently led to a production variant, as the R.A.F.1a, which, with further development, resulted in a series of different engines being produced at Farnborough in experimental and full production form. The R.A.F.1a and R.A.F.4a types became the most widely produced variants from some 45 different prototype, experimental or proposed developments.

In February 1913 Cody had completed his VB 'Military Trials Biplane' No 2, and this

Amongst the trees on Ball Hill is the wreckage of Cody's water-plane, which crashed on 7th August 1913, killing the intrepid aviator and his passenger, the Hampshire cricket captain, W H B Evans. Cody was given a full military funeral, with some 50,000 people lining the streets of Farnborough and Aldershot. He is buried in the Aldershot Military Cemetery.
FAST collection

was delivered to the RFC on 20th February as No 304. It was damaged in March and was not flown again and in November 1913 it passed to the Science Museum where it is still exhibited, being allocated BAPC.62. The next aeroplane from the Laffan's Plain 'production line' was the Cody VI 'Waterplane', powered by a 100hp Green engine, which was basically built to compete in the 1913 Circuit of Britain Float-Plane Race around the coast of the British Isles, where a prize of £5000 was at stake. Fitted with floats it was taken to the nearby Eelmoor Flash on the Basingstoke Canal in June 1913, where Cody demonstrated its buoyancy by standing on the lower mainplane wingtip. In July 1913 it was fitted with standard wheels and was demonstrated as a hospital aeroplane in what was perhaps the very first attempt at an Air Ambulance.

Then came disaster for S F Cody and his passenger, Hampshire cricketer W H B Evans. Both met an untimely end on Thursday 7th August when Cody's 'Waterplane' crashed in the Ball Hill area, this being on the northwestern corner of the present airfield. Cody was given full military honours for his funeral on 11th August with many military and civilian personnel (given as around 50,000) lining the streets to pay tribute to this pioneer, whose coffin was laid on a gun carriage. He is buried in the nearby Aldershot Military Cemetery. Although the cause of this accident has been a subject of debate for many years, it appears that the wing struts may have failed leading to the aircraft breaking up at 300ft above the ground. Two crosses, known as 'the Cody stones', marked the crash site near the junction between Range Road and Valiant Way, but efforts in recent times to locate the exact spot have proved fruitless. The stones were probably taken away or buried during the 1940s when the area was re-developed. The 'Waterplane' was to have competed in the Circuit of Britain Float-Plane Race a few days later and was due to be positioned to Southampton Water.

Just over a month after Cody's death there was a Sale by Auction, billed according to the catalogue as 'Col S F Cody, deceased Catalogue of the Contents of the Aircraft Works, Laffan's Plain, Aldershot, which Messrs Kingham & Kingham will sell by auction on Monday, 8th September 1913 at 12 o'clock precisely'. This consisted of 213 lots

and included engines, wood, part-built wings and a fuselage, a Cody glider, tyres, tools and propellers etc; plus of course the shed itself, complete with workshop and office. Only one lot was not sold and the total accrued from the auction was £667 10s 6d. The shed was sold to Leon Cody for £90. He had said he would keep the business going, but this did not happen and it appears from press reports that the shed was sold on to someone else. Where it exactly went remains unknown to this day, but the other parts and equipment were snapped up by a variety of bidders at the auction.

Aeronautical Inspection Department (AID) was formed at Farnborough this year, as an Aeroplane Testing and Inspection Establishment, set up after a number of fatal accidents. The AID headquarters was in the 'Black Sheds' until October 1915 but the department was closed at Farnborough in 1917, as the Royal Flying Corps had by then introduced its own Aeroplane Acceptance Parks, (later, under the RAF, to become known as Maintenance Units), although the AID continued to operate from offices in London.

1914
The building and testing of airships was terminated at the factory in this year, the last being the *Eta*, which was handed over to the Royal Naval Air Service on 1st January 1914 but was wrecked at Redhill on 19th November 1914 when it broke away from its moorings. Although construction of the *Epsilon* had started it was never completed, and all airship production and flying was handed over to the Royal Naval Air Service on 1st January.

Experimental Squadron was probably formed around this time, under the leadership of Geoffrey de Havilland. It would serve to control all the new aircraft and

those fitted with test equipment and various modifications.

The R.E.5 No 613 first flew during January and this type entered production with 24 examples being built, which were powered by either the 120hp Austro-Daimler or Beardmore (licence built) engine. R.E.5 No 380 achieved an altitude record of 18,900ft on 14th May flown by factory test pilot Norman Spratt.

HM King George V and Queen Mary continued the trend and visited the Factory on 19th May 1914 to view the work being undertaken and see aircraft being assembled on the production line.

The first purpose-built RFC hangars were constructed at this time, one of which still exists today as a Grade II listed building. This is one of the famous 'Black Sheds' (G29 building), which is still in use now by TAG Aviation as a store for airfield equipment. The other part of this building was demolished in February 1978.

War clouds were now overhead and Britain was perhaps ill prepared, from an aeronautical point of view. The B.E., R.E. and S.E. types were slowly evolving for production in quantity, but the Royal Aircraft Factory was really not capable of undertaking large-scale aircraft production. However, at this time, much research and development work was still ongoing at Farnborough, concerning many of the prototype and production aeroplanes. Many experimental types had been built since 1910 and some production was commenced by the Royal Aircraft Factory to help meet the ever-growing demands of aeroplanes to serve with the RFC. To this end, such types as the B.E.2, F.E.2, R.E.8 and the later S.E.5, were produced from the Farnborough workshops, although many of the more successful types were also produced by 'outside' industry in large numbers, and entered RFC front-line service – such were the high

demands for aeroplanes during the aeroplane's first conflict.

War between Britain and Germany was declared on 4th August and by now approximately 50 aircraft had been built for prototype development. At the beginning of the war, it was some of these types that were the only aeroplanes really suitable for immediate production. Consequently, the early Royal Aircraft Factory examples, such as the F.E.2b and the B.E.2c, were put into large-scale production by various private companies.

Amongst the malaise of a wartime footing, a world record was set for a passenger flight on 19th August when B.E.2 No 225 of No 2 Squadron RFC, with Capt C A H Longcroft as pilot and Col F H Sykes as passenger, flew the 520 miles from Farnborough to Montrose in 7hr 40min. Later, on 22nd November, Capt Longcroft flew B.E.2 No 218 from Montrose to Portsmouth then on to Farnborough, covering 550 miles in 7hr 20min, thus being awarded the Britannia Trophy for the outstanding flight of the year.

The prototype B.E.2c (No 602, later re-serialled as 1807) was flown on 30th May 1914 by test pilot Mr Spratt, but still with a 70hp Renault engine that had been converted from a B.E.2b. A second B.E.2c prototype had now been produced (No 601 an original B.E.2), but a 90hp R.A.F.1a engine had been installed and it appears that this aircraft flew before No 602 on 19th May

1914. However this was basically a new design and the first production examples were handed over to Farnborough in December for further trials. There were over 2,000 examples built of this type before the B.E.2d and 2e variants followed. Unfortunately E T Busk lost his life on 5th November, when the B.E.2c he was flying (No 601) caught fire in the air over Aldershot and crashed on Laffan's Plain whilst endeavouring to get back to the aerodrome. A plaque known as 'The Busk Memorial' was erected in the rose garden, adjacent to the Headquarters administration building (later Q1), in 1915 to commemorate his contribution to flying. It was moved in July 1970 and placed with a water feature just inside South Gate of the RAE, alongside R21 building. The plaque reads: 'The Busk Memorial. In memory of Edward T Busk pioneer of the stable aeroplane, who died in an aircraft accident at the Royal Aircraft Factory 5th November 1914'. With the later redevelopment of the site it was again moved and has been displayed in the garden at Trenchard House, the FAST Museum, since 2000.

Following on from the S.E.2, the S.E.4 No 628 was the first aircraft built with a cockpit canopy and made its initial flight on 27th July 1914, powered by a 14-cylinder Gnome 160hp rotary engine. This aircraft was subsequently taken over by the RFC but was written-off in an accident on 12th August and

Royal Aircraft Factory S.E.4 No 628 is seen here parked outside the hangars at Farnborough during June 1914. This aircraft was subsequently delivered to the RFC, but crashed on 12th August 1914 and was not repaired. In the background can be seen what became Q1 Building, Q3 (the old Balloon Shed) and the Beta Shed. *FAST collection*

was not repaired. The S.E.4a (No 1 but to become No 5611) then followed with four examples being built, the first of which flew on 25th June 1915. All four were pressed into use by the RFC, these aircraft being the first British types equipped with forward-firing machine guns.

The prototype F.E.6, with a one-pounder quick-firing gun, first flew in late 1914, but suffered a heavy landing in an accident on 24th November under the control of Frank Goodden, and was not repaired. The R.E.3 first flew during 1913 but crashed on 27th September and was also not repaired.

Outside of the directly flying-related achievements of this year, 'Technical Classes' were started by O'Gorman as a precursor to the Trade Lads School, which later evolved into the RAE Technical College. It was also planned to have evening classes but these did not commence until 1917 and continued on this basis until 1957.

THE ROYAL FLYING CORPS

An Air Force is Born

With the formation of the Royal Flying Corps during April 1912, its Headquarters was established at Farnborough with Lord Trenchard taking over the Royal Engineers Air Battalion's Headquarters building close to the Farnham to Bagshot road – the present day A325. Today, this building is Grade I Listed and has been known as G1 Building (under the RAE numbering system) for many years. It is much the same today in appearance as it was in Trenchard's time and now serves as the Headquarters of the Farnborough Air Sciences Trust (FAST) Museum. It was in this historic building that some of the early RFC Squadrons were born. The first of these, No 1 Squadron, RFC, was formed with airships and kites on 13th May 1912, having basically been renumbered from No 1 (Airship) Company Air Battalion Royal Engineers. This quickly led to additional squadrons being formed on the aerodrome between 1912 and 1917. Of course, the Royal Flying Corps became the Royal Air Force in April 1918 and remains as such today.

FARNBOROUGH'S RFC UNITS
The RFC Squadrons formed at Farnborough were numbered as follows:

**No 1 Squadron
(Motto: *Foremost in everything*)**
Formed at Farnborough on 13th May 1912, the squadron was initially equipped with airships and kites. With responsibility of airships being transferred to the Royal Navy on 1st January 1914, however, the unit continued to operate at Farnborough as the Airship Detachment RFC from 1st May 1914. Miscellaneous training types were added,

Built circa 1910 as the Royal Engineers Air Battalion building, this building was later to become the headquarters for Lord Trenchard during the formation of the Royal Flying Corps. This view shows how the building was circa 1918, with its entrance directly onto the Farnham to Bagshot (A325) road. This building (G1) serves today as the headquarters for the Farnborough Air Sciences Trust and is known as Trenchard House. *FAST collection*

The airships and personnel of No 1 (Airship) Squadron of the Royal Flying Corps Military Wing during Army manoeuvres in 1913. *FAST collection*

Bristol F.2B Fighters J6730 and J6703 of No 2 Squadron, seen outside the Black Sheds at Farnborough during 1923, these being the squadron hangars. The tree in the background became famous as Cody's Tree but at this time was still flourishing with leaves. J6730 was converted to a 'J' type and went on to serve with the RAF in India, whilst J6703 was written off as a result of a forced landing near Battle, Sussex, 3rd February 1924. *FAST collection*

Three Tornado GR.1As from No II (AC) Squadron, ZA401 'R', ZA367 'II' and ZA370 (no code, but wearing Gulf War mission marks), and three Harriers of No 3 (F) Squadron, GR.7s ZD378 '26', ZD379 '27' and T.10 ZH656 '104', came to Farnborough on 13th May 1997, in order to commemorate the 85th anniversary of the formation of both units. No 2 Squadron was formed as part of the RFC on 13th May 1912. On the same day, No 3 Squadron was also formed by the RFC, although it was to be based at Larkhill. Apparently both squadron commanding officers were present at the RFC headquarters on that day and deliberately took to the air in their BE aircraft in line abreast, from the grass in front of the black sheds, so that neither could claim priority into the air although rivalry still exists in this respect. This was re-enacted this day by a Tornado GR.1A and a Harrier GR.7 performing a paired take-off. *Falcon*

Hawker Audax K1998 of No 4 Squadron, seen at Farnborough during 1932, when the Squadron became an Army Co-operation unit. This aircraft was delivered to the squadron on 14th December 1931. After passing to 2 Squadron, and then various training units, it was struck off charge during November 1943. *via B Kervell*

Opposite page: **The Royal Aircraft Factory S.E.2 (later to become No 609) is seen here on Farnborough Common with Geoffrey de Havilland in the cockpit. This aircraft went into service with No 5 Squadron during January 1914 for service trials. It was later rebuilt and served with No 3 Squadron RFC.** *FAST collection*

namely, Boxkite (serial 641) and Farman (19), and on 14th August 1914 it moved to Brooklands to commence exclusive fixed-wing operations.

No 1 (F) Squadron is currently operational with Harrier GR7/GR7A/GR9/T10 aircraft and is based at RAF Cottesmore, Rutland.

No 2 Squadron (Motto: *Hereward*)
Formed at Farnborough on 13th May 1912 equipped with a variety of aeroplanes that included a Cody biplane, B.E.1 (201), B.E.2 (217), B.E.2a (235) and Farmans (352 and 207). It moved to Montrose on 26th February 1913 before very briefly returning to Farnborough on 5th August 1914, en route to France, and was there again from 27th September 1922 until 17th September 1923 with Bristol F.2B Fighter Mk.IIs (including J6689 and J6743). Became known as No II (AC) Squadron in the 1930s.

No II (AC) Squadron is currently operational with Tornado GR.4A aircraft and is based at RAF Marham, Norfolk.

No 4 Squadron
(Motto: *To see into the future*)
Formed at Farnborough during August 1912 and flew a variety of types including a Cody aeroplane (304), B.E.2a (220) and Farmans (216 and 352). Moving to Netheravon on 14th June 1913, the squadron was to return to Farnborough on 30th April 1920 as part of the Inland Area attached to No 22 Group, equipped with Bristol F.2B Fighters. Next, 'A' Flight moved to Ireland and the entire squadron moved again (to Turkey) in August 1922. Returning to Farnborough once more on 18th September 1923, it traded its Bristol F.2B fighters for Atlas I aircraft (including J9541) in 1929 and transitioned to Audax Is (including K1998, K2022) aircraft in 1932 when it began to operate as an Army Co-operation unit with the British Army at nearby Aldershot. The squadron made a short-distance move to RAF Odiham on 16th February 1937. It became known as No IV (AC) Squadron from 1939.

No IV (AC) Squadron is currently operational with Harrier GR.7/GR.7A/T.10 aircraft and is based at RAF Cottesmore, Rutland.

No 5 Squadron (Motto: *Thou mayst break but shall not bend me*)
Formed at Farnborough on 26th July 1913 flying a variety of types that included S.E.2 (609), B.E.8 (377), Farman (342 and 461), Voisin (1867), DH.2 (4732), and B.E.2a (1784) aeroplanes. The squadron moved to Netheravon on 28th May 1914.

No 5 Squadron was disbanded in September 2003 having latterly been operational with the Tornado F.3 from RAF Coningsby. However this squadron will re-form with the Sentinel R.1 at RAF Waddington, Lincolnshire, in 2006.

FARNBOROUGH'S VC PILOTS

During World War One, four RFC pilots who had served at Farnborough during their squadron formation received the Victoria Cross (VC) for bravery or action in the air over the frontline.

Prior to his deployment to France, Lt W B Rhodes-Moorhouse was an RFC pilot serving at Farnborough with No 2 Squadron. Before this, Lt Rhodes-Moorhouse had served as the Officer Commanding Southern Aircraft Repair Depot, also at Farnborough. He was posthumously awarded a VC for action on 26th April 1915 when he was flying a B.E.2 over Kortrijk, Belgium, and was wounded by a heavy barrage of ground fire when bombing a railway junction. Further wounded on his way back to Allied lines he managed to land his crippled aircraft and make his report before being taken to the casualty area. He died from his wounds the following day.

Capt L G Hawker DSO had begun his service with No 6 Squadron at Farnborough, although he was awarded the VC for action over Passchendaele on 25th July 1915 when he alone, in his Scout C 1611, attacked three German aeroplanes whilst in action from the squadron's base at Abeele. He also went on to many further combats until he was killed whilst serving as Commanding Officer of No 24 Squadron, flying a DH.2 on 23rd November 1916. He had become the eleventh victim of Baron Manfred Von Richtofen. Hawker himself had achieved eight victories in aerial combat. Incidentally the DSO awarded was for attacking the German Zeppelin shed at Gontrode with hand grenades on 22nd April 1915.

Seconded to the RFC from the 3rd Battalion The Argyll and Sutherland Highlanders and serving at Farnborough with No 7 Squadron, Capt J A Liddell was awarded the VC for action on 31st July 1915. He was on a reconnaissance mission over the Ostend-Bruges-Ghent area, flying an R.E.5 when he was severely wounded in aerial combat. The aircraft had dropped altitude whilst Liddell was unconscious but he came to and managed to regain control and brought the aircraft back to Allied lines, thus saving his observer and the machine. However he died from his injuries on 31st August 1915.

The fourth VC was awarded to 2nd Lt G S M Insall, at the age of 21, whilst serving with No 11 Squadron on 7th November 1915, although he had previously been Farnborough-based with another squadron. He engaged the enemy near Achiet, France, whilst on patrol in his FB5 Gunbus, forcing the German aircraft to land in a field. The crew were seen to scramble out but were preparing to fire so Insall positioned his aircraft so the gunner could fire and the crew fled. He then dropped a bomb onto the aircraft and flew through heavy fire from nearby German trenches. With his fuel tank hit, Insall managed to make a forced landing over Allied lines, and after making temporary repairs to the aircraft during the night, he returned to base the following morning.

No 6 Squadron
(Motto: *The eyes of the Army*)
Formed at Farnborough on 31st January 1914 with an assortment of B.E.2, B.E.2a (229), B.E.2b, B.E.8 (636) and Farman types (653 and 9157). The squadron moved to Dover on 6th October 1914, then on to Belgium.

No 6 Squadron is currently operational with the Jaguar GR.3A/T.4 and was based at RAF Coltishall, Norfolk until the unit moved to RAF Coningsby on 1st April 2006.

The last time a No 10 Squadron aircraft landed at Farnborough was on 23rd July 2004, when VC.10 C.1K XV105 'Albert Ball VC' arrived for the static display at Farnborough International 2004. The backdrop of the old buildings is somewhat different from the views of aircraft landing here during the Farnborough hey-days of the 1950s/1960s. *Falcon*

No 7 Squadron
(Motto: *By day and by night*)

Formed at Farnborough on 1st May 1914, this was the last of the Royal Flying Corps units to be formed before the outbreak of World War One. Initially engaged in experimental flying with types such as the B.E.8, Farman, Voisin and R.E.5 (631), the squadron moved to Netheravon on 22nd October 1914 and later briefly returned to Farnborough on 19th November 1919, equipped with R.E.8s, before being disbanded on 31st December 1919.

No 7 Squadron is currently operational with Chinook HC.2 helicopters and is based at RAF Odiham, Hampshire.

No 10 Squadron (Motto: *To hit the mark*)

Formed at Farnborough on 1st January 1915 from the nucleus of No 1 Reserve Squadron and flying an assortment of different types, the unit soon moved to Brooklands on 8th January 1915. The early aircraft flown included Farman, Martinsyde, Bleriot and B.E.2 types.

No 10 Squadron disbanded on 14th October 2005 having operated the VC-10 C.1 (and latterly the C.1K) from July 1966 from RAF Brize Norton, Oxford. The remaining VC-10s were absorbed into No 101 Squadron.

No 15 Squadron (Motto: *Aim Sure*)

Formed at Farnborough on 1st March 1915 from the nucleus of No 1 Reserve Squadron, this B.E.2c-equipped unit moved to Hounslow on 13th April 1915, before heading to France as a reconnaissance unit. Later became known as No XV Squadron.

No XV (Reserve) Squadron is currently operational as the Tornado Operational Conversion Squadron, with the Tornado GR.4 and is based at RAF Lossiemouth, Moray.

No 30 Squadron (Motto: *All out*)

Formed at Farnborough during October 1914 for service in Egypt, the Farman-equipped squadron departed for its destination on 4th November 1914, though actually did not adopt the squadron number until 24th March 1915.

No 30 Squadron is currently operational with the Hercules C.4/5 as part of the Lyneham Transport Wing, and is based at RAF Lyneham, Wiltshire.

No 31 Squadron
(Motto: *First into Indian skies*)

Formed at Farnborough on 11th October 1915, specifically for service in India. Was initially equipped with a few B.E.2c aeroplanes before it actually left for its destination on 27th November 1915.

No 31 Squadron is currently operational with the Tornado GR.4 and is based at RAF Marham, Norfolk.

No 70 Squadron (Motto: *Anywhere*)

Formed at Farnborough on 22nd April 1916 as a fighter squadron, initially equipped with Sopwith 1½ Strutters (such as A1514). 'A' Flight of the squadron moved to France for operations on the Western Front on 21st May 1916, and was shortly followed by the remaining Flights.

No 70 Squadron is currently operational with the Hercules C.1/3, as part of the Lyneham Transport Wing, and is based at RAF Lyneham, Wiltshire.

No 101 Squadron
(Motto: *Mind over matter*)

Formed at Farnborough on 12th July 1917 as a night bomber squadron, equipped with F.E.2b and F.E.2d aircraft, the squadron moved to France for operations on the Western Front on 25th July 1917.

No 101 Squadron is currently operational with the VC-10 K.3/4 and C.1K and is based at RAF Brize Norton, Oxford.

Seen on the 'A' shed tarmac on 22nd November 1995, in support of the then Aldershot-based Parachute Regiment, are three Hercules aircraft of the Lyneham Transport Wing (LTW), two of whose squadrons were formed at Farnborough many years before. Nearest the camera is C.3 XV209, with C.3 XV294 and C.1 XV187 beyond. The RAF Hercules were a common sight at Farnborough, collecting Army personnel for parachute drops on the nearby Hankley Common drop zone. *Falcon*

Sopwith 1½ Strutter bombers of No 70 Squadron (B Flight) RFC, seen lined up at Farnborough in front of the RFC/SARD sheds. This 'Flight' left for France on 29th June 1916. *via No LXX Squadron*

Other Early RFC Squadrons

Three further squadrons were briefly based at Farnborough, namely No 53 Squadron, No 100 Squadron and No 108 Squadron. Equipped with B.E.2e aeroplanes, No 53 Squadron arrived from Catterick on 11th December 1916 and departed again on 26th December 1916 en-route to France for reconnaissance duties. On 28th June 1937, the squadron was reformed at Farnborough as an Army Co-Operation Unit specialising in night reconnaissance, equipped with Hector Is (including K8149), before relocating to Odiham on 8th April 1938. No 53 Squadron was disbanded on 14th September 1976 having latterly operated the Belfast C.1.

No 100 Squadron was very briefly based at Farnborough after arriving from Hingham on 23rd February 1917, equipped with F.E.2bs and F.E.2ds, before moving to France as a night bomber unit on 21st March 1917. This squadron is currently operational with the BAE Systems Hawk T.1/1A/1W and is based at RAF Leeming, Yorkshire.

No 108 Squadron was very briefly based at Farnborough arriving from Upper Heyford on 19th February 1937 equipped with Hinds (such as K6730) before moving to Cranfield on 7th June 1937. The Squadron disbanded on 28th March 1945 having latterly operated the Mosquito NF.XII.

INITIAL INFRASTRUCTURE

Outside of the RFC's fledgling formations, Farnborough's importance as a nucleus for aerial development was mirrored by a flurry of additions within its boundaries, along with their necessary support.

Units added to Farnborough during this period included the School for Wireless Operators, which was formed on 24th August 1916, becoming No 1 Wireless School during October 1917 equipped with Armstrong Whitworth F.K.3s, F.K.8s and

An aerial view taken from a balloon by the School of Photography, showing the No 1 RFC Mess, during 1915, not long after it had been opened. *FAST collection*

Over the years many photographs of RAF personnel were taken outside the frontage of the No 1 RAF Mess. The very last photograph taken of a group of serving RAF Officers shows the current RAF contingent in June 1998, with Air Commodore A N Nicholson, the Air Officer for Farnborough, in the centre front. At left can be seen a model of a Cody aeroplane, whilst, at right, is a model of the Eurofighter. *Falcon*

No 1 Anti-Aircraft Co-operation Unit (AACU) was formed at RAF Farnborough in 1938 and remained there until 1942. Seen here is a newly delivered Henley 1 L3251 at Farnborough for target-towing duties with them, circa 1938/1939, against the black sheds, albeit then camouflaged. *via B Kervell*

Bristol F.2B Fighters. The RFC formed the School of Air Photography at Farnborough circa 1917 and undertook courses for photographic officers and air mechanics as well as camera repairs. This school had its Headquarters building on the southeast corner of the airfield, although hangars were shared with No 1 Wireless School, which were situated on Jersey Brow, west of the Factory area. The Wireless School moved to Flowerdown in the 1930s and the School of Photography later moved into temporary accommodation in Heath End, Farnham and then on to Wellesbourne Mountford in 1948.

The RFC workshops became an Aircraft Park for repairs and rebuilds, whilst an Administration Wing was formed to control the RFC Depot, Records Office and the Reserve Aeroplane Squadrons, the latter responsible for forming new operational squadrons as soon as equipment and personnel were available.

Some aircraft were originally housed in canvas tents; with the obvious expansion of the Royal Flying Corps, further room was required within the Royal Aircraft Factory for aircraft construction and repair. Accordingly, ten sheds were erected on Jersey Brow, some of these being transferred from Larkhill following the Military Trials of 1912. These were allocated to the No 1 (Southern) Aircraft Repair Depot (SARD), along with two airship sheds, and were used to house the aircraft that had arrived after being damaged in action, or for those undergoing routine maintenance for re-issue to the squadrons. At the same time, during February 1915, additional tree clearance was undertaken in order to enlarge the aerodrome area for further building work and aircraft movement as the airfield continued to grow in stature.

During 1914 the Officers Mess and quarters, known as No 1 RFC Officers Mess (even

though the first for the RFC was at Upavon), was also added at this time, being built in a unique colonial style to overlook the aerodrome on a site parallel to the Farnborough Road. (There was also a secondary RAF/RAE Staff Mess added behind the Swan Inn around the same time, which was demolished in 1996.) The Mess opened in the spring of 1915 and continued being referred to as the Royal Air Force No 1 Officers Mess right up to its final closure on 31st December 1998. During this time, with so little accommodation available to the ever-

The RAF flag and Wing Commander's pennant, flies over the RAF Mess for the last time, as seen here during a lowering winter sun in November 1998. *Falcon*

growing RFC contingent, further barracks were built on the south-east corner of the airfield and the RFC personnel moved in there from the previous tented encampment and from the temporary housing within the nearby Army camps. This accommodation later became the RAE Apprentice Hostel with the cessation of RAF use at the end of World War Two.

The RAF's links to Farnborough were further cemented on 15th April 1988 when it received the Freedom of the Borough with the presentations of a vellum scroll and a Wilkinson Sword during a ceremony at Farnborough Recreation Centre conducted by the Mayor of Rushmoor, Cllr A J Callan.

With regard to the other early RFC establishments, No 1 (Southern) Aircraft Repair Depot, now known as the RAF Repair Depot and part of the South Western Area, was receiving large numbers of DH.4s, DH.9s, DH.10s, S.E.5as, Dolphins and Martinsyde F.3s for repair or disposal at the end of World War One. This and similar repair depots led to the formation of a Home Aircraft Depot in the 1920s, and during the early 1930s there followed Aircraft Storage Units, which led to the widespread establishment of the Maintenance Units (MUs) in 1938. Local rumour has it that many of these surplus aeroplanes were dumped in the ground on the present site of the light industrial estate and Council Depot in Eelmoor Road, off Arrow Road in Cove. During September 1919 the Repair Depot came under the control of 7 Group RAF Southern Area and was disbanded shortly thereafter. The facilities were taken over by the 2nd Battalion Royal Tank Corps and the ten sheds were eventually demolished in the early 1970s.

On 23rd August 1939 a Physiological Laboratory was established on the site as part of the RAF Medical Service, which eventually evolved into the RAF Institute of Aviation Medicine in May 1945. In turn this became the RAF School of Aviation Medicine in 1994 and moved from Farnborough to RAF Henlow in 1998 where it was renamed the RAF Centre for Aviation Medicine (see chapter 11). The two CAM Hawk T1s, XX162 and XX327, still operate from Boscombe Down.

With this move, the RAF contingent at Farnborough was greatly reduced in numbers. The very birthplace of today's RAF now has a minimal service presence, consisting solely of personnel detached to the QinetiQ research laboratories.

1915 to 1924

A Change in Direction

So much had been achieved during that first pioneering decade and many lessons had been learnt. High prices had been paid with loss of lives during the steep ascent of the learning curve of controlled flight, which had now put Farnborough at the forefront on the aeronautical map.

The UK was now in the bloody throes of its first World War and the Royal Aircraft Factory saw further funds released for aircraft production, test and development, and things began to move ahead at a rapid pace. Additional Royal Flying Corps Squadrons were now being formed, most moving quickly on to the frontline for action in France. The Royal Aircraft Establishment (RAE) came into being in 1918 to avoid a clash of initials between the Royal Aircraft Factory and the formation of the Royal Air Force.

1915

Further tree clearance was undertaken, commencing in February, to allow for enlargement of the aerodrome and facilitate the addition of more buildings and aircraft movement areas. As outlined above, the No 1 Officers Mess and quarters were built during this period on the eastern edge of the aerodrome perimeter, next to the A325 road.

As World War One raged, more facilities were urgently required to support the rapidly expanding RFC. By now the Southern Aircraft Repair Depot (SARD) had become established on Jersey Brow and ten sheds were erected on the site, some having been moved from Larkhill, where the RFC workshops were now engaged in aircraft repair and rebuilds. By the end of hostilities,

No 1 (Southern) ARD, then known as the RAF Repair Depot (a forerunner of a maintenance unit or storage unit), was receiving large numbers of damaged or surplus aircraft. Many of them were disposed of, with some – accordingly to local rumour – being buried in the ground on what is now the Invincible Road industrial area. The depot was disbanded in 1919 and clearance

included a convoy of barges on the nearby Basingstoke Canal transporting assets away from the site. These facilities were taken over by the Royal Tank Corps 2nd Battalion and the ten former RFC sheds were then in use by the Army, before being eventually demolished in the early 1970s.

At the mid-year point, the Royal Aircraft Factory had expanded considerably for

B.E.2c 1695 is seen in pristine condition parked outside the RFC hangars at Farnborough on 20th May 1915 adorned with the title OVERSEAS, this being a presentation aircraft from the Overseas Club. Note the RFC No 1 Mess, which can be seen beyond. The aircraft went on to serve with No 12 Squadron and subsequently crashed in February 1916. *FAST collection*

Unidentified, but probably the first Royal Aircraft Factory F.E.2a, No 2864, is seen here on Farnborough Common on 17th March 1915. First flight of the type had been made on 26th January with Frank Goodden at the controls. Twelve F.E.2as were produced by the Factory. *FAST Collection*

the war effort and had now run day and night for the past year, engaging some 4,000 personnel.

In order to retain many of the Factory's key personnel, and to establish a number of mobile repair units, the Hampshire Aircraft Parks RFC (TF) Reserve was formed during October, with approximately 1,600 men from the factory put under military discipline. The purpose was to establish a number of mobile repair units so that, if and when an advance was made in France, a sufficient number of repair units would be available in the field to keep aircraft in the air. O'Gorman, Superintendent of the Royal Aircraft Factory, was the Commanding Officer of the unit and, in accordance with the practice of giving ranks to heads of departments, he went under the title of Lieutenant-Colonel. This operation continued to the end of hostilities and was deemed a success.

Pinehurst Cottages were built to the north just outside the factory fence, with the assistance of German prisoners of war, whilst Army accommodation was built in the North Camp area, known as 'Squares'. All these were built to provide accommodation for the factory workers, as many were being brought into the area to assist with the expansion of the Royal Aircraft Factory. Similarly, the construction of a housing estate known as Rafborough (Royal Aircraft Factory Farnborough – a name still used locally) for the factory workers was commenced in Cove and was the first development of its kind in southern England. It was built by constructors, with prisoner of war assistance, but had not been completed by the end of World War One. Roads on this estate are named after pioneers of Farnborough from those early days, for example, Cody, Busk, Fowler, Goodden, Keith Lucas and Weir. All of these

houses are now in private hands, but, to begin with, all those living here were employees of the factory; even up to the 1980s, a large proportion of the houses were homes to workers within the RAE.

On the aircraft side, the next in line of the B.E. series, the B.E.8a, first flew in 1915 and 42 were produced by industry with no prototype. The B.E.9 prototype (No 1700, a converted B.E.2c) followed on 14th August with Frank Goodden at the controls, whilst the B.E.12 (No 1697, a converted B.E.2c) made its maiden flight on 28th July, powered by an R.A.F.4a 140hp engine. This type was developed for bombing and reconnaissance duties and went into mass production for the RFC, the prototype having undergone service trials in France. The B.E.10 and B.E.11 variants were conceived but not proceeded with beyond the initial design concept stage.

Having been designed and built in 1914, the F.E.2a (No 1) made its first flight on 26th January in the hands of Frank Goodden under the power of a 120hp Austro Daimler engine. The improved F.E.2b followed and the first example was delivered to the Royal Flying Corps in October. The F.E.2c prototype (No 6370, a converted F.E.2b) was a departure from the norm, with the crew positioned in reverse (pilot in front). It was flown at Farnborough on 31st March 1916 but written off in a crash on 9th May 1917, and the type was not adopted for full-scale production. A second example, No 6371, was, however, sent to France for evaluation by the RFC but crashed in May 1917. The F.E.8 prototype (No 1, later becoming No 7456) was a single-seat fighter with 100hp Gnome Monosoupape rotary engine that first flew on 15th October, with Frank Goodden at the controls again. This type was deemed a reasonable success and, after

the first two (Nos 7456 and 7457) were built by the factory, industry constructed a further 300 examples. The prototype was sent to the Central Flying School for evaluation on 8th November 1915 but, upon its return to Farnborough on 15th November whilst being flown by Mr B C Hucks, it crashed on landing and was effectively written off. The second example, No 7457, made its first flight on 16th December 1915 and was flown to France for RFC evaluation by No 5 Squadron three days later. Back at Farnborough it was decided to resurrect the prototype (No 7456), with various modifications and it made its post-rebuild flight on 9th April 1916, again flown by Frank Goodden. This example was used for various tests including fitment of a 110hp Le Rhone and a 110hp Clerget engines, new elevators and rudders with steel ribs.

1916

Designed by Henry Folland in 1915, the S.E.5 prototype fighter (A4561), known as a Scout and fitted with an Hispano-Suiza 8A engine, took to the air on 22nd November 1916, in the hands of Goodden. The second prototype (A4562) made its first flight on 4th December, while the third example (A4563) followed into the skies on 12th January 1917.

The R.E.8 No 7996, powered by a Royal Aircraft Factory R.A.F.4a 140hp V-12 engine, first flew on 17th June 1916, with Goodden as pilot. The second prototype (No 7997) first flew on 5th July 1916 and was sent to France for RFC evaluation on 16th July being returned to the Factory in August for various modifications. This type proved a success and some 70 examples were produced at Farnborough, and some 4,000 by outside industry.

Development of the B.E. series led to the B.E.12a (No 6511, converted from a B.E.12), which first flew on 13th November, with a hundred produced by industry, and the B.E.12b followed in 1917, also seeing a production run of a hundred by industry.

The F.E.2d, No 7995, was first flown on 7th April 1916 with a 250hp Rolls-Royce Eagle V-12 engine. Some improvements were made and production by the Royal Aircraft Factory and industry continued. Many other enhancements were proposed and some incorporated into the F.E. series, which led to further designations, but they did not reach full-scale production.

Construction of the A.E.1 (Armed Experimental) two-seater was commenced at Farnborough in 1913 and it became the F.E.3

The production line for the F.E.2 series aircraft in what was known as F1E workshops, this view being dated 8th January 1916. 124 F.E.2 series aircraft were produced at Farnborough, the remainder by outside industry. *FAST collection*

The S.E.5 prototype A4561 is seen here with Frank Goodden in the cockpit on the day of its first flight, 22nd November 1916. Goodden was regrettably killed in the second prototype S.E.5, A4562, on 28th January 1917. *FAST collection*

prototype No 603, which flew only a few times. A twin-engined pusher biplane was designed by H P Folland and S J Walters for ground-attack and bomber roles. It became known as the F.E.4 and the prototype (No 1 which later became No 7993) made its maiden flight on 12th March 1916, powered by two R.A.F.5 140hp engines. It left for evaluation by the CFS on 11th May 1916 returning on 3rd June to Farnborough, who advised that the aircraft was considerably underpowered. There then followed the second example, No 7994, first flown on 5th July 1916 powered by two 250hp Rolls-Royce Eagle engines. Both examples were flown by Frank Goodden but, like many others of the time, the project did not live up to expectations and was abandoned, the production order for one hundred examples being cancelled.

The Royal Aircraft Factory commenced design in 1916 of a radio-controlled pilotless aircraft, which was intended for defence against Zeppelin airships and for use as a flying bomb. This was a relatively secret project and was referred to as the Aerial Target. Powered by an ABC Gnat 35hp engine, six examples were built (A8957-62) and trials commenced with the first flight of prototype A8957 on 6th July 1917 at Northolt but this resulted in a crash. This project was none too successful, as early trials resulted in accidents (the second and third examples also suffered accidents on 25th and 28th July respectively) and it was later abandoned. Nonetheless it paved the way for future target and pilotless projects (see later) and indeed areas of this work and technology continue with QinetiQ today.

During September 1916, Henry Fowler, the former Chief Mechanical Engineer of the LMS Railway, became Superintendent of the factory and, during this period, the number of personnel employed totalled over 5,000, just over half of these being women. During this period of World War One, the scientists and engineers at Farnborough constituted what, at that time, was the greatest concentration of aeronautical knowledge within the UK. The female work force played a large part in aircraft production and repair, being responsible for much of the fabric, sewing, stitching and doping work.

The Royal Aircraft Factory produced an early radio-controlled pilotless aircraft for use as a potential flying bomb. Known as the Aerial Target, six examples were built. Seen here is the first, after assembly at Farnborough during 1917. Flight trials were conducted at Northolt. *FAST collection*

The School for Wireless Operators was formed by the RFC at Farnborough on 24th August, which later became known as No 1 Wireless School during October 1917.

1917
The RFC, later RAF, School of Air Photography was formed in this period, with their headquarters buildings positioned on the southeast side of the aerodrome, where they remained until 1947.

Following from the R.E. series there then came the R.E.8a (A95), with a 200hp Hispano-Suiza V-8 engine plus other modifications, which first flew on 24th September 1917. The R.E.9 (A4600, converted from an R.E.8 and fitted with B.E.2d wings) made its first flight on 11th June 1917 and underwent handling and performance trials. Both the R.E.8a and R.E.9 were not adopted for production. The R.T.1 evolved from the R.E.8 being built by Siddeley-Deasey and basically having an R.E.8 fuselage, with six prototypes

built from the last batch of R.E.8s (B6625-30). The first of the R.T.1s arrived at the Factory from Coventry on 11th October 1917 for performance trials. It departed for Hounslow on 26th October and continued onward to France for RFC evaluation, whilst B6625, B6627 and B6629 also underwent engine and performance trials at Farnborough. This type similarly did not enter production.

The F.E.9 prototype A4818 first flew 14th May 1917, three being completed: A4819 making its first flight during October 1917 and A4820 taking to the air on 7th November 1917. On 5th June the first prototype was flown to France for evaluation by the RFC but was considerably criticised and was returned to Farnborough on 14th June. The Factory incorporated various modifications into the next two examples but these were still none too successful and the design was abandoned. The prototype continued to operate from Farnborough for various tests at least during 1918, the second was written

Built by Siddeley-Deasey, the R.T.1 evolved
from the R.E.8. Six of these were built and
the third, B6627, is seen on Farnborough
Common during October 1917. The type
did not enter production, although this
example underwent engine and
performance trials with the Royal Aircraft
Factory. *FAST collection*

off whilst with the RFC in early 1918 and the third was still in use as an engine testbed in early 1918.

The N.E.1, for Night Flying Experimental, B3971 was developed from the F.E.12 and made its first flight on 8th September 1917, flown by Maj Roderic Hill. Five others (B3972-76) were built, with B3972 making its first flight on 19th November 1917 and B3973 on 3rd December 1917. B3974 was used as a test airframe and not flown, B3975 was flown at Orfordness, while B3976 was never completed. Although various trials were made, including bomb dropping, the type was not adopted for production.

A4563, the third S.E.5, first flew on 12th January 1917, powered by a 200hp Hispano Suiza engine: with this engine it became the S.E.5a. However, on 28th January, the second prototype S.E.5 (A4562) suffered an in-flight strut failure while being flown by Frank Gooden and crashed onto the aerodrome, killing the famous test pilot. Failure had occurred in the compression rib and interplane strut attachments, which led to a rapid redesign. The S.E.5b (A8947) made its first flight on 12th April 1918. The S.E.5 type, arguably, became the best-known production aircraft built during 1917/1918 as a total of 5,269 examples of the series were built; 75 S.E.5s and over 200 S.E.5as were produced by the Royal Aircraft Factory at Farnborough, the remainder from outside industry.

A proposal for a larger, and two-seat, version of the S.E.5 was considered by the Factory, which saw the evolution in design of the T.E.1 (Tatin Experimental). Three prototypes (A8951-53) were actually ordered, with a further three (A8954-56) planned for later production. As the first example was nearing completion it was cancelled and the project was abandoned.

A 7-foot wind tunnel was built for use in aerodynamic research. Known originally as 'wind channels', a second example was built in 1918 and these were successfully used for various aerofoil sections and model research. This line of research has continued at Farnborough right up to the 21st century, with the 5-metre wind tunnel on the QinetiQ site still undertaking these duties on behalf of outside industry.

Royalty again visited the Royal Aircraft Factory, with King George V being shown the latest products during this year.

During 1916/17 the Royal Engineers extended the standard gauge railway within the establishment, with the assistance of prisoners of war, to connect with the main London and South Western Railway line at Farnborough station. The track was laid, running through the marshland area adjacent to Marrowbrook Lane and along the centre of Elm Grove Road, right into the station goods yard. This therefore enabled freight, coal and other goods to be moved to and from the Establishment with ease. In the early days of operation the Factory 'Baby' tractor was used to haul coal into the facility from Farnborough Station goods yard, the tractor being fitted with heavy angle shoes to run on the track and this continued until 1918 when a locomotive was purchased. Henry Fowler, of LMS background, acquired an 0-4-0 saddle tank locomotive, known as a '1515' and 'Baby' was converted back to an ordinary roller. Two new locomotives arrived with RAE in 1918, another 0-4-0 saddle tank known as 'loco 93' with a tall chimney and spark arrester, and a further 0-4-0 side tank Andrew Barclay 1602, the latter continuing for many years and ending up as a spares source for the next steam locomotive 'Invincible', this too an 0-4-0 saddle tank of the Kitchener Class, built in 1915 by Hawthorn and Leslie. 'Invincible' came to RAE from Woolwich Arsenal after re-conditioning in 1959 and was the stalwart of the railway operations until the end. Although a 150hp diesel locomotive was added in the late 1940s, it was still 'Invincible' that operated the majority of the goods trains until the demise of the RAE railway. The last service occurred on 10th April 1968, then the line

The famous RAE railway locomotive
'Invincible' is seen here crossing Union
Street in Cove on its very last journey to the
goods yard at Farnborough station on 10th
April 1968. This was the last day of the
railway operations that had commenced in
1917. Vestiges of the track are still present
today to the left of where this photo was
taken. *G P Cooper*

This aerial view of the Royal Aircraft Factory, seen in March 1918, shows the two large airship sheds in the foreground, (the one on the right being B Airship shed also known as the Lebaudy Shed and to the left C Airship shed), whilst the 'Beta' shed and the original Balloon shed can be seen beyond. F1E workshop, where aircraft were in production, is the long building seen at the mid-centre left. Note the tent on the edge of the roadway, which was for housing RFC aircraft 'in the field'. *FAST collection*

was closed, becoming redundant mainly due to the conversion to oil-fired boilers, although some coal was still brought into the RAE by large road vehicles. 'Invincible' was sold initially for scrap but was purchased whilst still at RAE by T Jeffries of the Docks Haulage Company and was taken away by road on 10th December 1968. 'Invincible' was taken to the Isle of Wight Steam Railway in June 1971 where it underwent a full overhaul in 1972 and commenced tourist train operations the following year.

1918

The only flying-boat design from the Royal Aircraft Factory was the C.E.1 (Coastal Experimental), a two-seat biplane with a wooden hull designed to help combat the threat to shipping of German submarines. Two prototypes were built (N97 and N98), the first making its maiden flight on 17th January 1918 on Southampton Water, powered by a 230hp R.A.F.3a engine, having been transported from Farnborough to Hamble. The second example was powered by a 260hp Sunbeam Maori engine and first flew during this year.

On or about 13th June, the most famous name in aeronautical research came into being when the Royal Aircraft Factory was renamed the Royal Aircraft Establishment, to avoid a clash of initials with the newly formed Royal Air Force, that had now evolved from the Royal Flying Corps, with the reorganisation of the RFC and RNAS from 1st April. This heralded a new and important era and, with the cessation of aircraft design and production, the RAE progressed with research and development, experimental trials and tests, both to improve types already in service and to research into future projects. This legacy set the tone for the next 76 years of flying from Farnborough, and is still there today with QinetiQ in regard to their research and

Known as the C.E.1, two flying boats were produced by the Royal Aircraft Factory with the intention of countering the German submarine threat. Seen here is N97, the first of the two prototypes, on Southampton Water at Hamble during January 1918. Other flying boats were superior to these and production did not ensue. *FAST collection*

development programmes, ongoing for Government and industry alike.

Experimental Squadron, with over fifty aircraft on strength, was now under RAE control and made up of four different Flights: namely 'A', 'B', 'C' and 'U'. It appears that 'C' Flight was first recorded on 14th August, 'B' Flight and 'U' Flight on 18th September and 'A' Flight on 19th September. Research and development into aerodynamics, stability and control, performance and propellers were conducted by 'A' and 'B' Flights, whilst 'C' Flight was tasked with engine development, fuel systems etc; and 'U' Flight (Unallocated) undertook acceptance of new types for handling trials and general development work prior to aircraft being issued for specific research work with the other RAE Flights. By 1920, with further expansion of

the aircraft fleet and facilities, Experimental Squadron had been renamed as the Experimental Flying Department (EFD). The respective Flights under its control undertook all flight testing of aircraft, for stability, control, spinning, vertical flight, engines, wireless communications, aircraft handling and early deck-landing trials.

The hostilities of World War One ceased on 11th November 1918. During the war period between 1914 and 1918, more than 500 aircraft of approximately 30 different types, were produced at Farnborough, the majority being in prototype form, although some went on to see massive production by private industries.

Towards the end of the war, the factory also produced 24 Handley Page 0/400 bombers (B8802-13 and C3487-98) plus ten

Twenty-four Handley Page O/400 bombers were produced by the Royal Aircraft Factory and the second-to-last example, C3497, is seen here parked on the grass outside the RFC hangars on 24th June 1918. Note the handling trolley for ease of ground movement. *FAST collection*

During World War One some captured German aircraft were sent to Farnborough for evaluation. Seen here outside the Lebaudy shed is an AEG G.IV G 1125/16 (G105) which arrived on 12th March 1918 from Martlesham Heath, having been brought down by British ground fire in France on 23rd December 1917. It is seen here shortly after arrival, still wearing its lozenge colour scheme, but with RAF roundels on the upper mainplanes and the tricolour on the rudder. *FAST collection*

Vickers FB.27 Vimys, (from serial allocations H651-70, although ten of these were cancelled) to assist the demand of industry. They were the last aircraft to be built at Farnborough, as the Armistice led to many surplus aircraft and a considerable fall in demand for production.

Before the end of World War One a number of German aircraft had found their way to the Factory where they were test flown and evaluated. These included Albatros A374 (XG2) on 22nd September 1915; LVG C.II (XG7) on 14th June 1917; Albatros D.V D4545/17 (G97) arriving from Lympne on 11th January 1918; AEG G.IV G1125/16 (G105), which arrived on 12th March 1918 from Martlesham Heath, and an Albatros two-seat variant (XG8) on 5th July 1918.

Apprentices were first taken into the establishment in 1910 but in 1918, under the 'Trade Lads' scheme, this was put on a more structured basis and constituted an early form of apprenticeship, which was further expanded over the years whereupon it set the trend for years to come, with apprentices

being taken in by the RAE annually up to 1992. The early apprentice intakes also resulted in commencement of the RAE Technical School, which later changed its name to the RAE Technical College in October 1945.

April saw a new Superintendent appointed, W Sydney Smith, and this led to some reorganisation within the various RAE departments. Due to the increasing demand of aeronautical research and experimentation, specific areas were defined for specific tasks. Aerodynamics, Engine Experimental, Physics and Instruments, Metallurgical, Mechanical Test, Chemical and Fabric Departments were all created or reorganised at this time.

1919

Some of the personnel of the Royal Flying Corps were originally housed in tented accommodation on the southeast corner of the aerodrome. Completed early in 1919 were new barracks and domestic accommodation for RAF Farnborough (as it had become on 1st April 1918) and these

buildings were in use for RAF personnel accommodation up to 1946, when they became the RAE Apprentice hostel accommodation blocks.

RAE was undertaking more and more varied research work and a number of specific activities, with the aircraft experimental and research departments, were taking shape. However, during this stage, the workforce was dramatically cut back after the cessation of hostilities to around 1,000 and financial budgets were also somewhat curtailed.

By now thoughts were being given to civilian aircraft and RAE expertise was sought by a number of manufacturers to assist with design and handling characteristics of their products. The first civilian Certificate of Airworthiness was issued by RAE to the Austin Whippet G-EAGS, which arrived from Bristol on 2nd December, this being tested by 'U' Flight in December for a few days. It was returned to civilian life and was subsequently withdrawn from use in November 1921

The Royal Air Force station at Farnborough originally came under the control of South Western Area and, during September, this came under the control of No 7 Group Southern Area. Further changes in the group structure occurred in 1920, and it became known as No 22 Group Inland Area during April 1926.

Measurement of engine power output was being investigated and data collected assisted further development of engines. At this time a B.E.2c, 2029, was fitted with a thrust-meter; a Sopwith Snipe, E8097, had a special torque-meter; and a DH.9, D5755, was fitted with a dynamometer – all producing data for analysis.

Tarrant Tabor F1765, a large triplane bomber designed with the intention of being able to bomb Berlin from aerodromes in southern England, powered by six Napier Lion 450hp engines, was transported by road to Farnborough from Byfleet, where it had been constructed by W G Tarrant Ltd.

Seen outside the airship hangars is F1765, the giant Tarrant Tabor triplane. Produced by W G Tarrant Limited at Byfleet, it was transported to Farnborough, assembled, and commenced its initial flight on 26th May 1919, shortly after this photograph was taken. Unfortunately the aircraft tipped forward on take-off and impacted the ground, nose first, killing both pilots.
FAST collection

The wooden components had been produced in Byfleet, with the metal parts made at RAE. Once assembled and re-rigged, and following ground runs, this massive aircraft (for the time) was rolled out of the airship shed for its first flight, all six engines were started, and it commenced its take-off run on 26th May. Unfortunately, due to the top two engines being powered up first, the aircraft tipped forward and impacted the ground, nose first, regrettably killing both pilots, although the five passengers escaped unhurt. The aircraft was not repaired and the project was abandoned, with the second example (F1766) uncompleted.

1920

Structural testing had now taken a step forward, far from the early days of loading the aircraft with lead shot bags, with a dedicated test frame having now been built, although more sophisticated structural frames were to be added later.

Wireless and Photographic departments were formed and had soon become engaged in High-Frequency (HF) Radio Research, and development of aircraft-mounted cine and still cameras. Air-to-air gunnery cameras and air survey cameras were developed during this time and were improved upon over the following years. Other work undertaken by these departments included radio valve research and aircraft radio transmitter developments, which led to very high frequency (VHF) and different forms of signal decoding (frequency modulation), to improve reception and reliability. Also commencing development during this time was an early form of radio direction-finding (RDF) equipment. The expertise of this department was also responsible for redesign of several RAF airfield wireless stations and radio installations.

A Sopwith Camel, F6456, was strengthened in order to undertake spinning tests to

Early structural load testing was conducted by use of sand or lead shot bags: the aircraft, in an inverted position, being loaded until the structure failed. An R.E.1 is undergoing testing with sand bags to 4,000 lb in the aeroplane erection shop (later Q27 building) on 21st July 1913. Better test equipment was brought into use in the 1920s, with structural testing conducted within a specialised frame.
FAST collection

study the behaviour pattern of the aircraft under such conditions as a number of accidents had befallen the type in service use. Further spinning tests were also conducted by S.E.5a D5923, Bristol F.2B Fighter A7260 and Avro 504K F3269.

Aerodynamic and stability research was ongoing in an endeavour to improve various aircraft characteristics. Various tests were accomplished during the 1920s including a Sopwith Camel being modified with wings moved rearwards in an effort to bring the centre of gravity forward but this proved none too successful. Stall tests were conducted on a DH.9 (H9120) that was fitted with a slotted wing and it was proved that there was a marked decrease in stalling speed, this slotted wing system later being further developed with moveable slots and was adopted by the Air Ministry for fitment to service aircraft. An HP 0/400 (C9773) was used for directional and longitudinal con-

trol research eventually leading to automatic elevator and rudder controls. At this stage an early autopilot, codenamed 'George', had been developed from this automatic control research.

Parachutes, with suitable ballast attached, were being dropped from DH.9A J597 in an attempt to experiment the bale-out conditions from an aircraft in level flight and during a spin. To achieve the latter Sopwith Camel F6456, with controls locked for a spin, was suspended from a kite balloon raised to 1,500ft over Laffan's Plain and then released. On the first occasion the parachute, with suitable weight to simulate the pilot, fell clear from the aircraft but failed to open. However during 1921/22 further experiments followed which proved successful escapes could be achieved but a more reliable parachute was required. Live pilot drops were also successfully made from a tethered kite balloon.

The first all-metal aeroplane was the Short Silver Streak, seen here at Farnborough during June 1921. It was powered by a 240hp Siddeley Puma engine and made its first flight on 20th August 1920. *FAST collection*

1922

Although allocated 'Flights' came into being in 1918, during 1922 subtle changes occurred where the four Flights were specifically named in conjunction with their specialised tasks; 'A' became Aerodynamics Flight; 'B' became Instrument, Wireless and Photographic Flight; 'C' became Engine Research Flight (all with a first recorded entry of 10th April) and 'U' became Equipment Flight (first recorded entry of 6th May). Wireless and Photographic Flight became its own entity, first recorded on 24th September 1923 – the same date as Instrument Flight became stand-alone. DTD Flight (Director of Technical Development) was first recorded on 10th September 1924. In May 1924 W&P Flight became Wireless, Photographic and Electrical Flight (WP&E), changing again to just W&E Flight in July 1928. Instrument Flight became Instrument & Photographic Flight (I&P) in July 1928.

Wind tunnel development continued now under the Aerodynamics Department and one of their early tasks was that of undertaking aerodynamic and stability tests on the Hill Pterodactyl. Early forms of helicopter designs were also tested, along with radiators to check drag characteristics, and a model of the Supermarine S.4 was tested prior to the actual aircraft being built for competing in the Schneider Trophy.

A total of 1,316 personnel were employed at the RAE, including 270 scientific, technical and RAF officers, plus 85 clerical, 626 skilled mechanics and 335 labourers and general workers.

An early form of catapult was designed at RAE during this year, using a compressed air powered hydraulic telescopic ram configuration and this was installed on Jersey Brow, where the first successful launch occurred during July 1925.

Development of the original pilotless aircraft project was resurrected and an improved design, powered by a 45hp Armstrong Siddeley Ounce engine was built. It was concluded that the tests had been a reasonable success: remote control of an aircraft had been achieved and found to be worthy of future development. Success in

1921

1st February saw the arrival at Farnborough, from the Isle of Grain, of the first all-metal aeroplane, the Short Silver Streak (later to become J6854, but allocated G-EARQ in March 1920). The aircraft was tested by 'U' Flight of EFD, although only six flights were conducted before a forced landing on 6th June 1921 resulted in damage being occasioned to the airframe. It was not repaired and went on to be used for ground vibration tests.

Engine Department experiments continued on a variety of engines, including British, French and American. Research into air-cooled cylinders, aluminium cylinder heads, early superchargers and fuel systems were all undertaken at this time. RAE also designed a variable-pitch propeller, but due to various problems the development was shelved as being none too successful but, some fifteen years later, the Hamilton Company of the USA designed and built a successful variable-pitch system.

Engine fires were researched in respect of endeavouring to extinguish them in flight. S.E.5a E5927 from 'C' Flight was employed

for this, the aircraft being deliberately set alight in the air and the in-flight extinguishing system then putting the fire out. This was conducted on a few occasions, with the fire successfully extinguished, but during one specific flight on 9th July the aircraft ran into a hollow on landing and was wrecked. The pilot, G H Norman, escaped, but died a short while afterwards. A plaque to commemorate this was placed on R141 Building and was relocated to the Kuchemann Building in 1996 on the QinetiQ site.

The Instrument Design Establishment moved to Farnborough from Biggin Hill and the Technical Contracts and Wireless Departments were transferred from the Air Ministry to Farnborough.

An 'A' Flight DH.10 Amiens Mk.III (E6042), powered by two USA-built 400hp Liberty engines, was modified for use by RAE with the fitment of a large servo rudder to improve flight characteristics and single-engine handling. It was later fitted with twin fins and rudders for handling trials. This aircraft was still in use in 1926, by which time it was the last serving example of the type.

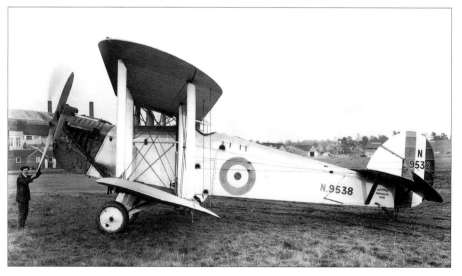

Blackburn T.2 Dart torpedo bomber N9538, the third production aircraft, came to Farnborough from Gosport on 16th October 1922 for fitment and test of short wave telephony equipment before returning to Gosport on 29th November 1922. It is seen here on 10th November. *FAST collection*

Seen during its first flight on 6th September 1923 is the RAE Light Aeroplane Club Zephyr G-EBGW. It was powered by a Douglas 500cc engine. This was the start of recreational flying at Farnborough, which still goes on today with the Farnborough Aero Club. *FAST collection*

these areas led to WPE Department equipping an Armstrong Whitworth Wolf, J6923, with automatic controls in 1924 and flight trials were successfully accomplished. Instrument Flight was formed in 1924 and this work continued with Armstrong Whitworth Tadpole J6585, DH.9A E746 and Avro 504N Lynx J7555 & J7556.

Oleo undercarriages were under research at this time and Vickers Vimy H651 and DH.9A E775 were both testing these pneumatic systems that had been developed from the earlier bungee-rubber shock absorber type.

Technical Publications, part of the Air Ministry, was transferred to RAE during this year and remained at Farnborough until 1944. During this period many Air Publications and Air Diagrams, were produced, giving technical, operational and maintenance data of all types of aircraft, engines and equipment, to the Services. Moreover, there was a small Technical Publications section that remained in RAE until 1994, in support of the various aircraft operated, including their onboard research equipment.

The Accident Investigation Branch was formed during this year (see chapter 14), which led to a close liaison with all test departments, including Aerodynamic, Mechanical and Metallurgical, assisting the Branch, with special advice and research, under laboratory conditions. This still happens today, with QinetiQ assisting the AAIB when requested.

Structures Department was formed but was contained within the Airworthiness Department: work on structural strength testing and general material research was part of their early responsibilities. Electrical Engineering Department and Wireless Department were formed. Airworthiness Department was established at Farnborough during this year, being transferred from the Air Ministry Headquarters. This department became responsible for checking all Airworthiness aspects of military and civil aircraft and laying down the guidelines for official standards, where contractors' military proposals would be scrutinised before the Air Ministry would procure a new type. This department also had the responsibility of research into the strength of structures and aero-elastic problems.

Following from the Zephyr was the RAE Light Aeroplane Club Hurricane G-EBHS. It is seen here on the aerodrome in its rebuilt form, in which it won the 1925 International Handicap at Lympne. *FAST collection*

The airfield covered an area of 300 acres, but further groundwork was under way to level areas to the southwest, to give extra runway length and provide other grass landing vectors.

Cove Radio Station was established at this time, along Ively Road, being an outstation of Radio Department, to provide a site for research and development connections with radio communications and navigation. The site began operations soon after being built. A rotating wireless navigation beacon was installed and accurate bearings could be established by flying aircraft. Further equipment followed with HF aerials for medium and long distance communications installed along with wireless telegraph and radiotelephone equipment. Tests with the RAE WE Flight aircraft continued resulting in the quality of transmissions being improved. In the early 1930s Morse transmissions were relayed here by the Fairey Monoplane, which paved the way for TR9 equipment installa-

tions in many aircraft and was still in use at the end of World War Two. A representative RAF Fighter Station section was installed at the beginning of World War Two where VHF, radio transmission services and a direction finder underwent trials to improve these services. In 1939 television pictures transmitted from an Avro Anson were received at Cove and this trial was undertaken for possible development for military aircraft use in the future. Successful single sideband trials led to improved communications between aircraft and ground stations. Long-range directional aerials were installed at Cove to give ground communication coverage worldwide along with the ability to measure signal strength and determine the radiation pattern of an aircraft aerial. High-speed automatic digital communications systems, fed into a computer system for Air Traffic Control purposes, were also trialled here. Work on recording identity, position and altitude without input by aircrew resulted in the 'Transponder',

which has been adopted worldwide for many years. Cove Radio Station eventually closed in the mid-1990s and the equipment was dismantled to make way for a housing estate, although some was re-erected within the QinetiQ site on the northwestern corner of the airfield where radio communication systems are still being evaluated.

1923

The RAE Light Aeroplane Club (LAC) was formed during October 1922 to design and fly its own indigenous aircraft. Built by club members, the first aircraft was known as the Zephyr. It was a pusher biplane, registered on 13th June 1923 as G-EBGW, and first flown on 6th September powered by a 500cc Douglas Flat-Twin (Bristol Sprite) engine. The Zephyr was eventually scrapped during November 1925. Next came a design known as the Hurricane, a single-seat ultralight aircraft powered by a 600cc Douglas engine. This was selected by the Air Ministry, along with four other types, for trials at Farnborough. Registered as G-EBHS on 10th September, the Hurricane took part in trials at Lympne, but was considered underpowered. It was subsequently rebuilt, now powered by a 32hp Bristol Cherub III engine, and the aircraft won the 1925 International Handicap at Lympne, with an average speed of 78.2mph over the 50-mile course. The Hurricane was eventually scrapped in 1927. Both types were designed by Sammy Child, a founder member of the club, who in 1934 became Chief Designer at RAE.

Many of the RAE aircraft and their pilots were tasked to display their aircraft at the RAF Hendon pageant which saw flying skills being honed at Farnborough and various aircraft put through their paces prior to being flown to Hendon for this prestigious event.

An Avro 549 Aldershot II (J6852, later converted to a Mk.IV), first flown as a Mk.I from Hamble in early 1922 and as a Mk.II on 15th December 1922, came to Farnborough on 10th January 1923, undergoing rudder and aileron tests, and departed back to the manufacturers on 2nd July after an appearance at the Hendon display. It returned to RAE on 30th October 1923 for ER Flight where engine endurance tests and engine/radiator development of a Napier 1,000hp Cub I engine were undertaken. Returning to Avro on 10th November 1924, it was converted to a Mk.IV with a 850hp Beardmore Typhoon engine, making its first flight as such on 10th January 1927 from Hamble. It returned to RAE on 17th June 1927 where it served testing the endurance of steel wings until 13th December 1927.

1924

An early helicopter design of 1919, by Louis Brennan, was assembled at Farnborough, under considerable secrecy, for redesign and test, although it was not on RAE strength. The engine was initially a 150hp Bentley BR-1 Rotary, driving small propellers at the rotor blade tips. The initial tethered flights were undertaken in the Gamma airship shed in November 1921, with a 'car' fitted. By this time, the Brennan had been re-engined with a 230hp Bentley BR-2 Rotary and had a rotor diameter of 62ft, with a forward speed designed to be 30mph. Three flights were made from Jersey Brow during May 1925, but these confirmed the Brennan was unstable. An early automatic control system was devised to correct the instability, but following a crash in 1926 due to control failure the project was abandoned. Some 200 flights had been made in the six years of development, although not

all of these were at Farnborough. In honour of these early trials one of the buildings, within what is now the BAE Systems headquarters, has been named Brennan House after this rotary pioneer.

A competition was held for a helicopter that could fly a 1-kilometre closed circuit. The sole entrant was the ungainly Covered Wagon. Needless to say, it did not fly.

During this year a committee was appointed to examine the current organisation of the RAE and its findings confirmed that the primary function should be to provide full-scale aeronautical activities for the Air Ministry, its main activities being defined as follows:
- Experimental and development work on aeroplanes and engines.
- Testing of experimental instruments and accessories.
- Flying instrument development, for which there is little commercial demand.
- Investigating failures within aircraft and components.
- Liaison with industrial contractors for research purposes.
- Technical supervision during construction of experimental machines.
- Approach for approval, design and stressing, of new aeroplanes and the issue of Airworthiness Certificates.
- Issue of technical publications, where applicable.

Ignition and Electrical Department was formed, originally as part of the Engine Experimental Department, and research work was undertaken on transformers, alternators, magnetos, generators, improved ignition systems, high-tension booster coils, spark plugs, electrically-heated aircrew clothing, light beacons, navigation lights and the like.

Air-to-air refuelling trials, the first in the UK, were carried out by Aero Flight at Farnborough between 7th February and 4th March. A weighted wire, and later a cable, was successfully passed between two Bristol F.2B Fighters (A7260 and F4675). Eventually the cable was replaced by a hose and water was passed between the aircraft whilst flying at 70mph. These tests proved that making initial contact between the two aircraft was difficult, but achievable. However no further trials were undertaken until 1930.

Experimental Flying Department also commenced high-altitude flying experiments during this year; they were to continue for many years to come.

Seen suspended inside the Gamma Airship shed at Farnborough is the Brennan early helicopter design, with the 'car' fitted beneath. Following tests in the airship shed, the helicopter made further flights on Jersey Brow. *FAST collection*

1925 to 1934

Helicopters, Pilotless Aircraft, Catapults and In-Flight Refuelling

Looking back over the past two decades gives one the impression that a lot of activity was going on at Farnborough. This is true, although during these years there were many prototype aircraft built and not proceeded with, let alone those design projects that did not proceed further than the drawing board. A hive of activity this place was during those years, but with the end of World War One, and the formation of the Royal Aircraft Establishment, things would dramatically change. A centre of excellence for all things aeronautical was now in the making.

1925

The early helicopter tests in 1924 paved the way for further rotary trials. A Spanish-built C.6A, the first Cierva Auto-Gyro, which was basically an Avro 504K with wings removed and fitted with a four-bladed rotor, was demonstrated at Farnborough, making its initial flight on the 15th October 1925. The flights, which continued until at least 10th November, proved successful and the Air Ministry ordered the Avro 574, a licence-

Spanish-built Cierva C.6A autogiro about to make its first demonstration flight during October 1925. The old RFC hangars can be seen beyond, whilst the RAE coal-burning power station emits pollution from its chimney. *FAST collection*

Cierva C.8L-1 (Avro 575) J8930 flew from Farnborough between September 1927 and June 1930 on handling trials. It is seen here during October 1927. It was written off in a crash during June 1930. *FAST collection*

DH.53 Hummingbird J7326 is seen at Farnborough on 1st December 1925 with the trapeze installation fitted for launch and reattachment trials to the R-33 airship. This aircraft was eventually registered G-EBQP and crashed on 21st July 1934.
FAST collection

built example of the type, whilst Juan Cierva himself set up his business at Hamble the following year. The Cierva C.6C J8068 (an Avro 574, later modified as an Avro 587 to become G-EBTW) arrived at RAE from Hendon on 14th July 1926 and underwent handling trials with Aerodynamics Flight until it crashed on take-off on 25th September. It was rebuilt, but on 7th February 1927 it lost a rotor blade in flight, crashed at Hamble and was destroyed.

Cierva C.8L-1 J8930, (basically an Avro 575) arrived from Hamble, via Worthy Down, on 30th September 1927 being flown by Senor de la Cierva. This Rotaplane had first flown during June 1927 and came to Aerodynamics Flight for general research and investigation into full-scale rotaplane characteristics. It crashed at Farnborough on 11th January 1928 but was repaired by the manufacturers and returned to RAE on 20th February 1929. It then undertook trials at Farnborough and Andover, before crashing during June 1930 and being struck off charge. Cierva C.9 J8931, an Avro 576, first flew in September 1927 and arrived to begin its research programme into the investigation of full-scale rotaplane handling and performance on 18th July 1928. It was eventually struck off charge in June 1930. Further tests were conducted during August 1929 with Cierva C.17 Mk.II Autogiro G-AAGK on Certificate of Airworthiness trials, followed by similar tests for the Cierva C.19 Mk.II K1696, (an Avro 620). This arrived from Hamble on 27th August 1930 for C of A tests and investigations into a full-scale autogiro with Aero Flight but was damaged in a forced landing on 10th September and struck off charge in February 1931. Further tests included Cierva C.19 Mk.III G-AALA arriving from Hamble on 6th December 1929 and undergoing its C of A tests that month, returning to Farnborough on 13th March 1930 for full-scale rotaplane investigations and being written off in June 1930. A further Mk.III, K1948, came from

Hamble on 5th January 1931 for rotating-wing research with Aero Flight, including deck-landing practice, before being struck off charge on 14th March 1934. All variants were eventually issued with their respective C of A documents.

August saw the RAE Light Aeroplane Club enter the diminutive Hurricane in the Lympne races, where it surprisingly won the Grosvenor Trophy and £300 prize money: its speed on the day being 81.19mph. The Hurricane was scrapped during 1927.

The first RAE Mk.1 catapult was designed in 1921, but the first launch of an aircraft therefrom was made on 21st July 1925, when a Seagull I N146, converted from a Seal Mk.II, was successfully launched from Jersey Brow with an acceleration of 2G.

Aerodynamics Department were carrying out trials at Cardington with the R-33 airship, with a view to launching an aircraft from beneath the airship envelope and receiving it back beneath the airship during flight. The R-33 was repositioned to the Airship Establishment at Pulham in Yorkshire, and two DH.53 Humming Birds, J7325 and J7326, were used for these experiments, one being successfully launched from the trapeze system on the airship for the first time on 15th October although re-attachment could not be successfully made. However the first successful release and attachment was made on 4th December. During 1926, following the success of the Humming Bird trials, RAE was requested to study the use of a fighter type. This resulted in Gloster Grebe IIs J7400 and J7408 being prepared for similar flights, both to be carried beneath the R-33 together and these were also successfully launched individually on 21st October 1926. However, further experiments were eventually abandoned.

A Hill Pterodactyl that had been built at nearby Brookwood had undergone early wind tunnel tests and was first flown as a glider on 31st December 1924, in Sussex, by Capt G T R Hill. The powered version of the

Pterodactyl was a joint development with Westland Aircraft at Yeovil. Built as the Westland-Hill Pterodactyl Mk.1, it was completed in the autumn of 1925, being powered by a 34hp Cherub engine. It came to Farnborough for taxying and flight trials on 28th October making its first flight on 2nd November, flown by Geoffrey Hill. At Farnborough it was originally referred to as a Hill Tail-less and was allocated serial J8067. There followed a number of subsequent flights, including a display at the RAF Pageant at Hendon in July 1926.

A Mk.II and Mk.III (two-seater) variant were proposed but not built, although the Air Ministry requested further development of the type that resulted in the Mk.1A, to Specification 23/26, powered by a 34hp Bristol Cherub engine. It was first flown in June 1928, from Andover, and allocated serial J9251. After various flight trials it came to Farnborough from Yeovil on 11th September 1928, by now re-engined with a 70hp Armstrong Siddeley Genet as the need for more power was apparent. Now known as the Mk.1B, successful trials at Farnborough resulted in a C of A being granted for this variant. It was returned to Yeovil on 16th January 1929 for modifications to be implemented, including a different undercarriage, after the aircraft was damaged during landing. In its modified form it was known as a Mk.1C and it returned to Farnborough on 8th July for controllability trials, making its final flight at RAE on 31st July 1930.

There then followed the Pterodactyl Mk.IV K1947 powered by a 120hp de Havilland Gipsy III engine, which first flew on 9th June 1931 at Andover. After various manufacturer's trials this example came to RAE from Yeovil on 18th June 1931 for stability and control trials and returned to Yeovil on 2nd July, then appearing at the 1931 and 1932 RAF Pageants at Hendon, painted to represent its prehistoric ancestor. It was struck off charge in August 1938. The Pterodactyl Mk.V (P8, but later K2770) was the fourth and last of this family. Powered by a 600hp Rolls-Royce Goshawk engine, it made its first flight in May 1934 from Andover. It was intended to send this example to RAE for flight trials, but very shortly after take-off from Yeovil on its delivery flight in the summer of 1935, the engine seized and a dead-stick landing was successfully accomplished. There were no spare engines available and thus no further development or testing was accomplished. Instead this example came to Farnborough

Seen on a snowy Farnborough aerodrome on 3rd December 1925, is Captain G T R Hill's Pterodactyl, referred to at this stage as a Hill Tail-less and eventually to become J8067. It is still extant in the Science Museum, South Kensington. *FAST collection*

During 1931, Pterodactyl Mk.IV K1947 came to Farnborough for stability and control trials. It is seen here outside one of the RAE hangars in June 1931. *FAST collection*

by road, on 8th June 1936, for storage and was eventually struck off charge during July 1937. Overall the Pterodactyls provided considerable information in respect of engineering and flight characteristics, which was of benefit in years to come with research into the jet tail-less types.

During the mid-1920s various civilian aircraft were test flown by RAE pilots, at Farnborough or the manufacturers facilities, where a variety of trials were undertaken and suggestions for modification and improvement made.

1926

The prototype Fairey Ferret N190, designed as a reconnaissance aircraft for the Fleet Air Arm, arrived at Farnborough from Northolt, on 25th June 1926, and was successfully launched from the Farnborough catapult on 9th July, whilst undergoing proving trials with Instrument Flight, this being the second launch from the catapult. The Ferret departed for Martlesham Heath on 17th August 1926. Parnell Peto N181 was also launched at this time, on or around 6th July 1926. This light reconnaissance aircraft was intended for operations from HM Submarine M2, which was fitted with a Carey catapult. Thus the RAE Mk.1 catapult proved successful and the same design was installed in HMS *York*, with the first successful launch being made during May 1928. A further catapult was then built at Farnborough, during January 1929, and this was tested before installation in HMS *Hood*. The third catapult launch was a Flycatcher S1278 on 31st January 1929. These catapults at Farnborough were the precursor of many seaplane catapults installed in battleships and cruisers at that time.

The Light Aeroplane Club designed an ultralight monoplane, called the Sirocco, as a projected entry for the Grosvenor Trophy race at Lympne this year. The aircraft was registered as G-EBNL on 26th January, but it was not completed and the project was abandoned. A Hawker Cygnet G-EBJH was presented to the LAC by Messrs Sopwith and Sigrist.

The three-engined Fokker F.VIIA/3m, J7986, is seen at Farnborough during September 1926 and was used for low-speed stability and control trials. It was scrapped in 1935. *FAST collection*

A DH.56 Hyena J7781 arrived at Farnborough from Stag Lane on 25th October 1926 and was fitted with an uncowled Jaguar IV engine. This aircraft was used for engine, carburation, altitude control and exhaust manifold tests and the development of an exhaust-driven generator. It was sent for service trials with the resident No 4 Squadron and returned to RAE Engine Research Flight in late 1927.

On 30th August 1926 a Fokker VII/3M J7986 arrived from Martlesham Heath and was engaged on low-speed stability and control studies along with an Armstrong Whitworth Ape J7753, which had arrived from Coventry on 1st June 1926 but crashed on take-off on 8th May 1928. It was rebuilt by the manufacturers and was re-engined with a Jaguar III and returned to RAE for engine trials. The Fokker was later fitted with a Stieger Monospar wing made by Glosters and was eventually struck off charge around 1934. These aircraft obtained many results that were useful in the study of aerodynamics.

Further changes occurred within the Royal Air Force element at Farnborough. During April it came under No 22 Group Inland Area and responsibility for the School of Photography, Experimental Section, and the resident No 4 Squadron came under this Group.

A A Griffith, of RAE Engine Experimental Department, undertook early gas turbine studies during this year, which led to various experiments being conducted at Farnborough during 1927 and 1930 on testing aerofoil-shaped compressor and turbine blades in a cascade wind tunnel. Probably as a result of a financial restraint, nothing further was researched in this field from 1930 up until 1936.

1927

Still continuing with the pilotless aircraft projects, with the advancement of radio and successful development of basic autopilot equipment, Instruments and Aerodynamics Departments had produced the Larynx. Originally designed as a 300-mile range bombardment weapon, it was fitted with a 200hp Armstrong Siddeley Lynx engine that gave it a top speed of 193mph. By now, catapult launching had come a long way forward and this small unmanned aircraft was developed into a reasonable flying target for operation from a catapult on board a destroyer. This Larynx was successfully launched from HMS *Stronghold* on 20th July, followed by further flights from ships in the English Channel during 1927 and 1928. Six aircraft underwent range tests at Shaibah, Iraq during 1929, with four being lost during these tests. All these tests proved satisfactory but, due mainly to lack of funds, the Larynx Project was eventually abandoned, although development of further pilotless aircraft continued at RAE for many years thereafter.

Engine research continued with ER Flight and a Bristol F.2B Fighter J6721 flew with an experimental steam-cooled Rolls-Royce Falcon III engine on 4th November 1927 to conduct tests to improve the efficiency of a liquid-cooled engine, the steam radiator being positioned on top of the engine cowling. Hawker Horsley II J8001 had arrived on 10th September 1931 and

was dispatched to Rolls-Royce at Tollerton on 16th September for fitment of a Buzzard III engine. After trials with the manufacturer it returned to ER Flight on 30th May 1934 and continued with the development work until 5th September 1934. A further Horsley II, J8620, had arrived for ER Flight on 8th June 1932 from Brooklands, and was subsequently fitted with a Junkers Jumo IV engine. It appears to have made its first flight with this engine on 16th December 1933. In 1933 another Horsley II, J8003, came in for engine development work and made its first flight, possibly on 13th June 1933, with a Rolls-Royce Condor C.1 compression-ignition (diesel) engine installed for various trials with ER Flight. This aircraft participated in the RAF Pageant at Hendon during late June 1933.

Dr A A Griffith started turbine engine experiments at RAE in 1927. This led to testing a model single-stage turbine and axial compressor, produced by engine experimental department and tested in 1929. *FAST collection*

Seen on board HMS *Stronghold* is an RAE Larynx No 3, ready to be launched from the ship's catapult on 19th October 1927. After further sea launch trials and range tests in Iraq during 1929 the project was abandoned. *FAST collection*

De Havilland DH.56 Hyena J7781 first flew on 29th June 1926 and came to RAE for engine research on 25th October 1926. It was used for thermo-coupler, exhaust collector, carburation, exhaust manifold, engine-driven generator, cylinder temperature, and cockpit heating tests, and was then transferred to I&P Flight during 1931, where trials for airspeed indicators, revolution indicators and air temperature thermometers, were carried out, until the aircraft crashed on the airfield on 23rd April 1931. *FAST collection*

1928

September saw the Contracts Technical Supervision Department and the Airscrew Design Department merging with Airworthiness Department, which led to the evolution of the Mechanical Test Department, with research into aircraft construction methods. This Department became principally engaged in stressed skin and monocoque construction, and testing of airframes. Wireless and Photographic Department was renamed Experimental Wireless Department during this year and work continued on improving radio equipment, including radio wave-length trials.

The German-designed Beardmore Inflexible J7557, initially registered as G-EBNG on 29th December 1925 but not taken up, was powered by three 650hp Rolls-Royce Condor engines and, at the time, was the largest aircraft in the world. It first flew on 5th March 1928 but did not make many flights and was eventually withdrawn from use in 1930 and used for early structural tests at Farnborough.

Further spinning trials were being conducted using a Bristol F.2B Fighter Mk.III H1417. This had its mainplanes moved rearwards by four inches, and was fitted with a larger fin and rudder and leading edge slots. Gamecock I J8047 arrived from Brockworth on 28th November 1928 and was in use with Aero Flight for general tests and spinning trials. This aircraft was returned to the Gloster factory at Brockworth on 1st March 1929 and was modified with a variable incidence gear on the tailplane. It returned to Farnborough on 10th August 1932 for further spinning trials. However, the tests conducted were not conclusive except that the aircraft was difficult to recover from the spin.

1929

By now, problems were recurring with the British national economy and therefore research work at RAE began to suffer and consequently the staff was reduced in numbers. A period of recession followed, and it was not until the mid-1930s that the workforce at Farnborough began to increase again.

After the completion of the Larynx pilotless target trials, attention was now being turned by the Physics & Instrument Department (renamed during 1930 as the Instrument & Photographic Department) to developing a more realistic full-scale target aircraft for use by the Royal Navy. The Fairey IIIF, to be fitted with floats, was chosen for conversion and a new autopilot and a radio control system was designed during 1929. Meanwhile during 1931 Fairey IIIF Mk.III S1317 underwent various tests at Farnborough including a launch from the RAE catapult on 24th February 1931, and various radio transmission/receiver tests as well as general wireless and instrument work. A second example, Mk.IVB K1698, came to Farnborough on 12th June 1931 and was used for various radio trials, long-distance flying and catapult trials.

Work continued on this design, and in 1930/31 three Fairey IIIF Mk.IIIBs (S1490, S1497 and S1536) were allocated for conversion. The Fairey Queen, as it was now known, was able to obtain all the flight characteristics of a manned aircraft and a fully automatic landing system was also embodied. The float-equipped aircraft had the advantage that it could land successfully on the sea and be recovered to a 'mother' ship, thus being available for further flights. The first of the three aircraft, S1490, arrived at Farnborough from Heath Row on 10th November 1930. By 2nd December, I&P Department had installed some of the equipment and it commenced extensive flight trials, including a catapult launch at Farnborough on 20th May 1932. The second aircraft, S1497, arrived from Martlesham Heath on 26th May 1931 and was operational after conversion on 13th July 1931 for the necessary flight trials. The third aircraft, S1536, arrived from Hamble on 22nd July 1931 making its post-conversion flight on 6th November 1931. There then followed much target flying, with pilots on board, of all three examples before they were ready for trials in the auto-radio-controlled mode.

Fairey Queen S1536 was the first to leave Farnborough when it was dispatched to Gosport on 7th January 1932, and then on to Lee-on-Solent for fitment of floats, whereupon it was flown from the Solent to HMS *Valiant* for its first catapult launch. The launch was made on 30th January but the aircraft crashed into the sea immediately after. S1497 followed on 4th April 1932, was launched from HMS *Valiant*'s catapult on 19th April but it too crashed into the sea after launch. The third, S1490, left Farnborough on 18th August, and made a successful launch from HMS *Valiant*'s catapult on 14th September 1932. HMS *Valiant* sailed for Gibraltar, the remaining Fairey Queen being sent with the ship to be engaged in Naval gunnery practice, from which it remarkably survived. However during May 1933 it was sent to Malta, only to succumb to the Royal Navy on board HMS *Shropshire*, being shot down on 30th May. Thus the three Fairey Queens were all expended but much had been learnt which would be useful in the Queen Bee development of the de Havilland Moth/Tiger Moth.

Dr A A Griffith ran bench tests on the embryo axial flow turbo-machinery, the early gas turbine engine, which had commenced work in the mid-1920s. This gathered further pace in 1936 and eventually led to the RAE/Metropolitan Vickers F.2.

A catapult, for installation on board HMS *Hood*, was successfully tested on Jersey Brow and was dismantled and fitted to the ship.

1930

The first of the large test frames, known as 'The Temple', was constructed for Mechanical Test Department. Using it, many airframes and structural components could be tested under flight load conditions.

The first recorded in-flight-refuelling experiments were carried out in the USA during 1923 and again during 1929. Following the trials of 1924, there was now a requirement for further trials and the resumption of these trials on 6th August, this time by Instrument and Photographic Department, engaged Vickers Virginia IX

Having arrived from Martlesham Heath on 28th March 1930 Virginia IX J8236 was first launched from the RAE portable catapult on 13th June 1930. The aircraft was successfully launched a number of times, including demonstrations at the RAF pageants at Hendon. This Virginia was withdrawn in September 1933.
FAST collection

J8236 as receiver and two DH.9s, DH.9A H3588 and DH.9 D2825, as tankers. The tanker flew with a 300ft length of weighted wireless aerial, and later a hosepipe, which was trailed and 'hooked' up. This eventually led to the successful transfer of 50 gallons of fuel, using a 1.5" diameter hose. Another Virginia VIII, J7275, was modified to a tanker, first flying as such on 3rd June 1931, to refuel J8236. Further tests were accomplished in 1931/32 including the first public demonstration, at Hendon in June 1931, using two Virginias: J7558 as receiver and J7275 as tanker. The last RAE demonstration at the RAF Hendon display took place in June 1937 with the Vickers Vannock I J9131 as tanker and Boulton & Paul Overstrand J9770 as receiver.

Well-known RAF pilot Sqn Ldr Atcherley visited the USA a number of times during the early 1930s to participate in air displays and air races, where he witnessed air-to-air refuelling demonstrations, and, whilst posted in Jordan, he considered there to be further potential for these refuelling methods. In 1934 he was posted to Farnborough, by now having devised procedures for this using grapnels in flight, and various experiments were conducted by EFD. These early methods of in-flight-refuelling were researched for a further eight years, utilising an assortment of aircraft, including: Vickers Venture J7277; Westland Wapiti Mk.IIA K1142, Mk.II K1386, Mk.IIA J9604 and Mk.V J9728; Valentia K3168; Fairey Seal K3576; Vildebeest I K2820; Hawker Hart K1436 and K3014; Wallace I K4344 and K3673; Vickers Vannock I J9131; Handley Page Heyford III K4021; BP Overstrand J9770; Vickers Vincent K4105 and HP.51 prototype J9833. Various permutations were also considered, including wingtip-to-wingtip, wingtip-to-cockpit and cockpit-to-cockpit methods, as well as the earlier trailed line caught by the observer in the rear gunner's position of the Virginia who then hauled the hose onboard. How-

ever the Air Staff decreed in 1938 that all further work in this field, and future development, would be undertaken by Flight Refuelling Limited of Wimborne and work continued with them, initially even using some of the aircraft that performed the tests with RAE. Consequently the last Farnborough trial was carried out on 24th August 1937 and the last demonstration a few days later on 31st August, this being a comparison between the RAE method and that of FRL, being flown from Ford. Reporting on the Hendon display of 1937, 'The Aeroplane' said, 'Refuelling in the air is one of those strange pastimes practised in secret at Farnborough and revealed every year to an admiring concourse of taxpayers at Hendon'. On 5th August 1939 the first in-flight refuelling of a scheduled flight occurred, this being between London and New York. The tanker aircraft was a Harrow and the receiver a Short 'C' Class flying boat. Sixteen of these flights were accomplished before the outbreak of World War Two. Thus further work on in-flight refuelling with FRL eventually led to the adoption of the 'Probe & Drogue' in-flight refuelling technique, which was introduced in 1949, and is still an important asset of today's operations in the RAF and elsewhere.

The largest aircraft to be launched so far from the RAE Portable Catapult was Virginia IX J8236, which was launched at an acceleration of 1G on 13th June 1930. This catapult was designed to launch aircraft up to 18,000 lb at 60mph in 100 yards. Further launches of this aircraft occurred on 16th June and 19th September, but it was also demonstrated at the RAF Pageant at Hendon during 1931. Other types launched by the Jersey Brow catapults during this period included Fairey Fleetwing N235, and Fairey IIIF Mk.IIIs S1317 and S1351. Later to become J9682, the sole Hawker Hornet, built to Specification F.20/27 and first flown during March 1929, arrived from Martlesham Heath on 1st July 1930 and was successfully launched from the catapult on 19th July, leaving for Brooklands on 25th July. It came back again on 15th September from

In-flight refuelling trials recommenced during August 1930. Seen here are DH.9A H3588 as tanker and Virginia IX J8236 as receiver. These trials involved many other aircraft and continued until August 1937.
FAST collection

The R-100 Airship is seen overhead Farnborough aerodrome on 20th January 1930, with Venture J7277 at the rear. The area of the airfield at this time extended from the main Farnborough road, running from an angle just left of lower centre westward to the grass at the extreme right-hand edge. *FAST collection*

Brooklands, for use by WE Flight for wireless transmission trials, and also heated clothing tests, and returned to Brooklands on 20th October 1930.

The R-100 airship flew over Farnborough from Cardington on 20th January 1930 for assessment of the envelope at speed, (that is, flapping and bulging). It was photographed by Venture J7277 of I & P Flight, which flew alongside for over an hour to record the condition of the airship envelope during speed runs over the airfield. With Barnes Wallis on board, it returned to Cardington completing a flight with a duration of 7 hours.

A seaplane tank was constructed at Farnborough during this year, for the hydrodynamic testing of model seaplanes and flying boat hulls for their water characteristics under speed. The tank had a length of 660ft and a carriage speed of 40ft/sec, and became operational in 1933.

During the early part of this year, a new wind tunnel design had been recommended for installation at the Royal Aircraft Establishment. Work was commenced during this year on what became known as the 24ft tunnel. It was designed with an open section of 24ft in diameter and was required for testing full-scale aircraft, propellers, engine cowlings and various other aircraft parts.

During 1930, Parnell Parasols K1228 and K1229 arrived. Powered by the 226hp AS Lynx engine, they had been built at Yate, Bristol for use as flying laboratories to test wing incidence and modified various lift devices. The first of these high-lift aircraft arrived on 20th August 1930 from Yate and made its first RAE flight on 30th September 1930 with Aero Flight. The aircraft was used for wing section experiments, lift devices, including Zap flaps, tests of a flight-path recorder and latterly with an RAF Wing 38 section. This wing section was one of a number of aerofoil profiles provided by 'Factory' research. This Parasol last flew on 22nd Sep-

tember 1936 and was struck off charge during January 1937. K1229 arrived from Yate on 15th October 1930 and made its first flight with Aero Flight on 31st October. This aircraft was used in much the same way as K1228, although latterly it was testing a Gottingen 387 section wing. It made a forced landing at Sutton Green on 31st March 1936 and was damaged beyond repair.

Another unusual type of helicopter came to Farnborough in January 1930. Known as the Isacco Heligyre, the type was originally built in France and an example, to be built by Saro, was ordered for the RAE. K1171 had 35hp Bristol Cherub engines fitted to the tips of each of the four rotating wings, whilst an Armstrong Siddeley Genet 100hp engine supplied forward power. It appears this

Heligyre did not actually fly, but it made some tethered hovers in one of the RAE hangars. It was damaged beyond repair on 30th December 1931, when one of the retaining wires was not released when the rotors were engaged.

1931

Experimental Flying Department commenced research on aircraft endurance with Bristol Type 109 G-EBZK (registered 4th July 1928, but also marked as R.2); a long-range biplane fitted with a 490hp Jupiter XIF engine. The first flight was made on 7th September 1928 from Filton and after various trials with the manufacturer it was sent to Farnborough, arriving there from Filton on 12th September 1930. Here it underwent

Having arrived from Northolt on 16th March 1929 for WE Flight, Fairey IIIF S1317 was originally used for general wireless transmission tests but on 13th August 1930 was launched from the RAE Mk.1 catapult. It made many other launches between 1930 and 1933 and this undated photograph shows the aircraft having just left the launch trolley. This early catapult was laid in a shallow pit on what was to become the famous Jersey Brow launch site. *FAST collection*

an extensive programme of endurance trials with ER Flight. On 30th September it spent a continuous 8.3 hours in the air, whilst other days would see a total airborne time of between ten and twelve hours, encompassing three or four flights. The programme went without any real problems until 22nd January 1931 when a forced landing was made at Lympne due to a broken valve-rocker tie-rod. Repairs were accomplished and the aircraft was returned to Farnborough on 11th February. Endurance tests resumed and continued until 11th March 1931. The programme covered some 300 hours; some engine de-icing investigations being undertaken during this period. The aircraft underwent a C of A test on 12th March and was flown back to Filton on 17th March.

The first two DH.60M Moths to be used by the RAE arrived from Stag Lane on 28th January 1931. Allocated to E Flight, these were basically to be used as 'hack' aircraft by the then Director of Technical Development (DTD) as well as on other general duties. K1877 was transferred to the resident RAF School of Photography during February 1937, eventually being struck off charge during July 1939; K1876 was used for slot and spoiler trials, passing to Handley Page at Radlett from 28th August 1931 until 27th November 1931, whereupon it returned to RAE to continue the slot experiments until it left for Martlesham Heath on 11th September 1937. Further DH.82 Tiger Moths gradually appeared and one example, K2567, which arrived from Grantham on 12th January 1933, made its first RAE flight on 7th February 1933 and went on to spend many years with I & P Flight undergoing research including: petrol gauges, atmospheric turbulence, pressure relay gauge, altimeter and air speed indicators, artificial horizon, mail pick-up, a target hack, camouflage tests, blind flying, directional gyro indicator and wind direction turn indicator

installation. It eventually left RAE for Kirkbride on 2nd March 1940. Other examples followed and perhaps it was rather fitting than even up to 2004 there was still a privately owned Tiger Moth, G-ANNG, based on the airfield with the DERA Aero Club, so on numerous occasions the unmistakeable sound of the Gipsy could still be heard in the circuit.

Aerodynamics Department were undertaking spinning tests with Bristol F.2B Fighter F4587, which had arrived from Radlett on 9th December 1931, basically replacing C4776, which had served in this role for some time. These tests carried on until the end of 1936 with the aircraft departing for Hendon on 10th January 1937. Spinning tests also included a model suspended in a small vertical wind tunnel, and further tests were continued when a specially constructed 12ft diameter tunnel was built in the old Beta shed. This was used for all subsequent spin research conducted at Farnborough until the late-1950s.

1932

After the success of the Fairey Queen a new, cheaper target aircraft was sought and the de Havilland DH.82B, based on the Tiger Moth, was chosen for this, fitted with floats, and installed with the radio and autopilot equipment under specification 18/33. This was a radio-controlled target aircraft and, although externally similar to the Tiger Moth, the mainplanes, undercarriage and fittings were the same but the fuselage was based upon the standard spruce and plywood structure of the Moth. All the early examples came direct from the Moth Major production line and from 1935 it was entirely Queen Bee production, alongside the standard DH.82 Tiger Moth. The standard front cockpit was retained but it was modified so that a fairing would cover it over during radio-controlled flying whilst the rear

cockpit was faired over as it contained the RAE-designed radio equipment. To increase range a larger fuel tank was fitted.

The prototype Queen Bee K3584, then known as a 'Special Moth', came from Stag Lane on 26th April 1933 for trials as a target aircraft, and first flew as such on 3rd May 1933. It was returned to the manufacturers on 25th April 1934 for full conversion to Queen Bee status and first flew as such at Hatfield on 5th January 1935, being later struck off charge during February 1935. The first full production-status aircraft was the second of the type, K3597, which arrived from Stag Lane on 17th October 1933, making its first flight after equipment installation on 20th November 1933. This example made its first auto-flight on 29th January 1934 and undertook target trials at Lee-on-Solent and Roborough, but was struck off charge on 14th March 1934. There then followed the third example, K3598, which arrived from Stag Lane on 20th October 1933, making its first flight at Farnborough on 8th January 1934. This aircraft was used for control and catapult trials including detachments to Lee-on-Solent, Roborough and Portland. It departed from Farnborough for Sealand on 10th April 1934, eventually being shot down off Gibraltar on 17th April 1936.

Three more aircraft, K4044, K4045 and K4046, followed from Stag Lane and all three arrived on 19th February 1934, and made their first flights at RAE after having the equipment installed, on 20th March, 13th April and 5th April 1934 respectively, these three being used as trials aircraft, both in the UK and overseas. Four more examples, K4226, K4227, K4228 and K4229, followed in quick succession, arriving from Stag Lane on 18th May, 23rd May, 28th May and 30th May 1934 respectively. These made their first flights at Farnborough on 1st June, 11th June, 15th June and 28th June 1934 respectively and were soon put to good work by I & P Department. K4044, K4045 K4228 and K4293, were deployed for target trials at Rosyth during September/October 1934. The first auto-flight at Rosyth occurred on 28th September with K4044. Meanwhile another example, K4046, had departed to Sealand on 24th April 1934 for shipment overseas. Further trials at Lee-on-Solent were accomplished with three of these aircraft, K4226, K4227 and K4229, whilst K4228 remained at Farnborough. Two further examples, K4293 and

Fairey IIIF S1536 was converted to a Fairey Queen target and, after trials at Farnborough, it was then dispatched to Lee-on-Solent for fitment of floats to embark on HMS *Valiant*. It is seen here on the catapult, awaiting launch on 30th January 1932 ... although immediately after launch the aircraft crashed into the sea.
FAST collection

K4294, arrived from Hatfield on 11th August 1934 and made their first Farnborough flights on 29th August and 27th September respectively.

Instrument and Photographic Flight had been operating all these aircraft, which from 8th June 1934 were officially referred to as the Queen Bee in the RAE Flight Log books, and on 25th August 1934 the operating Flight became known as GC (Gunnery Co-operation) Flight. The next nine examples from the production line came to Farnborough direct from the manufacturer's plant for equipment fitment, or trials, prior to being assigned to a Gunnery Co-operation Flight, Anti-Aircraft Co-operation Unit or the School of Naval Co-operation, most eventually being shot down, which is what they were intended for.

A demonstration was given at Farnborough on 26th June 1935 with Queen Bee K4227 being controlled by commands from a ground station transmitter, although there was still a safety pilot on board, this being repeated at the RAF display at Hendon a couple of days later. During 29th, 30th and 31st July 1935 Queen Bees K5100, K5060 and K5100 respectively made three auto-launches from the catapult installed at Watchet in Somerset.

This secret project had been known as 'Project Queen Bee', and this name was officially given to the converted Moth/ Tiger Moth radio-controlled aircraft. Overall 404 Queen Bees were built and over forty of these were either delivered to RAE or underwent trials work at Farnborough or participated on the numerous trials detachments. Many trials were flown with this type and these proved highly successful, including those fitted with a standard undercarriage for land-based operations. In 1947, when there was no need for these any more, the survivors were declared as surplus and sold on the general market, many finding their way into eventual civilian use.

DH.82B Queen Bee K4229 is seen here on Jersey Brow during January 1935. It arrived at Farnborough on 30th May 1934 and, after various radio-control trials, passed to the Gunnery Co-operation Flight at Gosport. *FAST collection*

DH.82B Queen Bee K5114 arrived at RAE on 16th August 1935. It is seen here about to be loaded onto its catapult at Watchet, Somerset for operation with 3 AACU. It was shot down during August 1937. *FAST collection*

Hawker Osprey I K2779 is seen here at Farnborough during January 1934. It arrived from Netheravon on 14th November 1933 for receiver and transmitter trials with WE Flight, still wearing its code '208' of 800 Squadron, returning to Netheravon on 23rd January 1934. *FAST collection*

The spinning tower was constructed during this year for testing of full-scale propellers. It proved to be very noisy, but needless to say it was a useful installation and remained in use until the 1960s.

1933

The seaplane tank commenced research operations and the first model used was that of a Shorts Singapore III flying boat, whose behaviour characteristics were recorded. Many other model flying boat types were tested in this tank during the years, including the Saunders-Roe Princess, and it was not until the late 1950s that the tank became redundant. However the building was converted to offices, being cut into two basic sections, where laboratories, workshops and offices were present. This building (Q120) was demolished in March 2005; it was strange to see the water tank area exposed after all these years, albeit without water. A small 20ft section of this tank has been retained, at the eastern end, for eventual development as a water feature within the Business Park currently under construction.

1934

Heinkel He 64c K3596 arrived from Martlesham Heath on 20th February 1935 to undergo flap research at RAE with Aero Flight. This aircraft, previously in Germany as D2305, was registered as G-ACBS in December 1932 but was given serial number K3596 whilst it was on loan to RAE. It undertook general handling trials, flap research and landing experiments and its last RAE flight appears to have been on 9th

May 1935 as it was struck off charge six days later. It eventually returned to civilian life and was sold in Southern Rhodesia as VP-YBI in January 1937.

First flown on 23rd March 1934 was the Westland F.7/30 prototype K2891, designed as a multi-gun, single-seat fighter, albeit in a biplane configuration, as opposed to the other contenders in this Specification. It came from Yeovil on 22nd June 1934 for a brief spell with Aero Flight before returning to Yeovil on 3rd July. At the same time the Westland PV.7 prototype, built to Specification G.4/31, first flown on 30th October 1933 and not allocated a serial number, came to RAE on 20th June 1934 and returned to Yeovil with the F.7/30 on 3rd July 1934. Neither of these projects proceeded any further and the F.7/30 was dismantled and sent to Halton for the School of Technical Training in May 1935, whilst the G.4/31 was written off in a crash while with the A&AEE on 25th August 1934.

A further contender for the F.7/30 contract was designed by Supermarine as the

Type 224 (K2890). This low-wing monoplane with a cranked wing first flew on 19th February 1934 from Eastleigh and was flown to RAE on 24th July 1935, making its first Farnborough flight on 12th August. Used by ER Flight for evaporative cooling trials and by Aero Flight for spinning research, it left for the A&AEE at Martlesham Heath on 15th June 1937 and ended its days as a gunnery target at Orfordness. Interestingly this aircraft, designed by R J Mitchell, had previously been unofficially known as the Spitfire, but due to various problems, including it not being accepted by the Air Ministry, Mitchell and his design team concentrated all their future efforts in Specification F.5/34, which ultimately became the true Spitfire. The third contender in the F.7/30 battle, which was actually won by the Gladiator to a slightly different specification, was the Blackburn F.3 K2892. This was never flown and remained at the Brough works until it was transferred to Halton as an instructional airframe as 874M.

Development of the first safety crash barriers were started at Farnborough and the first trials followed in 1937.

'A' shed (hangar), which later became P71 building, was completed this year and has been used to house many different types of aircraft over the years. This building is still extant. It is leased to BAE Systems by TAG Aviation and is in current use as a store.

One of the two Blackburn CA.15C monoplanes, K4241 was purchased by the Air Ministry and came to RAE Farnborough in 1934 for trials with WE Flight. These included experimental direction finding equipment and radio azimuth trials. It was also used for fog landing and airfield lighting trials and left Farnborough for Cardington on 16th February 1937. *FAST collection*

SBAC DISPLAYS AT FARNBOROUGH

The World's Premier Aviation Trade Show

The Society of British Aircraft Constructors (SBAC) was formed on 29th March 1916 and originally exhibited aircraft as static displays at Olympia, London, in conjunction with the annual exhibition by the Society of Motor Manufactures and Traders. The first exhibition attracted 28 aircraft to Olympia and SBAC continued to support these shows until 1929.

In previous years the RAF had started its own displays at Hendon, the first being in 1920, and these continued until 1937. In 1932 the SBAC obtained permission from the Air Ministry to use the Monday following the RAF event for a new static aircraft park and flying display of the new types. Thus the first SBAC show, which was a display for potential British and foreign buyers, took place on 27th June 1932, with 34 aircraft present and no cameras permitted. Fortunately, after much pressure from the Press, this restriction was lifted for the 1933 event and thereafter. The last Hendon event was 1st July 1935. Due to the growing number of aircraft and interest, the SBAC moved its event to de Havilland's airfield at Hatfield for the 1936 display. This venue also staged the two-day 1937 event, which turned out to be the last before the outbreak of World War Two. These occasions had been open to both British industry and foreign guests, but with war clouds looming it was considered inappropriate to allow foreigners to view the latest aircraft.

At the end of hostilities, the SBAC shows resumed in 1946, with one day for static aircraft inspection and one day for flying demonstrations, now at the Handley Page airfield at Radlett, where, during 12th and 13th September, some 55 aircraft of different types were on display from the British aircraft manufacturers – many for the first time. Such had been the advancement of the British aviation industry during the non-show years of World War Two that this was seen as the largest aviation industry show to date.

The next year, 1947, saw Radlett again as the venue and this was even larger and better attended than before, with three days allocated and all including flying demonstrations. By now the SBAC was thinking along the lines of finding a suitable, more permanent home. Up to now the public had not been admitted, so there was more pres-

This view from the Farnborough control tower shows the SBAC line-up during September 1948, the first of the displays at Farnborough. At left can be seen Hastings C.1 TG527, Marathon G-AILH is at centre, whilst beyond are Sealand G-AIVX, Brigand B.1 RH809 and Bristol Freighter 21E G-AIFO, plus a whole assortment of other types, including Lincolns, Lancastrian, Viking, AW.52, Air Horse and Nene-engined Viking. Further development of the airfield was yet to occur, as there would shortly be tree clearance at the left of the photograph and further hangars constructed in the background at right. *FAST collection*

sure on SBAC to open up the gates, and to extend the duration of the display.

Thus, having considered a number of options, SBAC chose Farnborough for the venue of its ninth display, which was held between 7th and 12th September 1948, with public admission on the final weekend. A 'Technicians Day' was also introduced, this being basically the rehearsal day where those who have helped design and build the aircraft and equipment on display can see the results of their labours, as well as their competitors' efforts, at close quarters and free from the general public. Consequently the benchmark had been set for a week-long display, with a Technicians' Day followed by three trade days, public admission on the Saturday, and an RAE employees' day on the Sunday. This natural display arena has remained the SBAC venue to date, although some fundamental changes have been implemented over the years.

Although the RAE airfield at Farnborough was a busy operational base, its size lent

itself to being suitable for a large array of static aircraft and the 1948 display saw a large number of aircraft present. An estimated crowd of 100,000 attended on the public day, such was the interest in the new aircraft and the test pilots that were now becoming household names. The static display of this show occupied the 'A' shed, hangar and apron, with some 200 trade stands situated in 'K1' and 'K2' sheds, the 'Black Sheds', occupying an area of 55,000ft^2. Suitable deckchairs were provided for the guests, to afford comfortable viewing, ranged on the north side of the runways.

The 1949 event continued in the same format but, as the size and scope of the show and its exhibition grew, a more permanent site was allocated for the 1950 display. This was located on the southeast area of the airfield, with the exhibition tent situated on the threshold of the cross-runway 29, very close to where Cody made his first flight. This area proved ideal for viewing and afforded much more space and of course meant that the visitors would be kept away from the main RAE site. Later the exhibition marquees were moved to a new permanent site on top of Danger Hill. Thus the area where today's exhibition halls stand has been the designated site for the past 53 years but has grown considerably during that time.

Up to and including 1962, the show had been held annually, but from 1964 it became a biennial event. During the same year, the society became known as the Society of British Aerospace Companies, which reflected the changes within the aerospace industry but retained its established initials. From the 1966 show, foreign aircraft with British equipment were permitted to participate by SBAC, this later developing into a true International show from the 1974 display when over 200 exhibiting companies were present.

Weather conditions have also had a part to play at the SBAC displays; some days being gloriously sunny, where aircraft have been able to perform in clear blue skies and show their stunning manoeuvres to the full with tell-tale smoke trails, whilst other days have seen extreme weather and storms curtailing the flying programme somewhat, the 1968 display being particularly spectacularly affected!

Although ownership of the airfield has now changed, SBAC has secured the current site for future exhibitions and these events, now entitled 'Farnborough International', attract many hundreds of thousands of visitors to Farnborough. The town, airfield, and the local road structure all become very busy and are packed with visitors for the duration of the display, which has now been moved from early September to the third week of July. Notwithstanding the fact that RAE Farnborough had been the UK's largest aeronautical research centre, it is probably in the air display guise that it has become so widely known throughout the world in recent years. Indeed, when travelling to

many foreign parts, as soon as you say you come from Farnborough, it usually opens up conversations – either about RAE or SBAC, or both!

Early Farnborough displays have become legends in their own right with fantastic flying, fabulous and futuristic aircraft, famous pilots and notable firsts and, in more recent times, a fun day out for all the family on the public days. There have been many notable aircraft and achievements at the Farnborough displays – far too many to record here as this would probably require a book in its own right – but the more notable aircraft for each of Farnborough's SBAC displays are recorded here.

1948

With much technical advancement in the aeronautical world, the stage was set to display new aircraft at Farnborough at the start of a new era. The static aircraft display was held on the 'A' shed apron where the 64 aircraft on show were ranged in neat lines, and what's more they were all British! Spectators were also on the north side of the main runway. Most of the aircraft on show were of interest but notable attractions included the world's largest helicopter at the time, the prototype Cierva Air Horse G-ALCV; the two prototype Armstrong Whitworth AW.52 'flying wings' TS363 and TS368; Hawker P.1040s VP401 and VP413; and the Saro SR/A1 TG271 jet flying-boat fighter, which made an inverted pass at 200ft during the display. Examples of aircraft on show included:

Avro Tudor 8	VX195	first flew 6 Sept 1948; the day before the show
Vickers Viking	G-AJPH	Nene-engined
Handley Page Hermes IV	G-AKFP	first flight 5 Sept; two days before the show
Vickers Viscount	G-AHRF	prototype
Bristol 170 Freighter 21E	G-AIFO	
Miles Marathon	G-AILH	
Airspeed Ambassador	G-AKRD	

Saro Skeeter	G-AJCJ	prototype
Fairey Gyrodyne	G-AIKF	prototype
	G-AJJP	prototype
Planet Satellite	G-ALOI	registration not carried
Short Sealand	G-AIVX	prototype
Supermarine Seagull	PA143	prototype
DH Vampire F.1	TG278	
DH Vampire F.5	VV218	
	VV219	
Gloster Meteor F.4	VT256	
	RA490	with Beryl engines
Gloster Meteor T.7	G-AKPK	prototype
Avro Lancastrian	VM732	twin Avon engines

1949

Held between 7th and 13th September the SBAC show was already expanding in size and the public attendance over the two days saw over 225,000 people present. There were 58 aircraft on display and 39 participated in the flying demonstrations. There were really two 'show-stoppers' at this display. The de Havilland DH.106 Comet 1 G-ALVG prototype, which first flew 27th July 1949 from Hatfield, made its debut at this display as the world's first jet airliner. Also making its debut at Farnborough on 8th September was the mighty Bristol Brabazon G-AGPW, the largest British-built aircraft, which had undertaken its maiden flight from Filton on 4th September. Other notable aircraft of interest included:

AW Apollo	G-AIYN	prototype, first flew 10th April 1949
Avro Athena T.2	VW892	third prototype
Avro Shackleton GR.1	VW131	second prototype
Avro 707	VX784	first flew 4 Sept 1949
DH Vampire FB.5	VV454	reheated version
Gloster Meteor F.4	RA435	
DHC Chipmunk T.10	WB549	first UK production example
DH Vampire NF.10	G-5-2	prototype, first flew 28th August 1949
EE Canberra	VN799	prototype, first flew 13th May 1949
Gloster Meteor F.8	VZ438	
Handley Page Hermes	G-ALEU	first flew 23rd August 1949
Hawker P.1052	VX272	prototype
Short Sturgeon TT.2	TS477	
Supermarine Attacker F.1	TS409	prototype
Supermarine 510	VV106	prototype
Vickers Varsity T.1	VX828	prototype

Seen during the SBAC flying display in September 1949 is the ungainly Cierva Air Horse, VZ724, which is flying with its front door open in this view. With its three large rotors, this was the largest helicopter in the world at the time, capable of carrying a load of 5,460 lb. Unfortunately the helicopter was written-off in an accident at West End, near Eastleigh, on 13th June 1950, when the forward rotor hub failed after high-frequency vibration led to failure of the swashplate drive. The three crew were regrettably killed. *FAST collection*

Handley Page Hermes V G-ALEV is seen here in the SBAC static display during September 1951. This was the second Hermes V; it first flew at Radlett on 6th December 1950, then passing to Boscombe Down for various trials. It then undertook trials with the manufacturer and came to RAE from Radlett on 20th February 1952 for automatic Maxaret braking trials, before being grounded and used for wing fatigue tests from April 1952 and finally being scrapped in September 1953. *FAST collection*

1950

The exhibition area covered some 66,000ft² and some 7,500 technicians visited whilst a further 21,900 people from the industry and foreigners were also in attendance. The public figure reached 43,750 on the Saturday and 76,100 on the Sunday. This display was moved to the south side of the main runway and the exhibition marquee was situated on the threshold of the cross-runway 29 with the aircraft ranged along Runway 25 for inspection prior to participating in the flying display, a tradition that continued until 2002. This change afforded better viewing with more space for aircraft static displays and exhibition space, which even at this time were rapidly expanding toward what they have become some 56 years later. Thus the famous RAE 'Factory' landscape became a familiar sight in photographs, newsreels and film footage over the years, though there is now very little left of the scene that dominated the backdrop and commentary all those years ago. Examples of notable aircraft on display this year included the Bristol Brabazon I G-AGPW, which was seen both on the ground and flying, and the English Electric Canberra B.2 prototype VX165. A military aerial refuelling demonstration was given during this show with Meteor F.4 VZ389 simulating taking on fuel from Lincoln B.II RA657, both aircraft being from Flight Refuelling Ltd. Other notable aircraft included:

Avro Lincoln B.II	SX972	with two Proteus turboprops
Gloster Meteor NF.11	WA547	second prototype
Gloster Meteor F.8	G-AMCJ	prototype ground-attack variant
Vickers Viscount 663	VX217	with Tay engines
DH Comet 1	G-ALVG	prototype
DH Heron	G-ALZL	prototype
Blackburn Universal Freighter	WF320	prototype
Hawker P.1081	VX279	prototype
Avro Ashton 1	WB490	prototype
Supermarine 535	VV119	prototype
Hawker Sea Hawk	VP413	prototype
Blackburn YB.1	WB797	prototype
Fairey GR17	VR557	second prototype
Percival Sea Prince C.1	WF136	
Percival P.56	WE530	second prototype
Bristol 171 Mk.3	WA576	prototype

1951

Fifty-one aircraft were displayed in the air at this show, ranging from the Blackburn Universal Freighter WF320 to the Auster J/5F Aiglet Trainer G-AMKF. The largest aircraft at the show, Bristol Brabazon 1 G-AGPW, remained on the ground, as did de Havilland Comet 1 G-ALYS. A good public attendance of around 300,000 was seen at this event with the exhibition area seemingly coming to a standstill during the public days due to a gridlock of visitors! Clearly, interest in the British aircraft industry was high with many new types still appearing. Aircraft on show included Hawker P.1067 prototype WB188, which gave the fastest speed demonstration yet seen in public and later went on to exceed the World Absolute Speed Record; along with the prototype Supermarine 508 VX133, which first flew on 31st August 1951 from Boscombe Down, just a few days prior to the event. There was an RAF flying demonstration, with four Vampire FB.5s from No 54 Squadron participating in the show. Other notable aircraft included:

Boulton Paul P.111	VT935	prototype
DH Vampire Trainer	G-5-7	statically displayed, first flew 15 Nov 1951
Auster B4	G-AMKL	
Avro 707A	WD280	
Fairey Firefly AS.7	WJ216	
EE Canberra PR.3	VX181	prototype
EE Canberra B.5	VX185	prototype
Miles Marathon	VX231	with two Mamba engines
Vickers Viscount 700	G-AMAV	
Fairey Gannet AS.1	WE488	third prototype
Westland S-51	G-ALIK	

1952

This was the 13th show and the fifth at Farnborough. Aircraft types, both civil and military, were rapidly increasing as the British aircraft industry was developing the platforms of the future, though not all would make it into full-scale production. Some 220 exhibitor stands were representing the UK aviation industry along with 50 aircraft on show. Guided missiles and rocket motors

were also on display. A high level of security surrounded the aircraft industry in these days and some of the aircraft types shown at Farnborough had never before been viewed in public. There were over 338,000 attendees during the week-long event.

Some notable aircraft accidents have occurred at Farnborough during the SBAC displays over the years, catching the limelight due to the nature of the event and also the fact that many of the world's press were present at the time. Thankfully these have been relatively few, although they have included the sad loss of test pilot Sqn Ldr John Derry and his flight test observer Tony Richards when their DH.110 prototype WG236 broke up just north of the airfield on 6th September 1952. The wreckage was projected into the SBAC crowd, where 27 spectators were also killed and a further 63 injured, this being the worst accident in SBAC history. Despite this tragic accident, the 1952 event is heralded as one of the best of the time with many, varied types on display, including the very first Avro Vulcan B.1 VX770, which had made its first flight on 30th August, two days before the show opened. Other notable aircraft included the prototype Short SA4 Sperrin VX158, the second prototype Hunter F.1 WB195 and a fly-by of the Saro Princess G-ALUN. Other aircraft of particular interest included:

Avro 707A	WD280	
Avro 707B	VX790	
Bristol Britannia	G-ALBO	prototype
Bristol Freighter Mk.31	NZ5906	for RNZAF
DH.110	WG236	prototype
	WG240	prototype
DH Comet 1	G-ALVG	prototype
DH Comet 1A	CF-CUM	for Canadian Pacific Airlines
DH Sea Venom NF.20	WK385	
EE Canberra T.4	WN467	
EE Canberra B.5	VX185	
EE Canberra B.2	WD943	with reheat
Miles Marathon T.11	XA250	
Hawker Sea Hawk F.1	WF147	
Scottish Aviation Pioneer 2	G-AKBF	

Two great British airliners are seen here in the SBAC static display at Farnborough during September 1952. Vickers Viscount 701 G-ALWE, in British European Airways markings, is seen in the foreground, whilst de Havilland Comet I prototype G-ALVG, in BOAC colours, which made its first flight on 27th July 1949, is seen beyond. The Viscount, the fourth built, first flew on 20th August 1952, just a few days before the SBAC display, but was later written-off in an accident on approach to Ringway Airport, Manchester, on 14th March 1957. *FAST collection*

The graceful lines of the Saunders-Roe SR.45 Princess G-ALUN can be seen in this view, showing a very low-level flypast down Farnborough's 25 runway on 11th September 1953. Clearing the runway are the two Vulcan prototypes, VX770 and VX777, whilst the four Avro 707s can be seen beyond. The Princess weighed 100 tons and was powered by 10 Bristol Proteus turbo-prop engines, with contra-rotating propellers on the inboard four engines. It made its first flight on 22nd August 1952, taking off from the Solent, but unfortunately the project was abandoned after three aircraft had been built, although this example was the only one to fly. All three were cocooned in storage during 1954, two stored at Calshot, where they remained for many years and were broken up during 1965. This example was stored at Cowes until it was towed along Southampton Water for scrapping on 12th April 1967. *FAST collection*

Seen here about to touch down on the Farnborough runway during the September 1954 SBAC display, is the Canberra B(I)8 prototype, VX185, finished in an all-black scheme. This aircraft carries a 30mm gun pack in the rear of the bomb bay and an F.24 high-level camera in the nose. This example was originally built as the B.5 prototype, making its first flight on 6th July 1951 from Samlesbury and was converted to a B(I)8 and first flew as same on 23rd July 1954. It was later used by Ferranti for air interception target trials and was then transferred to Short Brothers for development of the PR.9 version. It was eventually allocated to No 4 STT at St Athan as 7631M, for ground instruction duties and was finally broken up at Filton during April 1964. *FAST collection*

Opposite page: One of the first overseas-produced aircraft to be seen at an SBAC display was the Avro (Canada) CF-100 Mk.48, two of which appeared at the 1955 display. The type is powered by two Orenda engines and one of the aircraft, 18321, is here on approach to land on 9th September 1955. First flight of the type was made on 19th January 1950 and some 692 examples, in various marks, were produced, the type being finally retired from RCAF service in 1981, with this example being struck off charge in June 1958. The impressive Beta shed looms beyond, with the old original Balloon shed also in view and the RAE Q1 administration building to the right. *FAST collection*

Supermarine Swift F.1	WJ965	second prototype
	WK194	
Supermarine 529	VX136	prototype
Vickers Viscount 701	G-ALWE	
Westland Wyvern TF.4	VZ750	

1953

For the 1953 display there were 244 exhibitor stands, the exhibition marquee had expanded to cover 110,000ft^2, and 56 aircraft were on view. During this year's display Sqn Ldr Neville Duke set the new world speed record of 727.6mph on 7th September flying off Littlehampton in the all-red prototype Hawker Hunter WB188. The year saw a varied display that also included an unusual delta-wing formation comprising the four Avro 707s: blue 707B VX790, red 707A WD280, orange 707A WZ736, and silver 707C WZ744, with two of the new Avro Vulcans VX770 and VX777. The following aircraft were also displayed, with a high number of prototypes on show:

Short Seamew AS.1	XA209	prototype, first flew 13th August 1953
Hawker Hunter	WB188	prototype
	WB202	prototype
Handley Page Victor B.1	WB771	prototype
Blackburn GR17	WB781	YA7 and
	WB788	YA8 prototypes
DH.110	WG240	prototype
Vickers Valiant B.2	WJ954	prototype
Gloster Javelin FAW.1	WT827	prototype
Blackburn Beverley	WZ889	prototype
Bristol Britannia	G-ALBO	prototype
Saro Princess	G-ALUN	prototype
Bristol 173	G-AMJI	in BEA markings
Vickers Viscount 700	G-AMAV	
DH Comet 1	F-BGNX	for Air France
Scottish Aviation Pioneer	G-ANAZ	

1954

Popularity of the SBAC displays was now growing and on the last day of this show there were over 160,000 visitors and more than 20,000 cars and coaches present. The exhibition marquee moved this year from its previous site on Runway 29 to a new and more permanent position on the hill overlooking the airfield, where it remains today. Many prototype and early production aircraft were present at this show including Javelin FAW.1s WT827 third prototype, WT830 fourth prototype, WT836 fifth prototype, XA544 first production example and XA546; plus the second prototype Victor B.1 WB775; Short Sherpa G-14-1 and SB.5 WG768; and the sole Comet 3 G-ANLO. Aircraft of note at this display included:

Airspeed Ambassador	G-AKRD	two Proteus engines
Avro Vulcan B.1	VX770	Sapphire-engined
Bristol Britannia	G-ANCA	first production example
Bristol Freighter Mk.31E	G-18-166	for Pakistan Air Force
DH Comet 2	G-AMXD	
DH.110	WG240	second prototype

EE Canberra B.2	WD933	with Sapphire engines
	WD952	Olympus testbed
EE Canberra B.6	WJ771	
EE Canberra PR.7	WJ820	
EE Canberra B.8	VX185	prototype
Fairey FD.1	VX350	research prototype
Folland Midge	G-39-1	prototype
Gloster Meteor T.7	G-ANSO	
Gloster Meteor F.8	WA982	Soar engine testbed
Gloster Meteor NF.14	WS848	
Hawker Hunter F.1	WT631	
Hawker Hunter F.2	WN909	
Hawker Hunter F.6	XF833	
Percival Provost Mk.53	UB201	for Burmese Air Force
Hunting Jet Provost T.1	XD674	prototype
Percival Pembroke C.51	RM-8/	
	OT-ZAH	for Belgian Air Force
Vickers Viscount 720	VH-TVA	for Trans-Australia Airlines
Vickers Valiant B.2	WJ954	prototype
Supermarine Swift F.3	WK195	
	WK247	
Supermarine Swift F.4	WK273	
Supermarine 525	VX138	prototype

1955

The exhibition area had been increased for this show by a further 10%, with more terraces constructed for the exhibition area and additional pavilions built for company hospitality. All of this was situated in the elevated area of Danger Hill, which has now become the permanent SBAC exhibition marquee site. There were 307 exhibition stands in the indoor marquee covered area. This year saw service participation now becoming part of the display and a formation of 12 Vickers Valiants took part in a flypast, as did a formation of 64 Hawker Hunter F.1s, F.2s, F.4s and F.5s from various RAF squadrons, plus an aerobatic team of four Hunters from No 54 Squadron. Highlights of the display included the first production Avro Shackleton MR.3 WR970; the prototype English Electric P.1 WG760; the Fairey Delta Two WG774 research proto-

type; and the prototype Hunter T.7 XJ615. Other notable aircraft included:

Airspeed Ambassador	G-ALFR	with Eland turboprop engines
Avro Ashton	WB491	second example
Avro Canada CF-100 Mk.4Bs	18321	RCAF
	18322	RCAF
Bristol 173	XH379	second prototype
DH.110 Sea Vixen 20X	XF828	
EE Canberra PR.9	WH793	prototype
Fairey Ultra-light helicopter	XJ924	
	XJ930	
Folland Gnat 1	G-39-2	
Handley Page Herald	G-AODE	prototype
Hawker Hunter F.4	WT780	
	WV385	
Hawker Hunter F.6	WW593	
Percival Provost T.53	382	for Iraqi Air Force
Percival Pembroke C.52	83012	for Swedish Air Force
Scottish Avn Twin Pioneer	G-ANTP	prototype
Short Seamew MR.2	XE172	
Vickers Viscount 724	CF-TGV	for Trans-Canada Airlines
Westland Whirlwind HAR.5	XJ396	

1956

This year was the first display to host a delegation from the Soviet Union, with both civil and military missions present. Display teams at this show consisted of four Canberra T.4s from No 231 OCU at Bassingbourn and four Hunter F.4s from No 43 Squadron at Leuchars. Amongst the display aircraft a number of prototypes were to be seen including Hunting Jet Provost T.1 XD674 and Folland Gnat F.1 XK724. Other aircraft on show included:

Scottish Avn Twin Pioneer	G-AOEO	
Avro Lincoln B.2	G-37-1	Rolls-Royce Tyne testbed
Avro Vulcan B.1	XA892	
Fairey Ultra-light helicopter	G-AOUK	
Bristol 173	XH379	
Auster Agricola	ZK-BMK	
DH Comet C.2	XK695	

DH Heron 2	393	for Iraqi Air Force
EE Canberra B.2	WD930	Avon RA29 testbed
EE Canberra B.2	WK163	Scorpion rocket-motor testbed
EE Canberra B.2	WJ582	
EE Canberra B (I) 8	XK951	
Fairey FD.2	WG774	research prototype
	WG777	research prototype
Fairey Firefly U.9	WB257	
Gloster Javelin T.3	WT841	
Hawker Hunter F.6	XF833	with reverse-thrust Avon engine
Vickers Valiant B.1	WB215	with Sprite RATOG
Supermarine 544	WT854	prototype
	WT859	prototype

1957

A larger service display was presented this year from the Royal Air Force and the Fleet Air Arm. This consisted of aerobatics from the Hunter F.6s of No 111 Squadron, RAF North Weald; Provost T.1s from the Central Flying School at RAF Little Rissington and Sea Hawk FB.3s of 738NAS *The Red Devils* from RNAS Lossiemouth. Flypasts were performed by 36 Javelin FAW.2/4/5s from Nos 23, 46 and 141 Squadrons and No 228 OCU; 27 Hunter F.5s from Nos 1, 34 and 41 Squadrons; two Valiant BK.1s from No 49 Squadron; two Vulcan B.1s from No 230 OCU; 12 Gannets from the Fleet Air

Arm's 737, 796 and 825NASs, and a helicopter display from the Fleet Air Arm using two Whirlwind HAS.22s and three HAS.5s. Both the research prototype Saro SR.53s, XD145 and XD151, appeared at this display, as did the prototype Aviation Traders Accountant G-ATEL. Other aircraft included:

Miles Student	G-35-4	
Miles Aerovan	G-AHDM	
EE Canberra B.2	WK163	Napier Scorpion rocket motor
Bristol 173 Mk.1	XF785	
Bristol Britannia Srs 101	G-ALBO	Bristol Orion and Proteus testbed

The silver-finished prototype Fairey FD.2 research aircraft, WG774, is seen here lined up on the rain-soaked runway to commence its performance at the SBAC display on 6th September 1956. This example made its first flight on 6th October 1954 at Boscombe Down, with Peter Twiss at the controls, and it was on 10th March 1956 that an average speed of 1,132mph was achieved, this constituting a world record at the time. After trials with the manufacturer, the aircraft passed to RAE Bedford and in 1961 was converted to the BAC 221, to undertake trials in respect of the Concorde ogee delta wing. It later returned to RAE Bedford for trials and was withdrawn in 1973. It is now in the Fleet Air Arm Museum at Yeovilton. *Rawlings Family collection*

Above: **The spectacular 'Black Arrows', Hunter F.6s of No 111 Squadron, performed a superb 22-aircraft formation display and loop sequence at the SBAC display during September 1958. This was the greatest number of aircraft looped together at the time, and may still be the case today. Note the wing-tip vortices from the aircraft as they pull up through the moisture-laden air.** *FAST collection*

Left: **Thirty-six Gloster Javelin FAW.1/2/4 and 5s are seen in this view, heading north-to-south over the airfield, during the SBAC display in September 1957. There was large-scale Service participation during the 1950s/1960s, which gave a considerable added interest to the aviation enthusiasts of the time.** *R L Ward*

Bristol Britannia Srs 301	G-ANCA	for BOAC
Bristol Britannia Srs 313	4X-AGB	for El Al Airlines
DH Vampire T.55	L160	for Lebanese Air Force
EE P.1A	WG760	prototype
EE P.1B	XA847	prototype
Folland Gnat	GN101	for Finnish Air Force
Gloster Javelin T.3	WT841	
Gloster Javelin FAW.7	XH710	
	XH714	
Hawker Hunter F.4	XF310	
Hawker Hunter F.6	XE587, XF378, XK147 & XK148	
Hawker Hunter T.7	XJ615 & XJ627 prototypes	
Percival Pembroke C.54	AS+554	for West German AF
Supermarine Scimitar F.1	XD218	
Vickers Viscount 803	PH-VID	for KLM
Westland Whirlwind Srs 2	G-AOCZ	

1958

A further mass flypast was also performed this year with all three 'V Bomber' types: Valiant B.1s from No 90 Squadron, Victor B.1s from No 10 Squadron and Vulcan B.1s from No 83 Squadron, plus two Valiant BK.1s from No 214 Squadron giving an air-to-air refuelling demonstration. Also flying were nine Canberra B.6s from Nos 9 and 12 Squadrons; 45 Hunter F.6s from various squadrons; and 45 Javelin FAW.2/4/5/6s from Nos 46, 89 and 151 Squadrons. Aerobatic displays were performed by the Hunter F.6s of No 111 Squadron, the *Black Arrows*, with 22 aircraft being famously looped in formation; Jet Provost T.1s from the Central Flying School; Sea Hawk FGA.6s of 800NAS (XE462 broke off from the display and crashed at Blackbushe on 1st September); and a fast bombing sequence by 803NAS with its Scimitar F.1s. The prototype Blackburn NA.39s, XK486 and XK487, were present this year as was the prototype English Electric P.1B XA847, Short SC.1 research prototype XG900, Fairey Rotodyne prototype XE521 and Bristol 192 prototype XG447. Other aircraft displayed included:

Airspeed Ambassador	G-37-3	with Tyne engines
Bristol Sycamore Mk.14	CC+063	for the West German AF
EE Lightning F.1	XG308	
EE Canberra U.10	WJ624	
EE Canberra T.11	WJ610	
Fairey Gannet AEW.3	XJ440	prototype
Fairey Gannet AS.4	UA+115	for West German Navy
DH Comet 4	G-APDA	for BOAC
Hawker Hunter T.7	XL564	
Hawker Hunter T.8	WW664	
Saro P.531	G-APNV	
Westland Wessex	XL727	
Westland Westminster	G-APLE	prototype

1959

Again No 111 Squadron, the *Black Arrows*, performed with 16 of its Hunter F.6s and the Jet Provost T.1s of the CFS put on their display routine. Scimitar F.1s of 807NAS HMS *Ark Royal* gave a display routine that was rounded off by a unique landing sequence which saw the members of the formation landing on the Farnborough runway from opposite ends, and passing each other in the centre. The Royal Air Force put on a set piece with aircraft from Transport Command; including a Britannia C.1 from No 99 Squadron, a Comet C.2 from No 216 Squadron, Beverley C.1s from No 47 Squadron, Hastings C.2s from No 24 Squadron, Pioneer CC.1s and Twin Pioneer CC.1s from No 21 Squadron; a Sycamore HR.14 and Whirlwind HAR.2s. The flypast also included three Victor B.1s from No 15 Squadron; three Vulcan B.1s from No 230 OCU; and six Javelin FAW.2/7s from Nos 46 and 25 Squadrons. The first Lightning T.4 XL628 was seen as was the red/white Hunter Mk.66A G-APUX, which was put through a stunning spinning routine by Bill Bedford where 12 spins were performed from altitude trailing white smoke in the clear blue skies. Other aircraft of interest at this year's show included:

Blackburn NA.39	XK490	
Avro Lincoln 2	G-APRJ	Napier de-icing test acft
Avro Vulcan B.1	XA902	Conway engine testbed
Commonwealth Aircraft Jindivik Mk.2	A92-107	
DH Comet 4B	G-APMB	for BEA
Folland Gnat T.1	XM691	
Folland Gnat F.1	XN326	
Handley Page Herald 2	G-AODF	
SRN-1 Hovercraft	G-12-4	
Vickers Vanguard	G-APEB	for BEA
Westland Wessex HAS.1	XM301	
Westland Whirlwind Mk.10	XJ398	

1960

The 21st anniversary of the SBAC displays saw exhibition space increased to 126,000ft², with 382 industry stands. Aerobatics were performed by 18 of the *Black Arrows* Hunter F.6s of No 111 Squadron; the Jet Provost T.3s of CFS and four of the newly delivered Lightning F.1s of No 74 Squadron also gave display routines. There were also 'Scramble' take-off demonstrations with four Valiant B.1s of No 148 Squadron, four Victor B.1s of No 15 Squadron and four Vulcan B.1s of No 617 Squadron. The RAF Bomber Command assets took alternate-day turns to perform their rapid and most impressive four-aircraft stream take-offs. Shackleton MR.3s of No 201 Squadron also rotated each day, performing a round-the-clock maritime patrol from and to Farnborough. Other attendees included:

HS.748	G-APZV	prototype, first flew 24th June 1960
Avro Vulcan B.2	XH534	
AW Argosy	G-APRL & G-APRN	
Handley Page Herald	G-APWA	
Saro P.531 Wasp	XN334	
Saro P.531 Sprite	XP165	
Vickers Vanguard	CF-TKB	for Trans-Canada Airlines
Auster D4/108	CS-AMA	
Auster D/180	G-ARDJ	
DH Comet 2E	XN453	from RAE
EE Lightning F.1	XG332	
EE Lightning T.4	XL629	
Handley Page Victor B.2	XH669	
Bristol Belvedere HC.1s	XG451 & XG452	
Saro Skeeter AOP.12	XM563	

Blackburn NA.39 XK490 is seen arriving overhead Farnborough for the SBAC display in September 1959. This aircraft was the 5th of the type built and made its maiden flight on 23rd March 1959 from Holme-on-Spalding Moor. It was retained for trials by the manufacturer and A&AEE Boscombe Down, from where it was operating when it crashed near Lyndhurst, in the New Forest, on 12th October 1959, after stalling at altitude and spinning, inverted, into the ground. Both the test pilot, from NASA, and the flight test observer from Blackburns, were regrettably killed. *FAST collection*

1961

This year again saw a large-scale service participation, which included nine Lightning F.1s of No 74 Squadron; 16 Hunter F.6s of No 92 Squadron, the *Blue Diamonds*; and the CFS Jet Provost T.3s. The Fleet Air Arm put on a mass flypast with Gannet AEW.3s from 849NAS 'C' Flight; Sea Vixen FAW.1s from 890NAS and 899NAS and Scimitar F.1s from 803NAS and 804 NAS – some of the Sea Vixens and Scimitars participating in a flight refuelling demonstration and simulated low-altitude bombing runs. Furthermore, 800NAS, from HMS *Ark Royal*, put on a nine-aircraft formation with its Scimitar F.1s. An airfield assault/attack set piece was undertaken by No 38 Group utilising Hunter F.6s from No 54 Squadron, Whirlwind HAR.2/4s of No 225 Squadron, Bever-

ley C.1s from Nos 47 and 53 Squadron, Belvedere HC.1s from the BTU (Belvedere Training Unit), Skeeter AOP.12s and Auster AOP.9s from the Army Air Corps, Twin Pioneer CC.1s and Pioneer CC.1s from No 230 Squadron. A further mass flypast was staged at high altitude overhead, with Bomber Command supplying ten Valiants, eight Victors, twelve Vulcans and ten Canberras.

Such service participation gave the showgoers good value and entertainment, as well as a chance to see new types of aircraft being put through their paces. The operational aircraft of the three services were shown doing what they do best, albeit under an enacted scenario, which nonetheless produced a thrilling spectacle for an appreciative audience. Other notable aircraft at this show included:

Gloster Meteor U.16	WH505	RAE Llanbedr
Beagle A.109 Airedales	G-ARNP, G-ARNS & G-ARKE	
Beagle AOP.11	XP254	
Beagle 206X	G-ARRM	
DH Comet 4C	LV-AIB	for Aerolineas Argentinas
AW Argosy	G-AOZZ	
DH Comet 4C	G-AROV	for Middle East Airlines
Gloster Javelin FAW.1	XA552	Gyron Junior engine testbed
HP.115	XP841	research prototype
Handley Page Dart-Herald 200	G-ARTC	in markings of Maritime Central Airways
Hunting Jet Provost T.51	G-23-1	for Sudan Air Force

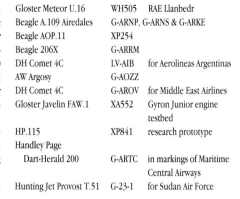

RAF participation during the 1960 SBAC display included 'scramble' demonstrations by all three V-bomber types. Seen here is Vulcan B.1 XH482 of No 617 Squadron, lined up on the Farnborough runway and about to depart on 9th September 1960. Beyond can be seen a Dart Herald G-APWA, Short SC.1 XG905 and Twin Pioneer G-APPH. *Rawlings Family collection*

Tiger Lightning line-up at Farnborough during the 1961 SBAC display. Twelve of 74 Squadron's Lightning F.1s are seen lined up on the 'A' shed parking apron, ready to commence their display during September 1961. Nine of these aircraft flew, with a stream take-off and vertical climb to altitude. After a series of formation manoeuvres the aircraft returned to beat up the airfield and break many windows in the town. The 12 aircraft consisted of XM167/H, XM144/J, XM164/K, XM165/F, XM140/M, XM166/G, XM139/C, XM142/B, XM146/L, XM163/Q, XM147/P and XM143/A. Most of these aircraft went on to serve with No 226 OCU and were finally withdrawn from use during the mid to late 1960s. *FAST collection*

This classic view of the BAC flight line on 10th September 1962 shows the Handley Page HP.115 research aircraft, XP841, in the foreground, with Lightning T.5 XM967 and T.4 XM974 plus Vickers VC-10 prototype G-ARTA beyond. The HP.115 can now be seen in the FAA Museum at Yeovilton. Lightning XM967 went on to serve with RAE Farnborough and XM974 eventually served with 74 Squadron and 226 OCU, before it crashed into the North Sea on 14th December 1972. The VC-10, G-ARTA, made its first flight on 29th June 1962 from Brooklands, and, after undergoing trials with the manufacturer, the aircraft was leased to Laker Airways and Middle East Airlines and was later sold to British United Airlines, which became British Caledonian, but it was damaged in a heavy landing at Gatwick on 28th January 1972 and was subsequently reduced to spares. *FAST collection*

1962

Again the Lightning F.1s of No 74 Squadron, Hunter F.6s of No 92 Squadron *Blue Diamonds*, Jet Provost T.3s of the CFS, and Scimitar F.1s of 736NAS provided the aerobatics, whilst Sea Vixen FAW.1s from 766, 893 and 899 NAS and Buccaneer S.1s from 700Z and 801NAS of the Fleet Air Arm gave a flypast. The Hawker P.1127 appeared at this display with the first development aircraft XP972 showing the versatility of this new VTOL/STOL technology, and the Bristol T188 research aircraft XF923 was seen for the first time. A number of preserved aircraft such as the SE.5a D7000, Bristol F.2B Fighter D8096 and Gloster Gladiator K8032 also flew during this year's show. Other notable attendees included:

Avro 748	C91-2500	for Brazilian Air Force
Avro Vulcan B.2	XL361	with Blue Steel
EE Lightning F.3	XG310	
EE Lightning T.4	XM974	
EE Lightning T.5	XM967	
Vickers VC-10	G-ARTA	prototype, first flew 29th June 1962
Westland Wessex HAS.31	WA202	for Royal Australian Navy

1964

Lightning F.2s of No 92 Squadron performed this year with a very impressive, rapid and noisy nine-aircraft streaming take-off, followed by a formation aerobatic display. The CFS provided the remaining aerobatic displays with six Jet Provost T.4s known as the *Red Pelicans*, whilst No 4 FTS displayed its newly delivered Gnat T.1s, which were then known as the *Yellowjacks* – the forerunners of the *Red Arrows*. This year's service demonstrations were from Argosy C.1s of Nos 114 and 267 Squadrons, Wessex HC.2s of Nos 18 and 72 Squadrons, Hunter FGA.9s of Nos 1 and 54 Squadrons, Canberra B (I) 8s of No 14 Squadron, Vulcan B.2s from No 9 Squadron and Victor B.2s from Nos 100 and 139 Squadrons. The Fleet Air Arm participa-

tion consisted of Scimitar F.1s from 803NAS, Sea Vixen FAW.1s from 890 and 766NASs and Wessex HU.5s from 848NAS.

The BAC.221 research aircraft WG774, modified from the first FD.2, was present at this show as was the first Super VC-10 G-ASGA. Other participants at this year's show included:

EE Lightning F.3	XP697	
BAC 1-11 Srs 201	G-ASJE	for British United Airways
Vickers VC-10	G-ASIW	for British United Airways
BAC Jet Provost T.52	603	for the Iraqi Air Force
Handley Page Herald		
Srs 400	FM1024	for Royal Malaysian AF
HS.748 series 200	G-ASJT	
HS 748MF Andover C.1	G-ARRV	prototype
HS.125	G-ASEC	
HS Trident 1C	G-ARPB	for British European Airways
HS P.1127	XP984	
HS Kestrel FGA.1	XS688 & XS689	
Hawker Hunter T.12	XE531	of RAE
Short Belfast C.1	XR362	
Westland Scout AH.1	XP910	
Westland Wasp HAS.1	XT414	
Westland Whirlwind HAR.10	XP299	
Westland Wessex HAS.1	XM837	
Westland Wessex HC.2	XR526	
Westland Wessex HU.5	XS484	

1966

This was the first year of European aircraft participation. The CFS' *Red Arrows* performed the only aerobatic display at this event, courtesy of the team's Gnat T.1s. A mass flypast put on by the Fleet Air Arm had the sky filled with 10 Sea Vixen FAW.2s from

Two of the aerobatic teams that participated in the SBAC display of September 1964 were the 'CFS Red Pelicans' from Little Rissington, with their Jet Provost T.4s, and No 4 FTS 'Yellowjacks' from Valley, with their Gnat T.1s. Both teams are seen here trailing smoke over the display area on 15th September 1964, flying over the static Vulcan B.2, XM595, from the Scampton Wing. By the next Farnborough display, the 'Red Pelicans' had disbanded and the 'Yellowjacks' had become the official RAF aerobatic team known as the 'Red Arrows', with their overall red Gnat T.1s. *FAST collection*

Trident 1E AP-AUG made its first flight on 24th August 1966 and, a few days later, it appeared at the Farnborough SBAC display, as seen here in this view taken from an RAE Hastings over the Hampshire countryside. The aircraft was delivered to Pakistan International Airlines on 14th February 1967 and was subsequently purchased by the Chinese Government and continued in service with the Peoples Republic of China Air Force as 50152 until withdrawn in October 1995. *FAST collection*

892NAS, and Buccaneer S.2s of 809NAS from HMS *Hermes*, three Gannet AEW.3s from 849NAS and five Wessex HAS.1s from 826NAS. Other notable participants included:

EE Lightning F.6	XR770	in Royal Saudi Air Force markings
Fiat G.91T	MM6432	Italian Air Force
Hawker Hunter FGA.9	708	for Royal Jordanian AF
HS Trident 1E	AP-AUG	for Pakistan International
Transall C-160	V1	French Air Force
Westland Wasp HAS.1	NZ3902	for the Royal New Zealand Navy

1968

The 1968 display was marred by the loss of Breguet 1150 Atlantic No 43, callsign F-XCVG, which had arrived from Le Bourget on 13th September. The aircraft crashed on the Friday of the show, 20th September, regrettably killing all five French crew as well as one onlooker and one RAE employee. Once again the Gnat T.1s of the *Red Arrows* gave their aerobatic display and Jet Provost T.4s from the RAF College at Cranwell staged a 20-aircraft flypast to form a '50' in celebration of the RAF's 50th Anniversary. The RAF also staged a simulated air-to-air refuelling demonstration utilising a Victor BK.1 from No 55 Squadron with two Lightning F.6s from No 5 Squadron. The Army Air Corps displayed its Sioux AH.1s of the *Blue Eagles*, whilst the Fleet Air Arm again staged a formation flying with six Sea Vixen FAW.2s, known as *Simon's Circus*, from 892NAS; five Buccaneer S.2s known as *Phoenix Five* from 809NAS; and four Phantom FG.1s from 700P NAS. Furthermore, Wessex HU.5s of 845NAS

and a Hiller HT.2 from 705NAS demonstrated an assault on the airfield.

Aircraft from Sweden, Saab J35F Draken 35346; Yugoslavia, Soko Galeb G2 23268 and Soko Jastreb 24031; and from Italy, Aermacchi MB.326G I-FAZE, Agusta-Bell 204B MM80473 and 205BG MM80503 participated during this show, giving a hint of what was to come from international attendees in the future. Other notable highlights included:

EE Lightning F.53	G-AWON/53-686 & G-AWOO/53-687	for Royal Saudi AF
BAC 167 Strikemaster Mk.80		
	G-AWOR/902 & G-AWOS/906	for Royal Saudi AF
BAC 1-11 series 501	G-AVML	for BEA
Avro Vulcan B.1	XA903	RR/Bristol Siddeley Olympus engine testbed
HS Andover C.1	XS601	
HS.748 series 2	ZK-CWJ	for Mount Cook Airlines
	A10-603	for Royal Australian AF
DH Comet 4C	XS235	of A&AEE
HS Trident 1E	G-AVYE	for Channel Airways
HS Trident 2E	G-AVFI	for BEA
HS Nimrod MR.1	XV226	
HS Harrier GR.1	XV739	
Short Skyvan III	VH-PNI	for Papuan Airlines
	VH-PNJ	for Papuan Airlines
Westland Wessex Mk.60	G-ASWI	
Sea King HAS.1	XV370	Sikorsky-built SH-3D
McDD Phantom FG.1	XT859	
McDD Phantom FGR.2	XT891	
Sud-Aviation SA.341	F-ZWRA	second prototype

1970

The highlight of this year's display was the large-scale airfield attack demonstration, which consisted of Wessex HC.2s from No 72 Squadron, a Belfast C.1 from No 53 Squadron, a VC-10 C.1 from No 10 Squadron, Hercules C.1s from RAF Lyneham, an

An air-to-ground view of the SBAC display during September 1968 shows a wide variety of types, ranging from the Beagle 206 to the Nimrod, Lightnings, Harriers, Phantom, Draken, Canberra, Strikemasters, Galeb and Macchi 326. They are lined up either in the static display or, for those flying later, in the temporary display on runway 25. *FAST collection*

Two LTV A-7E Corsair IIs, 156888 and 156889, attended the 1970 SBAC display. A-7E 156888, 'NH401' of VA-195 USS *Kitty Hawk*, is seen here posing for the RAE Hastings camera ship over the Hampshire countryside while en route to Farnborough. This aircraft was powered by an Allison TF-41A-2, which was a licence-built Rolls-Royce Spey turbojet. This basically heralded the commencement of many USAF and USN aircraft coming to Farnborough over the subsequent years. *FAST collection*

The 1972 SBAC display saw three Indian-produced aircraft participating in the show. Seen here en route to Farnborough are two of these aircraft, Hindustan Gnat Mk.1 E1070 (E1069 was also at the show) and the HJT-16 Kiran Mk.II U703. These aircraft were at the show because they had British engines: being powered by the Rolls-Royce Bristol Orpheus 701 and Rolls-Royce Bristol Viper II respectively. Many different nationalities, some with indigenous-build aircraft, have exhibited at Farnborough since this time. *FAST collection*

Andover C.1 from No 46 Squadron, Harrier GR.1s from No 1 Squadron and Phantom FGR.2s from No 6 Squadron; whilst a fly-by by a Victor K.1A from No 57 Squadron had Phantom FG.1s from No 43 Squadron and Buccaneer S.2s from No 12 Squadron in a simulated air-to-air refuelling demonstration. A Nimrod MR.1 from No 236 OCU also staged a fly-by. The Sioux AH.1s of the Army Air Corps *Blue Eagles* and the RAF's *Red Arrows* with Gnat T.1s flew display routines, while solo aerobatic demonstrations alternated between a Lightning F.3 from No 226 OCU and an F.6 from No 23 Squadron. Concorde 002 G-BSST made its triumphant SBAC debut during the flying display, which also included the first Jaguars – the first prototype being a French Jaguar E variant, E.01, which appeared alongside the third A variant, A.03, fifth M variant, M.05, and the sixth aircraft S.06: this being XW560, the first British prototype. Other highlights of individual aircraft attending included:

LTV A-7E Corsair II	156888
	156889 from USS *Kitty Hawk*
EE Canberra B.62	G-AYHP/
	B102 for Argentine Air Force
BAC 167 Strikemaster	
Mk.84s	G-AYHS/314 & G-AYHT/315
	for Singapore ADF
HS Trident 3B	G-AWZB British European Airways
BAC 1-11 Srs 475	G-ASYD
Vickers VC-10	G-AXLR RB.211 testbed
Grumman Gulfstream II	N804GA
HS Harrier GR.1	XV742
HS Harrier T.2	XW175 second prototype
Scottish Aviation Bulldog	G-AXEH first prototype
Westland Sea King HAS.1	XV666 & XV671
SA.330E Puma	XW241 prototype UK example, Aerospatiale built

1972

With 250 exhibitors, the exhibition hall was increased again to cover an area of 143,000ft². The flying this year saw a truly international participation in the aerobatic displays, with the CM 170R Fouga Magisters of the *Patrouille de France*, Fiat G.91PANs of the Italian Air Force's *Frecce Tricolori* and the Gnat T.1s of the RAF *Red Arrows*. Incidentally there has not been an SBAC show since that has had three international aerobatic teams attending! There were also the Army Air Corps *Blue Eagles* team with their six Sioux AH.1s. Another airfield attack was staged by No 38 Group; this one utilising Harrier GR.1As of No 3 Squadron, Hercules C.1s of No 30 Squadron, Phantom FGR.2s of Nos 6 and 41 Squadrons, Puma HC.1s of No 33 Squadron, Andover C.1s from No 46 Squadron, Wessex HC.2s of No 72 Squadron and Scout AH.1s of No 665 Squadron, Army Air Corps. Increased international representation at this display included Gnat Mk.1s E1069 and E1070 and HJT-16 Kiran Mk.II U703 from India, the second production Viggen 37002 and Saab 105s SE-DCX and SE-XBZ from Sweden, L-1011 TriStar N305EA for Eastern Airlines from the USA and Nomad N-22 VH-SUR from Australia. Other highlights included:

HS AV-8A Harriers	158699, 158701 &	
	158709	US Marine Corps
BAC 167 Strikemaster	G-AZXK/NZ6364	for RNZAF
Mk.88	G-AZYN/NZ6365	for RNZAF
BAC/Aerospatiale Concorde	G-BSST	UK prototype
SEPECAT Jaguar GR.1	XW563	second prototype
SEPECAT Jaguar T.2	XW566	first two-seat prototype
Fokker-VFW 614	D-BABB	Government Aircraft Factory
Hawker Hunter FGA.74	G-BABM/	
	526	for Singapore Air Force
Westland Sea King Mk.41	89+50	for West German Navy
Westland Sea King Mk.43	062	for Royal Norwegian Air Force
Westland Gazelle HT.2	XW845	
Westland Lynx WG.13	XW835	first prototype, first flight 21st March 1971
Westland Lynx WG.13	XW838	
Westland Lynx AH.1	XX153	prototype
Westland Lynx HAS.2	XX469	prototype

This display also included a selection of historic aircraft, including a Spitfire II, Hurricane IIC and Avro Lancaster I of the Battle of Britain Flight, as well as a Sea Fury from the Fleet Air Arm Historic Flight and aircraft of the Shuttleworth Collection. There was also a display by the Rothmans Team with its Stampe SV.4s whilst, on the Saturday only, a Daily Express handicap air race was won by Cessna 310 G-ASYV.

For the 1974 SBAC show, Farnborough became fully international and, for many, the awesome sight of a Lockheed SR-71A Blackbird was the highlight of the show. 64-17972, of the 9 SRW from Beale AFB, California, arrived on 2nd September, having achieved a new speed record from New York to London, covering the 3,400 miles in 1hr 55min 42sec, averaging a speed of 1,817mph. The aircraft is seen here having just landed and streamed its massive brake parachute. *FAST collection*

This Concorde, seen arriving for the 1976 SBAC display, is the first UK-built production aircraft, G-BBDG, which had made its maiden flight on 13th February 1974. Although wearing British Airways markings, the aircraft was retained by the manufacturer for trials. Later, it was purchased by British Airways for use as spares and stored at Filton, having made its last flight on 24th December 1981. The airframe hulk was eventually moved by road during May/June 2004 to the Brooklands Museum, where it can be seen today, undergoing restoration. *FAST collection*

1974

This was the first fully international display at Farnborough and with it came an increasing number of overseas participants. With 380 exhibitors there was an increase in exhibition area with two halls covering 246,000ft². The aerobatic teams that performed this year consisted of the Gnat T.1s of the *Red Arrows* and the Pitts S-2As of the *Rothmans Team*. There was also a large-scale Harrier demonstration, with eight GR.3s from No 1 Squadron, and the new RAF Jaguar GR.1s and T.2s from No 226 OCU took part in the service demonstration as did the Spitfire IIA, VA, Hurricane IIs and Lancaster I of the Battle of Britain Flight. The largest aircraft to be exhibited at an SBAC display so far was to be seen in the form of a USAF C-5A Galaxy 70-0454. Stealing the show, however, was the arrival of USAF Lockheed SR-71A Blackbird 64-17972, which broke the New York to London speed record on its flight into Farnborough. It had covered 3,400 miles in just 1hr 55min and 42sec, averaging a speed of 1,817mph. Other notable examples included:

Saab AJ37 Viggen	37052, 37053 &	
	37055	Swedish Air Force
Saab Sk37 Viggen	37808	Swedish Air Force
Airbus A300B2	F-WUAA	first widebody airliner on show
Lockheed L-1011 TriStar 1	N10114	for Pacific Southwest Airlines
Lockheed P-3C Orion	159327	US Navy
Lockheed S-3A Viking	158873	US Navy
McDD TF-15A Eagle	71-0291	second two-seat example
HS Hawk T.1	XX154	prototype
Aermacchi MB-326K	I-AMKK/MM54390	
SA.360 Dauphin	F-WSQX	second prototype
BAC/Aerospatiale		
Concorde 01	G-AXDN	
Boeing-Vertol		
CH-47C Chinook	71-20952	US Army
FBN BN2A-21 Defender	G-BCEM/	
	303	for Sultan of Oman AF
Dassault Falcon 10	F-BSQU	
Dassault Falcon 30	F-WAMC	first prototype
Alpha Jet	D-9594	second and
	F-ZWRV	third prototypes
HS Harrier T.52A	G-VTOL	
SEPECAT Jaguar GR.1	XX108	first British production aircraft
SEPECAT Jaguar T.2	XX136	first British production two-seater
Sikorsky S-67 Blackhawk	N671SA	prototype, destroyed in accident during display on 1st September
Westland Sea King Mk.50	G-17-2/	
	N16-099	for Royal Australian Navy

1976

The *Red Arrows* Gnat T.1s performed again this year, as did the *Rothmans Team* with its Pitts S-2As. The Battle of Britain Flight and the FAA Historic Flight also flew their usual routines, whilst the CFS *Vintage Pair* Meteor T.7 WF791 and Vampire T.11 XH234 also performed. Aircraft attending of note included a US Navy F-14A Tomcat 159855; the YF-17A Cobra 72-1570; YC-15A 72-1876; MRCAs (Tornado) XX948 and XX950 and Boeing 707-3J9C 5-249 for the Imperial Iranian Air Force. Other notable aircraft included:

Transall C-160	F54	French Air Force
BAC/Aerospatiale		
Concorde 202	G-BBDG	
Fairchild Republic		
A-10A Thunderbolt II	75-0264	USAF
Grumman E-2C Hawkeye	160010	US Navy
Aermacchi MB-339A	I-NOVE/	
	MM568	first prototype
HS.748 Srs 2A	CS-03	for Belgian Air Force
HS Harrier T.52A	G-VTOL	
HS AV-8A Harrier	159374	for US Marine Corps
HS Hawk T.1	G-HAWK & XX156	
Lockheed		
L-1011-200 TriStar	A40-TY	for Gulf Air
PZL TS-11 Iskra	SP-DOE	

1978

This display heralded the new title of 'Farnborough International' and, although still organised by the SBAC, it was now more in keeping with the multitude of overseas companies that were now displaying their wares or demonstrating their aircraft to a, by now, much wider audience. Indeed this year there were a record 350 exhibitors, representing more than 450 companies, with over a hun-

The last time an actual Comet appeared at an SBAC display was in September 1978, the first time having been 29 years earlier in 1949. Seen here from the old control tower, about to land at the end of its flying display, is Comet 4C XW626 (previously G-APDS), which was fitted with the Nimrod AEW.3 radar modifications during 1976 and first flew as such on 28th June 1977. It ended its days at RAE Bedford during August 1981 and was finally scrapped during 1994. *FAST collection*

dred aircraft on display. The aerobatic display contingent at this event was solely the Gnat T.1s of the *Red Arrows*, although this would prove to be the last using the Gnat as the team would shortly receive Hawk T.1s. A specially built ski-jump was first used for this SBAC display where Harrier T.52 G-VTOL/ZA250 launched itself skyward to demonstrate its fantastic STOL capability. Other aircraft of interest included:

FMA IA-58 Pucara	A-19	Argentine Air Force
Dassault Mirage F.1B	F-ZJTJ	
Dassault Mirage F.1E	F-ZJTK	
Dassault Mirage 2000	01	prototype
Aeritalia G-222TCM	MM62112	Italian Air Force
Alpha Jet	98+33	West German
	E2	French Air Force
DC-3 Tri-Turbo	N23A	
NDN Firecracker	G-NDNI	
Aerospatiale		
AS.350B Ecureuil	F-GBBQ	
Agusta A 109A	MM81014 for Italian Army
Agusta-Bell AB 212ASW	MM80954 for Italian Navy
Airbus A300B2	F-WUAD	
BAC 1-11 Srs 670	G-ASYD	
DH Comet 4C	XW626	AEW installation
BAe Sea Harrier FRS.1	XZ450	
BAe Harrier T.52	G-VTOL/ZA250	
CASA C-101 Aviojet	XE25.01/EC-ZDF	
DHC-5D Buffalo	C-GQUT	
DHC Dash 7	C-GNBX	
Embraer EMB-111	FAB-702 for Brazilian Air Force
Embraer EMB-121 Xingu	PP-ZCR	
Westland Sea King HAR.3	XZ586	
Westland Lynx AH.1	XZ179	
Westland Lynx HAS.2	XZ248	

1980

The *Red Arrows* once again performed the aerobatic display at this show, though this time with their newly delivered British Aerospace Hawk T.1s. The Fleet Air Arm with their new British Aerospace Sea Harrier FRS.1s of 800NAS from HMS *Invincible* gave a display with three aircraft, which included a mock ground attack. Notable aircraft included Mirage 2000 prototypes Nos 2 and 4, prototype Super Mirage 4000 No 1 and Tornado ADV ZA254 – the prototype of the F.2 variant. Other aircraft of note included:

DHC CC-132 Dash 7	132002	Canadian Armed Forces
GD F-16B Fighting Falcon	78-0089	
McDD TF-18A Hornet	160784	second prototype, two seater
Valmet L-70 Vinka	VN-2	Finnish Air Force
BAe Nimrod AEW.3	XZ286	
Dassault Mirage F.1C	241	French Air Force
Microturbo Microjet 2000	F-WJZF	prototype
Airbus A300B4-203	F-WZER/	
	9V-STA	for Singapore Airlines
BAC 1-11 Srs 201AC	XX105	Flight Systems, RAE Bedford
Boeing E-3A AWACS	77-0355	USAF
BAe Sea Harrier FRS.1	XZ457	
General Dynamics F-111F	70-2412	USAF
McDD F-15B Strike Eagle	71-0291	rebranded
Westland WG.30	G-BGHF	prototype

1982

The Hawk T.1s of the *Red Arrows* gave the aerobatic display at this event, although there was also a flypast by four Tornado GR.1s of No 9 Squadron. Aircraft of note included B-1A 76-0174, the fourth prototype, and TR-1A 80-1068 from the USAF; Sea Harrier FRS.51 IN601/G-9-478 for the Indian Navy; Boeing 757-225 N505EA for Eastern Airlines and Boeing 767-232 N102DA for Delta Airlines. Other notable aircraft included:

Dassault Super Etendard	31	French Navy
BAe Sea Harrier FRS.1s	XZ439, XZ457, XZ460 & XZ492
BAe Hawk T.60	604/	
	G-9-490	for Zimbabwe Air Force
BAe VC-10 K.2	ZA147	
McDD KC-10A Extender	79-0433	
Hughes YAH-64A Apache	73-22248	first prototype
Boeing 727-100	N199AM	
Airbus A310-221	F-WZLI	
BAe 146 Srs 100	G-OBAF	British Air Ferries
BAe 146 Srs 100	G-SSCH	Dan Air
BAe 146 Srs 200	G-WISC	Air Wisconsin
AS.332B Super Puma	F-WZLB	
Skyship 500	G-BIHN	prototype
BAe Nimrod AEW.3	XZ286	
Embraer EMB-312 Tucano	PP-ZDK	
Fairchild Republic		
A-10A Thunderbolt II	81-0009	
GD F-16A Fighting Falcon	661	Royal Norwegian AF
SEPECAT		
Jaguar International S	G-27-367	for Indian Air Force

Seen here about to touch down on the Farnborough runway, is a Sea Harrier FRS.1, XZ458 'N251' of No 800 NAS, as operating from HMS *Invincible*. Some eighteen months after this photo was taken, the aircraft was operational during the Falklands campaign, known as 'Operation Corporate', where it served with both 801 and 809 NAS. It returned safely to the UK, but it crashed as a result of engine failure near Fort William on 1st December 1984, and was written-off. *FAST collection*

The September 1982 SBAC display saw
Rockwell International B-1A 76-0174
statically displayed, having flown from
Edwards AFB, California. The type first flew
on 23rd December 1974 and the example
at Farnborough was the fourth prototype.
Now known as the Boeing B-1B Lancer, the
type is in service with the USAF Air Combat
Command, with some 90 aircraft on
strength with various Bomb Wings. The
B-1A is seen here departing from
Farnborough, en route back to the USA, on
13th September 1982. FAST collection

1984

This year, three exhibition halls covered an area of 415,081ft² and there were 269 hospitality chalets. The *Red Arrows* once again gave the aerobatic performance. From Russia, participating for the first time, the world's largest helicopter came in the form of Mil Mi-26 CCCP-06141, plus an Antonov An-72 CCCP-72000 and an Ilyushin Il-86 CCCP-86066, all wearing Aeroflot titles. Notable participants included:

Hindustan HTT-34	X2335	Indian Air Force
Hindustan HJT-16 Kiran II	U2462	Indian Air Force
SEPECAT Jaguar S	NAF710/	
	G-27-397	for Nigerian Air Force
SEPECAT Jaguar ACT	XX765	Active Control Technology demonstrator
Northrop F-20A Tigershark	82-0062/N4416T &	
	82-0063/N3986B	
Boeing 707-331C	N792TW	in tanker configuration
Boeing 737-300	N352AU	for USAir
Skyship 600	G-SKSC	
Agusta A 129 Mangusta	MM590	first prototype

Airbus A300-600	F-WZLR	
Airbus A310-203	G-BKWU	for British Caledonian Airways
Hawk Mk.60	G-9-518	for UAE Air Force
CNIAR/BAC 1-11 Srs 560	YR-BRC	for TAROM
Dassault Mirage IIING	01	first prototype conversion
Dassault Mirage F.1CR	602	
Dassault Mirage 2000C1	1	
Dassault Mirage 2000N	01	prototype
DH.88 Comet	G-ACSS	Shuttleworth Collection
DHC-5E Buffalo	C-GCTC	crashed on runway on 4th September
Panavia Tornado F.2	ZD901	
Saab-Fairchild SF340	SE-ISF &	Swedair and
	N340CA	Comair
Short 330 C-23 Sherpa	83-0513	for USAF,
Soko Super Galeb	23005	for Yugoslav Air Force
Westland Lynx 3	ZE477	prototype

1986

Whilst the *Red Arrows* were on hand to give their usual polished aerobatic performance, there were many different aircraft types present at this display from all around the world, and notable examples included the BAe EAP ZF534 technology demonstrator, Dassault Rafale A A01 and an Antonov An-124 CCCP-82005 in Aeroflot markings. Other notable exhibits included:

CASA 212s	ECT-131 & ECT-134	
CASA CN-235	ECT-100 & ECT-135	
Airbus A300B2	F-WUAD	Fly-By-Wire demonstrator
ATR-42-312	F-WWEC	for Cimber Air
Gulfstream SRA-1	F-313	Danish Air Force
Lockheed SR-71A Blackbird	64-17980	
Saab 340A	SE-E63	
	SE-ISV	for Swedair
BAe Sea Harrier F/A.2	XZ457	
BAe/Aerospatiale Concorde	G-BOAD	British Airways

1988

Apart from the Red Arrows, it was the Royal Navy that provided the interesting formation flying and noisy demonstrations. This consisted of four 705NAS Gazelle HT.2s, two Lynx HAS.3s from 815NAS and 829NAS, four Sea King HAS.5/HAR.5s from 706, 810 and 771NASs and six Sea Harrier FRS.1s of 899NAS. However, this year saw the start of a Russian fighter contingent coming to Farnborough, something which would have been unthinkable only a few years previously, with the arrival of two *Fulcrums*: MiG-29A 10 and MiG-29UB 53 of the Russian Air Force. They arrived at Farnborough escorted by two Tornado F.3s of No 5 Squadron. An Antonov An-124 'Ruslan' CCCP-82007 was also present and, as this required an engine change during the week, it had the effect of bringing to Farnborough a rare Antonov An-22 CCCP-09329 of Aeroflot, which carried the replacement engine and gave an unforgettable treat for all those that witnessed its arrival. Other notable aircraft included:

The world's largest helicopter, a Mil Mi-26
Halo, CCCP-06141, came to the SBAC
display in September 1984. This was a pre-
production example and more than 250
examples now serve throughout the world
in a heavy-lift capacity. The Halo is the
largest helicopter to have appeared at
Farnborough to date. It is seen here on 2nd
September 1984 in a low hover during its
flying demonstration, the main rotors
having a diameter of 105ft. Falcon

The British Aerospace Experimental Aircraft Programme (EAP) Technology Demonstrator, ZF534, first flew from Warton on 8th August 1986. This was built as an advanced technology demonstrator aircraft for the future European Fighter Aircraft (EFA), which later evolved into the Eurofighter/Typhoon. The EAP was powered by two Turbo Union RB.199 turbofan engines and was capable of a speed of Mach 2.0+. It is seen here just about to touch down on 5th September 1986. After its trials programme with the manufacturer it was retired and is now at Loughborough University for research work with the Department of Aeronautical and Automotive Transport Studies. *Falcon*

McDD CF-188A	188745 &	
	188756	Canadian Armed Forces
McDD TAV-8B Harrier II	162747	
European Helicopters		
EH101 Merlin	ZF641	prototype
McDD MD-81	N980DC	unducted fan
		demonstrator
Boeing 707-351B	N351SR	
Airbus A320-130	F-WWAI	
Airbus A320-110	F-WWDC	
Aeritalia/AerMacchi AMX	MMX595 & MMX599	
BAe Hawk 200	ZH200	
CASA/IPTN C.235	EC-011 &	
	EC-135	for Binter Canarias
Dassault Mirage 2000N	BX1	for Indian Air Force
Dassault Rafale	01	
GD F-16A Fighting Falcon	E-198	Royal Danish Air Force
GD F-16C	87-0239	for Turkish Air Force
Pilatus PC-7	HB-HMP	
Pilatus PC-9	HB-HPF	
	C-401	Swiss Air Force
Socata TB30 Epsilon	3	French Air Force
WS-70 Blackhawk	ZG468	

1990

The Hawk T.1s of the *Red Arrows* again performed their routine aerobatic display at this year's show. There was also an RAF display of six Harrier GR.5s from No 1 Squadron and other serving RAF aircraft gave fly-bys or demonstrations. The Russians returned with *Fulcrums* (Mikoyan MiG-29A 315 and MiG-29UB 304) and *Flankers* (Sukhoi Su-27A 388 and Su-27UB 389) of the Russian Air Force. Indeed it was during this display that the now relatively common tail-slide and 'cobra' manoeuvres stunned the Farnborough crowd with the sheer agility of these emerging aircraft. The Russian presence was also notable for the display of what is still the world's largest aircraft, the mighty Antonov An-225 Mriya CCCP-82060. Other notable attendees included:

IAR 99 Soim	708 & 709	Romanian Air Force
Dassault Mirage 2000-5	BY2	
Dassault Mirage 2000S	F-ZJSA	
Alpha Jet	F-ZJTJ	
Bell AH-1W Sea Cobra	161022	
Beech 2000 Starship	N1508S	
BAe C-29A (125-800)	88-0270	
BAe 146-300QT	G-BRXI	for TNT
BAe 146-100STA	G-BSTA	
Canadair CC-144 Challenger	144603	Canadian Forces
Embraer CBA-123 Vector	PT-ZVE	
Fairchild SA227AC Metro III	88003	TP88, Swedish Air Force
Lockheed TR-1A	80-1083	
NA TF-100F Super Sabre	N416FS	TRACOR Flight Systems ex-Hungarian AF, arrived inside An-26 for static display only and auction on behalf of the RAF Benevolent Fund
MiG-21PF	501	

The previously unthinkable happened for the SBAC display in September 1988. Two MiG-29 *Fulcrums*, MiG-29A '10' and MiG-29UB '53' of the Soviet Air Force, arrived from Wittstock in East Germany on 30th August 1988. The pair are seen here on approach to Farnborough over G1 building, now the FAST headquarters and museum, whilst the two escorting No 5 Squadron Tornado F.3s can be seen beyond. Although these were the first Russian fighters to be seen in a display at Farnborough, many others have been seen over the years since this historic occasion. *FAST collection*

The largest aircraft in the world is the Antonov An-225 Mriya, CCCP-82060. It was first flown on 21st December 1988 and is powered by six Lotarev D-18T engines, developing over 300,000 lb thrust in total. This view of the SBAC display area, in September 1990, shows the Mriya at left with a pair of Suhkoi Su-27 *Flankers* and MiG-29 *Fulcrums*. Other aircraft on display include Tornados, Hawk, Mirages, Alpha Jet, ATP, BAe146s, AMXs, F-16Cs and a CF-188. *FAST collection*

Sikorsky SH-60F Seahawk	164802	
BAe Jetstream 61	G-JLXI	
European Helicopters		
EH101	I-LIOI	
Valmet L.90TP Redigo	OH-VTP	
McDD F-15E Strike Eagle	90-0248	
Lockheed P-38J Lightning	42-67543/	flew in formation
	N3145X	with an F-16C
GD F-16C Fighting Falcons	91-0410 & 91-0416	
Boeing 747-438	VH-OJB	Qantas, flypast

1992

This was the 30th SBAC display at Farnborough and the Hawk T.1s of the *Red Arrows* again performed their routine aerobatic display at this year's show, as did the Battle of Britain Memorial Flight and the Royal Navy Historic Flight. Four British Aerospace 146s gave a formation flypast each day, operating from the Woodford factory.

The Russians totally dominated the show and gave a rare opportunity to see so many different former Soviet types in the UK. Participants included Sukhoi Su-24M 40; Su-25TK 10; Su-25UB 302; Su-27A 388; Su-27UB 389; Su-29 01; Su-29T 01; Su-35 703; Kamov Ka-50 020; Antonov An-72P 07; Mikoyan MiG-29M 156; MiG-29S 407; MiG-31 374;Tupolev Tu-22M-3 12112347; Yakolev Yak-38 38; Yak-141 141;Tupolev Tu-204 CCCP-64006; Ilyushin Il-78M CCCP-76701; Antonov 124 CCCP-82043; Mil Mi-17M CCCP-95448; Mil Mi-26T RA-06089; and Mil Mi-34 RA-13001. All this at one show! The numbers have never been quite like it since, however. Other notable attendees included:

IAR 330 Puma	105	Romanian Air Force
Saab JAS39 Gripen	39-3 & 39-4	
Airbus A340-200	F-WWBA	
Saab 2000	SE-003	
Douglas DC-3	N96BF &	
	ZS-LYW	turboprop conversions
FMA IA.63 Pampa	X-01	
Lockheed CC-130T Hercules	130339	Canadian Forces
Shorts Tucano	KAF112 & KAF115	
		for the Kuwait Air Force
GD F-16A	272	Royal Norwegian Air Force
Bell OH-58D Kiowa	87-0750	converted from OH-58A
Dassault Falcon 900B	F-GKDI	
PBN BN-2T Defender	G-BSPR/	
	MP-CG-02	for Mauritius CG
BAe ATP	G-BUKJ/TC-THZ	for THT

1994

Not only did the Hawk T.1s of the *Red Arrows* perform, there was also a flypast of 14 Hawks (T.1s/Mk.100/Mk.200) to depict the 14 different nationalities that were customers of the type. There was also a flypast of four Falcon 20s of FR Aviation. Several restored/preserved aircraft also took part during the public days, and a further selection was on display in the Historic Aircraft Park.

The Russians returned, this time with Sukhoi Su-27P 598; Su-29LL 02 (Su-32 demonstrator); Su-30MK 603; Su-31 RA-01404; Su-35 703; MiG-29S 999; MiG-29M 155 (MiG-33 demonstrator); Tupolev Tu-204 RA-64011 of Vnukovo Airlines; the D-27 engine testbed Ilyushin Il-76LL RA-76529; the prototype Il-96M RA-96000; Il-103 RA-10300; Il-114 RA-91002; Mil Mi-17MTV RA-70937 of Kazan Helicopters; and Myasishchev M-55 RA-55204. Other aircraft of note included:

Breguet 1150 Atlantic 2 NG 20		
Airbus A300F4-605R	F-WWAX/	
	N654FE	for Federal Express
Airbus A321-112	D-AVZB/	
	I-BIXU	for Alitalia
Airbus A330-342	F-WWKU/	
	VR-HLA	for Cathay Pacific Airways
Airbus A340-311	F-WWAI	
Vickers Vimy replica	NX71MY/	
	'G-EAOU'	departed for Australia
Saab 340 AEW	SE-C42/	
	100002	for Swedish Air Force
Atlas/Denel Rooivalk	ZU-AHC	
Panavia Tornado F.2 TIARA	ZD902	DRA
Bell AH-1W Super Cobra	165271	
Grumman C-20G		
Gulfstream IV	165094	
Dassault Rafale B	B-01	
Dassault Rafale C	C-01	
Eurocopter Tigre	F-ZWWW	
McDD C-17A Globemaster III	92-3294	
McDD AH-64D Apache	90-0423	

1996

The highlight for many during this show was the flypast of the USAF B-2A Spirit 88-0332 on the first day, operating directly from Whiteman AFB, Missouri. The Hawk T.1s of the *Red Arrows* again performed, while notable attendees included Aerostar/Elbit MiG-21MF 714 of the Romanian Air Force; USAF Boeing E-8C 92-3289; Airbus A319-114 F-WWAS; A330-332 F-WWKY/9M-MKY for Malaysian Airlines; A340-311 F-WWAI; Boeing 707-321B tanker N707AR; Boeing 777-200 N7771; and Embraer ERJ145 PT-ZJD. Other notable aircraft included:

Kamov Ka-50	024	
MAPO MiG-AT	81	
MiG-29SM	506	
Sukhoi Su-30MK	603	
Sukhoi Su-37	711	
Mil Mi-8 AMTS	RA-25755	
Tupolev Tu-214	RA-64501	
Aero Vodochody		
L.159T Albatros	0101	
Dassault Rafale M	M01	
Hawker 800	G-5-848/	
	U-125A	for Japan ASDF
Saab JAS39 Gripen	39111, 39116 &	
	39120	Swedish Air Force
Eurofighter 2000	ZH588	
BAe Harrier GR.7	ZD404, ZD463 & ZG533	
BAe Hawk Mk.102D	ZJ100	
EH Industries Merlin HM.1	ZH821	
Westland Lynx HMA.8	XZ697	
Grumman E-2C Hawkeye	163029	
Northrop F-5E Tiger IV	74-1568	
McDD AV-8B Harrier II	163676	

The Historic Aircraft Park also exhibited various aircraft such as Hurricane XIIB BE417, Spitfire T1X ML407, Vickers Vimy replica 'G-EAOU'/NX71MY and Sopwith Camel F1 replica B2458.

Appearing for the first time in the UK was the awesome Tupolev Tu-22M-3 *Backfire-C* of the CIS Air Force, which visited for the 1992 SBAC display. This aircraft, an advanced variable-geometry long-range bomber, flew a couple of routines during the week. It is parked on the runway static display on 7th September 1992. *Falcon*

This view of the 1994 SBAC display, seen on 8th September, shows the extent of the aircraft static park, chalets and the British Aerospace headquarters buildings beyond. In the lower foreground are the IIyushin Il-96 and Il-76, Sukhoi Su-27 and Su-30MK, together with a variety of other aircraft on display, including MiG-29s, C-17A, Airbus A300, P-3C Orion, F-15C Eagle, F/A-18 Hornet, Saab 340AEW, ATR-72 and DHC-8. *FAST collection*

Seen here on 5th September during the 1996 SBAC display, is the line-up of participating display aircraft on the western apron at Farnborough. Nearest the camera is Hawk Mk.102D ZJ100, the BAe demonstrator; Eurofighter 2000 ZH588; Su-30MK '603'; Su-37 '711'; Tornado GR.1 ZA321; and F-16C 92-3915. The Hawk and Eurofighter/Typhoon are still operated by BAE Systems at Warton. *Falcon*

1998

This was the 50th year since the SBAC display came to Farnborough and there were some extra displays incorporated within the flying programme to celebrate this event, utilising many of the older, preserved, aircraft and including jet types of the 1950s and 1960s. The Hawks of the 'Red Arrows' were of course part of the flying display. Two British Airways Concordes G-BOAE and G-BOAF visited during the show, whilst other notable types included Typhoon 98+30, Su-27P *Flanker* 598, C-130J Hercules C.4 N4242N/ZH873, YRAH-66 Comanche 95-0001 and Romanian Air Force MiG-21*bis* Lancer III 165. Other notable attendees were:

Grumman E-2C Hawkeye	164110	
MiG-29UBT	304	
MiG-29SMT	917	
Airbus A330-243	F-WWKA	
Boeing 777-3D7	N5028Y/	
	HS-TKA	for Thai Airways
Kazan ANSAT	02	non-flying prototype
Saab JAS39A Gripen	39132 & 39133	
Saab JAS39B Gripen	39801	
Saab 340AEW	100003 &	
	100006	Swedish Air Force Tp100B
BAE Systems		
BAC 1-11 Srs 479	ZE433	Ferranti Radar Trials
GD F-16C Fighting Falcons	91-0342 & 91-0420	
Sikorsky SH-60B Seahawk	164465	
Airbus A300-600ST	F-GTSD	
Gulfstream IVSP	N487QS	
Lockheed L-1011		
TriStar 100	N787M	flying hospital
Antonov An-74TK	UR-74038	
Dassault Falcon 50EX	F-GVDN	

C-17A Globemaster III 96-0007 of the 437AW is seen about to land, following its display on 13th September 1998. The familiar buildings behind were mostly demolished some two years later, leaving these familiar landmarks a thing of the past. British Airways Concorde 102 G-BOAF can be seen parked beyond on the 'A' shed apron. The 24ft wind tunnel looms in the distance. *Falcon*

A specially erected hangar housed:

Bleriot XI replica	G-AANG
Blackburn Monoplane	G-AANI
Blackburn B2	G-AEBJ
Avro Tutor	K3215/G-AHSA
Gloster Gladiator	423/G-AMRK
Westland Lysander	V9441/G-AZWT
Hawker Sea Hurricane IB	Z7015/G-BKTH
Sopwith Camel	B2458/G-BPOB replica
de Havilland DH.60 Moth	G-EBLV
de Havilland DH.2 replica	G-BFVH
Supermarine Spitfire Tr.IX	ML407/G-LFIX

The 50th anniversary static display included types such as:

Bristol Bulldog IIA	K2227/G-ABBB
DH.82A Tiger Moth	G-ANNG DERA Aero Club
DH Venom FB.50	G-DHUU/WR410
DH Vampire T.11	G-VMPR/XE920
Hawker Hunter T.7	G-BVGH/XL573
EE Canberra B.2	G-BVWC/WK163
VS Spitfire PR.XIX	G-RRGN/PS853
Lockheed	
C-121A Constellation	N494TW/48-0609
Gloster Meteor T.7 mod	WL419
Fairey Ultra-light	G-APJJ
Avro Avian	VH-UFZ
Beagle Airedale	G-ARNP
Percival Proctor IV	G-ANXR/RM221

2000

Farnborough's staple *Red Arrows* display took place, whilst some heavy military presence came courtesy of F/A-18F Super Hornets 165675 and 165676, Eurofighter Typhoon 98+29, WAH-64 Apache AH.1 ZJ173 and NH Industries NH90 MMX612. The public days saw the addition of a de Havilland formation flypast, which included the following representative types: DH.80A Puss Moth G-AAZP; DH.82A Tiger Moth G-AZZZ; DH.84 Dragon II EI-ABI; DH.85 Leopard Moth G-ACMN; DH.87B Hornet Moth G-ADKC; DH.89A Dragon Rapide 6 G-AGTM; DH.90A Dragonfly G-AEDU; and DH.94 Moth Minor G-AFPN. Other notable aircraft included:

Aero Vodochody L-159A	6004	
Aero Vodochody L-159B	5831	Czech Air Force
Sukhoi Su-32MF	45	
A300B4-608ST		
'Super Guppy'	F-GSTD	
Boeing BBJ 737-73Q	N737BZ	
Boeing 767-432ER	N76400	
Embraer ERJ-135	PT-ZJC	
Embraer ERJ-145	PT-ZJD	
Mil Mi-17	RA-70898	
Lockheed		
C-130J Hercules C.5	ZH888	

The Heritage Park contained:

Republic P-47D		
Thunderbolt	42-26671/N47DD	
Douglas C-47B	N47FK	
Gloster Meteor NF.11	WM167/G-LOSM	
NA B-25D Mitchell	G-BYDR	
Hawker Hunter F.6A	XF516/G-BVVC	
Fairey Swordfish II	W5856	
EE Lightning F.1A	XM172	

2002

Whilst the *Red Arrows* made their usual contribution, the Tuesday of the show saw a unique formation of four Eurofighter Typhoons (ZH588, ZH590, 98+29 and ZJ699), which flew over Farnborough from the BAE Systems facility at Warton. Handed over to Virgin Atlantic during the show was the ultra-long version of the A340 (a -642, registered F-WWCD/G-VSHY) whilst other notable attendees included Sukhoi Su-25KM 01 of the Georgian Air Force; Antonov An-140 UR-14001; a Super Lynx 103, ZJ905/M22, for the Malaysian Navy; and Typhoon T.1 ZJ699, which was used to officially name the type on 23rd July. Notable aircraft during this display included:

F/A-18F Super Hornet	165877 & 165894	USS *Nimitz*
DHC-8-Q400	LN-RDN	for SAS Commuter
Grumman C-2A Greyhound	162142	
Grumman E-2C Hawkeye	163849	
Aeritalia C-27J Spartan	CSX62127	
Airbus A318-122	F-WWIB	
Airbus A319CJ	A7-HHJ	Qatar Airways
Airbus A330-200	F-WWYN	for Qatar Airways
Airbus A340-642	F-WWCC	
Boeing 737-42C	N60669	
Boeing C-40A	165829	
Eurofighter	ZH588	
Aerostar MiG-21*bis*		
Lancer III	165	Romanian Air Force
Lockheed C-130J Hercules	99-1432	

Seen here outside 'D' hangar on 26th July 2000 for the SBAC Farnborough International display is Eurofighter/Typhoon (then known as the EF2000) 98+29 (DA1), which made its first flight from Manching on 27th March 1994. This aircraft is retained by the manufacturer for airframe, engine and flight control software development. The hangar is now used for aircraft maintenance by TAG Farnborough Engineering Limited. *Falcon*

Seen on the apron outside 'N' shed on 28th July 2002, are two Boeing F/A-18F Super Hornets: 165877 'NH101' of VFA-41 USS *Nimitz* nearest, and 165984 'NG104' of VFA-102 USS *Carl Vinson* beyond. The Super Hornet has been a superb display performer at the last three SBAC displays. *Falcon*

The Historic Aircraft Park contained a number of privately owned aircraft such as:

DH Sea Vixen D.3	G-CVIX/XP924
Folland Gnat T.1	G-NATY/XR537 &
	G-RORI/XR538
NA F-86A Sabre	G-SABR/48-0178
VS Spitfire Vc	G-AWII/AR501
HS Buccaneer S.2B	XX894
Lockheed T-33A	G-TBRD/21261
Hawker Hunter T.7B	G-FFOX/WV318
Hawker Hunter GA.11	G-BZPB/WV256

2004

The RAF's *Red Arrows* lent a military lift to a civilian-dominated show, which saw notable performances by South African Airways Boeing 747-444 ZS-SAZ on 24th July and Cathay Pacific Airways 747-467 B-HOY on 25th July. The show also saw the first example of the type ever to land at Farnborough, when ZS-SAK arrived from Heathrow on 14th July for a practice display. The PAC750XL ZK-KAY came from New Zealand and the EMB-190-100 PP-XMB from Brazil. Although the sight of a Boeing 747 cavorting around Farnborough's skies was one of the highlights at this year's event, there were also a number of fly-through performances by a B-1B Lancer, B-52H Stratofortress and F-117A Nighthawk from the USAF; and a VC-10 K.4 and Tristar KC.1 from the RAF. Other notable participants included:

Boeing F/A-18F	165916 &	
	165917	USS *Abraham Lincoln*
Embraer EMB170-100LR	EI-DFL	for Alitalia Express
Antonov An-140-100	UR-14007	for Kharkov
Antonov An-74TK-200	UR-74038	Kharkov
DC-10-40 tanker	N852V	Omega
Boeing 737-9B5	N6066U	for Korean Air
Bombardier BD700		
Global Express	A7-AAM	of Qatar Airways
Lockheed P-3M Orion	P.3B-09/	
	22-32	Spanish Air Force

Resplendent in Asia's World City special colours, this Boeing 747-467, B-HOY of Cathay Pacific, gave a flying demonstration on 25th July, the final day of Farnborough International 2004. It is seen here from the new Farnborough Air Traffic Control tower, commencing its taxi to the runway for departure. This aircraft had positioned to Farnborough from Heathrow, and returned there directly after it had undertaken its flying routine. In the background a P-51 Mustang, Spitfire, Hurricane, Domine T.1 and VC-10 C.1K can be seen in the Rolls-Royce Centenary Park. *Falcon*

This display also included a Business Aviation Park where a number of business/executive aircraft were exhibited, including:

Boeing 727-51	VP-BAA	
Embraer EMB-135BJ Legacy	PT-SIB	
Fokker 100EJ	G-MABH	
Bombardier BD700		
Global 5000	C-GLRM	
Bombardier CRJ700	C-FBQS	for Delta Connection

The Rolls-Royce Centenary Park, which was converted from the Business Park for the public days only to celebrate the 100th anniversary of Rolls-Royce engines, included:

EE Canberra PR.9	XH135
Typhoon T.1	ZJ800
Sea Harrier F/A.2	ZD579 & ZH796
Nimrod MR.2	XV244
Dominie T.1	XS736
Tornado GR.4A	ZE116
Vickers VC-10 C.1K	XV105
Spitfire LF.IXc	G-ASJV/MH434
Hawker Hunter T.7	G-BVGH/XL573
NA P-51D Mustang	G-BTCD/413704

2006

At the beginning of 2006 there were already a large number of exhibitors confirmed, with 93% of the exhibition and chalet space booked for 'Farnborough International 06': the 54th SBAC display and the 37th show held at Farnborough. The event held in 2004 created business worth some US$23 billion, confirming Farnborough as a top industrial summit that is still held in high regard in what has become a tough marketplace with strong competition from other trade events. The 'FI06' event is set to continue that trend, with a repeat of 2004's business aircraft area and, hopefully, a first appearance by the Bell/Boeing MV-22 Osprey. The humble beginning in 1948 has now turned into a multi-million-pound business and is set to continue, although some modifications and improvements to the layout and display will be implemented. Looking back over the decades, there has never been and never will be a better window on the aviation world than that provided by the world-famous Farnborough airshows.

1935 to 1944

Wind Tunnels, Monoplanes, Speed, Height and the War Effort

The previous decade had seen mixed fortunes at RAE, recession had set in and the workforce had been cut, but work by its dedicated scientists still continued with many experiments on aircraft, engines and systems progressing. The era of the biplane was passing but not totally finished, whilst that of the more sleek design of the monoplane, with its increased speed and engine development, was now moving forward in leaps and bounds. Indeed the very first jet aircraft would be entering service during this decade.

As tension now increased in Europe, a rearmament programme was instigated, which led to the RAE becoming involved with some urgency in development and research work, thus seeing the numbers of scientific and industrial staff increase yet again.

When World War Two was declared in September 1939, much work was already ongoing at RAE, but more research and test was required over the next few years as new aircraft, weapons, engines and systems appeared, some very rapidly, that required input from RAE for pre-service test, in-service modifications, initial design or redesign.

1935
The new 24ft tunnel was opened on 5th April by the then Secretary of State for Air, The Marquess of Londonderry. The aircraft shown therein was a Bristol Bulldog TM Trainer, K3183, fitted with a Napier Rapier engine. This underwent full-scale investigations on air-cooled engines and included aerodynamic and thermal airflows. However, prior to the official opening, Gloster SS.18/19 Gauntlet prototype J9125, having arrived from Martlesham Heath on 8th March 1935, was the first aircraft to be placed in the new wind tunnel for airflow research.

RAE was involved in the design of the large Mk.III hydro-pneumatic catapult, capable of launching a multi-engined heavy bomber up to 65,000 lb. There was no available space at Farnborough for this, so this new installation was earmarked for RAF Harwell, where work commenced in 1938. Construction of this ambitious project continued during the war years at Harwell, which involved a considerable amount of earthwork and building of the catapult structure and its operating equipment,

however, due to pressures of other work within RAE, no aircraft was ever launched on this system. With the advent of concrete runways the requirement disappeared and the project was eventually abandoned during 1943 and the installation removed in the late 1940s.

1936
The Bristol Type 138A K4879 was built at Filton as a high-performance monoplane, specifically for an attempt at the world altitude record. It was powered by a Pegasus IV engine and made its first flight on 11th May 1936 from Filton. It came to Farnborough on 1st August 1936 and, after installation of equipment, was immediately engaged in high-altitude tests with I&P Flight. Returning to Filton on 15th August for installation of a special two-stage supercharged Pegasus engine, the aircraft arrived back on 5th September. High-altitude research experiments were still being undertaken by Experimental Flying Department (I&P Flight) and an altitude record was attained on 28th September 1936, when the aircraft, flown by Squadron Leader F R D Swain, made a record ascent from Farnborough to a height of 49,967ft, (15,230m). Due to lack of oxygen the pilot made a precautionary landing at Netheravon after a flight of over 3 hours. The pilot's special pressurised suit, preshaped to the cockpit, had also been developed by RAE for this attempt.

The aircraft returned to the Bristol factory once again on 12th October 1936 for some modifications but was back on 20th October. A further world altitude record was achieved on 30th June 1937 when the aircraft reached 53,937ft (16,440m), the pilot this time being Flt Lt M J Adam and the aircraft landing back at Farnborough some 2hrs 15mins after departure. (Sqn Ldr Adam was regrettably killed on 12th September 1938 when the W&E Flight Whitley K7207 he was crewing crashed shortly after take-off

Bristol Bulldog Trainer K3183 arrived at RAE during 1934 for Rapier engine development. It is seen here within the open section of the 24ft wind tunnel on 1st March 1935, prior to the tunnel's official opening on 4th April 1935. *FAST collection*

Flt Lt M J Adam is seen here being suited up before he climbs aboard the Bristol 138A, K4879, for his altitude record attempt on 30th June 1937. *FAST collection*

Departing on 30th June 1937, Bristol 138A K4879 is about to obtain a World Altitude Record of 53,937ft, beating the same aircraft's 49,967ft achieved on 28th September 1936, flown then by Sqn Ldr F R D Swain. *FAST collection*

in the vicinity of Cove Reservoir.) The aircraft continued to be flown from Farnborough until its return to Filton on 26th August 1938. It was subsequently struck off charge and allocated for ground instructional use. A Bristol 138B L7037, a two-seater, was also built and the airframe was transported to Farnborough in 1937, but the Merlin engine was never installed and it ended its days as an instructional airframe allocated 2339M in September 1940.

July saw the RAF Farnborough element transferred to 24 Group, with No 4 Squadron moving to Odiham and No 53 Squadron taking up residence for a short period.

As a result of the type suffering a series of fatal accidents, a Mercer (Mignet) HM.14 Pou de Ciel or 'Flying Flea' G-AEFV, registered on 26th March 1936, was put into the 24ft wind tunnel at Farnborough for aerodynamic research into the cause of these losses. The first British-built example flew in July 1935 and they became popular as 123 were built in the UK. These tests found that, at certain angles of incidence with the stick hard back, there was an insufficient pitching moment to raise the nose, which could result in the aircraft entering an uncontrollable dive. Consequently, the Certificate of Airworthiness for the type was withdrawn in 1936. This particular example was cancelled from the register in February 1938.

A Fairey IIIF Mk.IVB K1726 came to Farnborough in late 1936 and was fitted with a Napier Culverin (a Junkers Jumo 205C) diesel engine and a metal variable-pitch propeller, to be used as a testbed. This engine was built in the UK for use in Army tanks while a later development was the Napier Deltic for use in the mine countermeasure vessels of the Royal Navy. RAE found that the engine was not suitable for aviation use so the aircraft was refitted with a Napier Lion and passed on to 2 CAACU at Gosport for target-towing duties, leaving Farnborough on 31st December 1938 bound for Lee-on-Solent.

Avro 616 Avian IVM G-AAXH was fitted with an undercarriage from British Landing Gears and came to Farnborough from Hanworth for evaluation from 9th October to 4th November, when it returned to Hanworth. It was flown by six different pilots for a total of fifteen flights, whereupon the RAE

report issued recommended the use of this aircraft for deck landings. However this was not followed up by widespread production or fitment of this new undercarriage.

Two General Aircraft ST-25 Monospar Jubilees were purchased from the manufacturer and fitted out with blind-landing trials equipment. The first aircraft (K8307) arrived from Hanworth on 27th January 1936, flying from RAE the same day, and the second (K8308) arrived from Hanworth on 6th February, also making its first Farnborough flight the same day. Both were assigned to WE Flight, where they were extensively engaged in blind flying to test the German Lorenz Beacon system, and useful data was gathered. They were technically transferred to the Blind Approach Trials and Development Unit (BAT&DU), but came under RAE/WE Flight control. Both aircraft undertook many flights within the UK and visited most airfields, making beam approaches to help enhance and develop the system further.

K8307 was also involved in general research, armaments, and British landing gear tests during its RAE service. It was returned to General Aircraft at Heston on 17th August 1938, probably by road, having made its last Farnborough flight on 28th September 1937. After fitment of new engines it went on to serve at Boscombe Down and was finally struck off charge in January 1941. Meanwhile the second Monospar (K8308) continued blind flying trials at Farnborough and was also briefly used for infra-red research, until it was flown to Exeter on 23rd October 1939. It saw some wartime RAF service, eventually being sold to Southern Aircraft on 22nd January 1946, registered as G-AHBK and was destroyed in an accident near Cirencester on 2nd June 1947.

Having made initial experimental tests between 1927 and 1930, in respect of basic gas turbine studies, Engine Experimental Department were now endeavouring to take this research a step further, with permission

Monospar Jubilee K8308 is seen on the 'A' shed tarmac during May 1937. This aircraft, assigned to WE Flight, was engaged in blind flying research. *FAST collection*

now granted to build an 8-stage axial flow compressor. This was known as 'Anne' and was completed in 1938, but suffered damage on its first test run and required a total rebuild. Work continued but this early compressor suffered further damage as a result of the German bombing of the airfield on 16th August 1940, when the engine test-beds were hit. However work had continued on a number of experimental compressor and turbine assemblies and, whilst the Whittle engine was under development at Rugby during 1938/1939, RAE sought co-operation from Power Jets to build an axial flow turbojet engine. Power Jets were not really able to assist in this project, as they were heavily engaged in completing their W.1 and W.2B engines for flight. At this time the RAE jet engine proposal was basically referred to as the Establishment F.1 and they then sought co-operation from Metropolitan-Vickers. Thus a joint venture was born, which resulted in the F.2/1 engine being first tested during December 1941. Flight tests then commenced in July 1943, with the engine being installed in the tail turret position of an Avro Lancaster BT308/G and this aircraft undertook research on this engine with RAE Turbine Flight. Later a second Lancaster, LL735, joined Turbine Flight; this also had an F.2/1 engine installed in the rear turret position.

Although much work on aircraft armaments and weapons had already taken place at RAE, Armament Department was officially formed on 1st January 1936. This was the start of much to follow over the next 58 years or so. Put into immediate action were trials on a buoyant bomb for sinking large ships, towed targets, and dropping of model bombs, torpedoes and flares to determine their ballistic behaviour before going into full-scale production.

1937

No 108 Squadron, operating Hinds, was detached to RAF Farnborough from 19th February to 7th July, whereupon the unit moved to Cranfield.

First flown as an HP.43, in a biplane configuration, on 21st June 1932 at Cricklewood, Handley Page HP.51 J9833 was rebuilt as a monoplane bomber/transport aircraft by the manufacturers making its (second) first flight on 8th May 1935 at Radlett. It came to Farnborough on 11th February 1937 for use as a hack, and for handling, performance and stability trials with Aero Flight. It then passed to W&E Flight for general radio development trials but was loaned to the War Office for troop-carrying exercises between Andover and Boscombe Down, departing for Odiham on 10th June and returning from Andover on 15th June. Dur-

ing June it was modified for use as a tanker aircraft and was briefly loaned to Flight Refuelling for trials, being flown to Ford on 9th August and returning on 2nd September. Back with RAE it was on strength with I&P Flight for blind landing trials, and W&E Flight for direction-finding homing tests, throat microphone, inter-communication and VHF trials. The aircraft was last flown at Farnborough on 3rd January 1940 and was struck off charge during May 1940.

Whilst the successful Queen Bee project was in full swing a further Air Ministry Specification Q32/35 was drawn up with a requirement for a faster and more adaptable radio-controlled aircraft. This resulted in the Airspeed AS.30 Queen Wasp: a cabin biplane that could operate from wheels or floats and was capable of being catapulted. Two prototypes, K8887 and K8888, were built, and a production order for 140 was initially placed but only five (P5441-P5445) were built, the remainder being cancelled. K8887 first flew on 11th June 1937 at Portsmouth and came to RAE on 9th October 1937 from there, first flying at Farnborough on 3rd November. It was fitted with the various onboard equipment and underwent handling and automatic control trials both at Farnborough and Lee-on-Solent during 1938. It went back to Airspeed at Portsmouth on various occasions but back at Farnborough, during 1938/1939, further work being undertaken included testing wireless transmission equipment, stalling characteristics, take-offs and landings, carburettor tests, auto-mixture controls and, of course, the role of aerial target. Departing Farnborough for Portsmouth on 4th October 1939 it was to return to RAE again on 29th December 1939 for further aerial target trials, which appeared to last until April 1940, whereupon the aircraft was probably stored until a test flight on 3rd August 1940 with delivery by air to Kemble two days later. It is believed that this example was written off when the Airspeed factory at Portsmouth was bombed by the Luftwaffe later that month.

The second example, K8888, arrived at Farnborough from Martlesham Heath, where

K5099, the Fairey P4/34 two-seat light bomber prototype, first flew on 13th January 1937. It arrived from Fairey's Great West Aerodrome (later to become Heathrow) on 25th May 1937, for wire barrage tests with A Flight. It later passed to IAD Flight for defence experiments and eventually ended up as an instructional airframe as 3665M, allocated during April 1941. *FAST collection*

Queen Wasp prototype K8887 arrived at
Farnborough on 9th October 1937 and
underwent radio and automatic control
trials with IAD Flight. It is seen here on the
'A' shed apron during March 1938.
FAST collection

it had been undergoing trials as a floatplane
variant, on 13th April 1938. It made its first
flight at RAE on 20th April when it underwent
general handling and engine tests with ER
Flight although officially operating with IAD
Flight. On the following day, the aircraft was
launched from the Farnborough catapult
with disastrous results. During the acceleration from the catapult the pilot's seat collapsed, resulting in loss of control and the
aircraft crashed to the ground and inverted.
It was wrecked in the process, although the
pilot escaped relatively uninjured. The
Queen Wasp was taken by road back to the
Airspeed facility at Portsmouth in June and
was rebuilt and returned to Farnborough on
23rd February 1939, making its first RAE
flight (again) on 19th April. Throughout 1939
this aircraft was engaged in wireless transmission tests, stability and handling trials and
aerial target development with IAD Flight
before returning to Portsmouth on 13th
November 1939. It was badly damaged in a
landing accident at Manorbier on 20th March
1941 but appears to have been repaired and
issued to 19MU at St Athan during May 1942.
It was eventually struck off charge on 7th July
1943, possibly as a result of an accident. Two
of the five production examples built also
had some Farnborough connections. An RAE
pilot flew P5441 at Farnborough on 14th May
1940 when the aircraft visited for the day
from Hawkinge, and again at Portsmouth on
17th May, then on 22nd May it arrived for a
short stay and departed for Portsmouth on
1st June 1940. It was on this day that the RAE
pilot also flew P5442 at Portsmouth, this
example not coming to Farnborough. Thus
ended a further chapter in the development
of target aircraft, with the Queen Wasp not
really being suitable for this role.

An Empire Air Day was held at Farnborough on 29th May 1937, being noteworthy
as a Hawker Audax K3066 of the Farnborough Station Flight/School of Photography
crashed onto the playground of the former
Farnborough Secondary School, adjacent to
Salisbury Road, on what is now the northern
car park of the Farnborough College of Technology. The Audax was one of three aircraft
flying in formation over the airfield making a
simulated attack when it over-corrected during a dive and was too low for recovery. The

two crew on board were killed and the aircraft was struck off charge on 29th August
1937. Two RAE aircraft took part in this display, the Fairey P.4/34 K5099 from Aero
Flight and Gladiator I K6143 from ER Flight.

Heinkel He 70G G-ADZF, W/Nr 1692 ex-
D-UBOF, an airliner with four passenger seats
registered on 18th December 1935, arrived
from Hucknall on 6th October 1936 for general handling and performance tests by Aero
Flight, including noise levels in a glide. It
returned to Hucknall on 24th December
1936. Rolls-Royce had purchased the type
directly from Heinkel at their Rostock factory
in 1935. At the time it was a very fast aircraft
and was of concern to the British politicians.
It was purchased on the basis of a requirement from Rolls-Royce for a Kestrel V engine
testbed and demonstration aircraft. It was
loaned to RAE for wind tunnel measurement
tests, arriving back at Farnborough on 10th
August 1937 to study its clean lines in order to
assist the knowledge of drag-reduced airliners. Whilst positioned in the wind tunnel dur-

ing August it had all the doors and windows
sealed up to prevent leaks and the results of
these tests were considered useful for the
future development of British civil airliners.
After a brief air test the aircraft departed back
to Rolls-Royce at Hucknall on 15th September
1937 where it was later re-engined with a
Kestrel XVI, which enabled a top speed of
463km/h to be achieved. In 1938, it was fitted
with a Peregrine I engine of 845hp that
increased the speed to 481km/h. Even the
design team at Supermarine acknowledged
that the He 70 was the influence behind the
aerodynamic form, and performance calculations, of the Spitfire. Its usefulness over, the
He 70 was withdrawn from use on 1st April
1940 and scrapped in 1944, but much had
been learnt from it.

By now the seaplane tank was being put
to good use. A variety of scale models were
tested, including a Roc during July, followed
by an Albacore in May 1940 and Hurricane,
Spitfire and Barracuda models, all fitted
with floats, in late 1940.

This four-passenger seat German-built
airliner, Heinkel He 70G G-ADZF is seen in
the open jet section of the RAE 24ft wind
tunnel during August 1937. This
streamlined aircraft was used for studying
airframe drag. *FAST collection*

Whitley prototype K4586 is seen here with engines running on the 'A' shed apron, during December 1937. Amongst other activities, it was used for taxying trials on grass, to measure the depressions of the wheels of this heavy aircraft. It became an instructional airframe in 1943.
FAST collection

At this time, albeit in the early design stage, RAE was looking at further development of the catapult for launching aircraft from aircraft carriers. The design was to be known as Assisted Take-Off Gear and as such became the BH.III accelerator. It was actually developed using the RAE Mk.II catapult on Jersey Brow in 1938. The first production unit began operations after installation in HMS *Illustrious* in 1940.

The prototype Armstrong Whitworth Whitley, K4586, arrived at Farnborough from Martlesham Heath on 24th March 1937 for directional stability trials with Aero Flight. It was also used for taxying trials on the grass airfield at Farnborough to examine the depth of depressions made by the wheels both during movement and whilst parked. The aircraft also undertook similar trials at RAF Odiham on 30th December, where it appears it initially got bogged down, but was returned to Farnborough on 11th January 1938 and further tests were accomplished at a weight of 40,000 lb. The conclusion was that there were no particular problems operating bombers from grass airfields at the weights tested, but by 1939 decisions had already been made for hard runways to be installed on RAF airfields and therefore these tests were no longer required. A lighter-weight Hawker Demon was also utilised for these trials without any problems.

Instrument and Photographic Flight was renamed Instrument Air Defence Flight (IAD) in October 1937.

1938

During the inter-war years, much had been learnt at Farnborough and passed to industry for further development on a mass scale. However since the earlier trial and error situation, where things were being learnt on a day-by-day basis, matters had by now taken on a somewhat different angle, as the Establishment had become well known and respected in the various fields of aviation. During this period a great deal of research, testing and learning had taken place in the fields of: aerodynamics, stability and control, engines, super-chargers, fuels, spark-plugs, radiators, variable-pitch propellers, auto-engine controls, autopilots, naviga-

tional instrumentation, cameras, photo reconnaissance, camouflage, bomb carrier and release experiments, aircraft safety barriers, the commencement of gas turbine research, fog dispersal, radio-controlled aircraft, VHF, HF and radio frequencies, intercommunications, airworthiness, structures, vibration and aero-elasticity. However, far from being complacent, the Establishment's scientists continued to learn and, during the forthcoming World War Two years, were in the forefront of further development of systems, or indeed the trials and tribulations of new aircraft and equipment.

Further Royal Air Force changes occurred during this year, with the control of RAF Farnborough reverting to No 22 Group on 1st June. No 1 Anti-Aircraft Co-operation Unit (AACU) moved to Farnborough from Biggin Hill on 11th April and two Wallace-equipped Flights were formed. The School of Photography was still lodging on the premises, although the AACU Flights moved away to various locations. However the AACU HQ Flight remained, converting pilots to the new Hawker Henley target-towing aircraft.

Although catapults had been in use for a number of years, the RAE Catapult Section came into being during September of this year, but with expansion of the department the title was later changed to Naval Aircraft Department in April 1945.

The Mechanical Test Department had installed a further large structural testing frame, known as 'The Cathedral'. This was later used for testing large aircraft and components such as Stirling, Halifax and Manchester, and others up to and including the TSR.2 in 1964. This Department had the responsibility for checking the structural strengths of all British civil and military aircraft. This was later to include the aircraft tested in the water tanks built along Tonks Terrace.

The second Gloster F5/34, K8089, with eight wing-mounted machine guns and powered by an 840hp Bristol Mercury engine, came to RAE from Brockworth on 6th December 1937 for use initially by W&E Flight on wireless transmission trials. It made its first flight at Farnborough on 17th

December. It was flown from Farnborough to Wolverhampton on 5th May 1938, for an aerial installation by Boulton & Paul, returning to RAE on 11th May. However it also underwent vibration measurements and spark plug research with ER Flight, pilot training, handling tests and high-speed research with Aero Flight until it made its last flight from Farnborough on 23rd January 1940. It was then transferred to instructional duties. Only two examples were built and these served as trials aircraft only, with no further production.

The prototype Hurricane K5083, which first flew on 6th November 1935, arrived from Martlesham Heath on 1st March 1938 for research handling and training of pilots with Aero Flight. This aircraft was originally built as a private venture but was produced to Specification F.36/34, and was soon to enter wide-scale production. This example was short-lived at Farnborough as it was returned to the manufacturer on 4th May 1938, although many examples of the Hurricane were to serve at Farnborough over the next ten years.

The prototype Spitfire, K5054, also arrived from Martlesham Heath on 7th November 1938 for handling tests. It was written off during landing at Farnborough on 4th September 1939 whilst undertaking sparking plug research with WE Flight. It had completed 151.30 flying hours.

Lockheed 12A G-AEMZ, c/n 1206, arrived from Croydon on 26th May 1938 and was allocated to Aero Flight for research handling trials. It was briefly used for camouflage experiments and radio development during early 1939 but its main usage with RAE was for Blind Approach research with WE Flight from 1939 to 1942. Its civilian registration was cancelled on 8th September 1939 whereupon it was allocated R8987, being recorded as such for its first flight under military conditions on 12th September. However it suffered a landing accident on 15th April 1942 when, returning from a routine ferrying flight to Lyneham, it veered off the runway and struck the DCTO track severing its undercarriage. There were no injuries but the aircraft was written off.

Messerschmitt Bf 108B-1 Taifun G-AFRN came from Heston on 29th November 1939 and commenced its type handling trials work with Aero Flight the same day. It appears to have made its last flight at Farnborough on 12th February 1940. Later, it was 'impressed' into RAF service as DK280 and was subsequently damaged beyond repair in an accident on 25th July 1944.

During the late 1930s, an area of Laffan's Plain, close to Berkshire Copse, was allocated for FIDO experiments, or 'Fog Intensive Disposal Of'. Oil burners were placed along the side of the runway, the heat being able to disperse the fog, these being trialled on the airfield at Farnborough by the Chemistry Division of RAE. Further research, by now known as Fog Investigation Dispersal Operations, led to many airfields adopting this system. The first installation was at Gravely, and the nearest installation to Farnborough was at nearby Hartford Bridge, later known as Blackbushe. Paraffin flares used for night flying – such as by the Vickers Virginia for searchlight training – first gave the idea of an intensified system that developed into FIDO.

1939

With the outbreak of World War Two, the trials and development work became more important and urgent. During the war period, the number of personnel at RAE was increased to approximately 6,000. Expansion of the airfield commenced again, with four sealed runways, taxiways, hardstandings and modern hangars being constructed, and the airfield was now enclosed. This work encompassed the remaining land that was Farnborough Common, Cove Common and Laffan's Plain. The original enhancements to the airfield were completed in 1941, with the airfield area consisting of approximately 800 acres. Pre-war, Experimental Aircraft Servicing Department was known as 11 Department and had approximately 170 engineering personnel, their main servicing hangars being F1E and 'A' shed. 'B' shed was added in 1939 and 'C' shed followed shortly after. At that time the general rule was to house the aircraft in the hangars overnight but as the size of aircraft increased this became impossible. 'G' and 'H' hangars came into being in 1942 and 'D' shed followed in 1943. In 1944 Vickers-Armstrong Aircraft Ltd were given permission to build 'E' shed for their use, this later being

passed to ETPS and RAE usage, as was E1, the ETPS hangar, built circa 1949. In 1944 some 300 or so detached RAF personnel were at Farnborough to assist with the aircraft maintenance under the classification of 'Flight Maintenance Wing', and this continued until 1946 with all maintenance then taken over by RAE aircraft engineers following a considerable recruiting campaign.

During August the RAF Medical Service had erected a physiological laboratory at Farnborough, close to Pinehurst Gate. Prior to the establishment of this building, various aircrew oxygen tests had been accomplished on the site, but now it was intended to investigate the physiological conditions of high-altitude flight, in order to develop these oxygen systems further. This work and the specialised equipment eventually evolved into the Royal Air Force Institute of Aviation Medicine.

With the advent of the tricycle undercarriage arrangement, a small fleet of aircraft with this new configuration underwent trials with Aero Flight at Farnborough to test their suitability. These included a Stearman-Hammond PH-APY that was hired from KLM, with whom it was undertaking experi-

ments and crew training duties, arriving at Farnborough on 9th November 1938; a Waco ZVN P6330, which later served with IAD Flight during 1940 but crash landed at Farnborough on 22nd August 1940 when the nose undercarriage collapsed and was written off; a Monospar ST.25 Universal N1531 that arrived from Heston on 24th June 1938; and a Cygnet 1 G-AEMA, which arrived from General Aircraft at Heston on 1st November 1939 and returned there on 9th January 1940. The Hammond went back to KLM on 23rd January 1939 but returned to RAE on 15th May when the airline had finished with it. It became R2676 with Aero Flight, remained in use up to 1940 and was struck off charge on 3rd February 1942.

Fitted with slotted wingtips, Hurricane I L1696 arrived at RAE from Brooklands on 23rd May 1939 for handling trials by Aero Flight. It was also installed for airflow trials in the 24ft wind tunnel during August 1939, with all gaps sealed up, in an endeavour to improve the airflow and speed of the type. The Hurricane departed from Farnborough on 10th June 1940 for Aston Down where it was issued to the RAF for squadron service. It did not last long as it was shot down over

This Stearman Hammond PH-APY, operated by KLM, came to Farnborough for tricycle undercarriage experiments on 9th November 1938. It is seen here on Jersey Brow during December 1938. It was later allocated serial R2676 and was in use with Aero Flight until 1940. *FAST collection*

Monospar ST.25 Universal N1531 came to Farnborough from the manufacturer on 24th June 1938 for tricycle undercarriage experiments, being fitted with a special nose undercarriage, as seen in this view taken during September 1939. *FAST collection*

GAL Cygnet 1 G-AEMA arrived at
Farnborough from Heston on 1st November
1939 for tricycle undercarriage
experiments, still in a camouflage scheme
but with a civil registration. *FAST collection*

Kent, during the Battle of Britain, by a Luft-waffe Bf 109 on 27th September 1940.

Aerodynamics Department were studying and evaluating new designs of aircraft. This included the proposed Westland F4/40 high-altitude fighter, DG558/G, which made its first flight on 1st November 1942 and became known as the Welkin. However, despite various performance improvements suggested by Farnborough, this new aircraft did not meet its expectations and the type was never introduced into squadron service.

Investigations also commenced into the detonation of magnetic mines, by means of being overflown by airborne magnets. These trials began with a Harrow I K6998, which arrived from Filton on 13th October 1939, and was fitted with a bar-shaped elec-tro-magnet in its bomb bay. The aircraft made its first flight at Farnborough as such on 5th December 1939, with E Flight, basi-cally as an aerial minesweeper. It was deployed to Gosport on 7th December, returning to RAE on 8th January 1940 and then being flown to Radlett three days later.

This proved so successful that improved sys-tems, employing large electro-magnetic rings of 48ft diameter, powered by a small aero engine driving a generator, were fitted to a number of Vickers Wellington aircraft and were successfully used.

Legend has it that a number of glass plate negatives from the RAE photographic department were crushed by the RAE steam-roller in order to be utilised as hardcore for the tarmac hardstanding in front of 'A' shed. This has not actually been substantiated, but over the years more have been crushed in similar circumstances.

1940

The RAF ensign had flown over Farnborough since formation of the service in April 1918 but as the RAE was transferred from the Air Min-istry to the Ministry of Aircraft Production, it was no longer appropriate to fly the flag over the Establishment. However the RAF presence at Farnborough continued as before.

Many aircraft types were now at Farnbor-ough, some receiving modifications or trial

installations of equipment, others with new engines or weapons; such was the urgency to meet the war effort. King George VI vis-ited RAE on 1st August and inspected some of the early captured German aircraft, as well as viewing RAE work at that time.

The 'Factory' was bombed by the Luft-waffe during the afternoon of 16th August, when eight Ju 88A-1s from 1/KG54 dropped twenty 50-kg and 250-kg bombs, of both instantaneous and delayed-action types. About half of these bombs fell on the RAE, in a line from the control tower, towards Syd-ney Smith Avenue, striking an old World War One RFC hangar, (which later had to be demolished), the engine test shops, and the mess grounds (behind The Swan Public House). The remainder fell outside in the residential areas of Albert Road, Church Road East, Reading Road and Canterbury Road, some hitting a local transport yard, whilst one bomb on the Factory did not explode for 49 hours.

The RAE staff were in shelters, but the two bombs that fell simultaneously on Sydney Smith Avenue caused the roof of a concrete shelter to collapse, killing three members of the local Defence Volunteers who had taken up duty there. These men belonged to the newly created 25th Battalion of the Hamp-shire Regiment of the Home Guard. They were the first casualties experienced by vol-unteers nationwide and were accordingly given full military honours at their burial. This area also contained the RAE Medical Department that was rebuilt on part of the bombed site and remained there until demolished in 2000.

The bombing disrupted work at RAE for only a few days. It did not cause a wide-spread problem, but lessons were learnt from this. Subsequently many RAE depart-ments were dispersed to sites outside the main establishment, in case another bomb-ing attack was forthcoming, which could have had far-reaching implications for the important work being undertaken. Sites such as Ambarrow Court, Bagshot and Bramshot came into being. The Performance

The clean-up is well under way after the
German bombing on 16th August 1940. This
view, looking east along Sydney Smith
Avenue, shows damage to the hangars on
the left and the roadway, whilst debris is
strewn across the airfield. RAE South Gate,
in the mid-distance, has been closed and the
people beyond are simply viewing the
damage to the Establishment. The last of the
delayed-action bombs detonated four days
after it had been dropped. *FAST collection*

Junkers Ju 88A-1 AX919, which was '9K+HL' of 1/KG51, arrived at Farnborough by road after having force-landed near Bexhill on 28th July 1940. Rebuilt, it is seen here during April 1941, allocated to Aero Flight for handling and performance trials. *FAST collection*

Section of Aerodynamics Department was dispersed to the Old Rectory in Rectory Road, and work on airfields, laminar flow, reduced drag, and various other aircraft performance improvements continued.

Experimental Flying Department immediately formed a Defence Flight, utilising their own Gladiator, two Hurricanes and Spitfires on air defence duties. Further aircraft were added, being allocated as and when necessary from the various RAE Flights. Between 17th August 1940 and 26th July 1944 the Defence Flight flew 340 sorties covering 114 days of action with 27 different aircraft of four types:
- Defiant I N3311
- Gladiator prototype K5200 and Mk.I K7946
- Hurricane Mk.Is L1778, L1780, L1788, P3864, V6809 and V7541; Mk.IIs Z2385, Z2691, Z2895, Z3564 and Z3887; Mk.IIBs Z4993 and BE145; and Mk.XIB BW953
- Spitfire Mk.Is K9796, N3053; X4258 and X4782; Mk.II P8781; Mk.VB W3248; Mk.VCs BR250 and EF644; and Mk.IXs EN498 and MA744.

However, extraordinary as it may seem, the RAE was not actually bombed again, although German aircraft were seen in the local area on other occasions.

The Short S.31 (M4) was built at Rochester and first flew on 19th September 1938 amid much secrecy. This was a half-scale wooden prototype of the Stirling bomber, powered by four Pobjoy engines, and was used for aerodynamic research by the company prior to commencement of Stirling production. The S.31 arrived at Farnborough from Rochester on 13th March 1940 and was engaged in general handling and undercarriage drag research making its initial flight with Aero Flight on 18th September 1940. Prior to this, during June 1940, it was placed within the open jet of the 24ft wind tunnel in order for turret drag and torque to be investigated in respect of a proposed development of the Stirling fitted with an under-fuselage 20mm cannon turret. The aircraft was returned to Shorts and eventually scrapped in 1943.

The Royal Air Force formed further AACU Flights at Farnborough with Hawker Henley aircraft, and other types were progressively added to the unit. Army Co-operation Command had been formed at Farnborough under 71 Group, but the Command and Group later moved away, with 70 Group now in charge of the station and the resident AACU.

The RAE Catapult Section main design team were involved in the design of a trolley launching system, an improvement on that in the wartime aircraft carrier HMS *Ark Royal*. This system had undergone development on Jersey Brow and sea trials were conducted in HMS *Illustrious* during this year. It was considered by the Admiralty that further launching systems should be installed at RAE, in order that development could be undertaken at Farnborough without requiring sea-going resources. The Jersey Brow site to the west of the factory was adopted for this work. During its lifetime some twelve catapult systems were developed at RAE by the Catapult Section and, later, the Naval Aircraft Department.

The very first captured World War Two German aircraft to come to Farnborough was on 14th May 1940, when a Messerschmitt Bf 109E-3, W/Nr 1304, flew in from Boscombe Down. This aircraft had force-landed in France on 22nd September 1939 and carried the German markings 'White 1' of JG76. It first flew at Farnborough the day after it arrived and underwent general handling, performance and engine cooling tests with Aero Flight, acquiring RAF serial AE479 in June. It then spent a couple of months at Northolt before returning to Farnborough on 20th November 1940, but it suffered a landing accident on 5th January 1941 and underwent repair, before departing from Farnborough on 23rd July 1941, bound for Northolt and onward to Duxford for the Air Fighting Development Unit. Whilst at RAE the aircraft had made 78 flights. The second captured aircraft to come to RAE was a Heinkel He 111H-1 (W/Nr 6853, later to become AW177), which was coded '1H+EN' of II/KG26 when it force-landed near Berwick on 9th February 1940 and was transported by road to Turnhouse. The aircraft was flown from Turnhouse to Farnborough on 14th August 1940 and undertook its first RAE flight on 27th October, being allocated to Aero Flight for handling trials. It spent a brief time at Duxford with the Air Fighting Development Unit between 12th September and 6th October 1941, when it returned to Farnborough, only to leave permanently to Duxford and 1426 Flight on 7th December 1941. 41 flights had been undertaken whilst the aircraft was with RAE.

Messerschmitt Bf 110C-5 '5F+CM' of AKG14 (W/Nr 2177, later to become AX772) was shot down near Goodwood on 21st July 1940 and was brought to the RAE, where it was repaired and made its first test flight on 25th October 1940. It was allocated to Aero Flight for handling and performance trials and was transferred to Duxford on 13th October 1941 for the AFDU, a total of 45 flights having been made with RAE.

Having run out of fuel, Junkers Ju 88A-1 '9K+HL' of 1/KG51 (W/Nr 7036, later to become AX919), force-landed near Bexhill on 28th July 1940 and was dismantled on site, arriving at Farnborough by road on 31st August 1940. It made its first RAE flight on 3rd April 1941 and left by road to Duxford on 12th June 1942, for use as spares for other aircraft operated by 1426 Flight. Only four flights were made by this aircraft whilst it was with RAE.

The first Italian aircraft to be captured and sent to Farnborough was a Fiat CR.42 (MM5701, c/n 326, later to become BT474), which was operating as '13-95' with 18 Gruppo/56 Stormo when it was shot down during the Battle of Britain, near Orfordness on 11th November 1940. It was taken to Farnborough by road on 27th November 1940, where it was repaired and made the first of two flights with Aero Flight on 26th April 1941. It was transferred to the AFDU at Duxford two days later, and is now displayed in the RAF Museum at Hendon.

Another early German aircraft to be captured and sent to RAE was a Gotha Go 145B, W/Nr 1115, later to become BV207. As '5M+NQ' of STAB/JG27, it had landed in error on Lewes Racecourse on 28th August 1940 and was flown to Farnborough on 31st August 1940. It was allocated to Aero Flight and made just three test flights before being passed on to Aston Down on 1st January 1941.

The RAE Radio Department came into being during this year, having previously been known as the Experimental Wireless Department. Work continued in very high

frequency (VHF) air-to-ground radio transmissions; development of Identification Friend or Foe (IFF); radio altimeters; VHF communications; aircraft aerials; auto-pilots; blind approach and radar development. Also a mobile ground control intercept (GCI) radar was successfully trialled.

During 1939 work on a new research installation, known as the Direction-Controlled Take-off (DCTO) system was commenced on Jersey Brow, with a long track being built across the airfield in a south-westerly direction along the old 'mile straight'. This was a proposed development for launching large multi-engined bomber aircraft without the need for runways. The track was nearly a mile (1472 yards) in length and was built like a very wide gauge (22ft 9in) railway, with twin rails either side. It was completed in 1940.

The system was first tested by a Heyford III, K5184, which arrived from St Athan on 10th July 1940. This was first launched from the DCTO track on 22nd August 1940 and for a second time on 10th September during 1940, at an all-up weight of 12,000 lb. This proved the system was perfectly capable of launching a heavy aircraft but the objective launch was to be by an Avro Manchester I aircraft of 38,000 lb. The prototype, L7276, had first flown on 25th July 1939 at Ringway and was delivered to Boscombe Down for tests. It came to Farnborough on 3rd June 1941 from there and was put to use by Aero Flight for take-off and landing tests, shimmy tests, stability and electrical research. It was then designated to continue with the DCTO trials, which the Heyford had accomplished by now some two years earlier. The Manchester was loaded onto the track during early September 1942, to check positioning, and during the early morning of 8th September it was successfully launched off the DCTO track, landing on the runway some five minutes later. Although proven, the DCTO concept, originated for the Norwegian Campaign, was not proceeded with and was abandoned. Vestiges of this track can still be seen today, some 66 years later,

buried in the grass adjacent to Mosquito Way on the airfield. Indeed many sections of this track were dug up from the ground on the airfield during 2001 when the airfield and its facilities were modernised.

Trials commenced on a Radio Direction Finding (RDF) System, which later became known as Radar, and early work proved a success with this equipment. Similarly work commenced on a gyro gunsight for fighter aircraft in combat and later a gyro bomb-sight for bomber aircraft, both of which proved to be a significant success and were used widely throughout World War Two.

Parts of the airfield at the Laffan's Plain end were mined as a protection against the enemy glider landings that were considered a real threat at the time.

Armament Department were undertaking tests to illuminate the night sky in order to light up enemy bombers, using candles from reconnaissance flares, trailed behind a Hampden. Later flares were fixed to the underwing bomb racks, but these were not too successful. Other work being carried out included incendiary devices, magnesium, petroleum jelly and phosphorous bombs and methane torch bombs.

1941

The Chief Superintendent, A H Hall, retired and was succeeded by W S Farren. The new Superintendent had been a scientist pilot in 1915 and was head of Aerodynamics Department during World War One. During his time as Director of the Establishment, he continued to fly various aircraft types from Farnborough and he established Technical Training Flight in October 1943 where scientists and engineers learnt to fly on Magister Is L5965, L8168 and L8284; Harvard IIBs FX216 and KF427; and DH.82A Tiger Moth R4752 to obtain a better understanding of handling aircraft on their own.

Chemical and Fabric Department were experimenting with aircraft camouflage, with various camouflage patterns being applied to aircraft, airfields, vehicles, buildings, tents and ships to suit the respective

environs. This department was also responsible for reducing the fire risk in aircraft by the installation of onboard fire extinguishers and indeed carbon monoxide indicators.

The first jet-powered aircraft to fly in the UK, the Gloster E28/39 Whittle W4041/G, made its maiden flight from RAF Cranwell on 15th May 1941. This was to be flown at Farnborough for evaluation during the following year.

Cordite rocket boosters, which became known as rocket-assisted take-off gear (RATOG), were being experimented with on various aircraft, including bombers and gliders, to gave a reduced take-off run. One of the aircraft used in these experiments was an SB2U Chesapeake AL912, it was intended that these aircraft could operate from the carriers with these booster rockets. However this would have caused a fire risk to the wooden decks of the American carriers and consequently use on this type was not proceeded with. Trials with other aircraft took place with reasonable success. Aircraft carrier deck landing trials were conducted on land by RAE at HMS *Condor* (RNAS Arbroath, Scotland), prior to the first arrester systems being installed on runway 04/22 at Farnborough in 1942. Vestiges of this equipment are still in place, their machinery pits alongside this former runway today.

On 17th January 1941 the prototype P.1 rocket-propelled catapult underwent its first trials on Jersey Brow with the launch of Fulmar I N4016, which had arrived from Lee-on-Solent on 9th January. This concept had been designed and built at RAE within just 25 days. Developed further, the P.1 remained in use until its removal from Jersey Brow in 1952. Installed alongside were the C.1 accelerator and the flywheel-operated K.1.

Wooden scale models of various aircraft were built and these were used for ditching tests by RAE, utilising a cooling pond of one of the wind tunnels that had been fitted with a wave-maker. These experiments continued for a number of years, utilising many different types of aircraft models.

Not only were intact enemy aircraft being brought to Farnborough at this time, but also many parts of captured German equipment. Examination of German radar units took place, which eventually enabled the RAF to jam German radar stations during the Allied mass bombing raids. Before

D-Day, a complete German radar set was sent to Farnborough and this enabled the scientists to generate much knowledge, which led to considerable jamming being possible during the actual D-Day landings.

Airworthiness Department joined with Mechanical Test Department and formed Structural Mechanical Engineering Department. Tests being conducted included undercarriage shimmy; tab controls; flutter; self-sealing tanks against enemy fire and reconstruction of German V-1 and V-2 rockets.

Following on from the seaplane tank tests of the floatplane Spitfire I, models of the Spitfire III were tested in the seaplane tank during May and June with redesigned floats, to determine the waterborne characteristics, wake and spray effects on the airframe if a floatplane variant were to be ordered by the Air Ministry. Trials were undertaken with a varnished balsa model, suitably ballasted, but these were none too successful. Flight and water trials on various full-scale Spitfire floatplanes were conducted by Folland but these never saw any production orders and the Air Ministry eventually decided to abandon the project, as a seaplane fighter would have inferior performance and limiting operational factors as opposed to a normal landplane.

Ditching tests for various types of aircraft were tasked to RAE during this period, as many aircraft were being lost in the sea, with a view to establishing the best way to ditch. The Lockheed Hudson was considered particularly vulnerable, as a large number had been lost without trace. Some tests had been carried out before World War Two on ditching aspects, to investigate the alighting of landplanes on water, using models in the RAE seaplane tank. This was unsatisfactory and it was concluded that it would be better to catapult models into a water tank. Many models were made for this work by the RAE craftsmen of the time. A B-17 Fortress was one example where the service ditching drill was improved as a result of the RAE tests, thus saving many aircrew. Tests of a Mustang model showed that the aircraft would dive beneath the surface when it had hit the water and RAE concluded that the Mustang should not attempt to ditch. Many other different types of aircraft were experimented on in this way over many years, including commercial models such as the Britannia. Indeed, during 1942, models of the Halifax and Lancaster were catapulted into the water tank for stability and yaw tests, which led to the Halifax being modified with larger fins, to give the Halifax improved stability.

The first B-17 Fortress to come to RAE arrived from Boscombe Down on 15th October 1941. Fortress I AN519 (ex-B-17C 40-2044) was one of the first in the UK, being operated by No 90 Sqn, and it was used at Farnborough for sky brightness measurements at high-altitude and gun-

firing tests, in conjunction with the Air Fighting Development Unit. It departed on 10th August 1942 for Burtonwood and issue to No 206 Sqn. Fortress IIA FK190 arrived from Burtonwood on 2nd May 1942 for long-range Air to Surface Vessel (ASV) radar trials with WE Flight and departed to Prestwick on 1st September 1942 with subsequent issue to No 220 Sqn. A further Fortress IIA, FK204, arrived from Burtonwood on 1st July 1942 but this was not accepted at RAE and returned on 11th July to be replaced by another example, FK202, which was ferried back the same day. This was used by WE Flight for long-range ASV work, autopilot and radio transmission trials before departing for Filton on 3rd October 1942. A Fortress GR.II, FA709, arrived from Prestwick on 2nd January 1943 and departed on 9th January 1943 for High Ercall, probably only undergoing ground tests at Farnborough, as it did not fly during its short stay with RAE. Yet another Fortress IIA, FL455, followed arriving from Prestwick on 18th March 1943 and also engaged on ASV and bomber radio transmission trials with WE Flight. It departed for Hamble on 20th April 1943 but returned, from Colerne, on 28th May 1943 to continue its previous work and finally left for Colerne 20th June 1943. Flame damping trials and static vent tests were conducted by ER Flight in mid 1943 using Fortress IIA FK187, which arrived from Boscombe Down on 6th April 1943 and later departed for Prestwick on 6th November 1943. Fortress III HB778 (a B-17G) arrived at Farnborough from Lichfield on 27th March 1945 and was engaged in trials for combustion heaters, handling, IFF (Identification Friend or Foe), and 'High Tea', being operated by WE Flight and SME Flight. This aircraft served at Farnborough until 9th September 1952 when it was returned to the USAF at Burtonwood.

Engine Research Flight, as its name suggests, was tasked to undertake research and development trials of all things pertaining to aero engines. However other elements of research also crept in under this title and consequently the Flight did lead a varied research existence. Work being undertaken during 1941 and early 1942, under Flight Commander Squadron Leader H C D Hayter, (from November Sqn Ldr G R Fielder, then from February 1942 Sqn Ldr W R Cox), included automatic boost control research on Tomahawk I AH797 and fuel tests in Tomahawk IIB AK184; endurance under tropical conditions in Swordfish I V4568; liquid oxygen in Spitfire II P8079; negative 'G' in Hurricane II Z2691; engine development in a Mohawk IV BJ449; fuel system vibrations and vapour-locking investigation in Airacobra I AH600; fuel tests on Spitfire II P8781; engine development and endurance tests in Wellington III X3224; engine development and cooling tests in a

Beaufort I N1095; RAE carburettor tests in Wellesley K7772; automatic air intake in Beaufighter IF R2066; air cleaner comparisons in a Chesapeake I AL912; oil-throwing tests in Martlet I AX825; carburettor jetwells, immersed pumps and high-altitude fuel research in Hurricane II Z2385; automatic boost control in Tomahawk IIA AH979; flame damping and carbon-monoxide tests in a Buffalo I W8133 and oil suitability tests in Anson I R9816.

During 1941 Research Department Flight, (Squadron Leader C R Hawkins, changing to Squadron Leader L D Wilson in April 1942), was based away from Farnborough at RAF Exeter. This was basically due to overcrowding at Farnborough, although RAF Exeter was an operational base, with two RAF Polish Squadrons, No 307 equipped with Beaufighter IIFs, and No 317 Squadron equipped with Hurricane IIs, both these units being fairly active. Work being undertaken at this dispersed site during 1941/1942 consisted mainly of research into dropping bombs. Various types of bombing experiments were conducted, using Wellington IA P9210 and Blenheim I L1146, whilst fuel tank endurance tests were undertaken with Spitfire I X4782 and Blenheim IV Z6189.

However, perhaps the majority of flights undertaken here during these years, were those flying aircraft into kite balloon and barrage balloon cables to test cutting equipment fitted to the aircraft and to determine the effects of cable impact on mainplanes and so on. Aircraft used for these experiments included Wellington IA P9210 and IC W5686; various Battle Is including K7698, L5003 and N2037; and Hurricane Is Z7066, AF979 and AG254. A Hurricane I P3585 was fitted with a camera and sight, for recording the cable impacts. These impact tests, which included critical velocity cutter impacts flown by the Hurricanes, were undertaken at Watchet and Pawlett in the Bridgwater area. The Flight moved to RAF Churchstanton near Taunton, where Polish No 306 Squadron with Spitfire VBs was based, during February, and became operational there on 16th February 1942 to continue with these experiments.

Armament Department had a close liaison with the Aircraft Torpedo Development Unit (ATDU) at Gosport, where torpedoes, mines, flares and sea navigation markers all underwent trials off Ryde, Isle of Wight.

Two further captured German aircraft arrived at RAE during this year, the first being a Junkers Ju 88A-5 (W/Nr 3457, later to become EE205), which was operational as '4D+DL' of 1/KG30 when it landed at Lulsgate Bottom, in error, on 23rd February 1941. It arrived at Farnborough from Wrington on 1st August 1941 and first flew with Aero Flight on 14th August 1941. It was engaged in handling and performance trials, also being operated by IAD Flight for dive bombsight, DF loop and de-icing trials. It passed to the AFDU at Duxford on 19th August 1941, returning on 1st September to continue the trials work, before finally leaving, after 75 RAE flights, for 1426 Flight at Duxford on 28th August 1942.

A Messerschmitt Bf 109F-2 (W/Nr 12764, later becoming ES906) was shot down over St Margaret's Bay, Dover on 10th July 1941, whilst operating with 1/JG26. It arrived at Farnborough by road during July 1941 and, after undergoing repair, made its first flight with Aero Flight on 19th September 1941, whereupon it was generally engaged in handling trials. After 14 RAE flights it passed to the AFDU at Duxford on 11th October 1941.

1942

Further runway extensions occurred, which gave runway 07/25 a length of 6,150ft, and runway 18/36, further extended during 1944, a length of 3,000ft, whilst runway 11/29 was 4,100ft and runway 04/22 2,500ft. The factory site by now covered approximately 56 acres, which accommodated various workshop, laboratory, specialist research and administration buildings.

The Instrument and Photographic Department was experimenting with a series of instruments for high- and low-altitude bombing, navigation and a high-altitude photo-reconnaissance camera. The latter, known as the F52, later became standard equipment for the Royal Air Force. Other work being conducted included a gyro-stabilised automatic bomb sight, which was introduced into service with great success; various camera upgrades, including the F8 which was put into production again; infra-red cameras; night camera development for low altitude, with pyrotechnic flash; compasses; oxygen

system development, including a portable oxygen kit for aircrew moving around the aircraft; emergency oxygen system; a low-altitude reconnaissance camera; drift recorder; low-level bomb sight; course-setting bomb sight; bomb teacher; air mileage measurement; air positioning and ground position indicators, giving fully automatic navigation; astro-navigation system development; Mk.8 auto-pilot; and film processing with rapid film development techniques, were all being researched during this period.

The 4,000hp high-speed wind tunnel was opened on 6th November, this tunnel being able to test models up to 6ft span in air speeds of 600mph. Much aerodynamic work on the scale models of new aircraft types was tested in this manner, which proved a great success for aerodynamic research.

No 653 (AOP) Squadron, then an RAF unit, arrived from Old Sarum on 8th July, as part of 53 Wing. This unit was equipped with DH.82A Tiger Moths, but the squadron quickly converted to the Auster Mk.1 before relocating to Penshurst on 7th September 1942.

During this year parts of German V-1 flying bombs and V-2 rockets had been brought to Farnborough for examination, in order to quickly learn more about these new weapons. Further captured aircraft were tested by the Experimental Flying Department.

Investigations into the effects of mine explosions; rocket catapult launching; impact with wire cables; glider towing; high G values on air crew; engine performance and high-speed dives, the latter to push the envelope further for high-speed flight, were all being undertaken by Experimental Flying Department at this time.

During late 1942 the Turbine Section of RAE Engine Department moved to Pyestock,

a specially built outstation, to become Turbine Division of RAE. However, during May 1944, this was amalgamated with Power Jets Limited and formed Power Jets (Research and Development) Limited. The Government decreed that all future gas turbine research was to be undertaken at Pyestock, which in 1946 became the National Gas Turbine Establishment (NGTE), in turn becoming part of RAE in 1983. Piston engine research remained at RAE under the Power Plant Division until 31st March 1946.

Experimental Engine Department was also undertaking examination of enemy aero engines such as Mercedes, Daimler-Benz and Junkers types, all being evaluated with much being learnt from them.

By the early 1940s, four catapult/accelerator installations had been built on Jersey Brow. The original Mk.I catapult had been dismantled in the late 1930s and the Mk.II unit, which had been in use for launching aircraft fitted with catapult spools, was also dismantled at this time. There was also the P.1 catapult, which was originally built at ground level but was later mounted on a raised structure, simulating the height of a ship's weather deck above sea level. Following various trials that were deemed a success with this catapult, the Admiralty fitted out

The UK's first jet aircraft, the Gloster E28/39 Whittle W4041/G, made its first flight on 15th May 1941 and came to Farnborough by road, amid much secrecy, during December 1942. Operating with Aero Flight, and later Aero T Flight, the aircraft made 52 flights from Farnborough. It is seen here, parked on the apron near what became 'H' hangar, during early 1945. *FAST collection*

three catapult aircraft ships followed by 33 further merchant vessels known as Catapult Aircraft Merchantmen (CAM) ships. The Farnborough catapult rig was also used for ab initio training of all pilots and ground crew, who had volunteered for this emergency measure in the defence of ocean-going convoy fleets. However, within a couple of years, with the advent of the Merchant Aircraft Carrier (MAC) ships, the system was superseded and the Jersey Brow rig was retained for spooled aircraft launches. The C.1 (Cordite accelerator) had also been installed on Jersey Brow and this took over most of the catapult launch trials at Farnborough. Later, a modified form of the BH.III trolley and shuttle was developed here. At one stage seven Albacore aircraft, from No 827NAS, were launched successfully in 20 minutes using the BH.III trolley system. This proved the ability of the installation to launch a mass of aircraft in quick succession.

Also designed, installed and tested on Farnborough airfield was the airfield emergency arrester gear, built for bomber aircraft in order to cut down overrun accidents on landing. L7246, a Manchester I, fitted with a basic arrester hook designed by the RAE, demonstrated this concept successfully during August 1942. The Manchester deployed to Woodhall Spa to carry out arrester trials on 21st and 22nd October 1942. However this project was terminated before it was adopted for full-scale use, as the development of airborne radar required the bomber aircraft to have equipment housed in the rear fuselage that left no space to accommodate an arrester hook. Originally it was intended to install six sets of equipment at the runway ends of the nominated bomber airfields of Elsham Wolds, Lakenheath, Linton-on-Ouse, Middleton St George, Swinderby, Waterbeach and Woodhall Spa. In the end some twenty airfields were equipped – but all to no effect.

By now the first jet engine had flown, Gloster E28/39 W4041/G making its very first flight on 15th May 1941 from Cranwell with the W.1 engine. During these pioneering days gas turbine engine development proceeded at Farnborough. The aircraft came to Farnborough by road and first flew with Aerodynamics Flight on 20th December 1942. It undertook 17 flights up to 15th February 1943, before it went back to Glosters by road for installation of the W.2/500 engine. It returned to Farnborough by road again and commenced further flight trials on 9th March 1944, completing a further 11 flights with Aerodynamics Flight. It then underwent some further modifications and recommenced its flight research programme on 25th August 1944, now with Aero T Flight, investigating Mach numbers. It undertook a further 24 flights up to 20th February 1945. It appears to have been returned to Glosters again sometime there-

after. This historic aircraft was transferred to the Science Museum on 28th April 1946, where it is still on display.

With the advent of the jet engine and the early research being undertaken at RAE in respect of aerodynamics, handling and general development, the scene was thus set for the next 52 years or so, during which many jet types have been used for a plethora of different trials, research and development duties at Farnborough.

On 13th July 1942, Aero Airborne Flight was formed at Farnborough under Flight Commander Flt Lt (later Sqn Ldr) W D B S Davie, as the programme of experimental gliding work, carried out by Aerodynamics Department, was increasing rapidly. After much deliberation Aero Airborne Flight was moved to Hartford Bridge on 11th August 1942, where the glider research was to be conducted. Work carried out from there included a triple-tow with three Hotspurs behind a Whitley; development of blind flying instruments for the Horsa I LG927 and Hamilcars DR853 and DR856; twin tug of Horsa Is DP341 and DG597, the prototype, using Whitley Mk.Vs Z9390 and BD504; short rope tows; Hamilcar DR852/G handling trials; Hotspur IIs BT833 and BT903 dive parachute tests; Hamilcar DR852/G with twin Halifax IIs DT502 and DT587 as tugs; RATOG with Whitley T4149 towing Horsa DP709, and RATOG with Hamilcar DR854/G towed by Halifax II DT502; flap droop tests with a Horsa I LG927; twin tug of Horsa I DP341 using two Master GT.IIs, one of which was DL308; and Hotspur II BT903 drag measurements. The twin towing experiments were handed over to AFEE to continue this research. Aero Airborne Flight moved back to Farnborough during March 1943.

Armament Department, during the course of World War Two, were extremely busy with their own ballistic and bomb developments, and future rocket projectile firing installations. The latter were trialled on various types of aircraft, although a Hurricane II Z3919 was the first to be fitted in this way at RAE followed by Mustang I AM130. This concept proved very successful against tanks and armoured equipment and was developed further as the years went by. Further development occurred of various guns; gunsights; bombs; bomb sights; gyro stabilised gun and bomb sights; rocket projectiles; underwater ballistics; gun fitments to aircraft; bomb carriage; parachute mines; cluster bombs; bomb containers; smoke containers and smoke bombs.

During the wartime period, Wireless & Electrical Flight was engaged in vital work on radio communications, radar, aerials, VHF, receivers and transmitters, and jamming equipment, to name but some. Under the command of Squadron Leader R J Falk, examples of the research work being undertaken included:

- radio clearance aerials in Hudson AE610;
- jamming counter-measures in Hudson III T9433;
- airborne radar in Beaufighter I X7672;
- airborne jamming equipment and VHF relay station in Beaufighter I X7821;
- cable noise, VHF range tests, beam approaches in Hudson I N7205;
- VHF clearance in Mustang I AG349;
- IFF equipment in Hudson III T9433 and Wellington Ic T2969;
- trailing aerials and 'Monica' warning equipment in Wellington II Z8440;
- VHF and blind approach trials in Defiant I N3377;
- radio clearance and VHF in Havoc I BJ462;
- AI radar and Turbinlite in Havoc I BB911;
- frequency modulation, transmitter tests and inter-com on Wellington Ic T2969;
- de-magnetisation of a compass in Anson I R9689;
- long-range precision radio altimeter in Wellington VIA W5802;
- oxygen tests in Wellington L4212;
- transmitter tests in Kittyhawk I ET580;
- American ASV equipment in Fortress IIAs FK190 and FK202;
- range tests in Hudson N7263 of the King's Flight;
- wireless transmitter tests in A-20B Bostons 41-3004, 41-3011 and 41-3031;
- VHF air homing in Beaufighter VIs EL156 and EL170;
- Coastal Command camouflage on Whitley VII Z9377.

Much of the radio transmission/receiver work undertaken by this department utilised the nearby Cove Radio Station.

The 10ft x 7ft transonic wind tunnel (R133 building) was completed this year and opened on 6th November; the tunnel being built inside a cylindrical pressed steel shell 140ft long and 37ft in diameter. This was a closed circuit tunnel and, whilst operating, cold brine was pumped through cascades of metal-turning vanes at the circuit corner to continually keep the tunnel cool. The four storage tanks collectively contained 1,000 tons of brine. Able to test scale models up to 6ft span in air speeds of 600mph, much aerodynamic work on scale models of new aircraft types was carried out, the first model being a Hawker Typhoon – many more fighter types were tested within the working section of the tunnel during the World War Two years. Then came the early jets and many of the new types were tested in model form at subsonic speeds. The new facility proved a great success for aerodynamic research.

A fair number of Luftwaffe aircraft had landed in the UK in error, the pilots thinking they were over their homeland or occupied France. Landing at Pembrey, South Wales on 23rd June 1942, whilst operating with III/JG2, was Focke-Wulf Fw 190A-3 (W/Nr 313, later to become MP499). It arrived at

Bell P-63A-9-BE Kingcobra, arrived at Farnborough on 20th September 1944 as 42-69423, but was later allocated the RAF serial FZ440. It undertook research into low-drag wings and high-speed laminar flow with Aero Flight. Note the US Army Air Force stencilling is still applied beneath the cockpit door. It was disposed of as scrap in March 1949. *via B Kervell*

Farnborough by road during late June and made its first flight at RAE on 3rd July, being allocated to Aero Flight for various handling and performance trials for fighter comparison. It flew at Farnborough for the 29th and last time on 29th January 1943 and was struck off charge during September 1943, with the fuselage used for firing trials and the wings for destructive testing.

1943

The second E28/39 Whittle, W4046/G, made its first flight on 1st March 1943 and was delivered by air from the Gloster facility at Edgehill on 3rd May. Fitted with the Rover W.2B engine, it commenced a research programme for Engine Research Flight on the same day, flown by Sqn Ldr W D B S Davie. It undertook 115 flights between 3rd May 1943 and 30th July 1943 and, on one day alone, made 10 flights, being flown by three different pilots. Unfortunately, on 30th July 1943, whilst at 33,000ft, the ailerons jammed, resulting in the aircraft entering an uncontrolled inverted spin. Squadron Leader Davie bailed out at 33,000ft and thus became the first pilot to bale out from a British jet aircraft, and at the highest altitude for a bale-out at that time. The aircraft crashed at Shalford, south of Guildford. The remaining E28/39, W4041, continued the research programme, which was completed in 1944. These early trials were the foundations of jet engine research and much was to follow over the next fifty years.

An arrester system known as the Drag Chain Arrester Gear (DCAG) was installed at Farnborough: Seafire Mk.IICs MB125 and MB299, with Mk.IB NX983 and Airacobra I AH574 successfully trialled this equipment. The Airacobra arrived on 23rd July 1943 from 51MU at Lichfield and was sent to Malcolms at White Waltham for fitment of an arrester hook, returning on 17th November. This aircraft was to be used for catapulting and arresting investigation with a tricycle undercarriage layout, this type being the first

high-performance tri-gear aircraft at Farnborough. The first trials commenced on 22nd December 1943 and on 20th June 1945 the aircraft was detached to Henstridge for trials on board HMS *Pretoria Castle* where touch-and-go landings were accomplished to check approach stability and touchdown. The Airacobra was struck off charge on 18th March 1948 but was retained by Naval Air Department for use as a catapult dummy. Two other Airacobras served with RAE, these being AH572 and AH600. Kingcobra FZ440 (P-63-9-BE 42-69423) arrived at RAE on 20th September 1944 as 269423 from Renfrew for research by Aero Flight into low-drag wings in flight and high-speed laminar flow. It remained at Farnborough until sold to International Alloys as scrap on 16th March 1949. Kingcobra I FR408 (ex-42-68937) also served at Farnborough, arriving from Speke on 17th May 1944 and operating with Aero Flight undertaking drag measurement trials until it was struck off charge on 18th October 1945.

The Ignition and Electrical Department of RAE was renamed the Electrical Engineering Department during this year and they continued much valuable research including into improved spark plugs; accumulators; bomb release and distribution; compass interference; magnetic sweeper for airfields to collect steel spikes, should these be dropped by the enemy; improved ignition systems; approach lighting for airfields and new cockpit lighting developed for both day and night operations.

Structural & Mechanical Engineering Department (SME) came into being as a result of various mergers within other departments, and both full-scale aircraft and component testing within the various test frames continued, whilst the development of the electrical strain gauge technique was introduced. Ongoing work included research on undercarriage shimmy dampers; dynamic loading investigations; trim and control tabs; drop tank developments; pressurised cockpits and self-sealing fuel tanks.

A new 11ft x 8ft wind tunnel was completed during this year, being capable of achieving speeds up to 400ft/sec (270mph). The high-speed wind tunnel, which opened during November 1942, was in use for dynamic testing of many aircraft models at speed, but the low-speed tunnel was first used for tests with the Miles E.24/43 supersonic project and further work on the early jets such as the Gloster E.28/39 Whittle and Gloster F.9/40 Rampage/Meteor. The earlier 7ft wind tunnel, built during 1917/18, was dismantled during this time and a 4ft x 3ft tunnel was built in its place.

Boundary layer and laminar flow research had commenced prior to the outbreak of World War Two and, during this stage, this work was further enhanced by wool tuft and wing section experiments being undertaken on various aircraft such as the Anson prototype K4771; Battle I N2183; Falcons K5924, L9705 and R4071; Magister I L5965; Hurricane I L1696, the latter being fitted with low-drag wings; Mustang I AG393 and Spitfire PR.XI EN409 with much performance data resulting from the flight research and wind tunnel tests undertaken.

The first Vickers Windsor prototype, DW506, intended to be a high-altitude bomber with a pressurised cabin, under specification B.5/41, was assembled at Farnborough in a specially built hangar, that later became known as E-Shed, this hangar later being extensively used by ETPS and RAE. (Brennan House, situated in the BAE Systems headquarters business park, now occupies the site of this hangar.) The first flight occurred on 23rd October 1943 and proved a success, but on 2nd March 1944 the aircraft made a forced landing at Grove, breaking its back, and was not repaired. The second aircraft, DW512, first flew from Wisley on 15th February 1944 and was broken up in June 1946. A third aircraft, NK136, also flew but, by then, technology had advanced so much that the project was considered outdated and was cancelled.

During this year a proposal to eliminate undercarriages was made, whereby take-off and ground handling was to be performed on specially designed trolleys and the aircraft would return to land and undertake a belly landing onto a cushioned surface. A 1:8 scale model was produced and various early trials were conducted, which led to this system being tested on a full-scale aircraft in later years.

The Vickers Windsor prototype, DW506, was assembled in the Vickers hangar, seen beyond the aircraft, that was later to become 'E' shed and made its first flight on 23rd October 1943. Here the aircraft has just been removed from the hangar, prior to its first flight. This Windsor was written off in an accident at Grove on 2nd March 1944. *FAST collection*

Turbine Flight, known as 'T' Flight, formed in February 1943 and commenced research during the year on the new generation of gas turbine-engined aircraft that were now entering service. Gloster F9/40 Rampage DG204/G made its first flight with 'T' Flight on 13th November 1943, completing only nine flights before it crashed on 4th January 1944.

By now the Americans had produced the Bell XP-59A, referred to by the RAE as a 'Toll-gate', although it eventually became the Airacomet. This made its first flight during October 1942, powered by two General Electric engines. The third aircraft (42-108773, becoming RJ362/G) came to Farnborough and after assembly was allocated to Turbine Flight, where it commenced flight trials on 20th December 1943 to gain engine data and performance statistics in comparison with the Rampage. It appears to have undertaken 20 flights at RAE, the last being on 26th April 1944, after which it was presumably returned to the manufacturer. Gloster Rampage DG206/G joined Turbine Flight and made its first flight on 2nd March 1944, whilst, from Hatfield, came 'Spider Crab' LZ548/G, later to become the Vampire. This made its initial flight with 'T' Flight on 10th February 1944. It was followed by a further example, MP838/G, which arrived from Hatfield on 7th March 1944. Avro Lancaster BT308/G arrived from Baginton on 1st July 1943, with a Metropolitan Vickers F.2/1 engine installed in the tail turret, for trials with 'T' Flight. A further example, LL735/G, arrived from Coventry on 28th March 1944 but repositioned to Bruntingthorpe on 12th September, for Power Jets to continue their research. Also operated by 'T' Flight was Dominie 1 R9550, which was in use as a general liaison and transport aircraft for the Flight. This Flight was based on the south-western side of the airfield and operated

from what is now 'H' hangar, this building still being extant today.

Aerodynamics Flight (Aero Flight) was arguably the busiest Flight at Farnborough for many years with diverse types of aircraft engaged in research work of a considerably varying nature. During 1942/43, work being undertaken included:

- investigation of cockpit heating in Typhoon IB R8943;
- tail vibration research in Halifax II BB390;
- handling and trim trials on Mosquito NF.II DZ294;
- buffeting in Spitfire VB P8753;
- performance with pressurised elevators in Lancaster III ED872;

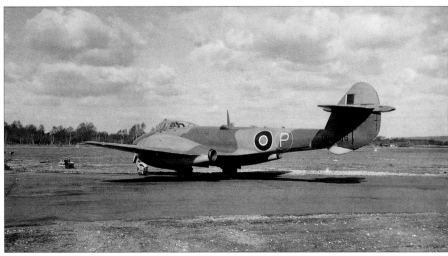

Bell XP-59A Airacomet RJ362/G, is seen here parked in what was then the 'secret' area of the airfield, where the early turbine aircraft operated with 'T' Flight. *FAST collection*

Gloster F9/40 Rampage DG206/G was powered by two Halford H.1 turbojets, and arrived for Turbine Flight on 2nd March 1944. It later passed to NGTE and was broken up during April 1946. *FAST collection*

- catapult trials with Firefly I Z1826 and Tarpon I FN792 (later Avenger I);
- tail parachute trials with Seafire IB AB205;
- compressibility research with Mustang I AG393;
- elevated catapult with Hurricane X P5187;
- suitability for deck landings on Airacobra I AH574;
- dive brake performance in Spitfire V BR372;
- plain aileron geared tabs on Spitfire I X4942;
- performance with contra-propeller trials on prototype Hawker Tornado R7936;
- RATOG trials at RAE and on board HMS *Chaser* with Seafire Ic MB141 operating from Machrihanish;
- RATOG on Hamilcar DR854;
- investigations of a Miles M.18 JN703, (ex-U2306);
- stability and G-forces in Beaufighter IF V8341;
- fuel jettisoning from Warwick C.1 G-AGFB/BV247;
- canopy hood jettisoning from Spitfire F.VII EN297;
- engine vibration in Corsair I JT118;
- performance research of Junkers Ju 88A-5 EE205 (W/Nr 3457);
- performance/ rate of roll on Focke-Wulf Fw.190A-4 PE882 (W/Nr 7155).

The Focke-Wulf Fw 190A-4/U8 had landed in error at West Malling, Kent, on 17th April 1943, whilst operating as 'H' of II/SKG10. It was flown to Farnborough on 18th April 1943 and flew two days later with PE882 applied. It flew 96 times with Aero Flight for performance and handling trials before delivery to Framlingham on 15th April 1944 for onwards transition to 1426 Flight.

An important acquisition was a Junkers Ju 88R-1 (W/Nr 360043, later to become PJ876) that had been operating in Norway as 'D5+EV' of IV/NJG3. It arrived at Dyce, Aberdeen, on 9th May 1943 from Kjevik, reportedly being piloted by a British agent, and was transferred to Farnborough five days later, the aircraft making its first flight at RAE on 26th May. This Junkers was equipped with the new German FuG202 radar installation and was immediately put to good use by WE Flight for radar trials, radio investigation and communication work, investigating the effects of chaff on the German radar unit and engine exhaust flame damping trials. After 83 RAE flights it eventually left Farnborough for 1426 Flight at Collyweston on 6th May 1944. This aircraft escaped the scrap man. After being stored at various units, it was dispatched to the RAF Museum at Hendon, where it has been on display since 1979.

Focke-Wulf Fw 190A-5/08 (W/Nr N5843, later to become PM679), operating as 'Red 9' of 1/SKG10, landed in error at Manston on 20th May 1943 and was delivered to Farnborough by road two days later. It first flew at RAE on 2nd July 1943, allocated to Aero Flight for performance trials and also

to WE Flight for testing of its German FuG 16Z radio equipment. Its service at Farnborough was relatively short-lived, just 17 flights, as it passed to the AFDU at Wittering on 17th July 1943.

A further Focke-Wulf Fw 190A-4/U8 (W/Nr 2596, later becoming PN999), operating as 'White 6' of 1/SKG10, also landed in error at Manston on 20th June 1943 and was flown to Farnborough next day. It first flew with RAE on 29th June, whereupon it was delivered to Boscombe Down, returning to Farnborough on 29th July 1943 for operations with WE Flight. Handling, radio trials and FuG 16Z 'Benito' research was undertaken, before the aircraft was transferred to the AFDU at Wittering on 28th September 1943 with a total of 34 RAE flights flown.

1944
General Duties Flight came into being around November 1944, being re-branded from E Flight.

Experimental Flying Department had a very busy time during these years, testing a variety of aircraft, engines and equipment. The total hours flown at RAE between 1939 and 1945 exceeded 43,000. The peak year was 1944, when 8,593 hours were flown, on a total of some 1,500 aircraft. A normal day on the airfield would see some 140 different aircraft ranged on the parking aprons and outside the various hangars, with some 160 aircraft flown each month, on trials that varied widely in purpose and duration.

On 28th March the first deck landing of a twin-engined aircraft, Mosquito VI LR359, was made on HMS *Indefatigable*. Detached from Aero Flight on 18th March and operating from Crail, it returned to RAE on 30th March. This was further followed by research into deck landings, lift and drag performances of jet fighters that were under development.

Aerodynamics Department were researching compressibility effects on aircraft performance, including dives by high-speed fighters; directional and lateral stability; stall research; and propeller development including blade tip Mach number effects being investigated within the 24ft wind tunnel. These design refinements were in an effort to gain higher speeds for the Spitfire, Hurricane, and other types. During this time further trials into gun turret aerodynamics; wing-drag effect measurements; spring-tab controls; aerodynamic loads; stability of towed gliders; and parachute research for men and equipment, were all being undertaken.

Power Jets (Research and Development) Limited came into being at Pyestock and all gas turbine research was subsequently undertaken by Power Jets, which later became known as the National Gas Turbine Establishment.

The airfield was handed over to RAE during this year by Wing Commander N H F Unwin, the last Officer Commanding RAF

Farnborough. Consequently RAF Farnborough stood down and the RAE took over the buildings, which included G1 (the original RFC building), G27 and G29 (the 'Black Sheds'). Up until now there had been a 'dividing' line, running basically along South Gate Road, separating the general 'Factory' site from the RAF element.

A well-known Farnborough pilot, Squadron Leader Davie, was killed on 4th January 1944 when the Gloster F9/40 Rampage (DG204/G) he was flying suffered turbine disintegration within the port engine during a high-speed flight test. The aircraft became uncontrollable and Sqn Ldr Davie abandoned it. With no ejection seat, he was thrown against the tailplane and, injured from impact with the airframe, he fell to earth with his parachute unopened and impacted through the roof of a store building close to the 'Black Sheds'. Thus he was the first British pilot to be killed in a turbine-engined aircraft. The aircraft suffered structural break-up and some of the wreckage crashed onto the airfield and 'Factory' buildings, with many other parts falling in the surrounding area away from RAE. Undeterred by this unfortunate loss, research work with the Metrovick F.2 engine continued and another F9/40 Rampage, DG206/G, was also being used for turbine trials as it was fitted with de Havilland H1 engines. In 1945 E28/39 Whittle (W4041/G) had resumed its turbine flight research at RAE, this time having the Power Jets W.2/700 installed.

During May 1944 the first production Meteors arrived at Farnborough from Moreton Valence for research with Turbine Flight, commencing operations on 10th May 1944. All the aircraft being operated by this Flight, except the communications DH.89 Dominie R7550, were of a top-secret nature and accordingly had the 'G' suffix, for Guarded, added to the aircraft serial. During June 1944 it appears that this Flight was called Tactical Flight and concentrated on the handling and jet performance of the Meteor. These Meteor F.1s (EE213 through to EE219) all participated in high-speed jet performance familiarisation, prior to joining No 616 Squadron for operational duties. Such was the urgency of the development of this new breed of aircraft that, on one particular day in mid-July, sixteen Meteor flights were made from Farnborough utilising four different aircraft. All these aircraft eventually passed to RAF Manston, where they joined the aforementioned Squadron, thus Tactical Flight ceased to exist after 23rd July 1944 and the jet engine research was now being handled by Aero T (Turbine) Flight.

Meteor F.1 EE211 then joined Aero T Flight, having arrived from Moreton Valence on 14th July 1944, and was used for jet performance and buffeting research before it was returned to Brockworth on 30th November 1944. Meteor F.1 EE215, which had arrived from Moreton Valence on 19th June 1944 and was delivered to Manston on 23rd July, returned to Aero T Flight from Manston on 1st September 1944. On 28th September this Meteor commenced new research into reheating, or after-burning, in order to produce a surge of extra power when required. This aircraft subsequently had the ammunition bay converted for an observer: a seat, covered with a transparent panel, was fitted at Farnborough, so the trials could be flown with an observer noting the performance. Consequently many of these trials from November 1944, with Turbine Flight, were flown with two POB, the aircraft then being dispatched from Farnborough to Power Jets at Bruntingthorpe on 20th February 1945. Aero T Flight continued to operate Meteor F.1s: EE212, EE219 and EE227 being used for 'snaking' trials; and EE211 for buffeting research. From mid-March 1945 Aero T Flight was integrated within Aero Dynamics Flight.

Many enemy aircraft were now arriving at Farnborough, including some jets. Some of the German aircraft were actually collected in Germany, or from German-occupied airfields, as the Allies advanced. Some were flown back to Farnborough in serviceable condition, whereupon Experimental Flying Department undertook many hours conducting detailed analysis of them.

During March, recommendations were made for the formation of a National Aeronautical Establishment (NAE), for research and development work on aerodynamic and structural aspects of aircraft. Although Farnborough was originally considered, the decision was ultimately made to encompass the existing airfields of Twinwood Farm, Thurleigh and Little Staughton, plus surrounding farmland, to form one large airfield north of Bedford.

Sqn Ldr A F Martindale suffered the loss of the propeller from Spitfire PR.XI EN409 on 27th April 1944 whilst in a high-speed dive from 40,000ft down to 27,000ft undertaking compressibility research. The reduction gear had disintegrated but, with the propeller separated, the aircraft was still under control and was brought back to Farnborough, gliding some 20 miles, where an emergency landing was made. On 15th September 1944 a further incident occurred whilst Sqn. Ldr Martindale was flying Spitfire PR.XI PL827, again on compressibility trials. While diving from 36,000ft at almost 600mph, the supercharger disintegrated

and the aircraft caught fire. The Spitfire force landed on Whitmore Common near Woking and the pilot escaped unhurt. For his bravery in respect of both of these incidents, he was awarded the Air Force Cross.

31st July saw the arrival at Farnborough of a German V-2 weapon. This example fell in Sweden during May and, although damaged, was still relatively complete. It was brought to Farnborough in a Halifax. Reconstruction of the V-2 by Accidents Section was very rapidly undertaken and this enabled the scientists to establish the effectiveness of this weapon before it was actually used against Britain: the first falling in the UK on 8th September. Further V-2s, and parts, arrived by rail for analysis

The first Farnborough catapult launch took place back in 1925 and various catapults had been tested over the years. Now, with the opening of runway 18/36, the shorter runway 04/22 was no longer needed and thus Jersey Brow, along with runway 22, became the centre for catapult launching and arresting activities. This was to continue for the next twelve years. During the wartime years, catapult launches had included the following aircraft:
- Fairey Seal K3576;
- Blackburn Roc L3058;
- Fulmar Is N1854, N4016;
- Swordfish I K5996 and II W5856;
- Seafire IIc AD371, MA970 and MB141, Mk.XVII NS487, Mk.XV PK245;
- Barracuda prototype P1767, Mk.I P9644, P9647, Mk.II BV692;
- Hurricane Mk.X P5187, Mk.I V7082;
- Martlet I AL247;
- Firefly Is Z1826 and DT985;
- Sea Otter I JM739;
- Tarpon I FN792;
- Hellcat I FN338;
- Avenger I FN793 and II JZ566;
- Airacobra I AH574;
- Firebrand I EK601;
- Albacore I BF658.

- Assisted take-offs, with the use of rockets, from the catapults, were made by: Fulmar II N4079;
- Martlet I AX825;
- Barracuda IIs P9791 and BV664;
- Swordfish IIs HS671 and NE954;
- Seafire IIc MB307.

Full rocket-assisted take-off (RATOG) experiments, with a runway take-off, were conducted by:
- Fulmar I N4016;
- Hurricane Is V7050 and V7301;
- Blackburn Shark II K5656;
- Vought Sikorsky Chesapeake I AL912;
- Seafire IIc MB141;
- Firebrand TF.III DK387;
- Firefly I MB561.

Aero Airborne Flight were busy undertaking glider research during this year, with handling and stability trials performed on examples such as Horsa Is LG921 and LJ271; Hamilcar DR853, blind flying trials; Hadrian I FR565; Hotspur II BT903 mainly being towed by Whitley Mk.VII EB409 and Mk.V LA893; whilst Tutor K3424 was used for towing the experimental Baynes Carrier Wing (Bat) RA809 and the Buzzard TK710, (a German Schleicher Rhonbussard). A Swordfish I L7678 was also employed for towing the Baynes Carrier Wing and a Dakota III FL519 joined the Flight to assist with the larger gliders. Lysander IIIA V9722 was engaged in general handling and performance trials for possible use as a tug for the Baynes whilst Whitley Mk.V LA893 conducted anti-spin parachute trials. Pick-up trials were being undertaken at Netheravon where the Whitley snatched from the ground a Hotspur and then a Hadrian, these trials proving successful.

Early in 1943 Miles Aircraft at Woodley, near Reading, were developing a radio-controlled pilotless target version of their Miles M.25 Martinet to be known as the M.50

Taken from a cine-film, Seafire IIc MB299 of Aero Flight is airborne from the elevated P catapult on 4th July 1944. Its service at Farnborough also included drag-chain arrester trials, before the aircraft passed to Lee-on-Solent on 31st August 1945.
via E Brown

Queen Martinet. The first installation for conversion was undertaken in Martinet I EM500, which became known as a Queen Martinet I. This arrived from Woodley on 29th November 1944 for flight trials with IAP Flight. It was damaged in a heavy landing on 26th April 1946 and was returned to the manufacturer but was scrapped during May 1947. Queen Martinet I PW979 arrived on 14th December 1945 for flight trials in connection with the pilotless aircraft development programme. It had been converted by Miles Aircraft at Woodley during late 1944 and had then been dispatched to the Pilotless Aircraft Unit at Manorbier during August 1945 prior to arrival at RAE. This aircraft was scrapped in May 1947. Some 82 Queen Martinets were built from new, whilst a further 11 were converted from standard Martinet Is.

The RAE Technical School was set up in 1944. However, from October 1945 this became known as the RAE Technical College where all RAE apprentices undertook studies associated with their respective disciplines.

Proposals to extend Farnborough Airfield to accommodate longer runways, up to 3 miles and 5 miles in length and 200 yards wide, were being considered, in order to take larger aircraft that were in the design stage at that time. The War Office would not release the neighbouring military land, but after a couple of years a National Aeronautical Establishment, that would have a long runway, was proposed. This eventually became RAE Bedford.

The High-Speed Track, as it became known, was built alongside Victoria Track, near Berkshire Copse, during 1943/1944. It was originally known as the 'Exeter Track', the actual rails being uplifted from the abandoned DCTO track and installed here. This was used for a series of trials, utilising a propelled sled, to investigate impacts of wing-mounted cutters on cables, bird impacts on windscreens, parachutes and (later) ejection seats, engines, arrester gear and missiles. In 1946 the track was replaced with standard

railway line sections obtained from the Long-moor Military Railway in Bordon, and was lengthened to 2,100ft. The eastern end was mounted on a concrete plinth and, during the 1950s, a rocket-propelled trolley was built to assist with various tests, the site now being designated as T16. By the early 1980s, the length was reduced to around 1,500ft. The track was not used so much throughout the 1980s/1990s and was actually last in use during 1998 by DERA. In 2000, it was severed for the erection of a new boundary fence to the airfield. The maintenance trolley, housed within a small shed at the eastern end of the track, was saved by FAST and is now in storage, whilst a section of track has also been cut away for retention by FAST.

Studies were being made at Farnborough into the possibility of landing aircraft with their undercarriage retracted, on the flight deck of aircraft carriers. This was designed to reduce the all-up weight of the aircraft, which could then carry more armament and be catapulted from the ship. The deck was to be a rubber carpet, also known as a flexible deck, stretched over shock absorbers, allowing the aircraft to pitch onto the carpet after engaging the arrester wire. Initial trials were conducted in model form in a Farnborough laboratory, followed by a small area of rubber matting placed on Jersey Brow, where a Hotspur III BT752 was dropped onto the carpet area. Further trials followed in 1947.

Between 1940 and the end of hostilities in May 1945, 17 ex-German aircraft had been taken to Farnborough and flown extensively on various trials work with RAE before passing to the Air Fighting Development Unit, 1426 Flight or the Enemy Aircraft Flight. The final four of these 17 arrived during 1944, the first being a Messerschmitt Me 410A-3 (W/Nr 10259, later to become TF209) that was operating as 'F6+OK' of 2(F)/122 when it landed in error at Monte Corvino, near Salerno, Italy, on 27th November 1943. The aircraft was dismantled and shipped to Farnborough, where it arrived on 14th April 1944. Reassembly began immediately, with its first flight being

made at RAE on 1st May. During a test flight from Farnborough on 5th June 1944, the aircraft made a crash-landing at Boscombe Down. After temporary repairs, it was returned to Farnborough on 29th June and underwent a full post-repair test flight on 12th August 1944. This aircraft did not undergo any specific trials at Farnborough, as it was allocated to E Flight for test flights only. It departed from Farnborough to Wittering on 14th August 1944, for analysis by the Fighter Interception Unit to compare this type with the Mosquito. 16 test flights had been made by this aircraft whilst with RAE.

Landing in error at Woodbridge on 13th July 1944, lost and desperately short of fuel, was a Junkers Ju 88G-1 (W/Nr 712273, later to become TP190), operating as '4R+UR' of III/NJG2. It was flown to Farnborough two days later. This aircraft was an important asset, as it was equipped with three different radars, FuG220, FuG227 and FuG350. It was immediately put to good work with WE Flight on radar trials and assessment of this equipment. It departed RAE, for the Enemy Aircraft Flight of the Central Fighter Establishment at Tangmere, on 17th May 1945, having made 33 flights with RAE.

A further Messerschmitt Bf 109G-6/U2 (W/Nr 412951, later to become TP814), operating as 'White 16' of 1/JG301, arrived at Farnborough on 26th July 1944, having landed in error at Manston five days earlier. The first RAE flight was made on 9th August 1944 with Aero Flight, the aircraft being used for handling. Its life at RAE was relatively short-lived, as it departed on 31st August 1944 for the AFDU at Wittering after just eight flights.

The last, and largest, of the captured Luftwaffe aircraft flown at Farnborough, was a Heinkel He 177A-5/R6 (W/Nr 550062, later to become TS439) that had been operational as 'F8+AP' of II/KG40. The French Resistance had captured it at Toulouse-Blagnac, where it was undergoing maintenance, in September 1944. It was flown from Toulouse to Farnborough on 10th September 1944 and made its first flight at Farnborough on 20th September 1944, this day being the date when the military serial was allocated. During its time at Farnborough, this aircraft was in use by four of the EFD Flights: Aero Flight for spring tab control and handling trials, SME Flight for heating system trials, altimeter trials with WE Flight, and bomb sight trials with IAD Flight. It departed Farnborough for Boscombe Down on 20th February 1945, having made twenty flights.

Messerschmitt Me 410A-3 TF209 is seen here at Farnborough during 1944, wearing RAF markings. It was allocated to E Flight for test flights only, and eventually departed for Wittering during August 1944. It was later scrapped at Brize Norton in August 1947. *FAST collection*

EMPIRE TEST PILOTS SCHOOL

Farnborough Takes on a New Lodger

With the Royal Flying Corps still in its infancy and its flying machines somewhat flimsy, it was not long before an Experimental Flight was formed on what is now known as Salisbury Plain, at Upavon Aerodrome, then the home of the Central Flying School. This Experimental Flight, formed in 1914, was an absolute necessity as there were no other aircraft test facilities in existence – many of the pilots literally learning the handling qualities of their steeds 'by the seat of their pants'.

A year after its formation, it was renamed as the Testing Squadron and was relocated to the somewhat bleak aerodrome of Martlesham Heath in 1915 where it became known as the Aeroplane Experimental Station. With the addition of armament testing to its repertoire, the unit adopted the official title of Aeroplane and Armament Experimental Establishment (A&AEE).

With the onslaught of World War Two came an almighty influx of new aircraft types into British service, both from the UK and US manufacturers. The new additions also included many one-off prototypes and captured enemy aircraft, which all demanded acceptance and clearance trials. This overloading was not only aggravated by rapid technological advancement but also further highlighted the shortage of properly qualified test pilots able to put these aircraft through their demanding trials work.

Excellence Imparted

Up to this time, the Royal Aircraft Establishment, A&AEE, RAF and the aircraft manufacturers' pilots had learned their professional skills through practical experience. These pilots were perhaps in a class of their own – the best available at the time. It is indisputable that their high levels of skill enabled them to cope with challenging situations that, in the hands of an average or operationally inexperienced pilot, could have been extremely difficult or even disastrous. It was clear that there was an urgent need for specialised test pilot training especially as the workload and shortage of suitable test pilots at Boscombe Down had become critical by late 1942.

Consequently the A&AEE Commandant, Air Commodore D'Arcy Greig, was tasked by the Controller of Research and Develop-

From its humble beginnings at Boscombe Down, ETPS soon became a worldwide leader in training test pilots. This view shows the Boscombe Down dispersal and office/classroom area of ETPS in August 1945. An array of Harvards, Spitfires and Tempests can be seen.
Rawlings Family collection

ment, Ministry of Aircraft Production, to establish the world's first test pilots school at Boscombe Down. Initially its terms of reference were 'To provide suitably trained pilots for test flying duties in aeronautical research and development establishments within the services and industry'. Accordingly, two of Boscombe Down's key figures were called upon to head the set-up. Mr G MacLaren Humphreys, a civilian Technical Officer, was appointed Chief Ground Instructor, whilst the Officer Commanding 'A' Flight, Sqn Ldr Sammy Wroath, was promoted to Wing Commander and thus became the first Commandant of the embryonic test pilot school, then known as the Test Pilots Training Flight.

Nissen huts on the southern side of Boscombe Down airfield were taken over as the classroom, operational and administration buildings ready for the 'No 1 Course' to commence. This landmark course started on 10th June 1943 with 18 student candidates, each selected from RAF and Naval officers (although five dropped out during the course). The first aircraft on strength consisted of Halifax I L9520, Master III W8537,

Mitchell II FL688 and Hurricane IIb Z2399. The Flight also borrowed various aircraft, including assets of the A&AEE, as and when required as the fleet grew on a gradual basis. The initial course ended in February 1944 without ceremony, injuries or crashes – these graduate test pilots being the first to have the honour of using the letters 'TP' after their names.

With the start of No 2 Course during 1944, further buildings were acquired and the course grew to 28 students. By now, the Commandant was Gp Capt J F X 'Sam' McKenna AFC and the Flight had become the Empire Test Pilots School, (as it still is today at Boscombe Down). The prefix 'Empire' was incorporated into the name in recognition of the many overseas and Commonwealth students that were being trained.

Whilst flying from Boscombe Down on 19th January 1945, Gp Capt McKenna was tragically killed when his aircraft, Mustang IV KH648, dived straight into the ground close to Old Sarum having suffered structural failure of the wing after gun panels had opened up in-flight. His memory is perpetuated to this day by the McKenna Graduation Dinner

The first ETPS course at Farnborough was No.7 in 1948. Seen here flying from Farnborough are three of the ETPS aircraft on strength at the time: Vampire F.1 VF313 arrived from Hatfield on 3rd November 1947 and departed to A V Roe on 6th July 1949; Lincoln B.II RF528 arrived at Cranfield from Coventry on 30th July 1946 and was transferred to Farnborough with ETPS, arriving on 28th May 1947, but later was allocated to RAE for parachute development on 12th November 1951; Tempest II PR622 arrived from Boscombe Down on 24th November 1947 and was dispatched to 6 MU on 21st November 1949. *Rawlings Family collection*

and a prestigious trophy, donated by his widow, is awarded annually to the most outstanding student of each course.

By mid-1945, the A&AEE had expanded considerably and, with some disruption to training schedules, it was decided that the ETPS would be relocated to the quieter airfield of Cranfield where the College of Aeronautics was in the process of being set up. The move took place in October 1945 and the next three courses, Nos 4, 5 and 6, were conducted from Cranfield. In early 1947, however, Cranfield airfield was purchased by the Ministry of Education, which had taken over the College of Aeronautics and it was decided that the unit should be relocated. Accordingly, Farnborough was chosen to accommodate the school. The first aircraft to arrive was Lincoln B.II RF528, relocated on 25th March 1947, though the majority of the school aircraft would arrive between June and August. They took up initial residence in the famous 'Black Sheds' and the initial fleet consisted of Auster AOP.V TJ524; Dominie I HG715; Lincoln B.IIs RF528, RF534 and RF538; Harvard

IIbs FX281, FX371, FX402 and KF333; Mosquito B.35s RS720, RS721 and T.III TW101; Seafire F.46s LA549, LA557 and LA558; Tempest IIs PR918 and PR919; Meteor F.IIIs EE397, EE398 and EE491; Vampire F.1 TG388; Oxford I AS504; Anson C.19 VP509; and Firefly Is PP639 and PP641. The staff and students moved in to the former School of Photography building that had been converted into a comfortable Mess on the southeast corner of the airfield, with the adjacent instructional block classrooms being very typical of the period. At the time of the school's relocation from Cranfield to Farnborough there were a few weeks where the course stood down but it was soon back to normal with the flying programme intensifying.

By the time of the commencement of No 7 Course in January 1948, the school had a fleet of 29 aircraft, with many different types continuing to arrive and depart over the years. Purpose-built accommodation was deemed to be required and construction began accordingly in 1948. This led to a further move in 1950 to the central southern side of

the expanding airfield, where two hangars, engineering facilities, an operations building and dispersal area were established adjacent to the Army Golf Course. This area has been disused since the 2004 SBAC display and is now under re-development.

Raising the Standard

It was during September 1949 that the official Armorial Bearings, '*Azure semée of Mullets Or on a Pale Argent a Torch enflamed proper. And for the Crest Issuant from an Astral Crown Or an Eagle wings elevated and addorsed Azure*', were issued by the College of Heralds, and the motto '*Learn to Test – Test to Learn*' was granted. Air Marshal Sir Alec William Coryton, Controller of Supplies (Air), presented the Bearings to the Commandant, Gp Capt L S Snaith, at a ceremonial dinner at Farnborough in December that was also attended by RAE Director Mr W G Perring. The list of VIPs attending the event did not end there, with Marshall of the Royal Air Force, Lord Tedder, stressing the importance of the scientific outlook of test pilots, and the need for them to understand the technical phraseology of scientific workers; 'There has always been a need for close co-operation and understanding between the scientist and test pilot and this is never more important than it is today'.

RAF personnel had previously undertaken aircraft servicing but all this was due to change with the ETPS' move to Farnborough. The RAE had its own comprehensive aircraft maintenance staff that had been used to undertake routine and installation servicing on an abundance of diverse aircraft types over the years. ETPS brought yet more aircraft to the already large Farnborough complement and thus it became a challenge to the RAE aircraft-servicing department to keep the fleet airworthy – a

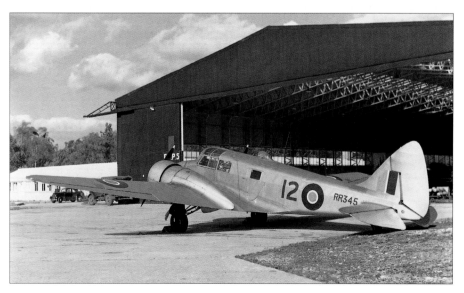

Oxford I RR345 '12' arrived from Portsmouth for ETPS on 28th August 1951 and was transferred to A&AEE on 1st April 1954. It is seen here outside the ETPS hangar on 30th September 1952. *FAST collection*

Avro 707B VX790 '19' is seen here on the ETPS apron on 3rd July 1956, with an instructor and a number of students from No.15 course. The aircraft was transferred from RAE to ETPS on 26th January 1956, but suffered a landing accident on 25th September 1956 and was dispatched to Bicester for storage on 27th May 1957, later being allocated to RAE Bedford for spares. Beyond is Canberra T.4 WJ867, which arrived at ETPS from Lindholme on 29th September 1954 (later coded '10') and transferred to Boscombe Down on 22nd January 1968. *FAST collection*

task that it rose to admirably. The varied portfolio of aircraft types swelled as many prototype, experimental or one-off aircraft joined the fleet. Each addition would present their own challenges, with such newcomers as the Armstrong Whitworth Apollo VX224 '15' (1955); Avro 707B VX790 '19', (1956); Avro Athena T.2 prototype VW890 (1951); Boulton Paul Balliol prototype VL892 (1953); Fieseler Fi 156 Storch VP546 (1950); Shorts SB.5 WG768 '28' (1965); Vickers Varsity T.1 prototype VX828 '12' (1954); and the first production prototype Westland Dragonfly HR.1 VX595 '29' (1957). All of these machines and more would keep the engineers, and pilots, on their toes, but in true RAE style it was 'all in a day's work'.

The ETPS was the first (and for a few years the only) test pilots school in the world and its world-renowned course and flying training syllabus had become legendary. Two previous Test Pilot graduates, one from the USAF and the other from the US Navy, had returned home to form the USAF Test Pilots School at Muroc AFB, California, (now Edwards AFB), and the US Navy Test Pilots School at Patuxent River, Maryland, respectively. Both schools were modelled on the ETPS and continue to this day. The exceptional British test pilots of this formative era were wartime survivors of a highly skilled nature and their flying demonstrations were outstanding at the time. Later generations of test pilots were skilled in a different manner, in accordance with updated aircraft instrumentation, systems technology and experience. Regrettably a number of accidents befell the school whilst at Farnborough and many students and instructors lost their lives with their aircraft destroyed. Furthermore, a substantial proportion of former ETPS graduates were killed while test flying prototype and developmental aircraft during their flying careers.

The prototype Varsity T.1 VX828 '12' arrived at Farnborough from Weybridge on 19th March 1952 and was used by ETPS until it was sold as scrap to R J Coley on 3rd July 1959. It is seen here on the ETPS apron at Farnborough on 3rd June 1958. *Rawlings Family collection*

Diversity to Develop

Helicopter flying was by now rapidly developing and the mid-1950s saw the arrival of early helicopter types such as Hiller HT.1 XB521, which arrived from Gosport on 25th May 1954. This was followed by a second example, XB476, also from Gosport, on 6th June 1955 along with Sycamore Mk.3 XH682 that was delivered on 13th July 1955 from Filton. Later arrivals were Dragonfly HR.3 WG662 '28' from Yeovil on 8th October 1956 and HR.1 VX595 '29' from Donibristle on 26th September 1957. These helicopters entered initial service with the school to provide continuation flying training for the school's embryonic rotary instructor cadre. More modern examples came in the form of a Whirlwind HAS.7 (XK907 '9') from Pershore on 17th December 1962 and an HAR.2 (XJ759 '4') on 23rd August 1963 from Boscombe Down. Indeed, with new models

entering service throughout the armed forces worldwide, the requirement for specific helicopter test pilots was becoming readily apparent. Consequently, at the commencement of No 22 Course in 1963, a full Rotary Wing course (No 1 RW course) was added to the ETPS syllabus in order to produce qualified test pilots for the growing number of roles that the versatile helicopter was establishing. It was not until 1974 – long after ETPS had departed from Farnborough – that a Flight Test Engineers Course was added to the syllabus.

Gliding had become a popular part of the syllabus as a means of furthering the students' aeronautical experiences as well as recreational flying. Indeed the first glider that was operated by ETPS, from Cranfield, was an ex-German Grunau Baby IIB 'LN+ST' that became VN148, having arrived at RAE in July 1945. It was passed to ETPS in

A Dragonfly HR.1, VX595 '29', is seen here on the ETPS dispersal during the late 1950s, with HR.3 WG662 '28' seen beyond. VX595 served with ETPS from September 1957 until it was struck off charge in October 1964. This helicopter is still extant in storage with the Fleet Air Arm Museum at Yeovilton. *E Fuller collection*

An ETPS Rotary Wing instructor is seen with two students of No 2 Rotary Wing Course on the School helicopter apron on 8th May 1964, framed by the tail boom of Whirlwind HAR.2 XJ759 '4', with Whirlwind HAS.7 XK907 '9' beyond. XJ759 arrived from Boscombe Down on 23rd August 1963, but suffered a heavy landing on 1st August 1966 and was eventually struck off charge for spares on 11th December 1967. XK907 arrived from Pershore on 17th December 1962, transferred to Boscombe Down on 6th March 1968 and was eventually sold to Autair on 30th March 1971. The cockpit/fuselage section is still extant, albeit in storage, with the Midland Air Museum at Coventry. *FAST collection*

1946, before it was sold to the College of Aeronautics in July 1947. Gliding continued after the move to Farnborough and the EoN Olympia 1 sailplanes VV400 and VV401, Sedbergh TX.1 WB920 and Slingsby Sky XA876 were all kept fairly busy throughout the years. Indeed, the gliders often operated away from Farnborough at places with a quieter airfield circuit: Detling, Odiham, Lasham, Chilbolton and Andover being favourites. During this period, a British altitude record for a glider was established by Flt Lt A W Bedford flying Olympia 1 VV400. He achieved some 21,300ft on 24th August 1950 flying from Farnborough to Driffield, during a flight that lasted 3hr 50min. Gliding was still part of the ETPS curriculum up to the early 1970s. Auster AOP.6 VF627, Fi 156 Storch VP546 (loaned from RAE), and later Chipmunk T.10s WB549 '7', WD321 '3', WD334 '3' and WD374 '3', were all employed for the glider tows and operated over a 20-year period.

Jet Age Skills

By 1957, with ETPS having been resident at Farnborough for 10 years, the fleet had changed dramatically. By now, there were more jets on the books although there were

Slingsby T.21B Sedbergh TX.1 WB920 was one of the stalwart ETPS glider types on charge, having been transferred from RAE on 17th March 1954 and relocating to Boscombe Down on 26th March 1968. It remained in service with ETPS at Boscombe Down until 22nd April 1975, whereupon it was dispatched to St Athan for storage. It is seen during the late afternoon on 25th November 1960, just prior to a sortie, outside the ETPS administration and office buildings. *FAST collection*

Here, flying in formation shortly before the retirement of the Shorts SB.5 WG768 '28' is Lightning T.4 XL629 '23', seen during 1966. The SB.5 served with ETPS from December 1965 until January 1968, whereas the Lightning transferred to Boscombe Down and is now the 'gate guard' at this QinetiQ facility. *E Fuller collection*

still some piston-engined types being put to good use by the school. During this time the fleet included this impressive mix of types:

- Avro 707B VX790 '19'
- Lincoln B.II RF456 '15'
- Devon C.1s VP979 '4' and XA879 '2'
- Chipmunk T.10 WB549 '7' and WD334 '3'
- Vampire T.11 WZ451 '16' and WZ475 '17'
- Canberra T.4 WJ867 '10'
- Gannet T.2 XA515 '24'
- Meteor T.7 WA638 '8' and WL488 '11'
- Meteor F.8 WF752 '1' and WK660 '9'
- Meteor NF.11 WD765 '5', WD769 '1' and WD797 '9'
- Javelin F(AW).1 XA547
- Sea Hawk F.1 WF212 '27'
- Sea Hawk FB.3 WF284 '8' that replaced Meteor WA638
- Sea Hawk FGA.4 WV910 '20'
- Sea Venom FAW.21 WM574 '18'
- Hunter F.1 WT572 '26' and WT621 '23'
- Pembroke C.1 WV710 '25'
- Provost T.1 WV425 '21' and WV577 '22'
- Dragonfly HR.1 VX595 '29' and HR.3 WG662 '28' and WG666
- Varsity T.1 VX828 '12', and WF381 '14'

By the turn of the decade, the ETPS had overcome many problems, specifically in connection with the development of the turbine-powered aircraft, turboprops and helicopters, and the availability of new types to the school in order to keep abreast of the then-advancing aviation industry. It had forged ahead under many different commandants each having a difficult job with this high-profile school with its ever-chang-

ing and challenging syllabus, lack of funds and a mixture of different aircraft. However the school moved forward into the 1960s – an era that brought its own set of challenges and equipment during a tough decade for British aviation that saw many changes in aeronautical development and production. More modern aircraft were by now joining the fleet as aircraft design evolved ever faster. The prototype Hawker Hunter T.7 XJ615 arrived from Dunsfold on 13th April

1959 (but was later lost in an accident on 24th June 1964) and the first production Hunter F.6, WW592, was transferred to ETPS on 28th February 1964 from the RAE Weapons Flight where it had been used for air-to-air ballistic trials. Delivered from South Marston for ETPS on 28th June 1963, was Vickers-Supermarine Scimitar F.1 XD216. At the time, this was the fastest aircraft in the fleet – although it did not last long as it crashed into the sea off West

Overall silver/natural metal Devon C.1 VP979 '4' arrived from Hatfield on 31st May 1949 and is seen here on the ETPS dispersal on 30th September 1952. It suffered a wheels-up landing at Chilbolton on 7th May 1957 but was road transported to Leavesden for repair. Returning to ETPS It was later transferred to the CDEE at Boscombe Down on 23rd September 1959 for trials into discharge of chemical substances. Devons remained in service with ETPS until 1967. *FAST collection*

Meteor NF.11 WD765 '5' arrived from 29 MU on 11th January 1957, but crashed at Mapledurwell, near Basingstoke, on 20th October 1958, after the rear fuselage detached, and was struck off charge 10th December 1958. Beyond can be seen Meteor NF.11 WD797 '9' at right, and Vampire T.11 WZ475 '17' at left. *Rawlings Family collection*

Wittering on 16th July 1964. Other new-comers were Scout AH.1 XP165, which arrived from White Waltham on 21st April 1964, and Twin Pioneer Srs 3 XT610, delivered from Prestwick via Llanbedr on 19th March 1965. The first of two ex-civilian Vickers Viscounts, Srs 744 XR801, arrived from Hurn on 16th January 1962 and was followed by Srs 745 XR802 from Cambridge on 8th May 1962. Transport and multi-engined aircraft types had been in use as 'flying classrooms' over the years, some borrowed from RAE, but the pair of Viscounts brought this element into a more modern environment. As well as being valuable assets for multi-engined training, and offering the ability to take students and staff on various overseas visits to test establishments in a good degree of comfort, they also enabled the school to provide long-distance and overseas continuation training flights.

The 21st birthday of the ETPS was celebrated on 3rd September 1964 – just prior

to the SBAC display of that year. The event saw a large gathering of current and former aircraft types operated by the school parked on the southern dispersal area at Farnborough, with many former graduates and invited guests being present for this prestigious occasion. Visiting aircraft that participated in the static display to represent previously operated types included: a Mosquito; Meteor NF.14 WS838; Spitfire VB AB910; Harvard IIb KF183; Valetta C.1 WJ491; Hurricane IIc PZ865; Rapide G-AHGC; Sea Hawk FGA.6 WV856; Lincoln B.II RF342; Anson C.19 TX213; Auster AOP.9 WZ672 and Sea Balliol T.21 WP333. From the RAE Farnborough fleet, across the airfield, came Javelin FAW.7 XH754, Meteor F.8 VZ438, Hastings C.1 TG619, Varsity T.1 WL679 and Shackleton MR.2 WG557.

The first Mach 2-capable aircraft to arrive at the ETPS was English Electric Lightning T.4 XL629 '23'. It was delivered from Warton on 13th May 1966, ostensibly to

A classic view of the ETPS apron at Farnborough, as seen during October 1961. The aircraft are, from left to right, Vampire T.11 WZ451 '16'; Meteor NF.14 WS845 '6'; Meteor T.7 WH231 '8'; Hunter F.4 XF969 '26'; Hunter T.7 XJ615 ('23' not carried); Dragonfly HR.3 WG662 '28'; a Devon C.1; Shackleton MR.2 WG557; Canberra B.2 WJ730 '18'; Swift F.7 XF113 '19' and Chipmunk T.10 WB549 '7'. *FAST collection*

replace the Shorts SB.5 WG768 '28', which itself had arrived from Bedford on 16th December 1965. This potent addition would now enable the school to give supersonic experience on a modern aircraft, as many of the students would eventually fly supersonic types when they returned to industry or their respective armed forces. The Lightning operated in a fleet which at that time consisted of two Canberra B.2s (WE121 '19', WH715 '27') and two T.4s (WH854 '30' and WJ867 '10'); a pair of Chip-

Hunter T.7 WV253 '24' has just returned from a training sortie, whilst T.7 prototype XJ615 '23' is seen beyond parked on the ETPS apron on 28th May 1964. WV253 arrived from Dunsfold on 12th June 1962, and relocated to Boscombe Down on 26th February 1968, but was written off on 15th July 1968 when it entered an inverted spin and could not be recovered over Lyme Bay, the student test pilot successfully ejecting. XJ615, the T.7 prototype, arrived from Dunsfold on 13th April 1959, although it was lost in an accident on 24th June 1964, due to a fuel transfer problem and struck high ground near Haslemere, Surrey, regrettably killing the French Air Force student test pilot. Beyond can be seen an ETPS Chipmunk T.10, Provost T.1 WV420 '21' and Dragonfly HR.1 VX595 '29'; with cocooned Comet fuselages in the distance. *FAST collection*

Viscount Srs 744 XR801 is seen here, resplendent in its new paint scheme, shortly before being delivered to ETPS from the BAC facility at Hurn. It arrived at Farnborough on 16th January 1962 and relocated to Boscombe Down on 29th January 1968, eventually being sold to Shackleton Aviation and delivered to Coventry on 18th May 1972. This aircraft, along with its sister-ship XR802, proved valuable assets to ETPS as flying classrooms and communications aircraft. *via Rawlings Family collection*

This air-to-ground view shows the line-up of aircraft on the ETPS apron at Farnborough, to celebrate their 21st birthday on 3rd September 1964. Many of the aircraft types previously operated by the School, or being flown at the time, are represented here in the 23 aircraft shown together on the dispersal area. *FAST collection*

munk T.10s (WB549 '7' and WD321 '3'); two Devon C.1s (VP980 '1' and XA879 '2'); two Hunter F.6s (WW592 '26' and XF375 '6') plus two T.7s (WV253 '24', XL579 '25'); a pair of Provost T.1s (WV420 '21', XF685 '20'); two Scout AH.1s (XP165 '5' and XR436 '4'); a Twin Pioneer Srs 3 (XT610 '22'); the Viscounts (XR801, allocated '12' and XR802, allocated '15' but not carried); as well as a Whirlwind HAS.7 (XK907 '9').

This writer, during the course of his aircraft engineering apprenticeship with the RAE at Farnborough, spent most of 1966 with the ETPS undertaking first- and second-line aircraft maintenance. Many anecdotes could be mentioned at this point but one in particular stands out... During a pre-flight inspection being undertaken early one morning on Hunter F.6 XF375 a six-inch crack was found in the upper wing skin of the port intake, thus grounding the aircraft. The apprentice supervisor may have been pleased that this young trainee had discovered a crack, but there was some consternation from the ground crew and aircrew in that nobody had spotted this before. Thus the aircraft became grounded pending repair – temporarily losing a valuable asset to the ETPS fleet!

Second to None

The 1950s and 1960s had seen the ETPS expand with great strides and it was during these years that the dedicated professionalism of the school and all that it taught was indeed heralded as second to none. Other nations have followed in establishing their own test pilot schools, broadly based upon the curriculum standardised by ETPS during this period. Then, amidst much controversy, having been resident at Farnborough for nearly 21 years, ETPS was given back to Boscombe Down during December 1967 at the end of the last courses at Farnborough –

ETPS Chipmunk T.10 WD321 '3' is seen here over the Hampshire countryside in this air-to-air view of the early 1960s. This aircraft arrived at Farnborough on 25th January 1956 from Aston Down and was used between the RAE outstations at Aberporth and Llanbedr for communications duties on the guided weapons test ranges. It arrived back at Farnborough on 1st August 1958 from Llanbedr for operation by ETPS, which it continued until it was relocated to Boscombe Down on 16th February 1968. It was later dispatched to 5MU for sale during February 1975 and became G-BDCC on 28th April 1975. *via G Allen*

The first Scout AH.1 built was XP165, which first flew on 29th August 1960. It served with Fairey, Westlands, RAE, Blackburns and A&AEE, before it arrived at Farnborough from White Waltham as 'Tester 12' on 21st April 1964. It is seen here on a damp apron on 10th November 1965, coded '5' in a two-tone grey/light blue scheme. It relocated to Boscombe Down on 24th January 1968 and continued in service until June 1971. It was later struck off charge and returned to Farnborough by road for spares use. It is still extant today within The Helicopter Museum at Weston-Super-Mare.
FAST collection

No 26 Fixed Wing Course and No 5 Rotary Wing Course. The majority of aircraft departed during late December 1967 and January 1968 with others following over the next few weeks and all being relocated by May. This resulted in the southern dispersal area of the airfield being quiet for a time, until the Radio and Avionics Flight, by then known as RAE Southern Squadron, moved in.

So ETPS had returned to Boscombe Down. Fixed Wing Course No 27 and No 6 Rotary Wing then commenced and, although most of the initial aircraft on strength had previously been at Farnborough, the facilities at their new home were somewhat modern compared with those that had been vacated during 1945! Today's ETPS is part of QinetiQ and still operates from this formidable and somewhat secretive airfield. As would be expected, the modern ETPS flies a mixed fleet of aircraft and is able to call upon others from the QinetiQ fleet when they are available. The types are as diverse as ever, with Andover C.1 XS606; BAC 1-11 Srs 479FU ZE432; Basset CC.1 XS743; Hawk T.1s XX154, XX341 and XX342; Alpha Jets ZJ645-650; Lynx AH.7 ZD560; Gazelle HT.2s XZ936 and XZ939; and AS.355F1 Twin Squirrel ZJ635. The school has also broadened its horizons with utilisation of flight time on two Swedish AF Saab JAS39 Gripens, flown in Sweden. These fourth-generation fighters bring yet another string to the ETPS bow under a contract that commenced in the autumn of 2005. During 2006 ETPS is set to branch out into the commercial sector with short flight-testing courses for wide-body airliners, such as the Airbus A340 and Boeing 777, plus a two-week course on operating unmanned aerial vehicles. In line with its current operations, the school is equipped with modern hangarage, classrooms, operational and recreational facilities. It is located only a few miles from where it all began during 1914 and, whilst its aircraft, support systems and infrastructure are a world away from that era, its basic principles remain exactly the same.

Some 522 pilots from 13 different national armed forces (including a small number of civilian and manufacturers' pilots) had undertaken the ETPS Fixed Wing or Rotary Wing Courses whilst at Farnborough. Only a very small number dropped out, whilst some others were killed in flying accidents during their year-long course. Whilst the rather quieter Farnborough circuit caused by the departure of ETPS was an ominous precedent for the future, the experience gained at the airfield produced many exceptional test pilots from around the world, who successfully graduated from the school.

After it was vacated, the excellent ETPS Mess (a legend throughout the services) became part of the RAE Hostel and until recently was part of the Farnborough College of Technology student quarters. Even the early classrooms are still in existence, just inside the airfield's Queens Gate. Owned by MoD Estates, this area is another addition to the list of sites scheduled for redevelopment, with the demolition of the buildings due to commence in 2006.

Seen here is a relatively rare photograph of aircraft being serviced in the ETPS hangar (E1) on 9th February 1967. Receiving attention is Viscount Srs 744 XR801, whilst to the right can be seen the tail boom of Scout AH.1 XP165, a tail rotor at upper right of a second Scout AH.1 XR436, and Hunter T.7 WV253 at left. Maintenance was performed by the RAE Experimental Aircraft Servicing Department, with routine line-maintenance undertaken within the ETPS hangar and any major servicing being performed in 'D' and 'N' sheds on the other side of the airfield. *FAST collection*

1945 to 1954

Concentration on the Jets of the Future

With the cessation of World War Two on 12th September 1945, the need for urgent research diminished and consequently the work force at RAE was again cut back. The establishment's record of war service was exemplary and, by the end of the war, the RAE had an extremely high reputation for work well done in respect of defence of the nation, thus justifying the Government's regard for RAE as the nerve centre of the UK's technical effort in the air.

Much had taken place at Farnborough during the previous decade and, with the introduction of jet aircraft, advanced research and development proceeded on new aircraft types and systems. Notwithstanding the jets, many different aircraft had been tested at Farnborough for a variety of research and development trials during these years and much had been learnt to good effect, which led to further enhancement in the years to come.

1945
A considerable number of USAAF American bombers and fighters also came to RAE during World War Two, for a number of varying tasks, some undertaking ground tests only and others only staying at Farnborough for short periods. These included the following:
- B-17E 41-2628 f Bovingdon 15.2.43, returning there 9.3.43
- B-17F 42-5745 f Alconbury 23.6.43 for communications and 'Oboe' trials
- B-17F 42-5788 f Molesworth 24.6.43 for HF/VHF comms trials until 2.7
- B-17F 42-29554 f Grafton Underwood 8.2.44 for range tests until 10.4
- B-17F 42-30034 f Chelveston 27.12.43, to Earls Colne 7.1.44
- B-17F 42-30145 f Thurleigh 7.1.44 for range tests, to Little Staughton 7.2.44
- B-17F 42-30328 f Alconbury 22.2.44 for 'Oboe', altimeters and 'supersonic' bomb trials

- B-17F 42-30639 for 'Monica III' tests
- B-17G 43-38150 f Eye 28.12.44
- B-24D Liberator 41-23721 f Exeter 8.7.43
- B-26B Marauder 41-31809 for static vent and directional control trials, to Crail 20.2.44
- A-26C 43-22479 f St Mawgan 18.12.44, to Boscombe Down 31.12

Fighter types were also undergoing trials at RAE:
- F-5A Lightning (P-38G) 42-12981 f Mount Farm 11.5.43, until 27.5
- P-38 '265' f Mount Farm 14.2.45 for powered control trials, until 20.2
- P-38 '301' f Mount Farm 25.2.45 for dive recovery and handling trials until 9.3
- P-38 '993' f Mount Farm 20.2.45
- P-47C 41-6226 for vibrograph tests
- P-47C 41-6252 f Grove 3.3.43 for handling and r/t work, to Honington 14.4.43
- P-47C 41-6324 f Broughton 13.10.43 for gyro gunsight trials until 3.11
- P-47D 42-75094 f Burtonwood 13.11.43 for handling trials, to Broughton 3.1.44
- P-51B 43-12413 f Benson 18.10.43 for gyro gunsight tests;
- P-51B 43-12425 f Bovingdon 21.10.43 for gyro gunsight tests
- P-51D 44-14061 f Bardney 11.9.43 for VHF tests, until 23.9
- P-61A 42-5496 f Speke 23.3.44 for spoiler control handling trials, to Boscombe Down 6.5.44.

The fighter types were evaluated in respect of their suitability for bomber escort duties and the P-51 Mustang proved best suited to this role, the type taking over USAAF escort duties for the remainder of World War Two.

In November, SME Flight broke away from Aerodynamics Flight and became a separate entity. During 1944/1945 some of the work carried out by this Flight included trials with:
- self-sealing tanks on Mitchell III HD370;
- turret heater and ventilation on Halifax B.III MZ472;
- handling and performance of Heinkel He 177 TS439;
- effects of 'G' on Vengeance IV FD169 and Spitfire HF.IX NH360;
- vibration on Spitfire F.21 LA191;
- stress, wing and undercarriage research with Lancaster B.III ED872;
- dropping of ASR equipment, dinghy and supplies from Barracuda III PM894;
- stresses, handling and controllability of Hoverfly I KL107;
- engine vibration on Lincoln B.1 RE254;
- engine-mounting stresses and undercarriage reaction on Warwick GR.II HG361;
- instrument layout in Oxford I HM767;
- comparative brake tests of captured German aircraft;
- de-icing with Halifax III HX246;
- vibrograph in Junkers Ju 88G TP190 and in Firebrand TF.III DK400;

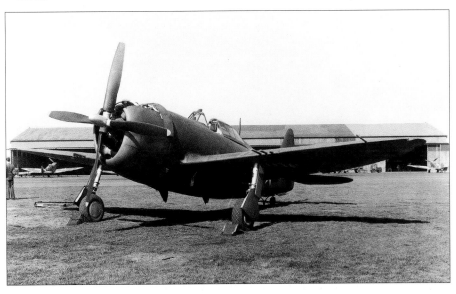

P-47C Thunderbolt 41-6252, is seen here parked on the Farnborough grass, in front of 'A' shed, with the top engine cowling removed during August 1943. This aircraft came to Farnborough for handling and radio transmission work, retaining its US Army Air Force markings throughout.
FAST collection

This B-17G Fortress III, HB778, arrived at Farnborough during March 1945 and was operated by WE Flight and, later, SME Flight. It served at Farnborough for the next seven years, undertaking a variety of trials, which included combustion heaters that were being researched when this photograph was taken in September 1946. It was returned to the US 3rd Air Force in September 1952. *FAST collection*

- undercarriage reaction in Albemarle GT.I V1599;
- power-operated controls in Lancaster B.I PP756
- cabin heating in Fortress III HB778.

Headquarters Flight was reformed as General Duties Flight on 27th November 1941 and further evolved into Transport Flight. During 1944, the Flight Commander was Flt Lt H J King (later Squadron Leader). His small band of pilots were responsible for not only ferrying RAE personnel around the UK and Europe but also collecting and dispatching various aircraft to/from Farnborough and other bases. This basically included all the aircraft that were being sent to Farnborough for their respective research Flights, but, in other cases, pilots from this Flight would still undertake various research duties on behalf of the other Flights. Communications aircraft being used at the time were Oxford II V3503 and Hudson V AM607. During 1945, as the Allies progressed through Europe, this Flight became very busy, being engaged in recovering many of the German aircraft that were

captured across Europe and ferrying them back to the United Kingdom.

RAE had been developing fuel injectors for a number of years and, during this year, the pressure fuel injector was taken over by H M Hobson Limited for development and production. Trials had been conducted at Farnborough with these injectors fitted in a Handley Halifax VI, Hawker Tempest and Vickers Viking aircraft. Early electronic ignition systems were also tested at Farnborough, on a Merlin engine in a Lancaster.

Testing and evaluation of captured German aircraft continued. As the Allies advanced through Europe, many more arrived at RAE. With the cessation of hostilities on 12th September, it was not long before the Royal Aircraft Establishment opened its gates, between 29th October and 9th November, to invited guests, including key figures from the Armed Forces, Government Ministries and the aircraft industry, to view the work of the Establishment during the War years. One of the main attractions was the Enemy Aircraft Exhibition, where most of the German aircraft captured and returned for evaluation at Farnborough,

including many parts from crashed aircraft, were on display for all to see, some to be viewed for the very first time. Over the weekend of 10/12th November the general public were allowed to view this fine selection of captured aircraft and RAE employees' families were also allowed in on one day. Visitors were even allowed to vandalise one aircraft, a Focke-Wulf Fw.190D (W/Nr 210079), to recover parts for souvenirs! The catalogue for this event is a rare commodity these days.

Aircraft ranged along the front of 'A' shed included: Arado Ar 232B-0 (W/Nr 305002, Air Min 17); Arado Ar 234B-1 (W/Nr 140476, AM26, VK877); Dornier Do 217M-1 (W/Nr 56527, AM106); Do 335A-12 (W/Nr 240112, AM223); Fieseler Fi 156C-3 (W/Nr 2008, AM100); Focke-Wulf Ta 152H-0 (W/Nr 150004, AM11); Fw 189A-3 (W/Nr 0173, AM27); Fw 190A-8/R15 (AM111); Fw 200C-4/U1 (W/Nr 176, AM94), the personal transport aircraft of Heinrich Himmler; Heinkel He 111H (W/Nr 701152; He 219A-5/R2 (W/Nr 310189, AM22); Junkers Ju 52/3m (W/Nr 641038, AM104); Ju 88G-1 (W/Nr 712273, TP190, AM231); Ju 188A-1 (W/Nr 230776, AM108); Ju 290A-2 (W/Nr 110157, AM57); Ju 352A (AM109); Ju 388L-1/V6 (W/Nr 500006, AM83); Ju 88A-6/Fw 190A Composite (Ju 88 W/Nr 2492, Fw 190 W/Nr 733759, AM77); Messerschmitt Bf 108B (W/Nr 1547, AM84); Bf 109G (VD358); Bf 110G-4/R3 (W/Nr 730037, AM30); Me 262A-1 (W/Nr 111690, AM80); Me 410B-6 (W/Nr 410208 AM.74); Reichenburg IV, a piloted Fieseler Fi 103/V-1 with cockpit and ailerons, as flown by German test pilot Hannah Reitsch; and Siebel Si 204D-1 (W/Nr 322127, AM4). Other aircraft, engines and weapons were on display in the adjacent hangar. Thirteen of the ex-German aircraft also made short flying displays on various days during the week, these being: Siebel

This aerial view of the aircraft exhibition at Farnborough on 29th October 1945, taken from a cine film, shows the extent of the German aircraft display, which includes some 20 captured ex-Luftwaffe types, along with many of the current British types of the time. In the foreground is Halifax C.VIII PP328, which is about to depart on a demonstration, being handled by General Duties Flight, having arrived from Radlett on 26th October and returning there on 6th November 1945. *via B Kervell*

The German aircraft and equipment display extended into 'A' shed and this elevated view shows a further selection of ex-Luftwaffe types, including Bf 109G-14 W/Nr 413601, He 162s AM64 and AM66, a Bv 155B prototype, Olympia sailplane 'LF+VO', Me 163B, Horten IV, Ju 88G-6 AM31 W/Nr 623193 and Fw 190A-4 W/Nr 171747. *FAST collection*

Si 204D-1 (W/Nr 221558, AM28); Fiesler Fi 156C-7 (W/Nr 475099, AM99); Bücker Bü 181C-3 Bestmann (W/Nr 120417, AM122); Messerschmitt Bf 108B-1 (AM89); Junkers Ju 52/3m (W/Nr 6567, AM103); Dornier Do 217M-1 (W/Nr 56158, AM107); Junkers Ju 88G-6 (W/Nr627461, AM41); Focke-Wulf Fw 190A-5/U8 (W/Nr2596, PN999); two Messerschmitt Me 262A-2a (W/Nr 112372, VK893 and W/Nr 500200, AM81); Arado Ar 234B (W/Nr 140356, AM226) and Heinkel He 162A-2 (W/Nr 120072, AM61). However, on the last day of the exhibition the He.162A-2 crashed at 14.55 hours. The pilot, Flt Lt R Marks, was unfortunately killed when the aircraft made a tight starboard turn, which resulted in the fin and rudder collapsing at low level and the aircraft entering a dive and crashing onto the Oudenarde Army Barracks in North Camp.

Nearly all of the current British types were on display and, with aircraft parked on the 'A' shed apron or Jersey Brow or on the top northeastern end of the airfield, there was undoubtedly an impressive array to be seen. Aircraft equipment and engines were laid out in 'A' shed, or within the various departmental laboratories and hangars, giving an insight into the research work that had progressed here during the War.

The flying programme included the following aircraft: Halifax C.VIII PP328, Avro Lancastrian I VM702, Lincoln B.II RE325, Tudor I G-AGPF/TT176, Windsor B.I DW512, Viking I G-AGOL, Dove I G-AGPJ, Shetland I DX166, Hornet F.I PX237, Mosquito PR.34 RG307, Vampire F.1 TG285, Fury F.I NX802, Tempest F.II PR739, Tempest F.VI NX117, Meteor F.4 EE360/G, Spearfish I RA356, Firefly F.IV Z2118; Brigand TF.1 MX991, Firebrand TF.IV EK680, Martin-Baker MB.5 R2496, Spiteful F.XIV RB521 and Spitfire F.21 LA216. The Heinkel He 162A VH513 and Messerschmitt Me 262A VK893 were both flown as a comparison with the British jets.

The RAE Catapult section was renamed Naval Aircraft Department on 17th April, thus recognising the extent of research work being undertaken on aspects of Naval aircraft, with specific attention towards launching and arrester gear on board ships. In June 1954 this work, along with that of the Carrier Equipment Division, was transferred to RAE Bedford where Naval Air Department continued its research in Naval aviation until its demise in 1981.

Earlier this year, German scientists began to appear at RAE Farnborough, initially as prisoners of war. Some were returned to Germany at the end of the War, many others stayed and worked at RAE alongside their British counterparts, while others were dispatched to the USA. An example of one of the best-known German scientists at Farnborough was Deitrich Küchemann, who eventually became head of Aerodynamics Department in 1966. He led the way in wing plan form design, Germany having appreciated the advantages of sweepback many years before the UK. Much of this work ultimately led to the design of the Concorde wing.

Arriving at Farnborough on 8th September 1945 was the twin push-pull engined Dornier Do 335A-12 'Pfeil' (W/Nr 240112, AM223), which had been 'liberated' from the Dornier factory at Oberpfaffenhofen, near Munich. Whilst undertaking its third test flight from Farnborough with GD Flight, on 18th January, it crashed on Cove School, along Fernhill Road, demolishing the headmaster's house and the school bicycle sheds. The aircraft had caught fire in the rear engine, which burnt through the elevator control system, resulting in loss of control. Regrettably the pilot, Group Captain A F Hards DSO, the Officer Commanding Experimental Flying Department at RAE, lost his life. There were no casualties on the ground. To this day the school retains an aircraft within its crest as a reminder of this accident. As a result of this accident, the flying of captured enemy aircraft at Farnborough was seriously curtailed, although there were a few further flights that took place during 1946/1947, before the majority were either scrapped or dispatched for storage or museum exhibition. Many of the German aircraft were scrapped at Farnborough and hearsay abounded during the 1950s/1960s that some of these old airframes and parts were in fact buried in a gravel pit just off the Frimley to Camberley road, in what is now the business area along Lyon Road, but this has never been substantiated and, with the area now all built up, the rumour will have to continue.

Dornier Do 335A-12 AM223 (W/Nr 240112), is seen here at Farnborough on 11th September 1945, three days after its arrival. This two-seat aircraft crashed on Cove Junior School on 18th January 1946, with Group Captain A F Hards losing his life. *FAST collection*

January saw the appointment of W A Perring as Director of RAE while, on 1st April, the Ministry of Aircraft Production became a part of the Ministry of Supply.

Martin-Baker built an aircrew ejection seat test rig during this year, positioned at the north side of R136 building. With a height of 33.5 metres it was designed for development and testing of ejection seat components such as guns and cartridges. The rig was used for the testing and evaluation of ejection seats and equipment, simulating the upward accelerations experienced when an aircrew ejection seat is discharged from an aircraft. Although the windblast was absent it did allow the vertical phase of ejection to be studied under controlled and repeatable conditions. The very last live test was conducted in 1971. The rig was laid down for modifications in 1948, was extended to 49 metres in 1953, and in 1971 it underwent replacement of some structural members. In 1980 a full overhaul was deemed necessary and the entire structure was examined, grit blasted and re-protected accordingly. The rig was first used on 24th April 1947 and by June 1980, by now under Engineering Physics Department control, some 7,700 tests had been carried out. At its peak use, in the mid/late 1950s, some 1,000 tests per year were carried out. With the structure impeding the airfield approach safety margin it was decided to move the rig and it was disassembled in 1982 by Lloyds British Testing and transported to Pyestock where further tests were carried out up to early 2005. During April 2005 it was again dismantled by Lloyds British Testing and taken away for inspection. It was re-erected on Foulness Island during late February/early March 2006 where, now sixty years old, it will continue to be used by QinetiQ for further ejection seat trials.

The Guided Projectile Establishment was created at Westcott to further the scientific and technological development of rocket propulsion. This was always linked to the Guided Weapons Department at Farnborough, in September 1957 it became known as the Rocket Propulsion Establishment.

On 1st May the Physiological Laboratory moved to the RAF station on the south side of Farnborough, in the area previously known as Danger Hill, and was now renamed the Royal Air Force Institute of Aviation Medicine.

March saw the end of the development of piston engines at RAE and all research of jet engines was transferred to the National Gas Turbine Establishment at Pyestock, to the northwest of the Farnborough airfield. NGTE had been established here on 1st April 1946 as a result of amalgamation of Power Jets Limited and RAE Turbine Division and Gas Dynamics Department, thus becoming a National Research station in its own right. NGTE rapidly acquired and built large research laboratories, and engine test cells and the like. Investigations into ramjet propulsion were commenced at this time for use in high-speed surface-to-air missiles. Some of the Pyestock testbeds were subsequently modified for ramjet work and research continued here for some time. The building of test cells continued into the 1960s and these culminated with Cell 4, necessary for the development of the Olympus engines and intakes for Concorde. Engine development work for new aircraft types such as the P.1127 and later Harrier, TSR.2, Jaguar and Tornado continued. NGTE became part of RAE in 1983 and continued throughout to QinetiQ days, although only a fraction of the site is currently operational under QinetiQ control. The site is about to be demolished for redevelopment in 2006 as a light industrial area to be known as Hartland Park.

Armament Research had previously been undertaken by AID Flight, but from January 1945 Armament Flight, under their Flight Commander, Squadron Leader R V Keeling (later Squadron Leader E J Spencer), became a separate entity and had a number of pilots, navigators and flight engineers attached to the Flight as the majority of aircraft undergoing research at this time were large multi-crew types. The diarist of the time said, 'We solely cater for the wants of war-loving boffins who drop bombs and the like': this

quote just about sums up Armament Flight, although the weapons being trialled were a diverse mix. Work being undertaken during this period included:
- structural distortion in a Windsor B.1 NK136;
- dive-bombing by Avenger II JZ625,
- rocket projectile trials on Hurricane Mk.IIc PZ772 and Mk.IV KZ706, Swordfish II NE957,
- air-photography from a Boston I AX926;
- boat drops from Dakota III FL510;
- 'Uncle Tom' firings from Mosquito PR.XIV MM173, FB.VI NT220 and FB.VI RF892;
- 'Village Inn' on Lancaster B.II LL737 and B.III RF268 plus Mosquito PR.XIV MM173;
- airborne field gun on Lancaster B.III JA938;
- 'Man Friday' on Lancaster B.III JA938 and B.I LL937;
- various bombing trials including blind bombing, 'Roman Candles', SV bombs, 4,000 lb 'Cookies' with proximity fusing, all flown from the Flight's Lancaster B.III JA938, B.I LL937, B.I ED842 and B.III RF288;
- rocket-sighting from a Mosquito NF.XIX TA193;
- mines being dropped from a Tempest II NV755;
- 25 lb field gun in a Halifax VII PN308;
- carbon monoxide tests in Avenger I JZ129;
- 'SV bombs' in a Lancaster;
- remote control turrets in Lancaster B.I LL780;
- panniers on Lancaster B.III RF288;
- rocket-sighting in Grumman Avenger JZ152 and Lancaster B.III RF288 with 10,000 lb of weight in canvas slings;
- photo-flash in Mosquito PR.XIV MM363
- bombing from Swordfish III NR933 and Barracuda II MX613.

The first Sikorsky R-4B Hoverfly Is, KL107, KL108 and KL109, arrived on 20th March 1945 from Martin Hearn at Hooton Park for various tests with Aero Flight, including stability and control, supply dropping and parachutes. During the following year, rotor downwash trials were undertaken. After the various trials, KL107 returned to Hooton Park on 15th June 1950, KL108 passed to the AFEE at Beaulieu for crop spraying experiments on 17th March 1948, and KL109 departed for Gosport on 3rd September 1948. Hoverfly II KN863 also underwent research work with RAE, arriving from Hooton Park on 22nd December 1948 and transferring to the AFEE on 27th February 1950.

During 1945, a smaller and simpler version of the 1940 direction-controlled take-off track was laid on Jersey Brow, to establish whether a light aircraft could benefit from this arrangement. The intention

R-4B Hoverfly I KL109 is seen here in the hover on 18th May 1946, undergoing handling and stability trials with Aero Flight, being flown by Lt Cdr E Brown. The test equipment above the tail rotor was used to measure airspeed and airflow gusts.
FAST collection

was for this to be used on a 'Landing Ship, Tank' (LST) in waterborne landing of troops. The aircraft chosen for these trials was Auster AOP.V TJ537, which arrived from Aston Down on 22nd April 1945. The idea was that the aircraft would take off by its own power, with all three wheels running in a channelled section, and it would lift off from the track with the tailwheel being held in a small trolley. The track was raised from the ground on concrete plinths and was 167ft in length. The Auster was first launched from the track on 4th May 1945 and a total of 20 launches were made during the year, before the project was abandoned. The Auster went on to undertake handling and stall trials with Aero Flight.

1946

Radio Department continued development with radio-controlled aircraft, as well as research and development of standard radio equipment. During this year four Vickers Vikings – C. (VVIP) 2s VL245, VL246, VL247 and C.2 VL248 – of the King's Flight had a special radio fit designed and installed by the Farnborough research team, prior to a Royal tour of South Africa during March 1947. The work of this department through subsequent years saw many different aircraft types equipped with various radio installations for communications and navigation trials.

The Meteorological Research Flight, following the scientific success of the High Altitude Flight, was formed at Farnborough during September 1946 and was initially equipped with Mosquito and Halifax aircraft (see chapter 9).

A new air traffic control building with modern facilities, the third on the airfield, designed by Radio Department during 1945 and built during 1946/1947 became operational in 1948, later becoming known as N1 building. It replaced the much smaller wartime brick hut (N2 building). The facilities in the new building are attributed to Radio Department, GPO Signals and Experimental Flying Department, who all assisted in the design and layout. Originally the earlier 'watch office' basically equipped with a telephone, then positioned beside 'A' shed, had been operational for many years with a duty pilot on 'watch', but had outgrown its usefulness and was moved to the brick hut for some seven years before the new tower became operational. During September 1944 a control system was introduced at Farnborough on an experimental basis with round-the-clock 'watches'. It was during this

time that Farnborough was receiving many RAF photo-reconnaissance aircraft, returning from overflying the continent with their precious films of ground activities for processing by the School of Photography. These activities were taking place throughout the day and night. On 1st September 1949 Farnborough had a full radar approach operational, by late 1950 it had become the first Radar Controlled airfield in the UK, and by 1952 was a Fighter Command diversion airfield, being mainly utilised by RAF Odiham. Throughout subsequent years this control tower had been slightly modified externally, and had further improved equipment installed. It remained in use until 21.18 hours on 25th November 2002 when it was closed down after the last flight of the day, thus ending an era of 54 years. It was demolished during January 2003.

The RAE Apprentices Hostel, owned by the Ministry of Supply, opened during October, these buildings being adapted from former RFC/RAF barrack blocks of 1915/1916 vintage, to provide accommodation for those apprentices who were from outside the area. The hostel was then run by the YMCA, and by 1952 some 250 apprentices were living therein at a full board rate of £1.17s.6d per week. These buildings, having recently been in use for live-in students of the Farnborough College of Technology, still exist today, although derelict and awaiting demolition during 2006.

Aerodynamics Department were researching tailless aircraft stability and control problems and one of the four experimental aircraft built by General Aircraft Limited, GAL.56 TS507, underwent wind tunnel and flight tests at Farnborough. This glider arrived at RAE from Dunholme Lodge on 22nd June 1945 and made its first Farnborough flight the same day, towed by a visiting Handley Page Halifax, but was damaged during landing on 24th July 1946 and returned to the manufacturers by road for repair on

14th August. It arrived back on 10th October 1946 and continued with the tests until it made its last RAE flight on 28th August 1947. It was dispatched to the manufacturer at their Lasham facility during October 1947. During its research at Farnborough, the GAL.56 was mainly towed aloft by Spitfire F.IX EN498 or LF.IX NH403, although Miles Master DM352 was also utilised at various times. However the glider crashed at Lower Froyle near Alton on 12th February 1948 whilst undergoing stall research with the manufacturer, after it entered a stall followed by a steep dive out of control. During August a scale model of the Armstrong Whitworth AW.52 tailless research aircraft was among many types tested in the RAE high-speed wind tunnel.

Gas Dynamics Flight came into being during January 1946, thus the initials GD Flight, previously General Duties, took on a different meaning with RAE Transport Flight officially formed during February from the original General Duties Flight. At its commencement, the Transport fleet included Hudson Mk.III V9034 and AE586, Mk.V AM666 and AM797; Oxford I RR349 and LX308; Dominie I X7375, Harvard IIB FS902; Anson C.XII PH622; Dakota III KG368 and Junkers Ju 352 AM8, the latter being put to good use as a transport aircraft since being captured by the Allies advancing through Europe.

To investigate transonic flight, trials were being conducted with a rocket-propelled model, built by Vickers and carried beneath a Mosquito of RAE Aero S (Supersonic) Flight. These trials were being conducted with Mosquito B.XVI PF604, which arrived at Farnborough from Edzell on 13th June 1946 to undertake research into high-speed and high-altitude flight. The aircraft would climb to approximately 36,000ft, then the liquid-propellant rocket motor would be ignited and the model, released at 400mph, would accelerate to supersonic speeds. This

Slung beneath the fuselage of Mosquito B.XVI PF604, in February 1948, is a rocket-propelled test vehicle that, after launch, would reach supersonic speeds. The launch of these models was made over a range off the Scilly Isles, the aircraft operating from St Eval. *FAST collection*

Sea Hornet F.20 PX214 was the first twin-engined aircraft to be launched from the Jersey Brow accelerator on 23rd January 1946. It is seen here prior to launch, in position on the accelerator track. It was struck off charge during October 1947.
FAST collection

model was successfully launched on a number of occasions over the range operating from St Eval in Cornwall. Mosquito PF604 was damaged in a ground accident at Farnborough on 13th April 1949 and was declared as scrap in July 1949.

Low-speed wind tunnel tests were carried out on the Miles M.52 earlier this year but this was actually cancelled in March 1946 as, supposedly, the rocket-propelled supersonic aircraft posed potential danger to the pilots. However a 40% scale model, a transonic bomb based on the M.52, was later produced and dropped over the range off the Scilly Isles by Mosquito B.XVI PF543, which had arrived from Edzell on 16th October 1945. After early problems, it achieved a successful launch on 9th October 1948 operating from St Eval. The model reached a speed of Mach 1.4 at this stage, but the programme was terminated, as very little useful data was being obtained. However this project eventually led to production of a series of ground-launched, free-flight models, all made at Farnborough, to continue research into supersonic flight. Mosquito PF543 ended its days at Farnbor-

ough, being withdrawn and dispatched to 49MU by road where it was declared scrap on 11th July 1950.

The first launch of a twin-engined aircraft from the Jersey Brow catapult, other than the Virginia back in 1930, took place when Sea Hornet F.20 PX214 was launched four times from the accelerator on 23rd January 1946. The aircraft arrived from Hatfield on 12th January 1946 and returned to the manufacturer on 29th January having made seven launches from Jersey Brow. During October 1946 the BH.V accelerator (also known as the BH.5 catapult) came into use at Jersey Brow. Built during 1945 this was capable of launching an aircraft at 30,000 lb AUW and consisted of much underground machinery in pits beneath the installation. Some of the underground pits, albeit now with no machinery present, are still extant to the side of Jersey Brow adjacent to the Farnborough Aerodrome Fire Station. The first launch from the BH.V was made on 25th October 1946 when Avenger I JZ298 from Aero Flight made a successful launch and recovery followed by four more on the fol-

lowing day. The Avenger had arrived from Renfrew on 9th February 1945 for use in proofing of arrester gear, replacing a previous example (FN911). Further catapult work proceeded with this aircraft but it was damaged during launch from the accelerator on 29th March 1947 and was dispatched by road to Stretton on 3rd July 1947. Bristol Brigand I RH748 arrived at Farnborough from Filton on 28th November 1949 for trials with Aero Flight in connection with arrester and catapult gear. It was launched from the BH.V for the first time on 6th April 1950 and transferred with NAD to RAE Bedford in 1955, being struck off charge in November 1955 for use in fire fighting training there.

The RAE staged a further air display this year with flying taking place on 27th, 28th and 29th June 1946. Aircraft giving demonstrations included: Avro Tudor II G-AGSU; Avro York C.1 G-AGNL; Handley Page Hastings prototype TE580; a Miles Marathon U.10; Bristol Freighter II G-AGPV; Viking 1A G-AGOM; DH Dove 1 prototype G-AGPJ; Sea Hornet NF.21 PX336; Bristol Brigand F.1 RH742; Firefly FR.IV TW687; Hawker Sea Fury second prototype SR666; Supermarine Spiteful F.XIV RB522; Meteor F.4 EE532; Martin-Baker MB.5 R2496; Blackburn Firebrand Mk.V EK746; Vampire F.1 TG285; Miles Gemini I prototype G-AGUS; Percival Proctor V G-AGTC; Auster J/1 Autocrat G-AHHD and Miles Aerovan II G-AGWO. Some of the RAE aircraft also gave displays including Seafire F.XVII SX314, which was launched from the accelerator; Seafire F.XV SW813, RATOG take-off; Gadfly (Hoverfly) KL108 and Vampire F.1 TG426.

1947

Aerodynamics Department was undertaking theoretical studies of swept-back, delta, slender and other plan-form wings. Following studies of German research undertaken into these futuristic designs, low- and high-speed wind tunnel testing occurred at Farnborough, using various models, as well as drag experiments on wings and dropping of aerodynamic bodies from high-flying aircraft. These led to greater understanding of

The RAE staged a further British aircraft display during June 1946 and this aerial view shows some 35 different aircraft, including the Tudor II prototype G-AGSU, Hastings prototype TE580, Martin Baker MB.5 R2496, Meteor F.4 EE532 and Gemini 1 prototype G-AGUS, to name but a few.
FAST collection

Hotspur II BT889 is positioned on its catapult in July 1947, to be launched onto the flexible deck that was installed near Meadow Gate to determine the flight trajectory, prior to use of 'live' aircraft experiments during the next stage of these trials. It was eventually scrapped at Farnborough. *FAST collection*

The first attempt to land on the flexible deck, with Vampire F.1 TG426, ended in disaster on 29th December 1947, as the aircraft struck the end of the deck, bounced, and then crash-landed on the grass beyond. Fortunately the pilot, Lt Cdr E Brown, escaped unhurt, but the aircraft was written off. *FAST collection*

stability and control at high speeds. Supersonic wind tunnel tests, investigating boundary layer, shock waves and temperature and kinetic heat were also undertaken. Flight tests to investigate high-speed dives and high Mach number performance were being conducted by Aero Flight, as the flight envelope of the new jets was constantly being increased. Ejection seat research was also being undertaken, utilising information that had been recovered from Germany.

In much the same way as they had undertaken previous work over the years, the RAE Structural Mechanical and Engineering Department, now comprising smaller sections, were utilising the various aircraft structural test frames for studies into fatigue and strength of materials, for fighter and training aircraft types. The Abbey test frame was built for airframe and component structural testing in 1945, whilst a new structural test frame, known as the Hercules, was also in the design stage at this time. This was, in fact, never completed, but the Cathedral test frame, which had been in use since the late 1930s, became the principal test structure for larger airframes, which eventually included many civilian types. Structures Department was formed from SME Department where tests into structural research, material strength testing, mechanical tests, flutter, vibration and fatigue and kinetic heating were being conducted.

During 1947 the civilian staff of the Aircraft Torpedo Development Unit (ATDU) at Gosport were transferred to RAE Farnborough as the research and development element had become part of Armament Department. Work on torpedo systems for aircraft continued. Even into the 1970s, Canberras and Wessex were deployed for torpedo trials at Culdrose, where the unit had re-located to some years earlier.

Rocket Propulsion Department of RAE came into being during this year, being renamed from the Guided Projectile Establishment at Westcott. Westcott became an RAE outstation, and the department became responsible for research and development on all forms of liquid- and solid-fuel rocket

motors. The RAE link continued until August 1958 when Westcott became known in its own right as the Propellants, Explosives and Rocket Motor Establishment.

Following the rubber deck investigation work, a larger area, alongside where 'Q' shed was eventually built off Meadow Gate, was allocated for Stage 2 of these experiments. The site was constructed in 1947 and various tests were carried out. In these, suitably ballasted and strengthened Hotspur III gliders (HH175, HH610 and BT889, which had all arrived from Shobdon on 27th November 1945) were launched by catapult to determine attitude and flight trajectory. The tests undertaken by the gliders were the precursor to the actual landings undertaken by the undercarriage-less jets.

The next stage, referred to as Stage 3, was to produce a full-scale flexible deck site on the airfield where a live aircraft could land. Consequently a flexible deck was constructed on the airfield, parallel to runway 07/25 and to the west of 04/22 near the intersection of the two, which was to be used as the main trial site for the intended undercarriage-less landings. The aircraft

allocated to this task was navalised Vampire F.1 TG426 that had arrived on 24th June 1946 but was returned to Hatfield on 3rd October 1946 for various modifications. It returned on 22nd May 1947 and was transferred to Naval charge on 1st August 1947. Commencing on 26th November, a number of practice approach flights were flown. The first actual landing on the flexible deck occurred on 29th December 1947, but this proved disastrous as the aircraft flew below its minimum speed during the final approach. Although power was increased, it was too late for the aircraft to respond and the Vampire struck the approach end of the deck, its arrester hook becoming jammed, the aircraft then bouncing and crash-landing on the grass beyond. The pilot, Lt Cdr E M 'Winkle' Brown, escaped unhurt but the aircraft was written off, being reduced to spares at Ford in February 1948.

The next development was to install a flexible deck on an aircraft carrier in order to conduct live trials on board ship. HMS *Warrior*, having been commissioned in January 1946 for the Royal Canadian Navy but returned to Royal Navy charge in March

Sea Vampire F.21 VT802 has successfully engaged the arrester wire on HMS *Warrior* on 17th February 1949, and is about to touch down on the flexible deck. *FAST collection*

1948, was designated to be so fitted. This was undertaken at Portsmouth in 1948 and, after much training at Lee-on-Solent and dummy approaches to the ship during November 1948, the flexible deck landing trials were conducted on board HMS *Warrior* between November 1948 and June 1949 utilising Vampire F.1s and Sea Vampire F.21s positioning from Farnborough to Lee-on-Solent. When a landing was completed, the crane on board HMS *Warrior* would lift the aircraft, the undercarriage would then be lowered and the aircraft taxied forward for a catapult launch.

The Vampire F.1s were: TG286, which had arrived from Hatfield on 6th February 1948 and was used for the flexible deck operations from 8th March, including on board HMS *Warrior*, before later being struck off charge for ground use on barrier trials; and TG328, which had arrived on 3rd March 1947, was in use for the trials from February 1949, but was damaged when the undercarriage collapsed during a conventional landing on 29th June 1949. Also used were five Sea Vampire F.21s from Hatfield: prototype VG701 arrived on 18th June 1948 and was used at RAE and on board HMS *Warrior* in February 1949, it transferred to

Culham on 23rd August 1949; VT795 arrived on 1st July 1948 and was used for the HMS *Warrior* trials, making numerous flexible deck landings, but suffered an accident at Farnborough when it missed the flexible deck wire and crash landed in the overshoot area on 1st May 1954; VT802 arrived on 19th February 1948 and commenced operations on 12th April, but was damaged during a handling test when it was caught by a gust of wind during a conventional landing at Farnborough on 2nd June necessitating a return to the manufacturer for repair, being returned to RAE on 19th October, whereupon it undertook much flexible deck work at Farnborough and HMS *Warrior* before entering storage in September 1955; VT803 arrived on 7th July 1948 and was in use both at Farnborough and on board HMS *Warrior* until it departed for Culham on 16th August 1949; VT804 arrived on 16th February 1949 for flexible deck trials but was also detached to Leuchars for Approach Dummy Deck Landings (ADDLs), on board HMS *Vengeance*, on 3rd/4th July 1950 before returning to continue the flexible deck work, finally transferring to Stretton on 11th August 1955; and, lastly, VT805 which arrived on 7th July 1948 for trials at Farn-

borough and on board HMS *Warrior* during February and March 1949, continuing with the work at Farnborough up to the end of the trials. It was later transferred to Brooklands Aviation at Little Staughton for refurbishing on 14th June 1955. Over 50 flexible deck landings were made at Farnborough and some 271 on HMS *Warrior* up to June 1949, when the trials were completed and the equipment removed. The ship was put into Reserve, but in 1958 it was sold to Argentina as the *Independencia*.

Deck landing trials on board the aircraft carrier HMS *Illustrious* were carried out by the first Naval prototype, Supermarine E10/44 Attacker TS413 on 14th October, with the aircraft operating from Ford. At this time safety barrier trials were also under way at Farnborough, with a number of aircraft being taxied into the new design of safety barrier to see what effect it had on the airframe. Some aircraft were accelerated into the net at speed, whilst others were taxied into it.

During August the RAE took over the former Convent School building, an early residence of Empress Eugenie, just outside the RAE boundary fence, along the A325 road close to the RAE main gate at the time. The RAE Technical College was officially opened by Sir Stafford Cripps on 10th February 1948 and offered a distinct improvement for academic and technical training. This building is still extant today, in private use by IBM as an office complex. The RAE Technical College became the Farnborough Technical College in 1959 and today is known as the Farnborough College of Technology.

The Empire Test Pilots School moved to Farnborough from Cranfield in July of this year (see chapter 7). Initially the ETPS staff, and aircraft, took up residence in the black sheds but by the end of the year the staff had moved into the former School of Photography buildings where their new Mess was established in time for No 7 course, with 23 students, to commence in January 1948. The aircraft were later moved to the southern area of the airfield where two hangars, an operational building and dispersal area were established, close to the Army golf course. This area was in constant use by ETPS / RAE until 1988, when the hangar and operations building were converted for use

Seen here in June 1949 in their Farnborough hangar, are two of the Sea Vampire F.21s, VT802 and VT805, which were in use for the flexible deck experiments. They are both on their ground-handling trolleys, as they would have been recovered after landing on the Farnborough rubber deck. *FAST collection*

by Carroll Aviation as the initial civilian enclave for business aviation development on the airfield.

The RAF No 1 School of Photography moved from Farnborough, firstly to temporary accommodation in Heath End, Farnham, then to Wellesbourne Mountford and later to Cosford.

Another unusual aircraft of German origin that came to Farnborough was the Brunswick LF1 Zaunkönig. It had been designed and built by the Braunschweig Technische Hochschule and had made its first flight on 3rd May 1944. At the end of World War Two, the aircraft, registered as D-YBAR with W/Nr NV2, was taken by the British and transported to RAE Farnborough, where it was first flown after assembly by Aero Flight on 18th September 1947. It was used for various handling trials in connection with its slotted wing configuration and was allocated RAF serial VX190 on 3rd February 1948, making its first flight as such on 12th February. The Zaunkönig left on 16th July 1948 for brief handling trials with the Ministry of Civil Aviation at Gatwick. It returned to RAE on 15th March 1949 but did not participate in any further trials work, only making brief handling flights with Transport Flight. It was loaned for the Royal Aeronautical Society's garden party at White Waltham on 6th May 1949, returning four days later although it undertook no further flying at Farnborough. It was registered to the Ultralight Aircraft Association as G-ALUA on 28th June 1949, and was flown from Farnborough to Pengam Moors, Cardiff, on 2nd July 1949. After a chequered career in its civilian life, it is still extant as D-EBCQ in Germany.

1948

The airfield at Farnborough was transferred to Ministry of Supply control on 1st June. At this time Experimental Flying Department recorded around 270 daily movements with 150 aircraft of some 50 different types based on the airfield. The 'Flights' were categorised as: Aerodynamics (A Flight), Aerodynamics-Supersonic (Aero-S), Naval Aircraft Section (NA), Structures and Mechanical Engineering (SME), Instrument, Armament, Radio, Transport, Scientific Technical Training (STT) and Meteorological (MRF).

The Society of British Aircraft Constructors moved their annual display to Farnborough from Radlett and the first at the new site occurred during September of this year, showing 50 of the latest aircraft (see chapter 5).

Armament Department continued their valuable research with bombs, guns, rockets and missiles all undergoing further upgrades and new types being introduced, which were tested at Farnborough or on the outstation ranges. A heavy universal freight container was also designed, for parachute delivery of guns, jeeps and heavy equipment up to a payload of 6,000 lb. These tests, with what was known as the Paratechnion, were first carried out on a Halifax VII, PP350, which arrived from High Ercall on 11th April 1947 and commenced drop trials in July 1947 with Armament Flight that continued until mid-1949. Hastings C.1 TG499 arrived from Radlett on 27th June 1949 to continue the trials with SME Flight, successful drops being made both at Farnborough and on Salisbury Plain. On 30th August 1949 the Hastings was returned to Radlett for fitment of a larger container for heavier drop trials. These continued with the A&AEE at Boscombe Down from 14th September but on 26th September, whilst flying at 4,000ft, the Paratechnicon broke away from its mountings and impacted against the starboard tailplane whereupon parts became detached. With control lost the aircraft crashed on Beacon Hill, just to the east of Boscombe Down, with the loss of the three crew. The project was terminated at this point.

Instrumentation Department were now improving and developing specialised instruments and equipment for determining aerodynamic, structural and engine characteristics; various recorders were undergoing experimental flying to give Instrument and Electronic in-flight measurements; special cameras were being developed for flash photography and various aircraft instrumentation was undergoing development and enhancement.

Electrical Engineering Department was heavily involved in improvements to airfield approach lighting systems, which eventually led to the standard line and bar system. This was installed at Farnborough during this year and, after various trials, was adopted throughout the UK at civil airports.

On 5th October 1948 the first prototype de Havilland DH.108 TG283, to specification E18/45, arrived from Hatfield to undertake low-speed research trials with Aero Flight. The second prototype, TG306, had broken up during high-speed flight over the Thames Estuary on 27th September 1946, killing Geoffrey de Havilland, the son of the early aviation pioneer. TG283, whilst undertaking sideslip and stalling trials with Aero Flight on 1st May 1950, entered an inverted spin and, although partial recovery was made, the aircraft crashed at Hartley Wintney. The pilot bailed out from the aircraft at low altitude but, being injured and his parachute only partly streamed, he lost his life. The third and final DH.108 built, VW120, arrived on 28th June 1949 and was used for high-speed trials with Aero Fight, before it too crashed on 15th February 1950, at Brickhill, near Bletchley, after disintegrating during flight. The pilot was killed.

There were also many dedicated engine testbed aircraft that served at Farnborough, notwithstanding those that were to serve with NGTE Flight. These included a Lancastrian C.III, VH737, fitted with two Nene engines that underwent engine icing trials during April/August 1947 and April/August 1948, and a Nene-engined Tudor 8, VX195, used for performance and high-altitude trials from April 1950 to January 1952.

The first issue of the 'RAE News' magazine was published in March 1948: it was to become both a factual magazine and the voice of the RAE staff. There had already been other magazines produced: the 'Sardian' by SARD/RAF 1917/1920; 'The Rafler' by RAE in 1919; 'Vortex' by the Technical College; while from Westcott there was 'Venturi' – these all fading away. However 'RAE News', with plenty of news, views, activities and features from all aspects of RAE and its outstations, continued until the combined November/December 1991 issue, nearly 55

years of publication, whereupon it was succeeded by a tabloid newspaper format 'DRA News', then 'DERA News' and, from 2001, a tabloid-style magazine called 'IQ'.

1949

Photographic Reconnaissance procedures and equipment were by now in use for high-speed recording by day and night, at both high and low altitude. The RAE Instrument and Air Photographic Department continued with the development of this equipment over the years, which eventually saw improved cameras and the use of TV imaging.

Further expansion of the airfield had occurred by now, with the lengthening of the runway westwards on Laffan's Plain towards the Basingstoke Canal. Three runways were operational, the fourth being previously declared surplus and downgraded for use by the Naval Air Department for catapult and arrester trials.

The RAE Technical College set up a Gliding Flight, formed on 28th February 1949, where engineering students were taught to fly. Since 1945 gliding had been on a private basis, but now had been sanctioned by the Ministry of Supply for professional training of fourth- and fifth-year students reading aeronautics. The syllabus would enable students to qualify to a 'Silver C Certificate' level. The first gliders to join the Flight were Kirby Cadet Is RA952 and RA967, both arriving from Weston-on-the-Green on 31st January 1949 and both dispatched to Fareham on 15th June 1954, having been sold to the Portsmouth Naval Gliding Club. Sedbergh TX.1 WB920 arrived at Farnborough from 9MU on 26th June 1951 and was transferred to ETPS on 17th March 1954; Sedbergh TX.1 WB973 arrived at Farnborough from Rufforth on 4th November 1950 and was returned to Slingsby's for repair after an accident at Farnborough on 3rd June 1951.

Some ex-German gliders were already being flown at RAE and at least two of these were subsequently allocated to the Gliding Flight. DFS 108-14 Schulgleiter 38 VP559, ex-38-371, and DFS 108-30 Kranich II VP591, W/Nr 1007, both arrived from Germany in July 1945 and were allocated for combined use by RAE pilots and RAE Technical College students for training and handling on 30th April 1946. On 15th June 1954, the Portsmouth Naval Gliding Club collected the former while the latter went to the RAF Gliding and Soaring Association. The tow-tug used for these gliders was the RAE's Fieseler Fi.156C-7 Storch VP546, which was allocated for these duties on 17th December 1949, although it still continued with trials and liaison work during the working week.

In January 1953, by which time some 115 apprentices and students had been trained in the art of glider flying, this element ceased to be part of the college's curriculum. In its place, a scheme of flight experiments was adopted for fifth-year engineering students. These were to be carried out on board an RAE powered aircraft in order to familiarise the student in routine handling tests and specialised research tasks. These flights took place on Friday afternoons, with four students on board each flight. Anson C.19 TX210 was modified for the Technical College requirements, with further instrumentation fitted. The Anson had arrived from Hendon on 5th May 1947 for flight endurance tests of flexible fuel tanks, known as crash-proof tanks, with SME Flight. These familiarisation flights, with the Anson being flown by an RAE Transport Flight crew, were of considerable benefit to the students in broadening their aerodynamic knowledge. They continued for a couple of years and then ceased altogether. The Anson, having completed its allocated trials, departed to Aston Down on 20th May 1955 for conversion to a C.21 variant.

RAE Transport Flight took on the first of its modern-era communications aircraft in the form of Devon C.1 VP959, when it arrived from Hatfield on 9th March 1949. This aircraft became the longest-serving

example with RAE, operating for 36 years until its last Farnborough flight on 11th December 1985. Although the others were not delivered for a while, the Transport Flight was eventually equipped with four Devon C.1s (VP959, VP975, XG496 and XM223), all later converted to C.2s. The second aircraft to arrive was XG496, which had been built as a Dove 1B and registered as G-ANDX on 28th September 1953 but sold to the Ministry of Aviation on 28th June 1954 and delivered on 21st July for use by Transport Flight. Its last Farnborough communications flight was on 9th September 1985. Devon C.1 VP980 arrived from Defford on 19th October 1956 for use by SME Flight but was transferred to Transport Flight on 27th June 1957, eventually going to ETPS on 21st June 1960.

Another Devon C.1, VP972, had been operating as a communications aircraft from the Royal Radar Establishment since 7th March 1957 but arrived from Pershore for Transport Flight on 28th October 1966. It was allocated to ETPS on 25th August 1967 as a stand-in until Basset CC.1 XS743 became operational. After a period in storage it was struck off charge for spares use on 6th May 1969. Arriving on 19th December 1957 from Hawarden, via Bedford, was Devon C.1 XM223 and this aircraft continued in service until its final return trip to Bedford on 17th January 1986. The last of the stalwart four was VP975, which arrived from Northolt on 2nd November 1959, and remained in service until 21st August 1985 when it undertook its final return flight to Bedford. The four aircraft were replaced in 1985, with the arrival of three Piper PA-31 Navajo Chieftains.

Other aircraft allocated to Transport Flight during 1949 included DH.89 Dominie 1s X7382, NR721 and NR728; Dakota IVs KJ836 and KJ993; Spitfire PR.IV R7034; Anson IX NL200; and Harvard IIB FX238 – all these aircraft being used for communications duties by RAE staff.

Avro Lincolns had been seen at Farnborough since 1946 with RAE and, since shortly after, with ETPS. The Lincolns, like the Lancasters before them, undertook a variety of research and development work with RAE; the type remaining in service at Farnborough until 1961. Some of the uses these aircraft were put to over the years are given in the table opposite.

A Blower Tunnel was built on the Ball Hill side of the airfield. Driven by four Rolls-Royce Merlin engines, this could achieve speeds of up to 250mph, and was capable of being raised or lowered at an angle to enable slipstreams to be directed where required. It remained in use until the late 1970s.

1950

Safety barrier trials for contra-rotating propeller aircraft were undertaken at Farnborough between October and December 1950 with a special raised platform strip, built on the first site of the experimental flexible deck, being utilised for the effects of these aircraft impacting with the safety barrier on board an aircraft carrier. The Seafire F.45s used for this work were basically non-flyers, all being damaged either on the raised platform, falling off it or overshooting the end. Although basic repairs were performed to allow their re-use, they were all eventually written off as a result of these trials. LA442 flew in from Culham on 18th February 1948, LA450 from Eastleigh on 9th April, LA439 from Anthorn on 20th September and LA448, also from Anthorn, on 4th October. The location for these trials was close to Meadow Gate, next to 'Q' shed, with the platform facing in a southerly direction. Once these trials had been completed the strip was removed and the area reverted to an apron dispersal for 'Q' shed, which was later to house the RAE helicopters until the mid-1960s.

An air display was held by the Royal Air Force on Friday 7th and Saturday 8th July 1950, being basically the first post-war RAF display. Many current types were shown, both on the ground and flying. This event was attended by HM King George VI and Queen Elizabeth with Princess Elizabeth (now HM Queen Elizabeth II) and other dignitaries. The static display included Lincoln B.4 RF562; Shackleton GR.1 VP255; Viking VL247; Lancaster B.7 NX773; Valetta C.1 VW860; York C.1 MW319; Washington B.1 WF442; Hornet F.3 PX309; Vampire F.1 TG307; Meteor F.4 EE595; Spitfire LF.16e TE210; Mitchell II FR209; and Prentice T.1 VR228. The many different flying displays included a flypast of 37 Harvard T.2bs in a formation spelling out 'RAF' and then

Examples of Avro Lincoln Trials

B.I RA633	bomb ballistic trials	Armament Flight 1949/1950
B.1 RA637	high-frequency ignition equipment tests	W&E Flight 1946/1948
	Air Traffic Control and UHF development, aerial icing and radio	
	warfare trials 1948/1954	
	to Lasham on 10.3.54 for ground research on aerials	
B.1 RA640	high-altitude bomb ballistic trials	Armament Flight 1950/1951
B.I RE284	multi-wheel undercarriage trials	SME Flight 1951/1952
B.2 RF368	armament trials	Armament Flight 1948/1950
	to Filton on 24.2.50 for Proteus development	
B.2 RF456	bomb ballistic trials	AIEU 1954
	bomb fuze trials	Armament Flight 1957/1958
	struck off charge for spares on 11.9.59	
B.2 RF528	parachute development and target towing	SME Flight 1951/1955
B.2 RF530	Mk.4 autopilot and power-operated controls	Aero Flight 1950
	radio warfare trials	IAP Flight 1951/1954
	to Rolls-Royce as testbed for the RB.109 engine	
B.2 RF533	armament and radar gunsight trials	Armament Flight 1954
	windscreens in rain, armament work	SME Flight 1955/1961
	parachute research and development testing	
	to Stansted on 27.6.61 for the MoA Fire School	
B.2 SS716	matching maps with radar presentations	IAP Flight 1949/1951
B.2 WD125	special dropping trials	Armament Flight 1950
	bombing development and pyrotechnic trials	Armament Flight 1951/1958
B.2 WD129	bombs, marine marker, missile guidance equipment and	
	pyrotechnic trials	Armament Flight 1950/1955
	transferred to the BTU at West Freugh on 7.6.55	
B.2 WD145	experiments with Aircraft Radio Laboratory	Armament Flight 1951
	special armament trials	Weapons Flight 1957
	damaged 15.8.57 landing at Farnborough	

Nene engine testbed Lancastrian C.III VH737 is seen here up against the blower tunnel, where it is undergoing icing tests of the Nene engine during July 1948. The blower tunnel was put to good use over a number of years and ceased operation in the 1980s.
FAST collection

At the Stansted Fire School, shortly after delivery from RAE Farnborough in 1961, is Lincoln B.2 RF533, with its faded Day-Glo markings and its nose modification seen to good effect. This aircraft, having spent some seven years at Farnborough, was delivered to Stansted by air on 27th June 1961 and burnt shortly thereafter.
E Fuller collection

This view from the Farnborough control tower during the morning of 26th April 1950 is taken after a heavy overnight snowfall. The Lancaster I PD137 in the foreground had only arrived from Cosford the day before, to undertake heavyweight parachute trials using Grand Slam with SME Flight. Beyond can be seen an array of aircraft, including a Mosquito, Vikings, Valetta, Lancasters, Sturgeon, Spitfire, Halifax and a USAF C-82 Boxcar. *FAST collection*

another pass to spell out 'GR VI'; a formation of twelve Vampire F.3s from Nos 601 and 604 Sqns; twelve Spitfire F.22s from Nos 610 and 613 Sqns; four Meteor F.4s from No 263 Squadron; and four Hoverfly IIs of the AFEE resembling elephants. There were also airfield attack demonstrations with twelve Vampire FB.5s from Nos 3 and 16 Sqns, including the CGS, hitting 'enemy' tanks, followed by six Vampires making a live rocket attack – which most certainly would not be allowed these days! Then came an airfield attack that included the defence of the airfield in a battle scenario. This involved a bombing attack by Mosquito NF.36s of Nos 23, 141 and 264 Sqns whilst seven Hornet F.3s of No 64 Sqn made a low-

level attack, but these were all intercepted by the 'home' Meteor F.4s of Nos 66 and 92 Sqns and chased off. Five Vampire FB.5s of No 54 Sqn, from nearby Odiham, gave an aerobatic display followed by a number of individual displays by a Canberra B.1 VN850; Hawker P.1081 VX279; Supermarine 510 VV106; and Meteor NF.11 WA546. There was also a staged 'Amiens' attack to represent the famous 1944 raid. Mosquito B.35s of Nos 14 and 98 Sqns escorted by Spitfire F.22s of No 613 Sqn attacked the mock-up prison; although they were hassled by Spitfire LF.16es of Nos 5 and 17 Sqns wearing German crosses and masquerading as enemy fighters. Supplies were dropped from a Hastings C.1 and a Dakota C.4

released a Hadrian glider to land troops. After being loaded with 'rescued' men the Hadrian was snatched off the ground by a Dakota with a hook, two Hoverfly IIs assisting with their rescue.

However perhaps the best was yet to come, at least in sheer numbers, with fly-pasts by six Sunderlands from Nos 201 and 230 Sqns; Dakotas from No 27 Sqn; a Valetta C.1, York C.1 and six Hastings C.1s; 27 Boeing B-29s of the 301 Bomb Group USAF; 47 Lincolns drawn from 14 different RAF squadrons plus an RAAF example; an RCAF Canadair C-54GM North Star; 24 Spitfire F.22s; 16 DH Hornet F.3s; 24 Vampire FB.5s; 24 Meteor F.4s; two Hawker Fury FB.60s of the Pakistan Air Force; six Vampire FB.5s of the French Air Force and 14 Meteor F.4s of the Belgian and Netherlands Air Forces. By all accounts this must have been a superb show to witness – ever get the feeling of being born too late? 'The Aeroplane' magazine had reported this as the 'Display of the Half Century' and it most certainly was. Two months later the same venue would host another superb SBAC display. Those were the days! However, this was the last full-scale RAF display at Farnborough. There had been Empire Air Days previously, and future events were staged as the RAF's participation in the SBAC displays, but never again has there been one like this!

A scale model of a Spitfire was unveiled, being donated by Supermarine as a tribute to RAE pilots for their work in connection with the development of the type.

Technical Training Flight ceased to exist in late 1949 and at a meeting of pilots and staff interested in recreational flying on 15th February 1950 it was decided, as agreed by the Treasury, to set up a flying club similar to that which had been operational in the 1920s as the RAE Light Aeroplane Club. Hence the RAE Aero Club was re-born and it was agreed in principle that negotiations would commence to purchase a Tiger Moth.

A number of Seafire F.45s were fitted with contra-rotating propellers, to investigate impacts with safety barriers. Seen here is LA450, which has fallen off its elevated catapult track, close to Meadow Gate, having been accelerated by catapult into the barrier on 13th November 1950. *FAST collection*

The RAE Aero Club Certificate of Incorporation was granted on 9th December 1950. The first official Aero Club meeting was held on 7th March 1951, the chairman being Group Captain Leonard Snaith of Schneider Trophy fame. Here it was reported that operations had commenced in January 1951 with DH.82A Tiger Moth G-AMCM, which had arrived from Boscombe Down and was housed in a small hangar near ETPS. At a club meeting of 22nd June 1953 committee members considered the offer made by Messrs Reid & Sigrist to present Tiger Moth G-AJHS to the RAE Aero Club free of charge. This offer was taken up, and it arrived from Desford on 30th June 1953. Both Tiger Moths were popular and were the mainstay of the club fleet, G-AJHS continuing until 1979 but G-AMCM was written off in an accident at Somerton on 25th September 1955.

As with other early jet types many Meteors found their way to Farnborough for research and development work whether it be for the airframe, engines, instrumentation, radio equipment, systems or armament. They became the most prolific jet type to serve with RAE, as the broad selection in the table on page 104 demonstrates.

The RAE gave 20th Century Fox permission to use part of the airfield, aircraft and facilities for the filming of *No Highway* during September 1950. Starring James Stewart as Mr Honey, the film was based on the classic book by Neville Shute. On 25th September a take-off and landing sequence was filmed utilising the prototype Gloster E1/44 TX145, which was flown by Sqn Ldr Smyth of Experimental Flying Department.

1951
During this year Experimental Aircraft Servicing Department occupied the following hangars (or sheds): 'A'; 'B', 'C', 'D', 'E', E1, 'G', 'H', 'K1', and 'K2'. 'L' shed followed in 1952 and 'N' shed/Base Workshops in 1954

along with the Ball Hill area in general. Upon the completion of 'N' shed, and utilising the already existing 'D' shed, this area became the main centre for aircraft servicing, installation and modification work which continued until the demise of research flying in 1994. EASD had a work force of approximately 700 personnel during early 1951 and there were no less than 43 different types of aircraft operational at RAE of some 70 different marks, and bear in mind that in some cases there were many aircraft of the same type and mark undertaking different tasks.

Throughout the 1950s, research into many civil aircraft types was undertaken at RAE. The Bristol Brabazon, Scottish Pioneer, Armstrong Whitworth Apollo, Avro Tudor, Handley Page Hermes, Miles Marathon and Saro Princess were some of the airframes being tested, some within the structural test rigs at Farnborough. The Princess, being the largest British aircraft of the time and too big to fit into the rig, was tested as a half-scale aircraft that was placed within the Cathedral test frame in Q153

Thirty-seven Harvard T.2s spell out 'GR VI' in the sky over Farnborough at the 1950 RAF display, which was attended by King George VI. *Author's collection*

Meteor F.3 EE445 arrived from Baginton on 3rd October 1947 for trials with the special Griffiths wing. It continued in this work with Aero Flight until it was declared as scrap on 1st July 1950.
FAST collection

Fitted with Red Hawk (OR.1056 specification) missile mock-ups on the wingtips, for aerodynamic investigation, Meteor F.8 WA982 looks a potent weapon. The missile was later downgraded and became the Pink Hawk and later the Blue Jay. The aircraft is seen here at Farnborough on 6th November 1951, before being dispatched to Boscombe Down for handling trials. The aircraft then passed to Rolls-Royce for Soar engine trials and in 1959 it was converted to a U.16 target drone and was lost in the sea off Llanbedr after a control accident during an unmanned sortie on 9th May 1961.
FAST collection

Examples of Meteor Trials

F.3 EE246	ejection seat parachute development	SME Flight 1949/50
F.3 EE337	arresting, deck-landing and pilot training	Aero Flight 1948/50
F.3 EE351	fire destruction tests of the airframe	1945
F.3 EE403	emergency arrester gear for airfields	Aero Flight 1952/55
F.3 EE445	Griffiths type wing research	Aero Flight 1947/50
F.3 EE454	high-speed flight testing	Aero Flight 1945/48
F.3 EE455	investigation of turbine engine vibration	SME Flight 1947/48
	high-speed low-level photography	IAP Flight 1948/49
	aircraft destructor trials	Armament Flight 1953
F.3 EE476	directional oscillation (snaking) investigation	Aero Flight 1946/52
	emergency arrester gear trials for airfields	NAD 1952/54
F.3 EE519	powered controls and development of artificial feel	Aero Flight 1954/55
F.3 EE522	smoke screening trials	1950/52
	investigation of wake effects on target aircraft	Radio Flight 1952/53
	smoke tests	NGTE Flight 1953/54
T.7 EE530	flight tests of type E auto-pilot	IAP Flight 1949/53
	auto-stabiliser development and target wake investigations	Aero Flight 1953/54
F.4 EE594	effects of precipitation static at high speeds and interference from jet engine exhausts	1947
	physiological effects of high-speed flight	1947/48
F.4 EE597	flight tests of power operated controls	Aero Flight 1947/50
	measurement of take-off and landing distances	1950/51
	cumulo-nimbus cloud investigation	1951/52
F.4 RA424	radar calibration trials	W&E Flight 1950
	investigation of aerodynamic flutter at high speed	Aero Flight 1950/52
	photographic duties in seat ejection trials	1952/53
	ground resonance tests	SME Flight 1953/55
F.4 RA479	investigation of high-lift at high mach numbers	Aero Flight 1948/49
	collision course and skew pursuit attack trials	Armament Flight 1952/53
	fitted with reflectors to test possible use in guided weapon trials	Guided Wpns Flt 1953/54
	drone radio aerial test installation	Radio Flight 1954/55
F.4 RA490	Nene engines, auxiliary stabilising fins, jet deflection system	Aero Flight 1956
F.4 VT108	high-lift at high mach numbers	1948
F.8 VT150	high-speed parachute test work	SME Flight 1954/59
F.4 VT340	guided weapons radar trials and VHF aerial installations	Guided Wpns Dept 1955
F.4 VW302	flutter characteristics of special VHF mast for B.35/46	Radio Flight 1952
F.4 VW303	transition of airflow, meteorological duties, effects of target wake on attacking aircraft	1952/53
FR.9 VW362	rocket development trials	Armament Flight 1951/54
T.7 VW411	continuation training and instrument rating flying	1967/68
T.7 VW412	aero-elastic distortion	Aero Flight 1948/49
	automatic dive brakes in conjunction with stabilising parachutes for ML automatic ejection seats and photographic work	Aero Flight 1950/51
	cumulo-nimbus and clear air gust investigation and spinning research	Aero Flight 1951/56).
NF.11 VW413	non-standard aerodynamic prototype	IAP Flight
	autopilot trials for drone Meteors	1955
T.7 VW414	stabilising parachutes for ML automatic ejection seats and photographic work	SME Flight 1950
T.7 VW441	A I Mk.17, and 'Red Ticket'	Armament Flight 1949/55
	flight tests of instrument systems	IAP Flight, 1958
T.7 VW443		NGTE Flight 1952/53
	guidance and control trials	Guided Wpns Dept 1953/59
T.7 VW470	airborne trials of automatic radar ranging equipment	1949
F.4 VW790	dropping supersonic models for transonic research	Aero Flight 1949/50
	in-flight investigation of collision and skew pursuit attack	Armament Flight 1951/52
F.4 VZ403	transition of airflow at high altitude and meteorological duties	Aero Flight 1952/54
F.8 VZ438	'snaking' trials and development of auto-stabiliser	Aero Flight 1952
	photography for seat ejection trials	SME Flight 1953/54
	investigation of transition at high altitude	Aero Flight 1954/57
	air launching of sleeve and banner targets	SME Flight 1957/60
	parachute opening tests at up to 400kts	SME Flight. 1960/62
	continuation training and general flying practice	Experimental Flying Department 1962/67
F.8 VZ460	fire bomb installation	Armament Flight 1954/55
	parachute testing	SME Flight 1955/56
F.8 VZ473	assessment of modifications to OR.946	IAP Flight 1959/62
T.7 WA690	type E auto-pilot	1954/56
	auto-pilot Mk.12 flight trials	IAP Flight 1956/57
F.8 WA788	'Blue Sky' sighting trials	Guided Wpns Dept 1953/55
F.8 WA982	aerodynamic investigation of Red Hawk mock-ups	1951
	wingtip-mounted RB.93 Soar flight tests	WE Flight 1952
FR.9 WB134	auto-damping tests	Aero Flight 1954/55
NF.11 WB543	A.I. Collimator and a blind predicting gunsight installation	Armament Flight 1952/55
NF.11 WD589	radio clearance of VHF and intercom equipment	Radio Flight 1951
NF.11 WD596	flight trials of ILS system	IAP Flight 1952
NF.11 WD634	'Violet Picture' for stage B approval	Radio Flight 1958
NF.11 WD797	source of compressed air on the ground, for supplying air-jets for rain dispersal tests	1960
F.8 WE919	rocket ballistics 3" and 3¾" OR.1099	Armament Flight 1953/55
	'Blue Sky' sighting trials	Guided Wpns Dept 1955
T.7 WF822	VT fuses for guided weapons	Guided Weapons Dept/ Armament Flight 1955/56
	continuation, conversion + instrument rating flying	Exp Flying Dept 1961/63
	continuation, conversion + instrument rating flying	Exp Flying Dept 1966/67
T.7 WH231	sight development trials	Armament Flight 1954/55
FR.9 WH535	rocket projectile trials	Armament Flight 1953
F.8 WK660	firing trials of Aden guns	Armament Flight 1952/53
F.8 WK878	flight flutter investigations	SME Flight 1953/57
NF.13 WM367	Hispano 5 gun firing trials	Armament Flight 1955
FR.9 WX979	F.95, GX.90, FX.101, FX100, FX.97 Mk.2, FX.99 cameras, infra-red strip light	IAP Flight 1952/58

building for structural fatigue testing. The Princess first flew in August 1952 and the three aircraft built were later cocooned and stored at Calshot. At one stage, during the early 1960s, these aircraft were offered to RAE for use but perhaps the logistics of returning them to flight were just too much as the proposal came to nothing. Not all of the types tested entered full-scale production, but valuable data was acquired throughout all the tests that were performed. Many military aircraft were also tested here, which led to further development and later-generation types, including technological input into some of the aircraft still in service today.

Arriving at Farnborough on 26th April was a specially modified Lancaster III ME540. It had previously been in storage at 5MU, before being flown to the Boulton Paul factory for fitting of a gust-alleviating device for flight tests in connection with the Brabazon I. The specially fitted nose probe carried sensors to detect vertical gusts and pressure changes, while strain gauges were fitted on the mainplane and tailplanes. It undertook many flights from Farnborough, including an overseas detachment to Idris in Libya for trials work. Leaving Farnborough on 8th October 1952 and routing via Tangmere and Istres to Idris, it returned on 29th October 1952 via Blackbushe. It appears that its last flight was made on 13th November 1952.

The Night Photography Section of the Instrument and Air Photographic Department (IAP Flight) was developing a high-altitude night pyrotechnic flash-bomb and, in co-operation with Armament Department, this was intended to improve photo-flashes from altitude. Lincoln B.2 SX974, with a faired-off tail and no bomb doors, arrived on

10th December 1948 from Baginton and modifications were undertaken for this task. Camera development work and the night photography trials were undertaken with IAP Flight, not only in the UK but throughout various overseas deployments, including Australia, but particularly to Cyprus where a photo-mosaic survey was undertaken during November 1951. On completion of its task the Lincoln was dispatched to 20MU at Aston Down on 11th March 1954.

Naval Aircraft Department had proposed an angled deck for carrier operations to allow more safety margin for aircraft recovery and take-off as aircraft speeds were now increasing and the space on deck was becoming more congested as more aircraft were being embarked on ship. A model carrier deck had been built at RAE in the late 1940s and after various refinements and tests this was adopted as standard for all aircraft carriers of the time. Trials were flown by Attacker F.1 WA471, which arrived from South Marston on 12th October 1951 and was detached to Ford from 11 to 13th February 1952 for touch-and-go approaches to be flown with HMS *Triumph* which had an angled deck painted thereon. After further use at Farnborough the Attacker was returned to the manufacturers on 24th July 1953. Visual landing aids were also being researched at this time, with the mirror landing sight being developed by NAD. Trials were conducted in 1952 that proved a great success and they were adopted for installation on all aircraft carriers, the first being in 1955. Sea Vampire F.20 VV151 arrived from Ford on 18th June 1952 for trials of approach aids, airspeed error and stall warning indicators. The aircraft was detached to Ford for deck landing trials on board HMS *Illustrious* during July 1952, and again on 29th September 1952 for trials on board HMS *Indomitable*. After further

work at Farnborough the aircraft was transferred to Ford for 703 NAS.

With the HMS *Warrior* trials completed in 1949, the last stage of the development of the flexible deck, by now given the codename 'Red Rufus', saw a new site built in 1950/1951 at RAE. This was further along runway 25/07 and parallel to it, south of the trees behind the western apron and 'C' shed. It was 400ft long and 80ft wide. Between April 1952 and January 1955, 302 landings were made on it by 23 pilots, utilising the modified Sea Vampire F.21s, and Hawker P.1040 VP413 (the Sea Hawk prototype). The Sea Hawk made its maiden flight from Farnborough on 3rd September 1948, operating from the Hawker Aircraft hangar, but was transferred to RAE for arrester trials that commenced on 11th April 1949. It also spent time at Boscombe Down for landing and assessment trials on board HMS *Illustrious*. Over the next couple of years the Sea Hawk made many demonstration flights on behalf of the manufacturer, interspersed with other trials at Boscombe Down and Farnborough, the latter including flexible deck development. It was returned to

Hawkers at Dunsfold on 13th June 1952 for conversion to the 'mat landing' configuration, returning to Farnborough on 17th July 1953, it undertook many of the flexible deck landing and catapulting trials for Naval Air Department. On 12th November 1953 VP413 was launched from the slotted ventral tube catapult on Jersey Brow and made an undercarriage-less landing on the flexible deck. The aircraft was transferred to RAE Bedford and was struck off charge and broken up during July 1956.

As with other trials of this period, the flexible deck proved successful but the project was abandoned. The deck equipment was dismantled shortly thereafter. Vestiges of both flexible deck sites are still extant today, although the earlier site where the Hotspur gliders were catapulted onto the deck is now under an office block situated adjacent to the Meadow Gate roundabout.

Helicopters had been in service at RAE since the Hoverflys arrived in March 1945 but by now other types were being flown on various trials work. These included the following: Sikorsky S-51 Dragonfly VW209 (ex-G-AJOP), which arrived from Beaulieu on

Sycamore Mk.1 VL958 came to Farnborough for auto-pilot and de-icing trials. It is seen here during September 1952, still with its prototype symbol on the tail boom and its photo-calibration marks on the fuselage. It suffered damage during October 1952 and was reduced to spares. *Rawlings Family collection*

Dispatched to Bristol by 49MU on 8th March 1955, the Sycamore underwent repair and returned to ETPS on 13th July 1955. It was transferred to RAE for SME Flight on 24th September 1956 where research into structural load problems relating to flight in wind gusts and landings; development of test techniques and equipment and general vibration survey was undertaken. The helicopter crashed on take-off at Farnborough on 13th March 1958 and was retained at RAE for spares use.

1952

Tested in the wind tunnel earlier in model form, the Armstrong Whitworth AW.52 (Flying Wing) was undergoing full-scale aerodynamic and laminar flow research at Farnborough during this period. Previously the Armstrong Whitworth AW.52G Glider RG324, a half-scale example of the powered variant, had flown on 2nd March 1945 from Baginton, towed by an Armstrong Whitworth Whitley. It had produced useful aerodynamic data exploring the flight envelope of the tailless configuration, in much the same way as the Pterodactyl had some years earlier. After many flights with the manufacturer, the Airborne Forces Experimental Establishment (AFEE) at Beaulieu and the Aeroplane and Armament Experimental Establishment (A&AEE) at Boscombe Down, the AW.52G arrived back at Baginton on 27th June 1953. The early data obtained from the glider experiments was put to good use and the first powered AW.52 TS363, built to specification E.9/44, made its maiden flight on 13th November 1947 from Boscombe Down, powered by two Rolls-Royce Nene engines of 5,000 lbst. The second example, TS368, took to the air on 1st September 1948, powered by two Rolls-Royce Derwents of 3,500 lbst each. Both were to be seen at the first SBAC display staged at Farnborough in September 1948, the second aircraft having only flown three days before.

TS363 was lost in an accident on 30th May 1949 after suffering violent oscillation in flight. The pilot ejected safely, the aircraft amazingly re-stabilised itself and slowly

10th October 1947 for various related experimental work, including stability and control, with Aero Flight and returned there on 23rd May 1950; Dragonfly HR.3 WG666 arrived from Boscombe Down on 8th October 1952 for WE Flight for trials of aerials, installations and landing lamp equipment, returning there on 10th June 1953. It was to return on 8th January 1954, from Yeovil, for rotor-flow and stability and control trials with Aero Flight and was transferred to RAE Bedford on 1st June 1955.

The prototype Bristol E.34/46 Sycamore VL958 arrived on 21st November 1951 from Boscombe Down for auto-pilot and de-icing trials with Aero Flight but was damaged in an accident on 22nd October 1952 and was subsequently written off as a source of spares. Second prototype Sycamore 1 VL963 (ex-G-ALOU) followed, arriving from Filton on 28th July 1950. It was used for experiments on rotor blades and aerodynamic investigations with Aero Flight before it suffered an accident at Farnborough on 8th September 1953 when the tail and main rotor blades struck the ground during take-

off. Third prototype Sycamore 2 VW905 (ex-G-AJGU) arrived from Filton on 14th October 1953 for general research work but was transferred by road to RAE Bedford for simulated deck movement tests on 18th June 1957. It returned by road on 30th September 1959 for use by Structures Department for structural research and was struck off charge on 20th November 1959.

The prototype Sycamore 3, WA576 (ex-G-ALSS), arrived from Weston-Super-Mare on 28th July 1960 for establishment of structural design and airworthiness criteria for rotorcraft with SME Flight. It was re-allotted on 15th November 1963 for continuation training, conversion training of pilots to rotor wing aircraft, communications and photographic duties. On 5th January 1966 it was dispatched to No 1 STT at Halton for instructional training, it is now with the Dumfries and Galloway Aviation Museum. The final Sycamore to come to Farnborough was Sycamore 3 XH682 (ex-G-ALSR), which was originally delivered to ETPS on 15th October 1954 and suffered a take-off accident at Farnborough on 31st January 1955.

Seen here at altitude is the second AW.52 TS368, which was in use with Aero Flight at Farnborough between 1950 and 1954 for aerodynamic research. Two examples were built, TS363 having crashed on 30th May 1949. *B Kervell collection*

North American F–86A Sabre 49-1296 is seen on the western parking apron on 15th August 1952, the day after it had been overstressed during high-speed flight. The Sabre was the first aircraft from Farnborough to achieve Mach 1. *FAST collection*

descended into a field near Leamington, where it slid along the ground and partly disintegrated. The manufacturer did not undertake any further flying wing development work after this accident. To continue research into the flight envelope, TS368, the remaining aircraft, was dispatched to Farnborough from Bitteswell on 25th October 1950 for use by Aero Flight. It was a fairly common sight in the Farnborough skies as it undertook many flights investigating pressure plotting of the wing, transition measurements and boundary layer experiments. It appears to have made its last flight on 25th November 1952 but was not struck off charge until 10th March 1954 when it was passed to the Proof and Experimental Establishment (PEE) at Shoeburyness.

A North American F-86A Sabre 49-1296 had arrived at Farnborough by December 1951 and was allocated to Aero Flight for stability and control trials of swept-back wings. On 14th August 1952, whilst in high-speed flight, the aircraft was damaged beyond economic repair when the airframe was overstressed. Notwithstanding this the USAF decided that the aircraft was repairable and instructed its return on 13th November 1952. Presumably the airframe left Farnborough in a dismantled state sometime thereafter. In order for the high-speed research trials to continue a further F-86A, 49-1279, arrived from Boscombe Down to replace its unfortunate predecessor on 21st October 1952. This example remained at Farnborough until April 1955, when the USAF instructed that it be flown to Short Brothers & Harland in Belfast. It was during this period that an F-86A was the first aircraft from Farnborough to pass through the sound barrier. There then followed a further Sabre, this time a Canadair Sabre F.4 XB620, which was one of the 370 examples supplied under the Mutual Defence Air Pact to equip RAF Squadrons with the type. This arrived from Kemble on 13th August 1953 and was used for the investigation of aerodynamic effects and armaments at supersonic speeds. It returned to Kemble on 30th August 1955, its research work having been completed.

To give added capacity for supply drop trials a USAFE Fairchild C-82A 45-57784 was

loaned to RAE for use by SME Flight. It arrived from Rhein Main, West Germany on 12th July 1951 and was engaged in supply drops and handling trials before it departed on 19th November 1951 for Erding via Blackbushe and Munich. Another example, 45-57740, was ferried from Rhein Main on 5th December 1951, by the same crew that had returned the previous example. This C-82A was involved in many parachute drops over Salisbury Plain and elsewhere with SME Flight before it was returned to the USAFE on 13th November 1952. On 23rd April 1953, to replace the C-82, a Fairchild C-119C Flying Boxcar, 51-2611, arrived from Rhein Main, via Blackbushe, initially on loan for 12 months but this was later extended. It was used for heavy supply dropping and equipment loading trials, including some overseas detachments with SME Flight. It was also utilised for general load transportation as required by RAE, being the largest and most capable transport aircraft on strength at the time. On 18th September 1956 it departed, callsign 'Nugget 20', bound for the 465 TCW at Evreux, France, having flown some 304 hours on supply drop tasks whilst with RAE.

Supply dropping trials continued for many years utilising Dakota, Lancaster, Halifax, Hastings, Beverley and Andover aircraft.

1953
Proofing trials with Naval Air Department of the catapult launching of a French Breguet BR.960 Vultur, No 02, the precursor of the Breguet BR.1050 Alizé, were undertaken on behalf of NATO. The aircraft positioned from Villacoublay on 4th February 1953 and undertook a total of fifteen catapult launches from Jersey Brow before returning there on 30th April.

Crash barrier research was still ongoing with Naval Aircraft Department at Farnborough and, with more jet aircraft types entering Naval service, various trials were conducted into the effects of the nylon net barriers on the airframe. Attacker F.1 WA483 arrived by road on 27th December 1952 from British Lion Production Assets, and this airframe was used for assessment of damage to the wings. It eventually departed for Arbroath by road on 10th February 1953 where it was used for instructional purposes. Sea Venom NF.20 WK379 arrived from Boscombe Down on 20th May 1954 for

Breguet BR.960 Vultur No 02 came to Farnborough for catapult launching proofing trials with Naval Air Department. It is seen here positioned on one of the Jersey Brow accelerators in February 1953 during its deployment from France. *FAST collection*

barrier engagement trials, but it suffered damage during this work and was struck off charge during January 1956. Arriving by road from RAE Bedford for similar trials on 18th March 1956 was Sea Venom FAW.20 WM503, it too departed Farnborough by road to Arbroath on 2nd October 1957.

Other than aircraft previously mentioned, there was a varied selection of experimental, prototype and pre-production jet aircraft that served at Farnborough during the early 1950s, some only for a short period but others for a longer duration. Avro 707B VX790 arrived at Farnborough for Aerodynamics Flight on 12th September 1952, for investigation by Aero Flight of the stability and characteristics of a delta-wing configuration. This aircraft transferred to the Empire Test Pilots School on 26th January 1956. Avro 707A WD280 arrived at Farnborough on 17th August 1953 for measurement of position error in connection with high-altitude and handling trials with powered controls, returning to Wood-

ford on 14th October 1953. Avro 707A WZ736 arrived at Farnborough on 16th June 1953 for aerodynamic research in respect of problems associated with its delta-wing configuration, later passing to RAE Bedford on 12th September 1955 for automatic speed control tests and automatic approaches. This example actually came back to Farnborough on 24th May 1962, by road, as a spares aircraft for sister-ship Avro 707C WZ744. WZ744 had arrived on 12th January 1956, returning to Woodford on 26th September for fitment of an electrical signalling system. Arriving back on 25th March 1959, the work done had effectively made it the first experimental fly-by-wire aircraft. It was also fitted with an RAE-designed side-stick controller, and, from July 1961, it was engaged in creating and evaluating the manoeuvre demand system. It was last flown during September 1966 and is now to be seen in the RAF Museum at Cosford.

The Boulton Paul P.111A VT935 arrived at Farnborough from Boscombe Down on

24th February 1954 for research by Aero Flight into problems associated with the delta-wing configuration. It passed to RAE Bedford on 16th February 1956. It can now be seen in the Midland Air Museum at Coventry.

The first prototype Sea Venom NF.20, WK376, arrived from Hatfield on 19th May 1951 for arrester and deck assessment trials with Naval Aircraft Department. After a period at Boscombe Down and Hatfield, the aircraft returned on 19th January 1952 for trials with an improved arrester hook damper and, after a further period at Boscombe Down and Hatfield, for catapulting and RATOG proofing trials. It crashed near Frimley Green due to structural failure on 27th August 1952. There then followed the second prototype Sea Venom FAW.20, WK379, which arrived at Farnborough on 24th September 1952 for catapult trials and, after a period at Boscombe Down, returned on 20th May 1954 for barrier trials. This aircraft was damaged in October 1955 during the barrier trials, with the fuselage being allocated to IAP Department and the wings to PEE Shoeburyness. The third prototype Sea Venom FAW.20, WK385, arrived from Hurn on 16th February 1953 for catapult and RATOG trials. It was eventually transferred to RAE Bedford for emergency barrier trials on 15th June 1955.

A French Navy SNCASE Aquilon 201 (No 05, F-WGVT) arrived at Farnborough on 12th October 1954 from Bretigny for proofing trials with the Naval Air Department catapult on Jersey Brow. Four Sea Venom FAW.20s had been supplied to France, being assembled by SNCASE at Marignane. No 05 was the first of the type actually built in France, with short-stroke undercarriage and fitted with ejection seats. The trials work on the catapult proved successful and the Aquilon returned to Marignane on 30th October 1954. Further Sea Venom trials were to take place when an export variant,

Seen on Jersey Brow for catapult proofing trials with Naval Air Department is a French Navy Aquilon 201, no 05 (F-WGVT), fitted with RATOG gear. These trials proved successful, with a number of launches being made during the eighteen days it spent at Farnborough during October 1954. *FAST collection*

FAW.53 WZ894 for the Royal Australian Navy, arrived from the de Havilland factory at Christchurch on 6th February 1955 to undergo catapulting and arrester trials. It departed on 3rd March 1955 for Boscombe Down whence it was to undergo a detachment to Khartoum for tropical trials.

The Canberra B.1 prototype, VN799, first flew on 13th May 1949. It arrived on 11th October 1950 from Warton for autopilot development trials, departing for the AIEU at Martlesham Heath on 4th March 1953. It subsequently crashed at Woodbridge due to failure of both engines. The second prototype Canberra B.1, VN813, arrived from Warton on 12th April 1950 for aerial and communications tests, returning there on 12th May. Canberra B.2 second prototype VX169 arrived from Warton on 22nd April 1953 for the installation and test of automatic 'window' launchers with Radio Flight. It departed for Marshalls of Cambridge on 11th May 1956 for further installation of equipment in respect of high-altitude spectroscopy, investigating propagation of UHF/VHF and high-altitude research, returning to Farnborough on 12th October 1956. It was eventually struck off charge during May 1960, the airframe going to PEE Shoeburyness.

The Gloster E.1/44 TX145 came on 2nd December 1949 from Moreton Valence for handling checks by RAE pilots. It was also used for research into high Mach numbers with Aero Flight. Whilst engaged on braking parachute trials this aircraft was damaged in a wheels-up landing at Farnborough on 15th May 1951, the airframe being dispatched to PEE Shoeburyness. The second example of this type, TX148, came to Farnborough on 14th February 1950 from Moreton Valence and was used for suppressed aerial trials with WE Flight and general handling with Aero Flight until it, too, passed to PEE Shoeburyness.

The Hawker P.1040 Specification N.7/46 prototype VP401 arrived from Langley on 10th March 1949 for catapult trials and performance tests. Having been damaged dur-

ing the accelerator trials, it returned to Hawker Aircraft on 25th April 1949 and was fitted, at the time of repair, with a Snarler bi-fuel rocket motor. It then went to Armstrong Siddeley at Bitteswell during 1950, for tests on the Snarler. It returned from Bitteswell on 16th April 1952 for storage, although during August of that year it was also allocated to Aero Flight for minimum drag flight tests. The second N.7/46, VP413, has been covered previously in this chapter; and the third, VP422, was undergoing trials with the manufacturer at Farnborough during 1950 (Hawker Aircraft rented a hangar at Farnborough, where a lot of their own trials work was undertaken), then passing to Boscombe Down for a period, making its last flight on 20th January 1953 when it suffered a landing accident after the port leg failed to lower. It came back by road on 17th July 1953 for barrier trials. In August 1955 this aircraft was involved in the development of ground resonance test techniques, and was subsequently struck off charge during January 1958.

The Hawker P.1052 VX272 arrived from Langley on 26th April 1949 for general

research flying, but whilst operating with Aero Flight it suffered an engine failure resulting in a forced landing in a farm at Cove on 29th September 1949 and was returned to Hawkers at Kingston for repair. Returning to Farnborough on 5th May 1950, the aircraft was handed over by Hawkers to Aero Flight on 24th May for wing-dropping experiments at high speed and longitudinal stability tests. On 17th July 1950 the aircraft suffered engine failure on approach and crashed into the bicycle sheds near South Gate whilst on approach to runway 25. It was returned by road to the Kingston factory once again on 10th August 1950 for repair. It also made a precautionary landing, due to the undercarriage being stuck in the 'up' position, during September 1951 and was returned to Dunsfold, this time for repair. Deck landing trials were carried out on HMS *Eagle* between 23rd and 27th May 1952, with the aircraft operating from Ford. It then returned to Dunsfold once again to be converted back to standard configuration and was again dispatched to Farnborough on 27th May 1953 for aerodynamic research on swept-wing aircraft. Having completed

Hawker P.1052 VX272 is seen here at Farnborough during 1949, for general research flying with Aero Flight. This aircraft led a somewhat chequered career, including deck landing trials and swept-wing research. It still exists, and is currently in storage with the Fleet Air Arm Museum. *FAST collection*

Seen here on Jersey Brow during September 1950, the third prototype Attacker TS416 is fitted with rocket-assisted take-off gear (RATOG). This aircraft spent four years at Farnborough, undertaking various tasks for RAE Naval Air Department. *FAST collection*

its flying duties, it was sent to 1 STT at RAF Halton on 8th February 1955 for ground instructional purposes. The aircraft is still extant and is stored with the Fleet Air Arm Museum at Yeovilton.

The second Hawker P.1052, VX279, arrived at Farnborough from Boscombe Down on 27th July 1949 for manufacturers' development trials. It was converted as the P.1081, fitted with a new tail unit, and was first flown as such on 19th June 1950. Flight trials continued from Farnborough with the manufacturer, including many demonstration flights. The aircraft subsequently crashed near Ringmer, Sussex on 2nd April 1951 whilst performing a general air test, with the pilot Sqn Ldr T S Wade being fatally injured. The precise cause was never established.

Hawker P.1067 Hunter F.1 WB195, the second prototype, arrived from Dunsfold on 25th October 1954 for barrier and overrun trials on behalf of the Central Fighter Establishment. It departed by road to Henlow on 28th September 1955 becoming 7284M.

The Short SB.5 WG768 first arrived from Boscombe Down on 17th August 1953, after handling trials at both locations it went to Bedford on 5th August 1955 for exploration of flow patterns over highly-swept wings. It was to return to Farnborough, from Bedford via Benson, on 16th December 1965 for use by the Empire Test Pilots School. After retirement in 1968, it entered preservation and can still be seen with the RAF Museum collection at Cosford.

The Vickers-Supermarine E.4/46 510 VV106 arrived at Farnborough from Chilbolton on 13th April 1950 for research into maximum lift and drag at high Mach numbers. This aircraft was basically a tail-wheel-configured prototype for the Swift. It returned to Vickers at Chilbolton for preparation for deck landing trials on 26th July 1950 and returned to Farnborough on 13th October 1950. There then followed many flights using RATOG from Farnborough, Chilbolton and Boscombe Down to prepare

the aircraft and pilots for the next trials. These were to be deck landing and take-off trials to assess the suitability of the aircraft for operation from aircraft carriers. It then made a series of deck landings on board HMS *Illustrious*, being the first swept-wing aircraft to land and take-off from an aircraft carrier on 8th November 1950, although it was damaged on board the carrier on 14th November when it suffered a RATOG failure on take-off – the port wing striking a gun turret. It was returned to Chilbolton after these trials and was subsequently fitted with a variable incidence tailplane. Returning to Farnborough on 26th September 1952, it continued its high-speed research, although it suffered an undercarriage failure and carried out a wheels-up landing on 14th November 1952. It was repaired and arrived back at Farnborough on 3rd September 1953 to continue high Mach number research until it passed to No 1 STT at Halton on 17th February 1955. The second aircraft to specification E.4/46 was originally designated Type 528 with a tailwheel but after modification with a nosewheel in May 1950 became the Supermarine 535. VV119 arrived on 14th September 1953 from Chilbolton to research the effects of carrying guided weapons on swept-wing aircraft. During September 1954 it was engaged in emergency overrun barrier trials on behalf of the Central Fighter Establishment, and eventually went to No 1 STT at Halton, allocated 7285M, on 28th September 1955.

The Vickers-Supermarine N.9/47 Type 508 prototype VX133 first arrived on 29th April 1952 from Chilbolton, and returned on 2nd May. It positioned to Farnborough again on 26th May 1952 and returned to Chilbolton again on 27th May for deck landing trials on HMS *Eagle*. On 17th July 1953 it returned to Farnborough and was engaged in the measurement of loads during arrested landings and was transferred to Bedford during August 1955.

The second N.9/47 prototype, VX136, was dispatched to Farnborough from

Chilbolton on 20th April 1953 for trials in a tail-down landing configuration. It returned on 22nd June 1953 for acceleration trials. Working-up deck trials on board HMS *Eagle* followed during October 1953, but it was returned to Chilbolton on 19th November 1953 and damaged in an emergency landing there on 2nd December 1953. The aircraft was subsequently dispatched to PEE Shoeburyness.

The prototype Vickers-Supermarine E.10/44 Attacker, TS409, arrived by road from Vickers on 26th September 1951 for barrier trials both at Farnborough and on board HMS *Eagle* – being pulled into the barrier by cables. It eventually was allotted A2313 as an instructional airframe and departed by road to Arbroath on 10th February 1952. The third Attacker, TS416, arrived for arrester trials on 27th March 1950 from Chilbolton, but returned to the manufacturer for RATOG fit on 5th May 1950, arriving back on 10th July 1950 to undertake RATOG trials. The aircraft returned to the manufacturer on 18th October 1950 for fitment of a steerable tailwheel and it was flown back to Farnborough on 21st August 1951 to continue its trials. It was subsequently used for ground tests in respect of deflected jet experiments during June 1953 before dispatch to St Merryn for ground instructional use on 12th August 1954.

1954
With the loss of BOAC Comet 1 G-ALYP in the Mediterranean Sea off Elba, Italy, on 10th January, followed by a second example, G-ALYY, off Naples on 8th April, a major investigation was launched to determine the cause of their losses. Many parts of the aircraft from the first accident were salvaged and brought back to Farnborough, where the Accidents Investigation Branch and RAE Structures Department conducted a massive investigation, which included the building of a large water tank by Braithwate & Co during April/May 1954 for cabin pressure fatigue testing. The water tank and its reservoir were located on the southern boundary of the airfield, behind the Empire Test Pilots School hangar, now the site of the headquarters of BAE Systems. The Comet wreckage was re-assembled, as much as possible, by the AIB / RAE Structures Department: this being undertaken in a hangar that was used by Structures Department for aircraft investigation at the time. The tests undertaken in the water-pressure tank, which simulated air-frame pressurisation, showed that the struc-

With much of the wreckage recovered from the Mediterranean Sea, BOAC Comet 1 G-ALYP has been reconstructed in a temporary hangar at RAE, where an extensive investigation is in process during July 1954. Much of the wreckage has been reconstructed around a special frame in order to piece the parts together, this method being still used today for investigation purposes by the AAIB. *FAST collection*

ture failed because of fatigue around the aerials and window frames of the fuselage. With the conclusions reached, modifications were undertaken to the remainder of the Comets and incorporated into new-build examples, where this failure did not manifest itself again. Other water tank facilities followed, including those for the Britannia and Herald aircraft where trials were conducted which provided information on the structures of these pressurised airliners, the tanks remaining in use until 1963. Some structural test frames were also built in this locality where other airframes were also tested.

As the investigations progressed various Comet 1 airframes found their way to Farnborough for structural analysis by RAE Structures Department. The prototype, G-ALVG, was placed within the structural test facility in Q153 building during June 1954, and tested until a wing failure in August 1954. G-ALYU was placed within the water tank on 19th May 1954 where tests continued unceasingly until a failure occurred in the fuselage adjacent to the forward escape hatch. A new section was inserted and testing continued, but wing cracks appeared and further repairs were made, before the fuselage was again torn open when the structure failed on 24th June 1955. The tank was drained and the airframe inspected in detail. The investigators and structural engineers saw what they had suspected, a massive rupture of the skin had occurred, emanating from a rivet hole below a window. ended on 10th August 1954. G-ALYR was also used for water-tank tests during 1955/1956 until failure of the structure occurred. The wings of Comet 1A F-BGNX, which had flown in from Hatfield as G-AOJT, were also used for structural testing.

These fuselages and others were later cocooned and stored on the Ball Hill site, forming a familiar part of the Farnborough landscape well into the 1960s.

DH.106 Comet 1 Arrivals:
- G-ALVG (by air 31.7.53) fatigue tests 6.54 to 8.54; scr late 1956
- G-ALYR (by road 6.55) fatigue tests 1955/1956; scr 1960s

Short SA.4 Sperrin VX158 is seen here over Farnborough in 1955, whilst undergoing navigation and bombing system research with Armament Flight. *FAST collection*

- G-ALYS (by air 14.4.54) fuelling and jet efflux trials; scr early 1960s
- G-ALYU (by road 5.54) fatigue tests 5.54 to 6.55; fuselage to Cardiff
- G-ALYW (by road 6.55) cocooned 1956; to Bicester 1969 as a travelling Nimrod nose marked as 'XV238'
- G-ALYX (by road .55) cocooned 1956; fuselage to Lasham 1969
- G-ALZK (by road 4.57) stored until early 1960s; aerial trials; equipment test airframe for Comet IV, fitted with a donor nose and tail, 1969; to Woodford early 1970s
- G-ANAV (by air 24.5.54) experimental flying 23.6.54 to 10th August 1954; static tests 1954/1955; nose to Science Museum 1962
- G-AOJT (by air 27.6.56) fuselage cocooned 1957; to Mosquito Aircraft Museum at London Colney 17.3.85

The transonic wind tunnel (R133 building) was rebuilt and modified from the original 10ft x 7ft section during 1954. It was returned to operations during late 1955, with a reduced working section of 8ft x 6ft and new 12,000hp electric motors that gave an increase in speed to Mach 1.24. Many more models of fighters, bombers and airliners, as well as weapons and the like, were tested in this tunnel, it being in continual use until 1991 when bombs were being tested for aerodynamic research. This is now a Grade II Listed building, as is R136 building, and will be refurbished as part of the new Heritage Centre on the former RAE site. A further wind tunnel, a smaller 2ft x 1ft 6in transonic tunnel, was built in 1954.

Continuing with rotary-wing research, Sikorsky S-55 Whirlwind HAS.22 WV202

ROYAL AIRCRAFT ESTABLISHMENT, FARNBOROUGH.

AIR SURVEY SECTION. I.AP R.AE.   A.S. 123. 23-4-53.

Aerial view of the RAE, taken by the Air Survey Section of Instrument and Photographic Department, on 23rd April 1953, showing the extent of the airfield, the industrial site and the surrounding environs. Much recent work to the airfield facilities can be seen. *FAST collection*

arrived from Yeovil on 12th May 1954 for IAP Flight to undertake trials on auto-controls and an early autopilot system. In October 1958 it was re-allotted for trials to determine the stability of a Black Knight separating head at subsonic speeds. The helicopter crashed at Farnborough on 11th December 1958 due to tail rotor drive shaft failure. Whirlwind HAR.1 XA871 arrived from Yeovil on 25th October 1954 for Sea Slug guidance receiver trials with Guided Weapons Department but was transferred to Brawdy on 15th August 1955 to continue these trials on the Aberporth range. Whirlwind HAR.1 XA864 arrived at Farnborough from Boscombe Down on 12th January 1959 to resume the Black Knight trials that the unfortunate WV202 had started. In June 1959 it was re-allotted for research into landings to check the touchdown rate of descent meter and in October 1960 it was re-tasked with IEE Flight to investigate the location and identification of submarines using a magnetic detector. It was next dispatched to RAE Bedford on 3rd February 1965 to undertake an assessment for preliminary investigations into V/STOL operations from restricted sites. It was withdrawn from service in 1969 and dispatched to the FAA Museum on 3rd March 1970, where it is still held in storage.

Rocket Test Vehicle 1, an RAE development, shot down a target aircraft over the Cardigan Bay range, this being the first demonstration of a missile firing for anti-aircraft use. RAE also assisted in the development of Sea Slug, Thunderbird, Bloodhound, Sea Cat, Firestreak, Red Top, Sea Dart and Sea Skua missiles over the years.

The Royal Aircraft Establishment Armorial Bearings (Coat of Arms) was granted to the Establishment by the College of Arms during this year. The blazon reads: '*Azure a Key in pale wards downwards Or on a Chief embattled of the last a Mural Crown between on a dexter a Naval Crown and on the sinister an Astral Crown of the first and for the Crest Out of an Astral Crown Or a Pterodactyl displayed proper Mantled Azure doubled Or as the same are in the margin hereof more plainly depicted*'.

Scientific research into space began in 1954, with the design of a rocket to fly at high altitudes of 50 miles or more. Skylark was born out of this early research and from that came the scientific payload carried on the six satellites launched between 1962 and 1979. Inter-continental ballistic missiles were being assessed by Guided Weapons Department during this period and a study was being undertaken into the use of satellites for reconnaissance purposes. In the late 1950s, whilst Blue Streak was being built, Black Knight, designed by RAE and built by the Saunders-Roe Division of Westlands, was being developed under the control of RAE Space Department. In 1960, Blue Streak was cancelled as a missile but was retained as the first stage of the ELDO satellite launchers that were developed during this period. Black Arrow was eventually cancelled during 1971, although it made a successful launch of the Prospero satellite during October 1971 from Woomera, Australia.

The prototype Short SA.4 Sperrin VX158 made its first flight on 10th August 1951 from Aldergrove, followed by the second example, VX161, on 12th August 1952.

VX158 was used for navigation and bombing system research, with an advanced H2S Mk.9 radar and electrical-mechanical computers, as part of the Optical Aiming System. The second example, VX161, came to RAE on 20th September 1954 and was used to investigate bomb ballistics, and dummies of the 'Blue Boar' (a free-fall TV-guided bomb) and 'Blue Danube' (atomic weapon) were carried for essential research in respect of the forthcoming 'V' force, these trials being undertaken by Armament Flight. During 1956 VX158 was used as a testbed for the de Havilland Gyron engines but at the end of the Gyron project it was sold to the engine manufacturer on 21st September 1959 and scrapped. In 1955 VX161 was part of the RAE display on the 'A' shed tarmac, fitted with a dummy 10,000 lb bomb. It returned to Shorts at Belfast on 16th July 1956 and was scrapped in 1958.

At the beginning of this year, the RAE had the following departments: Aerodynamics, Armament, Armament and Instrument Experimental Unit, Carrier Equipment, Chemistry, Electrical Engineering, Experimental Flying, Guided Weapons, Instrument, Instrument and Photographic, Mathematical Services, Mechanical Engineering, Metallurgy, Naval Aircraft, Radio, Rocket Propulsion and Structures. Most were further divided into Sections under the main departmental heading.

Over the past couple of years, Guided Weapons Department had been building an electronic-hydraulic calculating machine, or simulator, called 'Tridac' (Three Dimensional Analogue Computer) in a building adjacent to R134. This was quite an achievement and it was the largest calculating machine in the UK and could deal with problems in which a radar beam on an aircraft flying under autopilot moves with complete freedom in any direction and space. Tridac occupied 6,000ft^2 of floor space, used 8,000 valves and, whilst operating under peak condition, absorbed approximately 650 kilowatts from the mains power supply. Consequently Tridac could calculate the forward speed of an aircraft, its position, engine thrust, variation in direction of flight, detection of radar transmission signals from an aircraft, all these calculations being done on a 'real time' basis, thus creating useful research and specialised information gained for the future air combat scenario of aircraft and missile development.

METEOROLOGICAL RESEARCH FLIGHT

Probing the Atmosphere

Another of Farnborough's long-standing lodger units, until its departure in October 2003, had been the Meteorological Research Flight (MRF). It was, until recently, part of the Meteorological Office, who had their headquarters in nearby Bracknell for many years,.

In 1927 an early Meteorological Research Flight had been established at RAF Duxford but, mainly due to lack of specialised equipment, it was soon disbanded. Notwithstanding this early attempt to assist in weather research, there was by now a need for accurate forecasting for combat operations in World War Two, this being of considerable importance, particularly over the Atlantic Ocean. The Meteorological Research Committee was established in November 1941 to research into meteorological sciences. At this point it was thought a good idea to establish local meteorological reconnaissance flights at various RAF stations in the UK, to give an accurate picture of the weather situation over the whole of the country. Some flights were formed which led to a marked improvement in actual and

forecast conditions, using current RAF aircraft such as the Spitfire. In fact it was not until the early 1960s that the RAF Temperature and Humidity (THUM) Flight at RAF Woodvale, with its Mosquitos, disbanded.

In August 1942, the Meteorological Research Committee formed a High Altitude Flight (HAF) at Boscombe Down under the leadership of Dr A W Brewer. Initially the aircraft used were two Boston IIIs – AL480 joined A&AEE on 12th August and departed on 18th July 1943 while AL481 arrived on 29th August 1942 and departed on 14th July 1943; Spitfire VI BR287, which appears to have been used by 1401 Met Flight and 521 Met Sqn and was probably on loan to the HAF; and Hudson VI FK406, which arrived at Boscombe Down on 14th February 1944 and operated for seven months. None of them were considered too successful. Initially the HAF investigated the atmospheric conditions favouring the formation of contrails, as high-flying aircraft were giving their positions away to the enemy by the production of condensation trails. Furthermore measurement of temperature and humidity,

Seen parked on the grass near Jersey Brow on 28th May 1948 are two of the Meteorological Research Flight aircraft: Mosquito PR.34 VL621 and Halifax Met.6 ST817. These were the first two aircraft in use with the MRF, both arriving at Farnborough during 1946. *FAST collection*

which saw the early aircraft fitted with various specialised instrumentation, was also commenced. Mosquito XVI MM174 joined the HAF on 18th August 1944 but suffered an accident on 5th May 1945 and was not repaired. It was followed by a B-17E Flying Fortress IIA, FK192, which arrived on 11th June 1943 and served until 28th September 1944. This aircraft was installed with updated equipment and, for the first time, accurate samples and measurements could be taken from the upper stratosphere.

Following the scientific success of the HAF the Meteorological Research Flight (MRF) was formed during September 1946 at Farnborough with the main task of advancing meteorological science, but continuing to provide advice and collect data as

Seen here during 1949, Halifax Met.6 ST796 is seen dropping 'window' at altitude, whilst undertaking experiments from Farnborough in 1949. This aircraft was used for humidity investigations, research into rain and shower clouds and artificial nucleation of clouds, the latter probably being one of the experiments shown here. *via G Allen*

Metrological Research Flight Mosquito PR.34 RG248, is seen parked on the 'A' shed apron during September 1951. This aircraft was modified with a spectrometer reflector sight, positioned on the port side, just forward of the roundel, as seen here, and the aircraft would fly with the sun behind it, gathering data on the sun's rays through the reflector panel. An observer would be positioned within the rear fuselage, to operate this equipment. This aircraft was also used for investigation of rain clouds, hygrometers and humidity tests. *via G Allen*

Nose of Hastings C.1 TG618, seen here during September 1954, with various sensor and probe appendages for gathering meteorological data. This aircraft was later fitted with a detachable long nose probe and a chin-mounted weather radar. *FAST collection*

required on weather-related problems of aircraft design and operation. The first aircraft for the newly formed Flight, Mosquito PR.34 VL621, arrived at Farnborough from St Athan on 21st September 1946 and continued in service until its departure to Hullavington on 8th June 1955. Halifax MET.6s ST817 and ST796 arrived from Edzell on 4th October and 5th November 1946 respectively, while another Mosquito PR.34, RG248, arrived from Silloth on 17th December 1946 and remained with the Flight until May 1954. Thus the early Flight was complete with its four aircraft and work continued in much the same way as the HAF had done previously. The Halifaxes were used for Mk.II Hygrometer research, boundary layer studies, humidity investigations, construction of cumulus clouds, cloud nuclei measurements, artificial nucleation of clouds, cloud temperature and particle research, and rain cloud investigations. The Mosquitos were utilised for Mk.II Hygrometer research, high-level ascents, spectrometer trials, low-level and tropopause humidity investigations, high-level turbulence research, and pitch and yaw studies. Both these types were specially instrumented to undertake the necessary research, with the Mosquitos generally used

for high-altitude work whilst the Halifaxes maintained a lower altitude research profile. Mosquito PR.34 VL621 was fitted with an early infra-red radiometer and provided data on radiation within the troposphere. An additional Halifax Mk.III, HX246, joined the Flight from Radlett on 30th June 1948. This aircraft was initially used by SME Flight on thermal de-icing trials but crewed by the MRF. It departed on 27th April 1949 for Boscombe Down where it was used as a ground test rig for a thermal de-icing system. Mosquito PR.34 RG205 arrived from Lichfield on 15th August 1949 to operating with the MRF for four weeks. A further Mosquito PR.34A, PF673, arrived from Llandow on 19th October 1949. This aircraft undertook research into high-level ascents and cumulus cloud properties, departing for Benson on 31st January 1951.

In 1950 the original two Halifaxes departed: ST817 to High Ercall on 12th September and ST796 to Aston Down on 13th November. They were replaced by a pair of Hastings C.1s: TG619 from High Ercall on 21st July and TG618 from Aston Down on 3rd August. The Hastings were used for a variety of cloud physics research, including raindrop micropores, raindrop size, cloud water content, humidity and thermometer tests. TG619 was fitted with various sensors including hygrometers, thermometers and aerosol detectors, as well as a long nose probe. This research led to a better understanding into rain droplet-producing clouds and associated ice particles.

Hastings C.1 TG619 was transferred to the RAE fleet on 20th April 1955. Its replacement, Varsity T.1 WJ906, arrived from Sywell on 6th May 1955 and was fitted out with much internal equipment. The second Hastings C.1, TG618, was converted to carry weather radar, housed in a chin radome, which resulted in the Meteorological scien-

Canberra B.2 WJ582 arrived for the MRF during 1953 and undertook a variety of high-altitude research work. It is seen here at Farnborough, painted in a light blue scheme, parked on the dispersal area in front of 'A' shed during September 1956. Unfortunately it was lost in an accident on 21st February 1962. Note the sampling probes beneath the nose. *FAST collection*

Hastings C.1 TG618 is seen here on the western apron at Farnborough during 1966. This aircraft was used for a variety of meteorological experiments and it served with MRF at Farnborough from 1950 until 1967. In this view the weather radar has been removed. *Author's collection*

tists receiving valuable and accurate data of weather features.

The buildings initially occupied by the newly formed MRF were positioned on the southeast area of the airfield at the foot of the hill where the SBAC now have their site. They were moved in the early 1950s to pre-fabricated huts close to the RAE Control Tower and during the early 1960s they moved into a purpose-built brick building (Y46) in the Ball Hill area of the airfield site, where they were based until moving to Exeter on 3rd October 2003, along with the Meteorological Office from Bracknell, to a new modern headquarters building.

On 24th July 1953 Canberra B.2 WJ582 arrived from Radlett, and this aircraft soon became tasked with the high-altitude research work, including ozone sampling and radioactive particle sampling from atmospheric fall-out following nuclear testing in the USA and USSR. By now MRF aircraft were being tasked for overseas deployments around the globe for cloud research, monsoon, storms and pollutant sampling; the first deployment being the Canberra to Khartoum, Sudan.

WJ582 departed from Farnborough as 'Nugget 72' on 20th February 1962 bound for RAF Leuchars from where it was to operate on various trials. However on the following day, when returning from an Arctic stratospheric sampling mission, the pilot lost control and the aircraft hit the sea during approach to Leuchars in bad weather, coming to rest on the beach. The loss of this aircraft was a setback to the research programme and resulted in temporary curtailment of the high-altitude work until a replacement aircraft, Canberra PR.3 WE173, arrived from Samlesbury on 12th November

1962. This Canberra became distinctive in that it was fitted with a long instrumented nose probe, capable of taking sample measurements of the undisturbed air forward of the aircraft, and carrying wind vanes directly linked to the aircraft inertial navigation system. This aircraft became a useful asset to the MRF as it was deployed on many overseas detachments for research into clear air turbulence phenomena. A Selective Chopper Radiometer was later installed in this aircraft and it conducted overseas research into the sampling of radiation absorption from tropical climatic conditions.

Seen lined up along Wellington Way, the western taxiway at Farnborough, during May 1964 is the entire Metrological Research Flight complement of Canberra PR.3 WE173, Varsity T.1 WJ906 and Hastings C.1 TG618. These three types were the mainstay of the MRF fleet during the 1960s/1970s. *FAST collection*

Varsity T.1 WF425 of the Meteorological Research Flight is seen on the western apron at Farnborough during August 1974, wearing an MRF badge just aft of the cockpit. This aircraft was used for various trials throughout the 1970s, including dropsonde sensors, until its retirement to the Imperial War Museum at Duxford on 20th May 1975. Note the sampling probes under the nose.
FAST collection

Seen lined up along the 18/36 runway is the Meteorological Research Flight complement during April 1975. Hercules W.2 XV208 had arrived at Farnborough on 3rd January 1974 and the Varsity T.1 WF425 was shortly to be delivered to Duxford for the IWM, whilst Canberra PR.3 WE173 was retired on 31st March 1981.
via B Kervell

Dropsonde equipment was developed in the 1960s, and accordingly was fitted to Hastings C.1 TG618 and, later, Varsity T.1 WF425. It consisted of a metal capsule containing sensors and a radio transmitter that descended on a parachute from the aircraft, enabling various measurements and recordings to be taken that were transmitted directly to a computer on board the aircraft. During the mid-1960s the three MRF aircraft were actively engaged in atomic radiation sampling, upper atmosphere research including clear air turbulence, the latter involving overseas deployments to Entebbe, Uganda and Australia, as well as general atmospheric recording and analytical duties.

Hastings C.1 TG618 was retired in 1967 and Varsity T.1 WJ906 was dispatched to Kemble on 19th September 1969. Replaced by another Varsity, WF425, which arrived on 24th March 1970 from Kemble, the MRF now had just two aircraft: the Varsity and Canberra PR.3 WE173. The 'new' Varsity was fitted with an abundance of meteorological equipment and was usefully employed in the dropping of radiosonde capsules for the measurement of temperature, humidity and wind conditions associated with warm front conditions, along with other research duties.

In the early 1970s, with the Varsity nearing the end of its useful life, consideration was given to a replacement aircraft. A standard RAF Lockheed Hercules C.1, XV208 that had previously served with No 48 Sqn, was selected to become probably the most capable and advanced metrological research aircraft in the world. At Marshalls of Cambridge it underwent much modification, its conversion spanning a period of some 2½ years. These modifications included a 22ft-long extended nose boom, profiled to the forward nose bulkhead where the weather radar was previously positioned. The weather radar was re-positioned within a pod mounted above the cockpit. A Dropsonde ejector system was built into the rear loading ramp, although this was later modified and relocated to the rear of the cabin, whilst various other items of meteorological measuring and sensing equipment were fitted in numerous areas around the fuselage, nose and within the underwing pods fitted outboard of the No 1 and No 4 engines. Various other installations were fitted, including cameras and computer workstations for the onboard scientists, along with a special 'van' that was designed for installation in the cabin, to house the meteorological scientists plus their recording and monitoring equipment. This was a removable cabin, but in fact was rarely removed, perhaps only when a major overhaul of the airframe was being undertaken. The plethora of equipment installed in this aircraft certainly made this Hercules a very valuable aerial platform, a task that it took in its stride. These modifications led to official re-designation as a Hercules W.2. Less formally, it soon gained the nickname 'Snoopy', which stuck right to the end of its useful life, although the names 'Trunky' and 'Pinnochio' also referred to this aircraft.

Seen shortly before its retirement, the MRF Canberra PR.3 WE173 was operating an air-to-air photographic sortie with Hercules W.2 XV208 on 10th March 1981. Note the distinctive 'Barber's pole' nose probes on both aircraft. *FAST collection*

The specially adapted Hercules undertook its maiden flight from Cambridge on 21st March 1973. It then went to A&AEE at Boscombe Down for handling and release to service trials on 8th June 1973, before it returned to Marshalls for a brief period. It was delivered to the MRF at RAE Farnborough on 3rd January 1974 from Cambridge. 'Snoopy' was to be based at Farnborough for the next twenty years. After initial acceptance trials and crew training, the aircraft was deployed on its first overseas experimental sortie on 24th June 1974, when it left for Dakar, Senegal, as part of the Global Atlantic Tropical Experiment (GATE).

Varsity T.1 WF425 remained in use until retired on 20th May 1975, when it flew to Duxford for the Imperial War Museum. Canberra WE173 made its last flight on 31st March 1981 and was dispatched to Coltishall on 4th March 1982 for fire practice, thus leaving the MRF with the Hercules W.2 as its sole aircraft for all tasks, although no high-altitude work was to continue.

Capable of carrying two pilots, a navigator, flight engineer and loadmaster, plus up to fourteen scientists, 'Snoopy' soon became used for a variety of meteorological research tasks including cloud physics, boundary layer and turbulence studies, temperature latitude weather systems, satellite calibration, atmospheric turbulence chemistry, atmospheric radiation, and various other weather related phenomena and hazards, plus pollution sampling which included the effects of 'acid rain'. For some of these tasks further modifications were undertaken and other external sampling probes were fitted. By the early 1980s the aircraft had become a very capable weather reconnaissance platform, arguably the best in the world, and probably the most comprehensively instrumented meteorological aircraft anywhere. The demand for research work was by now increasing, so much so that overseas deployments were now commonplace.

Throughout the twenty years 'Snoopy' graced Farnborough, the aircraft visited many faraway, and not-so-faraway, places:

1978/9	Gibraltar and Dakar, Senegal for METEOSAT calibration work
1980	Gibraltar for volcanic dust sampling from Mount St Helens
1983	Bermuda for microwave sounding trials
1983	Machrihanish for investigation into frontal structures
1985	Bodø, Norway for polar lows research
1987	San Diego, California for marine stratocumulus trials
1988	Dakar, Senegal for water vapour research
1990	Trondheim, Norway for development of instruments
1990	Oulu, Finland for studies on microwaves
1990	Crete, Greece continuing with water vapour research

Seen about to depart from Farnborough on 24th March 1994, to relocate to Boscombe Down, is the MRF Hercules W.2 XV208. The area of trees is where the Farnborough control tower is now situated. *Falcon*

1991   Bahrain for sampling Kuwait oil smoke plumes after first Gulf War for radioactive properties and environmental impact

1991   Trondheim, Norway and the Ascension Islands for ERS-1 satellite calibration validation and wind research

1992   Santa Maria, Azores for marine stratocumulus research

1993   Honiara, Solomon Islands for studies into humidity fluxes

1993   Halifax, Canada for research into ozone production

1993   Rabat, Morocco

1993   Prestwick for research into cirrus cloud formations

1994   Tenerife, Canaries for experiments with small cumulus clouds

During these years much work was also conducted into various atmospheric and meteorological conditions that did not require deployments away from base. Indeed after 'Snoopy' was relocated to Boscombe Down on 24th March 1994 (changing ownership from the RAF to the MRF in 1995 and becoming part of the DERA fleet in 1998), a further thirty overseas deployments were accomplished, the very last being to Tromsø, Norway, for polar research, radiation, rain and atmospheric sampling. Upon its return from this trip on 29th March 2001 'Snoopy' was retired, with a total flying time of 14,123 hours, which is considered low by comparison with the remaining first-generation Hercules in the RAF fleet, thus bringing to an end 28 years of service with the MRF. After a period of storage, during which the Royal Netherlands Air Force expressed an interest, 'Snoopy' left Boscombe Down on 27th April 2005 for Marshalls of Cambridge, where the W.2 conversion had been undertaken 32 years ago. Reconfigured as a normal Hercules again, Marshall Aerospace will

convert it as a flying testbed for development of the Europrop International TP400-D6 11,000shp engine for the Airbus Military A400M freighter. The engine, along with the all-new eight-bladed Ratier-Figeac propeller, will be mounted on the port inner (No 2) position and will undergo flight trials late in 2006 ahead of anticipated certification due in late 2007.

No longer do the MRF have their own dedicated aircraft as it has been replaced with converted BAe146-301 G-LUXE, which is based at Cranfield. It is owned by BAE Systems on a ten-year lease deal, and operated by Directflight in the meteorological and environmental research role. During August 2001 the Meteorological Office, Natural Environment Research Council (NERC) and the University communities established a

joint venture called the Facility for Airborne Atmospheric Measurements (FAAM) to share the management and operation of a new airborne research aircraft. The aircraft has been fitted with many external appendages and sensor/sampling equipment as well as onboard data processing and recording systems and is shared on a 50/50 basis between the Meteorological Office and the NERC.

Many different aspects of meteorological research had been covered by the MRF, their findings bringing many benefits to the Meteorological Office, and other organisations, as they advanced and enhanced weather forecasting and climate prediction. Throughout their 57 years of operations at Farnborough, and later Boscombe Down, they have played a significant role in their dedicated research tasks.

Wearing DERA markings that were applied during 1998, along with the Meteorological Office emblem on its tail, Hercules W.2 XV208 made its last operational flight on 29th March 2001 and was then placed in storage at Boscombe Down. It is seen there on 23rd May 2001 with ETPS Andover C.1 XS606, another ex-RAE aircraft, beyond. The Hercules finally departed from Boscombe Down on 27th April 2005, bound for Marshall Aerospace of Cambridge, where it will be used as a flying testbed for engine development of the Airbus Military A400M freighter. Its extended nose probe and weather radar have now been removed. *Falcon*

1955 to 1964

More Sophisticated Weapons and Systems

Again much had happened at Farnborough during the past decade: jets had now come into their own, many different and sometimes obscure trials had taken place, further aircraft types had arrived and all in all Farnborough had become a busy place once again.

This decade would see more research into high-speed flight, paving the way for supersonic military and passenger flights, development of more rotorcraft technology, carbon fibre materials, early computers and space research.

1955

The Naval Aircraft Department at Farnborough moved to Bedford, into what was to have become the National Aeronautical Establishment (NAE). However, this did not materialise and the airfield at Thurleigh became known as the Royal Aircraft Establishment, Bedford. RATOG work was still ongoing at Farnborough with Hawker Sea Fury and Westland Wyvern, although this also included de Havilland Sea Venom and Hawker Sea Hawk aircraft before the work was transferred to Bedford. Progressively over the next two years all Naval research and the NAD assets were transferred from Farnborough to Bedford.

Varsity T.1 WL674 arrived at Farnborough for Radio Flight from Moreton Valence on 14th April 1954 for airborne equipment trials of the passive radar warning receiver 'Yellow Barley', the Mk.5 radio altimeter, AYF (an early version of an American frequency-modulated radio altimeter), ILS and radio compass. During 1961 it was equipped with a data transmission system, TACAN and an interferometer. A year later, it was trialling radio landing aids and an approach and guidance radiation pattern system and aerials, and in 1964 it was being used for tests of a take-off monitor. The air-

craft was released from research tasks on 31st March 1965 and went to the Fire Service Training School at Stansted on 16th February 1966. Another Varsity T.1, WJ937, had already arrived at Farnborough, being flown in from 20MU Aston Down on 10th February 1955 for navigation and autopilot development with IAP Flight. It was dispatched to Ferranti at Edinburgh for fitment of 'Blue Study' on 29th August 1955, returning to Farnborough on 11th October. During July 1957 it was re-allotted for flight tests of a Kelvin and Hughes azimuth gyro and a Ferranti gyro and these trials continued until 16th May 1958 when the Varsity was transferred to ETPS. It departed for major servicing with Brooklands Aviation at Little Staughton on 25th October 1961 as 'Tester 14'. It did not return to Farnborough until 23rd May 1968 when, replacing WL679, it continued the automatic approach and landing trials with a coupled autopilot system that it had been engaged in with the Blind Landing Experimental Unit at RAE Bedford. Its career ended on the fire dump at Llanbedr, being struck off charge on 12th December 1969.

On 2nd July 1954 Meteor F.4 RA479 arrived at Farnborough from 38MU at Llandow to join Radio Flight for testing of a drone radio aerial installation. This was the forerunner of the full U.15 drone programme and during January 1955 the first proof of concept flight took place from Farnborough. RA479 left on 2nd March 1955 for full U.15 drone conversion at Flight Refuelling's facility at Tarrant Rushton and the eventual and inevitable shooting down over the Cardigan Bay range whilst operating from RAE Llanbedr. During 1952/53 Radio Department had evaluated a number of Firefly U.8s, converted by Fairey Aviation from the AS.7 variant. WJ147, WJ149, WJ150, WJ151, WJ152 and WJ153 were sent to Farnborough to test the special equipment on board for drone development, albeit being flown with a safety pilot on board. These were the precursors of the pilotless drone types employed over many years at RAE Llanbedr and the Weapons Research Establishment (WRE) at Woomera, Australia.

On 13th January 1955 the ungainly Rolls-Royce Thrust Measuring Rig, more commonly known as the 'Flying Bedstead',

RATOG trials were still ongoing at Farnborough, although this work was shortly to be transferred to RAE Bedford. Here on the 'A' shed tarmac during May 1954 is Wyvern AS.4 VZ776, which arrived at Farnborough from Merryfield on 23rd September 1953 to undergo catapult, RATOG and arresting trials. It is seen here with the RATOG gear installed beneath the fuselage, and also carrying 16 rockets beneath its wings. *FAST collection*

Aerial view of the water-pressure tank at Farnborough, in March 1955, with Comet 1 G-ALYU installed therein. The tank was filled with water, both in and around the fuselage. With all openings sealed, a pressure differential was then created, simulating both flight and static loads. *FAST collection*

VP546 was allocated in May 1946 and it made its first flight with this identity on 15th May. It was initially engaged in landing distance experiments with Aero Flight, which included deck landings on board HMS *Triumph* on 28th May 1946 flown by Lt Cdr E Brown. The Storch made an excellent glider-towing aircraft and from 1946 through to 1950 it was engaged in towing operations for ETPS and the RAE Technical College. In 1946 it towed the German gliders such as the Horten Ho IV (LA+AC became VP543), Weihe (LO+WQ became BGA448 and G-ALJW), Grunau Baby IIB (LH+FT became VP587) and Olympia-Meise (LF+VO became BGA449), which were being evaluated by RAE. Apart from glider towing the Storch was also used for laying smoke trails, general communications duties, and as a photographic chase aircraft. It made its last flight during October 1955 and was offered for disposal on 1st November. Mercifully being found unacceptable for instructional purposes, it survived to enter the RAF Museum collection where it arrived in 1989 and can be seen displayed at RAF Cosford to this day.

By now two Devons had been delivered for Transport Flight but there was so much liaison and communications work required at the RAE outstations, and elsewhere, that the fleet was somewhat stretched. The first of two Miles Marathon 1As, XJ830, arrived at Farnborough from Woodley on 2nd March 1955 and operated with Transport Flight until it departed on 2nd October 1958, having been sold to Air Navigation & Trading Co at Blackpool as G-AMHS. The second example, XJ831, arrived at Farnborough from Warton on 20th May 1958 but operated only a short while, departing for the same owner on 6th October 1958.

arrived at Farnborough for VTOL research. XJ314 had made its first tethered flight at Hucknall on 9th July 1953 and its first free flight on 3rd August 1954. Powered by two Rolls-Royce Nene 4 engines, it was not only an early form of VTOL but in an elementary fly-by-wire configuration. It transferred to RAE Bedford on 21st June 1956 and eventually found a home in the Science Museum. A second example, XK426, was allocated to Bedford and did not come to Farnborough.

The RAE Golden Jubilee celebrations took place on 7th July, with HRH Princess Margaret attending the Establishment, having arrived from Buckingham Palace in Westland Whirlwind HAS.22 WV221 'GJ701' to tour various departments and witness a flying display. This was a large-scale event and included the 'Pelican Formation' of four Meteor T.7s from the Central Flying School at Little Rissington; a Canberra; Anson; Mosquito T.III RR303 from White Waltham;

Skeeter G-AMTZ from Eastleigh; a Lancaster from St Mawgan; Javelin FAW.1 XA544 from Moreton Valence; a Jet Provost from Boscombe Down; Swordfish from Lee-on-Solent and a Hunter from Odiham. Formation flypasts were given by Hunters, Canberras, Javelins, Shackletons, Sunderlands and Gannets, plus Hiller, Whirlwind and Dragonfly helicopters. In addition, a large number of the RAE/ETPS aircraft were ranged in a static display on the 'A' shed apron. This visit by HRH Princess Margaret, and the employees/public days for this event, were declared a great success.

The last of the captured German aircraft was taken out of service, this being the Fieseler Fi.156C-7 Storch VP546, which had latterly been in use as a low-speed training, trials and communications aircraft. It had arrived at Farnborough on 5th September 1945 from Knokke, via Hawkinge, along with two others AM99 and AM100. Its serial

The RAE Golden Jubilee celebrations were staged during July 1955. A large number of aircraft were statically displayed on the 'A' shed tarmac, followed by a flying display with service participation. The other work of the establishment was displayed by the various departments. Dominating this scene is Armament Flight Valiant B.1 WP209, which departed for Australia for weapons trials three weeks later. Other aircraft seen in this view include Short SB.5 WG768, Avro 707B VX790, Rolls-Royce 'Flying Bedstead' XJ314, AW.52G glider RG324, Ashton Mk.4 WB494, Apollo VX224, Lincoln B.2 RF533, Meteor FR.9 WB116 from No 2 Squadron and Sperrin VX161. *FAST collection*

1956

A Saunders-Roe SR.53 rocket-powered interceptor fighter was placed in the Structures Department test rig at Farnborough for airframe fatigue testing. This was a non-flying structural test specimen – the two development prototypes, XD145 and XD151, were still under construction at East Cowes and were later taken to Boscombe Down where they made their first flights on 16th May 1957 and 8th December 1957 respectively. Other structural test frames were also present on the airfield at this time, near the water tanks: Viking I VW218, previously engaged in aerial development at RAE, was undergoing structural tests; Venom FB.1 WE361, in use previously at RAE for air-launching containers for banner targets during 1955, had been allocated for fatigue testing on 11th September 1957; and Hunter F.2 WN893 arrived by road from RAE Bedford on 22nd July 1958, all being placed within these rigs for various fatigue and structural research with SME Department.

In 1946 the National Gas Turbine Establishment (NGTE) was set up at Pyestock. Much of the earlier engine research flying had taken place at Bitteswell but in mid-1952 NGTE flight-testing was transferred to Farnborough with the arrival from Bitteswell on 25th June of the first aircraft, Vampire F.1 TG421. The Vampire was used for combustion chamber efficiency tests and there then followed Meteor PR.10 WB164 on 26th June to undertake engine re-lighting tests at high altitude, and Meteor T.7 VW443 on 9th July for thrust measurements in flight and temperature controller and speed governor tests. Lincoln B.2 SX971 arrived from Bitteswell on 10th July 1952 for NGTE Flight where it was used for reheat

Seen here during April 1955 is the much-modified Lincoln B.2 RF533. It was operated by Armament Flight and seen hanging beneath the fuselage is a large dummy missile. This was the last Lincoln in service with RAE, being finally retired in May 1961. *FAST collection*

View from the Farnborough control tower, as seen on 26th June 1956, shows an 'A' shed apron with Varsities, Hastings, Meteors, Chipmunk, Vampire and Marathons, whilst at left is a yet to be delivered Peruvian Air Force Canberra B(I)8 No 476 (ex-WT367), which was visiting from the English Electric factory at Warton for an ILS installation to be undertaken by RAE. *FAST collection*

A unique formation of National Gas Turbine Establishment (NGTE) Flight aircraft, seen during 1956. It consists of Hunter F.1 WT633, Meteor F.8 VZ473, Canberra B.2 WK161 (stand-in for WH657), Lincoln B.2 SX971 and Ashton Mk.2 WB491. *FAST collection*

Examples of V-Bomber Trials

Valiants

B.1 WP201	special armament trials (1954/1955)
	OR.1132 Navigator System for Blue Steel (1956/1957)
	general research and development of loadings, flutter and vibrations, and development of equipment, shared with IAP Department (1958/1959)
	to St Athan for ground instruction as 7707M 28.11.60
B.1 WP202	radio trials (1955)
	testing of flight instruments, and store vibrations (1956)
	crashed at Southwick, Sussex 11.5.56 with the loss of the three crew after electrical failure and loss of control
B.1 WP203	various bombing trials (1955/1957)
B.1 WP209	bomb ballistic trials (1955)
B.1 WP214	'Blue Study', automatic blind bombing system (1955)
	aerodynamic assessments, 'Grapple' (1956)
	flight trials of RCM (Radar Counter-Measures) aerials (1957/1958)
B(PR)1 WP219	installation and flight trials of a 2,100 lb weapon (1962/1963)
B(PR)1 WZ383	trials with 6,000 lb bombs and a TMB (Target Marker Bomb) trial installation (1957)
	development and ballistic trials of 2,000 lb TMB and 7,000 lb HC bombs (1957/1961)
BK.1 XD813	brief trials with ARL (1958)

Victors

B.1 XA922	checks of a special wiring installation (9.58)
	armament clearance trials (10.58)
	development and clearance trials of nuclear weapons (9.59)
	measurement of parachute drag loads and study of general performance of special brake parachutes (10.63)
	returned to Radlett (3.5.66)
B.1 WB775	contractor's trials (20/22.6.55)
	fuselage returned for explosive decompression tests (4.11.59)
	struck off charge 27.6.60, but cabin section retained as 'space model'

Vulcans

Prototype VX777	preliminary bomb dropping trials (12.7.54)
	during a test flight on 27th July, an uncontrollable yaw to starboard was developed, which was caused by a runaway rudder. A higher than normal speed landing was made, whereupon the brake parachute shredded upon deployment and the aircraft overshot the runway collapsing the undercarriage. It was repaired and returned to Avro.
B.2 VX777	ground vibration trials of armament installations and equipment (27.4.60)
	struck off charge 18.10.62 and eventually scrapped during 1964
B.1 XA890	armament trials and development for ballistics and fusing trials with 'Red Beard', 'Yellow Sun' and 'Project E' development – the use of US weapons by the RAF (1958/59)
	continuation of armament trials (1960/1962)
	initial proving trials of 'Rapid Blooming Window' cartridges and infra-red decoys (1962/1964)
B.1 XA892	weapon-loading trials (1956)
	development and clearance trials of nuclear weapons (1960/1962)
	to No 1 STT Halton 21.6.62 for instructional purposes as 7746M.

development work and other research, fitted with a Derwent 5 engine, with afterburner, in an underslung pod. On completion of its research work it was dispatched to 10MU Hullavington on 4th December 1956.

Thus NGTE Flight now had a small nucleus of aircraft for engine development work and they began operations on 19th September 1952. A further Meteor F.8, VZ473, was added to the fleet when it arrived from Moreton Valence on 13th March 1953 for research of jetpipe heat radiation on special TRE equipment, followed by a Canberra B.2 WH657 that arrived from Boscombe Down on 4th June 1953 for research into high-altitude turbine engine problems until it was transferred to RAE on 25th September 1960. Hunter F.1 WT570 arrived from Dunsfold on 12th January 1955 for research with NGTE Flight into engine malfunctions caused by the use of air weapons, followed by a further F.1 WT633 which was transferred from RAE to NGTE Flight on 29th April 1955 for engine compressor stall and gun firing investigations in respect of engine parameters. Ashton Mk.2 WB491 was fitted with a Rolls-Royce Avon and later a Conway engine and came to Farnborough from Wymeswold on 4th September 1955 as a turbine engine flying testbed for NGTE Flight. It had been converted by Napiers at Luton, with an engine pod under the fuselage that had earlier housed an Avon but now contained a Conway. It was struck off charge at Farnborough on 13th February 1962 and the forward fuselage survives at the Newark Air Museum. NGTE Flight continued until around 1957, by which time the many engine test cells at Pyestock were operational and the need for airborne testing was not so great.

Over the years, other than the SBAC displays of the 1950s and 1960s, there have been a small number of V-bombers based at Farnborough, undergoing weapon research work with what was known as ARL (Airfield Radio Laboratory), or other derivatives thereof. ARL was built in the early 1950s. 'H' shed was already in existence from the early 1940s but was rendered unsuitable by being outside of the secure compound. There was even a further security post here, and if you did not have the right pass then you did not get in!

Consequently during the 1950s/1960s, parked on the apron in the southwest corner close to the ARL compound, could be seen Valiant, Victor and Vulcan aircraft that

Valiant B.1 WP214 is seen on the Armament Flight apron, on the southern side of the airfield, during May 1956. This aircraft had been used for various weapon trials, including radar counter-measures. It had arrived at Farnborough on 3rd August 1955 and returned to the manufacturers at Wisley on 13th August 1958. *FAST collection*

Vulcan B.1 XA890 arrived at Farnborough from Woodford on 7th February 1958 for various armament trials, including 'Red Beard' and 'Yellow Sun'. In May 1962 it undertook proving trials of rapid-blooming 'window' cartridges and infra-red decoys, before departing to RAE Bedford on 21st January 1964. *FAST collection*

were undergoing secretive work. They would frequently be towed or taxied into the inner sanctum, behind the sliding, corrugated green gates, for the weapons to be loaded/unloaded within the compound away from prying eyes. Probably last opened around 1964, these sliding gates were there right to the end albeit somewhat corroded with their wheels and tracks very much overgrown and impossible to move any more. The ARL compound was demolished during March, April and May of 2004.

The aircraft that were involved in this work are detailed opposite, they all being allocated to Armament Flight although these were locally referred to as belonging to 'V-Flight'.

It is also worth mentioning here that the remains of the first prototype Handley Page Victor, WB771, came to Farnborough after the aircraft suffered a structural failure and crashed on 14th July 1954 at Cranfield. The parts were analysed by RAE Structures Department and AIB. Flutter of the tail surfaces had led to a structural break-up and loss of the tail-plane and elevators in flight.

Other Vulcan B.1s (XA893, XA895, XA907, XH478, XH498 and XH532) were detached to RAE for trials with ARL. Furthermore an interesting visitor on 24th June 1958 was Vulcan B.1 XA900, which arrived from Wyton with HRH The Duke of Edinburgh on board. After his V-bomber flight he was transported back to Buckingham Palace in Whirlwind HAS.22 WV224 from Lee-on-Solent.

The prototype B.5/36 Vulcan B.1 VX770, the Rolls-Royce Conway engine testbed, disintegrated during a Battle of Britain display at Syerston on 20th September 1958, whereupon the parts were dispatched to

Farnborough for investigation by Structures Department and AIB. The aircraft was struck off charge on 29th September 1959 and the parts were disposed of during July 1961.

1957

A demonstration was given of an aircraft being arrested by a barrier strung out across runway 04. The aircraft used, Sea Venom FAW.20 WM503, had arrived by road from Bedford on 18th March 1956. It proved that this was a successful arresting system and the dignitaries invited to watch the demonstration were by all accounts suitably impressed. The aircraft was dispatched by road to Arbroath on 2nd October 1957 where it was allocated instructional serial A2447.

A number of different aircraft had been used post-war for various catapult trials, including the first twin-engined types. Examples of the aircraft conducting these trials, initially with Aero Flight and from 1952 with Naval Air Department Flight, are as follows:
- Hornet F.1 PX214
- Avenger I JZ298
- Firebrand MK.IV EK740
- Seafire F.XVIIs SX311, SX314, SX342
- Firefly Mk.Is MB417, MB718
- Firefly AS.6 WD857
- Sea Fury (second prototype) SR666

- Sea Fury FB.10 TF898
- Sea Fury FB.11 VW588
- Avenger Mk.IIIs KE436, KE446
- Spearfish (second prototype) RA360
- Sea Hornet F.20 TT191
- Sea Hornet NF.21 VV431
- Vampire F.20 VG701, VV142
- Vampire F.3 VT803
- Sturgeon (second prototype) RK791
- Brigand TF.1 RH748
- Attacker TS416
- Attacker F.1 WA475
- Sea Hawk (second prototype) VP413
- Sea Hawk F.1 WF144
- YA.7 (prototype) WB781
- Wyvern TF.2 VW876
- P.1052 (prototype) VX272
- Vultur No 02
- Gannet AS.1 WN372
- Aquilon No 05
- Sea Venom FAW.20s WK379, WM504
- Sea Venom FAW.21s WM568, WW200, XG656
- Sea Venom FAW.53 WZ894.

RATOG trials were still being undertaken throughout this period and aircraft being utilised included: Sea Otter I JM821; Seafire F.XV SW813; Firebrand Mk.IV EK741; Mosquito TR.33 TS449; Firefly I PP652, FR.IV TW735; Fury X (prototype) VB857, T.20 VX298; Sturgeon TT.1 TS475; YA.7 WB781; Attacker TS416, F.1 WA471, Supermarine 510 VV106, P.1052 VX272 and Sea Venom FAW.20 WM504 and FAW.21 WM568.

Thus the scene was set for the very last catapult launch from Farnborough, when Sea Venom FAW.21 XG656:'FD524' of 700 NAS was catapulted from the BH.V accelerator on 20th September 1957, bringing to a close some thirty or so years of catapult research on Jersey Brow, the fruits of which were to be found in installations on both

Sea Venom FAW.21 XG656, 'FD524' of 700 NAS, is seen being prepared on Jersey Brow for the very last catapult launch on 20th September 1957. Thereafter all catapult work was conducted at RAE Bedford. *FAST collection*

British and American aircraft carriers. Throughout the eleven years of its operation the BH.V had seen some 3,343 catapult launches, the first being made on 25th October 1946. This catapult served NAD well, as had its predecessors, and was a great asset to the trials and research being undertaken at the time, paving the way for the steam catapult fitted to today's aircraft carriers. All subsequent research in this field was undertaken by NAD at RAE Bedford.

The second Skylark rocket was launched from Woomera on 22nd May. This was designed as a special purpose high-altitude rocket carrying scientific instruments some 70-90 miles above the earth. The structural design and launcher system were the responsibility of Guided Weapons Department, whilst the Raven rocket motor was designed and developed at Westcott.

Around 50 Canberras have served at Farnborough from 1950 through to 1984 and have undertaken a variety of research duties. A selection of these aircraft, along with the work undertaken, is given herewith.

1958

The first Black Knight rocket was launched in September, RAE having a considerable involvement in this project. During the late 1950s a free flight model of a Mach 1.2 transport aircraft was carried on the back of two solid propellant rocket motors and launched at altitude. After separation, data was transmitted back to RAE via a telemetry system.

Structural testing of the Britannia and Herald was conducted in the water tanks, which provided information on the structures of these pressurised airliners.

The English Electric P.1 was officially named the Lightning at Farnborough during a ceremony in 'L' shed where P.1B XA847 was given the name by the Marshal of the RAF Sir Dermot Boyle whilst champagne crashed against the nose of the aircraft. The P.1B had arrived from Warton on 22nd October as 'Tarnish 6' and departed back to the manufacturers as a Lightning on 23rd October. Interestingly this same aircraft was to return to 'L' shed some eight years later when it was allocated for the soft ground arrester trials.

Many Hunters served with RAE Farnborough between 1954 and 1994, undertaking a variety of research duties. A selection of these aircraft, along with the work undertaken, is given opposte.

Canberra B.2 WH912 arrived from Belfast on 2nd April 1954, for use by Armament Flight on research into VT fuses. It is seen here on the western apron on 21st October 1955, with a modified nose for armament trials. It suffered a wheels-up landing at Bedford on 23rd November 1959, was repaired, and passed to Hunting Engineering at Luton on 1st December 1960. *FAST collection*

Examples of Canberra Trials

B.2 WD929	special navigation and bombing trials	IAP Flight 1951/1955
B.2 WD931	bomb container trials	Armament Flight 1951/1954
B.2 WD945	flight trials with 'Blue Devil', 'Red Cat'	
	further trials including instruments	IAP Flight 1953/1955
	development of target marker bomb	Armament Flight 1956/1957
	releasing of test vehicles at various altitudes in connection	
	with 'Green Flax' (renamed 'Yellow Temple')	Guided Weapons Flight 1958
B.2 WD947	armament development trials	Armament/Weapons Flight 1953/63
	experiments on satellite systems in a weightless environment by	
	flying ballistic trajectories	Space Department 1963/1966
B.2 WD953	fuse development and bomb trials	Armament Flight 1957/1961
B.2 WD962	ejection seats, including Javelin FAW.7 ejection trials	SME Flight 1952/1958
PR.3 WE146	FX96 and FX89 Mk.3 cameras and auto-stabilisers	IAP Flight 1964
B.2 WH657	development trials of parachute stabilising system, using articulated	
	dummy man dropped from the bomb bay; measurement of cosmic	
	radiation levels; satellite tracking	SME Flight 1960/1966
B.2 WH661	parachute mine, armament development and bombing trials	Armament Flight 1952/1955
B.2 WH715	bombs, pyrotechnic and fuses, fuse proofing trials, development of	
	instruments and testing a new range of equipment	IAP Flight 1960/1961
PR.7 WH776	tests of Mk.6 altimeter for accuracy, prior to service fit	1954/1955
	UHF/VHF/ILS investigations, TACAN trials, IR trials and Phase 3	
	Window research	Radio Flight 1955/1960
PR.7 WH777	trials on 'Blue Study' equipment	1954/1955
	modifications in respect of 'Green Satin'	1955/1956
	determining position and velocity using high-accuracy ballistic cameras	IAP Flight 1957
T.4 WH854	soft ground arresting trials	SME Flight 1966/1967
B.2 WH912	VT fuse trials	Armament Flight 1954/1960
B.6 WH952	aircraft response to bomb bay buffeting and general research and	
	development of air crew equipment, including parachutes	1964/1968
	Violet Fire detection system for Concorde and fuel vapour sensing	
	equipment, cabin pressure control systems tests	SME Flight 1968/1973
B.2/8 mod WJ643	Navigation Attack System for Harrier, later, laser-ranging equipment	
	for Jaguar	Weapons Flight 1969/1980
TT.18 WJ682	dropping radar-responsive parachute targets into Cardigan Bay,	
	for Bloodhound firings	Weapons Flight 1961/1962
PR.7 WJ818	flight trials of Mk.10 Auto-pilot	IAP Flight 1955/1956
PR.7 WJ820	moving topical display development – early moving map	IAP Flight 1961/1962
B.2 WJ994	trials of guided weapon recovery system and other guided weapon trials	Guided Wpns Flight 1959/1961
	flight tests at various altitudes and speeds, up to the maximum for the	
	Canberra aircraft	1961
	to ETPS and written off landing at Farnborough 1.4.63	
B.2 WK161	special armament trials	Armament Flight 1955/1956
	special coating for RAM radar assessment flight trials for air-to-air target	
	radar system development by RRE Pershore	1961/1962
B(I)6 WT308	general weapons trials, bombs and rockets	Weapons Flight 1955/1983
B(I)6 WT309	general weapons trials inc LABS and toss bombing	Weapons Flight 1957/1983
B(I)8 XH231	electrical system trials for 2,000 lb TMB	Weapons Flight 1957
B.6 XH568	low-level turbulence trials	SME Flight 1958/1966
	development trials	Weapons Flight 1967

On 17th May 1957, Canberra B.2 WH863 is seen on the diamonds parking area on the west side of Farnborough airfield, with its main wheels jacked up to allow clearance of a large bomb into the bomb bay. The bomb is probably an early 'Red Beard', of 2,000 lb, that was undergoing a trial fit only. This aircraft arrived from Belfast on 8th June 1953 and was in use by IAM and was later transferred to SME Flight until its departure to 33 MU Lyneham on 10th April 1958. The aircraft was later converted to a T.17 variant and was struck off charge during May 1981, allocated 8693M. The forward fuselage is with the Newark Air Museum. *via B Kervell*

1959

The first Comet to be assigned to RAE Farnborough, for use by Radio Flight, arrived from Boscombe Down on 15th April 1959 as G-AMXD, using callsign 'Evergreen 05'. This was a Mk.2E, XN453, which was previously registered as G-AMXD, built for BOAC but not delivered and purchased by the Ministry of Supply. The Comet underwent prolonged installation work at RAE with the fitment of an experimental radio installation for trials into radio propagation at very long wavelengths, navigational and communications equipment, including observer work stations, equipment racks and other onboard equipment for airborne experimental use. It made its first flight trial on 15th March 1960 and further equipment was installed over the years which also saw research and development by Radio & Navigation Department into the Omega navigation system, inertial navigation, Distance Measuring Equipment, Tacan, infra-red jammers, countermeasures and satellite communications. The aircraft made a number of overseas deployments including round-the-world trips during its RAE service. It undertook its last flight on 9th February 1973, being allocated as a Ground Experimental Vehicle shortly thereafter.

After the loss of Victor B.2 XH668 on 20th August, in the Irish Sea off St Brides Bay, a considerable investigation into the cause of the crash was undertaken by Structures Department and the AIB. Some 600,000 pieces of wreckage, equating to approximately 70% of the aircraft, were recovered by a fleet of vessels from depths of up to 400ft and were flown back to Farnborough in the various transport aircraft that were on RAE strength at the time. It was determined that the Victor had suffered fatigue fracture of the

The first Comet to arrive at Farnborough was Mk.2E XN453. After installation work, it undertook its first flight trial on 15th March 1960. It is seen here flying over the south coast during November 1963, whilst operating a radio and navigation trial with RAE Radio Flight. It continued in service until 1973. *FAST collection*

Examples of Hunter Trials

F.2 WN890	vibration measurement and flight flutter research	SME Flight 1956/1960
F.2 WN893	investigation of tightening into turns	Aero Flight 1954/1955
	airframe fatigue testing	1958
F.5 WN955	investigation of air-launched target banner	SME Flight 1958/1959
	ground infra-red trials	Radio Department 1959/1960
F.5 WP143	LABS and gunnery trials	Armament Flight 1955
F.5 WP150	gunnery, rocket and USAF LABS trials	Armament Flight 1955/1957
F.1 WT571	aerodynamic drag research at high mach numbers	Aero Flight 1954/1955
	area rule modifications	Aero Flight 1955/58
F.1 WT572	fighter armament development, Aden gun and sighting investigation	Armament Flight 1954/1955
F.1 WT564	auto stabiliser trials	IAP Flight 1954/1955
F.1 WT656	tests of a scheme for supersonic blowing of air over flaps	Aero Flight 1955/1956
F.4 WT706	trials of flight instrument system	IAP Flight 1955
	high-speed flight at low level	Guided Weapons Dept 1956/57
F.4 WT735	UHF suppressor aerials, Green Salad, high-speed aerials for Black Knight	Radio Flight 1956/1958
F.4 WV276	investigation into engine compressor stall and gun-firing trials	Armament Flight 1956
T.7 WV383	HUD, NVG, FLIR, PENETRATE system	Avionics & Sensors Flt 1971/1994
F.6 WW592	air-to-air rocket battery trials OR.1226, plus flight trials and function	
	tests of UTC 1957, air-to-air ballistic trials	Armament/Weapons Flt 1957/1964
F.6 WW598	Llanbedr chase aircraft with Jindiviks	1967/1968
	high-speed position of Rapier SAMs	1968/1974
F.1 WW605	fire control tests	Armament Flight 1955
	pressure cabin performance and air-blast vision	SME Flight 1956/1961
F.6 XF444	air-to-air rocket battery	
	OR.1126 clearance trials	Armament Flight 1956/1957
P.1099 F.6 XF833	fatigue testing	Structures Dept 1958/1962
F.6 XG290	DRLS, with counter-measures to optically-guided weapons	1974
	fly-by-wire target requirement	1977/1978

Various Hunter T.7s have also served with RAE on a short-term basis, mainly to replace based T.7s WV383 and XL563 for continuation flying training, instrument ratings and general flying practice; these included WV372, XL573, XL591, XL596, XL597, XL602, XL614, XX466 and XX467.

An unidentified Hunter is seen here on 13th July 1955 with Aden gun deflector modifications. For forty years, from 1954 until 1994, various Hunters of different marks have served at Farnborough in numerous roles. *FAST collection*

SE.5a D7000 was rebuilt at RAE during the late 1950s and made its first flight on 4th August 1959. It was retained at Farnborough for many years, later being re-serialled as F904 before being handed over to the Shuttleworth Trust at Old Warden. It is seen here flying over the Farnborough airfield on 14th January 1964. *FAST collection*

Meteor T.7½ WL375 is seen on the apron at 'A' shed during the early 1960s. This aircraft was fitted with an F.8 tail and FR.9 nose and was being used by IEE Department for development and test of an integrated instrumentation system. It ended its days at West Freugh but was rescued from there and is still extant with the Dumfries and Galloway Aviation Museum. *E Fuller collection*

starboard wingtip, including loss of the pitot tube, therefore setting up a trim runaway with the aircraft descending from over 50,000ft in a high-speed dive into the sea.

On 4th August 1959 S.E.5a D7000 made its first flight from Farnborough after rebuild, flown by Air Commodore Wheeler. The skeletal frame had been found in a barn during 1957 and was taken initially to Old Warden then to RAE, where it was originally designed, for rebuild over a two-year period by Aircraft and Apprentice Departments with much assistance from outside industry and private individuals.

1960

Meteor T.7 WL375, which had originally arrived at Farnborough from Glosters back on 12th June 1952 for investigation of auto-stabilisation with Aero Flight, transferring to IAP Flight on 1st May 1954, returned on 2nd February 1960 for flight tests and development of the integrated instrument system installed by the College of Aeronautics at Cranfield in respect of OR.343 – the Operational Requirement that led to the TSR.2. This aircraft was by now a standard T.7 fitted with an F.8 tail and an FR.9 nose, earning it an unofficial designation of T.7½! This work continued with IAP Flight, later becoming IEE Flight, until the aircraft was re-allotted to SME Flight on 25th January 1966 for comparison of braking friction and tyre wear on a normal runway with that on an experimental rough surface. It returned to IEE Flight on 28th November 1966 for flight assessment of individual instrument groups, aimed at developing a complete cockpit display. This evolved into an early Head-Up Display as trials by IAP Department were initially undertaken in a special flight

A rare colour photograph of Meteor F.8 VZ473 of IAP Flight, seen on a wet 'A' shed tarmac during 1961, fitted with an FR.9 nose. This aircraft was used for various instrument trials, having previously been in use with NGTE Flight and being transferred to RAE on 1st December 1959. It made its final trials flight during October 1961 and was struck off charge on 18th January 1962, being dispatched to MoA Fire School at Stansted for fire-fighting training. *FAST collection*

SME Flight Javelin FAW.7 XH754 arrived at Farnborough on 18th November 1960 and served until July 1964. It is seen here on the apron outside 'C' shed during March 1961. It is carrying a dummy missile beneath its port wing. In this view it wore an overall white scheme with black trim and silver undersides, but later had Day-Glo added to its nose and tail and black/yellow stripes to its undersurfaces. This aircraft was dismantled by the aircraft apprentices between January and March 1965, the airframe going to Spadeadam. *FAST collection*

simulator but then the basic HUD was installed in this Meteor. A statement at the time read, 'The development of the Head-Up system may well have an important influence upon future flying by instruments. The system relieves the pilot of the need for looking down at the information on his cockpit panel. The information he requires is seen through his windscreen, superimposed on the outside world right in front of him.' This system has been much improved over the years and has revolutionised the cockpit instrument panel, being in common use today on most jet combat types. From 10th November 1967, the Meteor was undertaking trials with a 'Kayser Raster' type electronic flight instrument display, (an early EFIS system), making its final research flight on 8th May 1969. It was dispatched to West Freugh on 9th June 1969 for fire-fighting training. It is currently extant with the Dumfries and Galloway Aviation Museum, displayed in spurious colours.

Meteor T.7 WA714 had arrived from Bassingbourn on 21st September 1959 for aircrew continuation training with Experimental Flying Department/Transport Flight for the benefit of RAF pilots based at Farnborough and West Freugh, as well as civilian pilots based at Llanbedr. Its last flight was on 23rd May 1968, the aircraft being delivered to PEE Shoeburyness shortly thereafter for vulnerability trials on their range.

Javelin FAW.7 XH753 arrived from Moreton Valence for SME Flight on 28th July 1960 for development of a windscreen rain clearance system, which consisted of air jets. However, this aircraft was not considered suitable for the task and was swapped with XH754 on 18th November 1960. This aircraft spent much of its time at RAF Changi in

Singapore, flying through tropical storms. From October 1961 it was also tasked with trials in respect of insect clearance from windscreens, plus parachute-towed targets and high-altitude photography. By now the aircraft had been repainted overall white with Day-Glo areas, and black/yellow undersurface stripes. It was last flown during July 1964 and was later dismantled by the aircraft apprentice training department and dispatched to Spadeadam for ground tests, being later scrapped in 1970.

The Ball Hill range, close to the area where Cody had crashed in 1913, was used for various gunnery and projectile trials. Parts of aircraft hulks and structures were fired upon to test the various armaments being used and to indicate the damage tolerance of the airframe systems and structures. Further work was also carried out in this connection at the outstations of the Pendine range and Shoeburyness, the latter still continuing in this type of work today.

The Beta shed was demolished during May, having stood as an RAE landmark since it was built in 1905. Its girders stretched to a height of 75ft, a legacy of its original use as an airship shed. In 1906 the first Cody powered kite was built in it, the *Nulli Secundus* airships and Cody's Aeroplane no.1 were to follow. At the start of World War One, it was partly used as an engine repair and test shop, the testbeds being just outside the west end of the building. Over the years it was converted and used as a block of offices and then as a stores building for RAE.

1961

Radio Department were using Lasham Aerodrome, the southernmost hangar and surrounding area becoming an RAE outpost for various ground tests involving radio aerials, away from the general electro-magnetic clutter that was present at Farnborough.

Having arrived from Brough on 16th September 1959, the SME Flight Beverley C.1 XB259 was engaged during the early 1960s, amongst other work, in trials dropping tanks from its spacious cargo hold. These trials took place over Salisbury Plain near Netheravon Down. On the first occasion the drogue chute pulled the tank rearwards from the hold but the main parachute did not deploy and the tank dived into the ground from some 2,500ft leaving a deep crater. Subsequent trials were more successful!

1963

The RAE Aircraft Apprentice Training
Department was set up in the western end of
'A' Shed (Building P82), with ex-ETPS Vampire T.11 WZ475 allocated for training purposes on 26th September 1963, plus a wing
from a Provost T.1 that had been undergoing
tests with SME Department. Various other
airframes were added over the years. A dedicated training classroom had been converted at the back of the hangar for in-house
aircraft engineering lectures, although the
apprentices (your author among them) also
continued with their day release studies at
various technical colleges.

On 2nd May 1963 Hunter T.7 XL563
arrived for the RAF Institute of Aviation Medicine. This was to be one of the longest-serving jet aircraft at Farnborough, making its
last flight before retirement on 9th July 1993.

Designed by Space Department and known
as UK3, the first UK satellite underwent climatic testing in the RAE environmental chamber in September. This chamber was built in
the USA and installed by Vickers Engineering
Ltd in the building on the corner of Range and
Brake Road. Meanwhile, up at Spadeadam, the
Blue Streak rocket was undergoing ground
tests that included engine firings. This was part
of the European Space Research Organisation
(ESRO) that was set up in 1961 between
Britain and France as a joint venture for a
multi-stage space launcher system, under the
European Launcher Development Organisation (ELDO).

A 4ft 6in x 3ft 6in wind tunnel was built in
RAE for the Farnborough Technical College
in order for students to learn aerodynamic
theory. Construction began in 1960, it was
test run in April 1961, became operational
during September, and was finally handed
over on 20th October 1961.

The wooden fan blades of the 24ft wind
tunnel were replaced by new blades made
from Honduras mahogany by RAE 40
Department. This was precision work and
each blade weighed 550 lb. The wind tunnel
operated at speeds up to 110mph and was
driven by a 2,000hp generator.

1962

Work on the new Structures Department
buildings at Ball Hill, designed by Sulzer
Bros, started in July being constructed by
Gilbert Ash Ltd under the Ministry of Buildings and Public Works. This £4 million, 90ft-
high structure to house the Concorde
structural test airframe was 'topped out' on
18th November 1964 and opened in 1965
although its official opening took place on
6th June 1966 with Her Majesty Queen Eliz-

abeth II undertaking the honours.

During the early 1960s Avionics Department had begun research into thermal imaging, moving maps and optical navigation
displays, which were trialled on RAE aircraft.
Eventually continued development and
refinements led to the widespread military
service of this equipment in the 1970s/1980s.

Another Meteor, this time T.7 WL405,
arrived from 5MU Kemble on 13th September 1962 for low-level flying with Weapons
Flight researching air-surface guided
weapon trajectories; this aircraft being capable of taking closed-circuit television pictures. It was reallocated on 29th June 1965
for low-level flying under CCTV control,
where the first pilot would fly the aircraft
normally whilst the second pilot would fly
'seeing' by television. It was released from
this task on 11th September 1968 and used
for spares. It then passed to the RAE Aircraft
Apprentice Department where it was used
for instructional purposes for many years,
before being taken by road to Chalgrove to
act as a spares source for the airworthy Martin-Baker Meteors on 28th June 1989.

To commemorate the last link with military ballooning at Stanhope Lines in Aldershot, where the Balloon School had been
established in 1892, a last Balloon flight was
made on 27th March 1963. The Balloon
shed was constructed in 1892 and was to be
demolished to make way for modern barracks, although it had not been used for balloons for many years. To honour this
occasion a balloon flown by local balloonist
Wing Commander G Turnbull, with Capt J R
Hill (Royal Engineers) and Barbara Cook
(RAE photographer) on board, ascended for
the last time from this historic site. Its flight
was relatively short, the landing near Frim-

ley drawing to a close another chapter of local aeronautical history.

During the mid-1960s there were a number of Provost and Hunter airframes stored in a dismantled state near to the water tanks on the southern side of the airfield. The Provost T.1s had been sold to the manufacturer and included WV577, WV603, WV604, WV662, WV683, WW449, XF556, XF602, XF606, XF610, XF890 and XF906; all eventually being scrapped or departing by the late 1960s. The Hunter F.5s, being sold to the Ministry of Supply or the manufacturer, with their fuselages and wings stored under the trees included: WN972, WN987, WP102, WP109, WP110, WP112, WP117, WP141, WP146, WP181 and WP183, although there were probably other fuselages or wings in this area that were not recorded. The majority of the Hunter fuselages still had No 41 or No 56 Sqn markings. These were also scrapped or removed by the late 1960s.

1964

SME Flight Beverley C.1 XB259, commenced ultra low-level approach trials at Farnborough and on the Lark Hill range on Salisbury Plain. This spectacular enterprise involved large parachutes drawing the sled from the cargo hold whilst the aircraft flew some 20ft above the ground. During the early stages of these trials, in order get the height right across the airfield, the Beverley would fly through an arc of water provided by the RAE Fire Service, enabling a precise height to be attained.

RAE Transport Flight Devon C.1 VP959 received its new blue/white colour scheme and the others progressively followed.

The Cody aeroplane scale model that was made in the RAE workshops was presented to the No 1 RAF Officers Mess on 6th September and was unveiled by the President of the SBAC, Mr E C Wheldon, to commemorate the first aeroplane flight in Britain

ETPS held a 21st birthday party on 3rd September, for which a large number of aircraft were gathered on the ETPS apron to commemorate the various types that had been flown since the formation of the school at Boscombe Down back in 1943.

The very last balloon to ascend from Balloon Square in Aldershot is seen here about to lift off on 27th March 1963. This flight brought to a close Aldershot's long association with balloons, the Balloon School having been originally established in 1892. *FAST collection*

During May, the new BAC TSR.2 came to RAE for airframe fatigue tests in one of the structural test frames in Q153 building. The first flight of the type was made from Boscombe Down on 27th September.

Rev John Rawlings, a well-known aviation author and historian, was appointed in 1964 as the Chaplain to the RAF element at Farnborough for service personnel and in 1966 as Chaplain to the entire RAE. He was also Curate at St Peters, the Farnborough Parish Church. Whilst serving at RAE he flew in many of the aircraft types over the years, culminating in the very last research flight of Varsity T.1 WL679 in August 1991. He had

flown in some 60 different aircraft types up to the time of his passing in 1997.

Carbon fibre was produced at RAE, this pioneering the way ahead in material technology. Research into plastic material was attractive to manufacturers, because of its light weight and low density plus ease of fabrication. However for any structural use, this would need to be reinforced with a load-carrying component like glassfibre. Studies commenced in 1963 and methods of production were researched. A substance called Polyairylonitrili fibre was used, known as Courtelle. This was turned into a carbonised fibre and the process then commenced, resulting in production of a large increase in the tensile strength of the material and thus greater stiffness. Further experimentation resulted in a greater and improved stiffness; in fact twice as stiff as but only a quarter of the density of steel. Production of a small quantity went ahead and evaluation proved excellent qualities. During 1966 production of carbon fibre was undertaken at Harwell and, in 1968, the Materials Department (Plastic Engineering Section) produced the first continuous carbon fibre plant. Carbon fibre reinforced plastic (CFRP) was then produced elsewhere in the UK in massive quantities and continues today. CFRP has a wide range of uses, both for general applications and for those of the aerospace industry.

During this year the Society of British Aircraft Constructors became known as the Society of British Aerospace Companies, the display now becoming biennial and being open to foreign aircraft with British equipment.

The 92-ton Blue Streak rocket made its first launch on 5th June 1964, as part of the European Space Programme, when it was successfully fired from the Woomera test range. The rocket left the UK by sea in December 1963 for Australia. A team of RAE scientists were present and were involved throughout the satellite launch vehicle project.

Scimitar F.1 XD229 of Weapons Flight was painted in a blue and white colour scheme during 1963. It is seen here on the parking apron outside 'C' shed, during September 1963, prior to dispatch for weapons trials at West Freugh. It arrived from Wisley as 'Limar 19' on 26th June 1958. It was used at Farnborough for general armament development for the type and spent the remainder of its life undertaking weapons development trials, between Farnborough and West Freugh, where it was eventually struck off charge as a source of spares on 10th October 1966. *FAST collection*

THE INSTITUTE OF AVIATION MEDICINE

Physiology and Medicine Make Their Mark

The early decompression chamber of the RAF Physiological Laboratory at Farnborough is seen here on 7th November 1940. These early experiments resulted in the formation of the Institute of Aviation Medicine in 1945. *via B Kervell*

Close to Pinehurst Gate, where building Q153 still stands, a temporary structure was erected on 23rd August 1939 to serve as a Physiological Laboratory. This humble residence, which was established at Farnborough as a branch of the RAF Medical Service, was intended to investigate the physiological conditions of high-altitude flight in relation to practical development of oxygen systems. At the start of its operation, the only piece of equipment it possessed was a simple decompression chamber.

With the onset of higher flight speeds and altitudes it soon became necessary to determine how pilots would react to the rapid changes in force that would be encountered during acceleration, along with the temperature and pressure variations at different heights. Consequently, investigation proceeded during World War Two into the many problems associated with aircrew physiological matters. In May 1945 the laboratory moved to the RAF station on the south side of Farnborough airfield in the area housing the Army polo ground, then known as Danger Hill, where it was renamed the Royal Air Force Institute of Aviation Medicine (IAM).

Human Nature

Dr Bryan H C Matthews and Sqn Ldr William E Stewart were the leading exponents within the IAM in its early days. Although aircraft appeared to have been borrowed from the various RAE Flights on an ad-hoc basis, a dedicated Medical Research (MR) Flight was established in May 1940, but was short-lived – it seems that the aircraft undergoing medical research were allocated back to other Flights by September of that year. A Gloster Gladiator (in fact the prototype, K5200) and later Fairey Battle Is (K9258 and K9289, both equipped with cine cameras) would be flown to investigate the 'new' forces of flight, with Sqn Ldr Stewart acting as the experimental, human subject.

The aircraft would be accelerated in a dive with the subject's reactions recorded during the onslaught of 'G'-force experienced in the pull-out from the dive. This originated in the classification of the 'eyeballs in' syndrome, or the diminution of vision through a physical 'black out' under high 'G' loadings caused by blood draining to the lower body

and starving the brain. MR Flight also operated two Spitfires, Mk.Ia L1095 and Mk.I P9448, both being used for high-G manoeuvres; whilst Hurricane Is P3089 and V7541 with a single Defiant I, L7024, were also engaged in medical work during the period. Research into the ideal ways of presenting oxygen to aircrew (after an oxygen economiser had already been developed by RAE); the development of aircrew clothing (including heating); the effects of severe cold and frostbite on aircrew; contamination of aircraft cockpits with carbon monoxide; air sickness; the ability to find targets at night and operational fatigue were further fields of investigation at this time. The flotation properties of lifejackets and their ability to orientate their perhaps unconscious wearers into a correct life-saving attitude after ditching or parachuting into the sea was another exploratory exercise, as were the effects on pilots during ejection seat firing. This latter research led to the further design of flying clothing restraints and personnel equipment for the new generation of seats, to which the most modern systems are related.

Perhaps one of the most bizarre experiments conducted by IAM was that of snatching live personnel from the ground. This research, undertaken in conjunction with RAE, arose as a result of the obvious dangers

imposed by missions into enemy-occupied territory to pick up downed airmen or recover secret agents. Enter here Flt Lt Roland Winfield, a rather eccentric character, who was posted to the Physiological Laboratory at Farnborough in 1940 and was by now known as Dr Winfield. He, along with Sqn Ldr Stewart (by now also a Doctor) and Capt P J Lee-Warner, volunteered for these daring trials. The idea was that the subject would be snatched from the ground without the aircraft having to land – a technique that had already been developed by the All American Aviation Company of Wilmington, Delaware, which had carried out successful live tests of this system in the USA.

The Ministry of Aircraft Production requested that experiments should be conducted at Farnborough and an Avro Anson X, NK234, was duly sent to R Malcolm Ltd at White Waltham on 22nd January 1945 to be modified for the task in hand. The installation of the pick-up gear saw the removal of the upper turret and a folding trapdoor

Anson X NK234 was modified with the installation of man pick-up gear. The aircraft is seen here during a 'live' pick-up of Dr Winfield from the grass in front of 'A' shed during May 1945. The Anson is approximately 30ft above the ground and the hook has engaged the wire and is about to snatch Dr Winfield, secured in his special harness, from the ground. A number of successful 'live' pick-up tests were performed in this way. *via G Rood*

being cut in the floor of the Anson, whilst a shock-absorbing winch with 200ft of nylon rope and a hook was fitted along with the other required equipment. The subject to be snatched from the ground was fitted with a specialised harness with a large nylon hoop, which was strung between two 18ft-high vertical poles. The Anson was to approach in a throttled-back shallow dive at between 120 and 140mph and, when some 50ft from the poles at an altitude of 30ft, the pilot would open the throttles and climb away as steeply as possible with the hook deployed. The subject to be snatched would then be caught by the hook and reeled into the aircraft through the trapdoor, whilst the aircraft was established in a positive rate of climb.

The Anson arrived at Farnborough on 14th April 1945 and the first trial run was carried out on 16th April 1945 at Henley, where much of this experimenting was conducted. It quickly became clear that this was not an easy task and it took some time to hone the accuracy of approach and positioning. Many pick-ups were made of ballasted containers and, later, rubber dummies including full-size weighted models, before it was attempted for real. At this point the acceleration was calculated to be 5G for a short duration (1.5 seconds) with a maximum of 10G for 0.25 seconds. These figures were considered as acceptable for the human body so the system was deemed ready to be tested on a 'live' subject.

The equipment was readied for the first live snatch, which took place on 1st May 1945 with Capt Lee-Warner being successfully picked up. This was followed by two more live snatches on 2nd May when Winfield and Stewart were both recovered from the grass in front of 'A' shed. Always wanting to do more, Dr Winfield requested a second snatch, which was agreed and scheduled in for 4th May 1945 before a gathered audience. This would actu-

ally be the 53rd snatch and the fourth live occasion. All appeared to be going to plan until the snatch hook did not engage cleanly in the loop, snagging the cable shackle located above it. It was due to the alertness of the winchman in the Anson that Dr Winfield was eventually recovered into the aircraft. He had seen what was happening and, using a long pole with a hook that was inside the aircraft to assist the reel-in, saved Dr Winfield from a potentially fatal situation.

Up to mid-July 1945 some 97 snatches had been accomplished, albeit only four of them 'live', and the Anson returned to R Malcolm Ltd for modifications to the equipment. However Winfield went on with Dr Stewart to perform some 15 more live tests after a further series of snatching dummies was successfully accomplished during 1946 with the modified equipment. Although this concept was proven as a practical solution for pick-ups, particularly in an emergency, the end of World War Two dissolved the requirement and the project was therefore abandoned. Incidentally, the Anson I was badly damaged in a gale during the night of

16-17th March 1947 and was struck off charge, being later consigned to the scrap dump at Lasham.

Need for Speed

Throughout the next 20 years or so the IAM undertook much aircrew research in respect of the advancing jet era, with work focussing on modern high-speed flight and experiments into the best pilot positions to withstand 'G' in particular. This had stemmed from trials by Capt Eric 'Winkle' Brown in flying the captured German Horten Ho 4 glider in the prone position, and IAM therefore continued with research into this pilot concept. It was considered that a 'knees up' position would be possible, with the pilot lying in a semi-backwards position. At this time the Reid & Sigrist RS.4 Bobsleigh VZ728 (ex-G-AGOS) was in use at Farnborough, having arrived from Desford on 23rd August 1951, and further prone research was conducted on this aircraft in conjunction with the RAE. It departed on 3rd March 1955.

The scientists were also looking at a more streamlined shape for the fighter aircraft of

Seen on the 'A' shed tarmac, during the RAE Golden Jubilee celebrations of July 1955, is the specially modified prone-pilot Meteor F.8 WK935. From August 1954 until April 1956, this aircraft gave IAM some valuable data to determine the effects of 'G' with the pilot lying in the modified nose in the prone position. It was eventually allocated instructional serial 7869M and can be seen today in the RAF Museum at Cosford. *via B Kervell*

the future. They were endeavouring to design a more efficient profile and cockpit, and perhaps dispense with the bubble-shaped cockpit altogether. To give a realistic picture for the jet era, further tests in this respect were carried out in the much-modified Prone-Pilot Meteor F.8 WK935, which arrived at Farnborough on 31st August 1954 from Baginton. This aircraft allowed the pilot to lie in the prone position in a modified nose to determine the effects of 'G', whilst a safety pilot sat in the normal cockpit. Although this research gave IAM some valuable data from the 55 hours flown, the next-generation jet fighters were being designed with seats raked rearwards at an angle, after this had proved to be a much more acceptable concept for 'G' manoeuvres in conjunction with the now-standard 'G-suit'. As a result, research into the prone/supine positions was abandoned and the Prone-Pilot Meteor was dispatched to Kirkbride on 20th April 1956. It is currently displayed within the RAF Museum collection at Cosford.

Human Factors

Whilst the prone-pilot experiments were being conducted, other research, in the 1950s and throughout the next two decades, centred on aircrew breathing systems. This included better oxygen systems for pilots; assisting with the development of the Onboard Oxygen Generating System (OBOGS) and altitude physiology, including hypoxia induced by rapid decompression. Further human-related research involved night-vision alertness; eye protection for aircrew when using laser designator systems; ejection seats; cockpit design; shape of control columns; design of instruments; development and evaluation of aircrew life support systems; immersing weighted volunteers into a water-tank to record cardio-vascular effects of weightlessness; development

of flying clothing, including thermal protectives; sea survival equipment including life-jackets and immersion suits; air-ventilated suits; liquid-cooled undergarments for future Space flights; assisting the American Space programme with various research; and 'G-suit' requirements for high performance jet aircraft types.

As the specification of aircraft continued to advance, so did the physical demands on their pilots – and none more so than in the dogfight. Obviously this research had first been considered during the aerial conflicts of World War Two with service aircraft used to determine the effects of 'G' in combat manoeuvres, particularly in high-speed turns and dives where the pilot would have a tendency to 'black out'. This research was none too successful at the time, however, and it became apparent that more sophisticated equipment would be required. Various designs were considered but, in 1947, the main features of a centrifuge were finalised. After further refinement, the RAF IAM commissioned the building of a man-carrying centrifuge system during 1952. Opened on 17th May 1955 by The Rt Hon Viscount Thurso KT, CMG – the wartime Secretary of State for Air – the centrifuge had a variety of applications but its prime use was for high-G research tests on aircrew. Mounted on a vertical axis at its centre and rotating clockwise, the centrifuge was built with a balanced rotating arm of 60ft span and has a rotating mass of 45 tonnes. This had a maximum rotational speed of 55rpm and was designed with a capacity of a maximum continuous radial acceleration of 30G with an onset of 1G per second. It incorporated the capability of simulating the range of centrifugal acceleration encountered by pilots when they change direction at high speeds. The centrifuge is powered by a single 1,000kw (1,340hp) DC motor coupled directly to the arm. A 'car',

built by ML Aviation at White Waltham, is attached at either end of the rotating arm in which the pilot 'under test' would sit. The cars, weighing 1,150 lb and capable of attaining a circumferential speed of 115mph (at 30G), could be interchanged with specialised compartments where other experiments could also be performed. The 'cars' or 'gondolas', as they are known, are both supplied with 240v mains electricity plus air, oxygen and mixed gases, whilst approximately seventy instrumentation lines are contained therein, which can record the various physiological parameters being tested. Each subject could be filmed as they undertook a variety of practical tasks whilst under the effects of 'G' loads, as a CCTV system is fitted within the 'gondolas' and is monitored from the control and recording rooms. Prone and supine tests were also carried out in the late 1950s/early 1960s using a special test rig designed for this specific purpose. Electrodes attached to the subject's body would record his reactions in the recording room, and he would also be in continuous contact via the communications system with an observer and a medical officer to ensure his well being, sitting near the centre of the arm as well as the centrifuge controller. Driven from the control room, still very much as it was in its original form, the speed of the centrifuge is determined by a Cam Profile Generator, this controlling the peak 'G' acceleration, the onset rate and duration of the run. Of course, safety factors were paramount right from the start, with duplicated braking systems, control systems, protective devices, safety interlocks and electrical emergency stop switches in place.

The centrifuge is still in operation today and during 2005 it operated a total of 3103 runs, although the grand overall total from commissioning until 31st December 2005 is a massive 88,314 runs in just over 50 years … and still rising! The RAF's Qualified Flying Instructors on the service's Hawk and Tucano training aircraft all undergo experience to 7G at the site but, with restriction applied due to its age (it was downgraded some years ago, for man-carrying runs, to a maximum rating of 9G), a new centrifuge is being planned for installation at RAF Henlow some time in the future. Meanwhile the centrifuge has recently been in use for anti-G trouser development; research into flight jacket and cold climate assemblies; head equipment assembly which incorporates a helmet mounted visor display; and aircrew

The IAM man-carrying centrifuge was opened in May 1955 and continues to operate today, under the control of QinetiQ. The centrifuge arm is seen here during December 2005, basically the same as it was when it was built 50 years ago. The 'car', built by ML Aviation, is of an aircraft-type construction, relating to the style of aircraft production in the early 1950s. *Falcon*

The last operational Spitfire at Farnborough was Mk.22 PK495. It served with the Institute of Aviation Medicine undertaking anti-G work from September 1950 until June 1953, then being sold as scrap. It is seen here at Farnborough on 30th September 1952. *FAST collection*

Seen on the western apron during 1966 is Canberra B.6 WT212 of the IAM, painted in overall white with Day-Glo nose, rear fuselage and wingtip areas. It also carries the IAM badge on the nose. This aircraft served with the IAM for over 17 years and undertook a number of different physiological and aviation medicine tasks before it was broken up in the mid-1970s. *Author's collection*

services package, all in support of the Typhoon programme. Recent work programmes included the RAF Typhoon pre-employment training, which incorporates an advanced anti-G system and pressure breathing for 'G' protection, which is somewhat different in the Typhoon compared with other fast jet aircraft. Indeed all aircrew posted to a Typhoon squadron will attend the centrifuge facility to receive instruction on the Typhoon life support equipment and will experience accelerations up to 9G. Research into G-tolerance assessments of anti-G trousers for the aircrew of future aircraft such as the JSF, as well as the Typhoon, is being studied. The centrifuge facility has also recently been utilised by inexperienced space tourists to enable them to experience '+G' and G-acceleration as part of their medical assessment. High-G acceleration training has also been carried out on pilots who have recently completed the Hawk advanced flying training course. Instruction is given in the use of anti-G straining manoeuvres, this being carried out at +8G and to the satisfaction of the supervisory medical officer, in order to reduce the risk of G-induced loss of consciousness of the pilot, particularly when flying the more advanced aircraft. He is thus able to tolerate the higher 'G' levels already experienced in the NFTC Hawk Mk.115. The RAF have recently incorporated familiarisation of G-acceleration at the centrifuge before pilots commence their Hawk

IAM Javelin FAW.6 XA831 is seen here parked on the western diamond dispersal area during November 1962. This aircraft never saw squadron service and operated with IAM for four years, undertaking a variety of tasks. *FAST collection*

Hunter T.7 XL563 arrived at Farnborough for use by the IAM on 2nd May 1963. It made its last flight some 30 years later on 9th July 1993. It is seen here outside 'C' shed during 1966, fitted with a long gust probe on the nose and finished in standard, for that time, silver and Day-Glo scheme. *Author's collection*

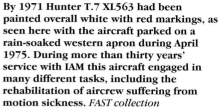

By 1971 Hunter T.7 XL563 had been painted overall white with red markings, as seen here with the aircraft parked on a rain-soaked western apron during April 1975. During more than thirty years' service with IAM this aircraft engaged in many different tasks, including the rehabilitation of aircrew suffering from motion sickness. *FAST collection*

Hunter T.7 XL565 was with IAM from February 1984 until September 1987, when it was returned to No 237 OCU. It is seen here, wearing RAF Institute of Aviation Medicine titles and badge, on the western apron on 2nd June 1986. The un-named lady in the foreground was an Air Traffic Controller about to embark on a familiarisation flight. *FAST collection*

- Meteor F.3 EE246 f White Waltham 21.11.49 for seat ejection work
- Harvard IIb FX238 f Hooton Park 5.6.44 for general communication duties; to High Ercall 28.7.53.

Over the years IAM Flight operated the following types:
- Spitfire F.22 PK495 (replaced PK513) 12.9.50 to 22.5.52
- Firefly I PP549 f Abbotsinch 11.12.52, to Anthorn for storage 7.54
- Sea Fury FB.11 VX608 f Langley 24.4.52 for 'anti-G' suit trials; to Donibristle 18.8
- Mosquito T.III TV974 f Andover 31.5.50 instrument presentation trials; to Wroughton 1.9.53
- Vampire FB.5 VV463 arrived 28.10.48 for anti-'G' work; to St Athan on 4.8.53
- Meteor T.7 WA636 f Hucclecote 24.1.50; crash landing Farnborough 10.4.52
- Meteor T.7 WA619 f Lyneham 3.3.55 until 19.11.62
- Meteor T.7 WL363 f Moreton Valence 7.5.52; crashed near Huckswagen in Germany 9.12.54 whilst on deployment from Farnborough
- Meteor T.7 WL405 f Kemble 13.9.62 shared with Weapons Flight until SOC 1.4.69
- Sea Hawk F.1 WF219 arrived 19.1.54 for cockpit communications work until 6.4.55
- Sea Hawk FB.3 WN114 arrived 4.4.55; until 7.8.57
- Balliol T.2 WG148 f Cosford 13.4.53 as 'hack' aircraft until SOC 8.12.58
- Canberra PR.3 WE145 f Wyton 2.5.55 until 16.8.56
- Canberra B.2 WH863 f Belfast 8.6.55; to RAE 29.3.57 (though IAM still had some use)

advanced flying training course at RAF Valley. They will be exposed to accelerations up to +7G and be instructed in the use of the anti-G straining manoeuvre.

Various other buildings and laboratories were also part of the IAM site, which also included the RAE Human Factors Group and Psychology Division and the Army Personnel Research Establishment.

IAM Machines

The RAF Institute of Aviation Medicine has operated its own aircraft from Farnborough throughout the years, although prior to February 1952, when IAM Flight came into being, aircraft were loaned to the unit for

their research work from SME Flight. Particularly notable was the 'anti-G' suit research carried out with probably the last Spitfire employed on experimental work during the early 1950s. Aircraft flying with the SME Flight on IAM work included:
- Spitfire F.22 PK513 f Aston Down 21.9.48 for 'anti-G' research but crash-landed at Abingdon 24.7.50 and reduced to spares
- Brigand B.1 VS854 f Filton 14.6.49 for tests of a nitrogen purging system with Varley valves until 21.4.50
- Meteor F.4 EE594 f Hucclecote 10.8.47 for instrument presentation factors and physiology work in connection with high-speed flight; to Andover 7.5.48

Hawk T.1 XX327 was transferred from No 2 TWU to the Institute of Aviation Medicine during 1988, and subsequently replaced Hunter T.7 XL563. The aircraft is seen here on the western apron on 24th March 1994, the day it relocated to Boscombe Down, where it is still operational today with the RAF Centre for Aviation Medicine. *Falcon*

- Canberra B.6 WH962 f Aldergrove 11.7.55; to Colerne 27.1.56
- Canberra B.6 WT212 f Wroughton 5.7.57; SOC 1.12.74 and scr Farnborough
- Javelin FAW.5 XA692 f St Athan 19.2.58; returning to St Athan 20.2.59
- Javelin FAW.1 XA549 f Moreton Valence 14.4.59; to St Athan on 19.8
- Javelin FAW.6 XA831 f Lyneham 14.7.59; to St Athan 21.10.63.

Other aircraft from the various RAE Flights have also been used by IAM over the years on an 'as and when required' basis, although these were mainly for communications or ferrying purposes. One particularly important aircraft was the first production Hunter T.7, XL563, which arrived from Filton on 2nd May 1963 and remained in faithful service with the IAM until it made its last flight on 9th July 1993 and was retired. During its long career, the Hunter's modifications for its research into flight envelope parameters included fitment with an On-Board Oxygen Generating System (OBOGS) and low resistance breathing oxygen plus a multi-channel recorder for measurement of physiological variables in breathing flow patterns under differing flight conditions. Aircrew chemical defence equipment was also trialled on this aircraft and proved successful with further development continuing over the years, as was cockpit altitude and 'G' research. Another of the Hunter's roles was the rehabilitation of aircrew suffering from motion sickness. Aircrew who suffered from this ailment would be sent to the IAM for 'desensitisation' and work undertaken to address this problem enjoyed an 80% success rate. During periods when the Hunter was undergoing maintenance, other T.7s (such as XL573, XL613, XL617 and XX466) were temporarily on loan, whilst XL565 served with the IAM for a

longer period, from 17th February 1984 until 16th September 1987.

This Hunter T.7, XL563, was subsequently replaced by a Hawk T.1, XX327, which was delivered from RAF Chivenor on 18th July 1988. A second Hawk, XX162, arrived from RAF Valley on 21st October 1992. These aircraft relocated to Boscombe Down on 24th March and 13th May 1994 respectively, from where they continue to operate wearing the titles RAF Centre for Aviation Medicine. The Hunter was subsequently mounted on a plinth in flying pose on 27th February 1995, outside the No 1 RAF Officers Mess, testifying to its 30 years of service at Farnborough in its specialised role with the IAM. However, with the closure of the No 1 Mess, the Hunter was sold to a private buyer and was removed from its plinth on 25th March 1999, being transported by road to Kempston before being moved into storage near Leominster.

Modern Medicine
During 1994, the RAF IAM underwent fundamental changes when the teaching and training function in aviation medicine for medical officers and aircrew, and the operational and clinical support to the frontline, streamlined

to become the RAF School of Aviation Medicine. The remainder of the set-up was absorbed into the Defence Research Agency (as it was at that time) on the northwestern side of the airfield, as the Centre for Human Sciences, which is now part of QinetiQ.

In 1998 the School moved to RAF Henlow together with the RAF Aviation Medicine Training Centre to form the new RAF Centre for Aviation Medicine (CAM), which is equipped and staffed to meet the era of the Eurofighter Typhoon. Work on 'desensitising' aircrews that have become prone to air sickness was commenced at Farnborough many years ago but this important activity is still being undertaken by the RAF CAM, operating its two Hawk T.1s from Boscombe Down, whilst high 'G' research is still being conducted in connection with the Eurofighter Typhoon's service entry.

This unit accomplished much important research and development work in the aviation medicine field during its near-60 years at Farnborough. The majority of the IAM/SAM buildings are now derelict and under the control of MoD Estates, but extant on top of Danger Hill – an area that is also destined for future redevelopment probably commencing late in 2006.

Hawk T.1 XX162 is seen undergoing maintenance in 'N' shed during March 1994. This aircraft arrived from 4 FTS during October 1992 for use by the IAM but retained its red, white and blue training markings, albeit with RAF Institute of Aviation Medicine titles. It relocated to Boscombe Down on 13th May 1994 and continues to operate there with the RAF Centre for Aviation Medicine, now painted overall black. *Falcon*

Having served IAM for over thirty years, Hunter T.7 XL563 underwent preparation by the DRA Aircraft Apprentices during 1994 for its new role as a plinth-mounted exhibit. The Hunter was mounted in flying pose outside the No 1 RAF Mess on 27th February 1995, where it is seen in this view taken during June 1995. The Mess buildings can be seen beyond. With the closure of the Mess, the Hunter was sold to a private buyer and was removed on 25th March 1999. *Falcon*

1965 to 1974

More Jets and Helicopters Arrive for Systems and Equipment Tests

The last decade had seen the introduction of more jets and turboprops, which had become more sophisticated than their predecessors. This was quite normal, however, and, as technology and systems advanced, so did the aircraft and their roles, with many now being able to perform a variety of multi-role functions.

Some of the technology that we take for granted today, had its roots in the 1950s, 1960s and 1970s. Fly-by-wire was first researched at Farnborough, as was the Head-Up Display (HUD) system, ultra low-level parachute dropping, low-light television, terrain mapping, night-vision goggles and radio-navigation equipment to name but a few, amongst a constant flow of research and development that kept the Air Fleet aircraft and the scientists busy throughout these years.

1965

The first of the Buccaneers to arrive at Farnborough was a Development Batch S.1 XK530, which was flown from Holme-on-Spalding Moor on 19th February 1965 for armament development trials, having been modified for carrying the WE177 weapon. It continued with these trials, operating from both Farnborough and West Freugh, until it was struck off charge on 26th August 1971 for spares, but was later allocated to RAE Bedford for ground running trials.

S.1 XK528 arrived on 24th November 1965 from Holme-on-Spalding Moor for weapons delivery trials. However, whilst undertaking a low-altitude bombing system (LABS) trial on the Luce Bay range, the aircraft suffered disintegration of the starboard engine, causing the main fuel tanks to rupture, followed by an in-flight fire. The aircraft crashed into the sea, southeast of West Freugh, on 30th June 1966, the pilot and navigator both losing their lives. There then followed Blackburn NA.39 second prototype XK487, which had originally been designated to pass to ETPS when the research and development commitment had ended. This did not happen, although the aircraft was flown to Farnborough from Holme-on-Spalding Moor on 14th December 1966 for spares use for the RAE fleet.

Arriving from Holme-on-Spalding Moor on 19th October 1966, was the RAE's first Buccaneer S.2 XN975, and this arrived for weapons development trials with Weapons Department. It left for Boscombe Down on 20th October 1967, then went back to the manufacturer and was redelivered to Farnborough from Holme-on-Spalding Moor on 11th October 1968. It then departed for the Royal Radar Establishment (RRE) at Pershore for radio/radar trials on 7th November 1974, passing to RAE Bedford on 26th May 1977 for radio/radar and navigation trials, and returning back to Farnborough again on 11th April 1978, as callsign 'BlackBox A', for high-frequency communication trials. However, having departed from Farnborough on 12th June on a trials detachment to Germany, this Buccaneer crashed near Laarbruch, on 14th June 1978, when control was lost after a mid-air collision with a German civilian helicopter. Also lost was Buccaneer S.2A XT285 that was detached to West Freugh in 1978, undertaking flight test trials for avionics of the MRCA (later Tornado) aircraft. However, whilst operating from West Freugh, it crashed shortly after take-off on 5th July 1978 and was destroyed.

Buccaneer S.2 XN975 arrived initially in October 1966, but returned to the manufacturer and served with the RRE until it returned to Farnborough during April 1978. It is seen here parked on the western apron at Farnborough on 12th June 1978, but it was lost in an accident in Germany two days later. *FAST collection*

Buccaneer S.1 XK525 is seen during April 1967, having recently arrived for weapons development trials with Weapons Flight. It continued to serve with RAE until March 1973. The colour scheme was dark sea grey, with white and red areas on tail and nose. *Author's collection*

Beverley C.1 XB259, of SME Flight, is seen making an ultra low-level drop over the Larkhill range on Salisbury Plain during 1965, with the sled pulled out of the hold by a large drag chute. Much of the parachute work undertaken by this aircraft involved drops over Salisbury Plain or Henlow. *FAST collection*

Seen here on the western parking apron at Farnborough during 1966, is Canberra B.6 XH568, in its white and Day-Glo colour scheme, with its nose gust probe. This aircraft was affectionately known as 'Flook', due to its long nose, and 'Flook', a cartoon character from the Daily Mail, duly appears on the tail. The Canberra arrived from Marshalls on 18th February 1955, being allocated to SME department for low-level turbulence trials. It was temporarily on loan to Weapons Flight from 1st January 1967 and eventually departed, bound for the RRE at Pershore on 28th December 1967. After being withdrawn from use in 1993, it was registered as G-BVIC and was flown to Bruntingthorpe for Classic Aviation. *Author's collection*

The next example to arrive was Buccaneer S.1 XK525, which arrived at Farnborough from Holme-on-Spalding Moor on 4th April 1967 for weapons development trials with Weapons Flight. This aircraft had also previously been in use for manufacturer's weapons trials at West Freugh. It continued to undertake a variety of weapons tasks between Farnborough and West Freugh and was eventually struck off charge during March 1973 for spares recovery.

The arrival of the NA.39s and early Buccaneers at Farnborough aroused much interest in the type's rotating bomb doors, even though perhaps they were an engineer's nightmare for servicing with all those hydraulic leaks! The type became affectionately known as the 'Brick', due to its flying characteristics. Buccaneers continued to fly from Farnborough from 1965 until 1994, being operated from either 'C' or 'L' sheds, with the second prototype, early pre-production (development batch) or early production examples, followed by three dedicated new-build examples and lastly the famous 'Nightbird' example all serving with RAE, the type enjoying a service time-span of nearly 30 years.

Aircraft providing the RAE scientists with airborne flying laboratories or aerial test platforms for their various trials at this time included:
- Avro 707C WZ744 IEE Flight
- Auster AOP.9 XK419 SME Flight
- Beverley C.1 XB259 SME Flight
- Buccaneer S.1s XK528 and XK530 Weapons Flight

- Comet 2E XN453 Radio Flight
- Canberra B.2 WD947 Weapons Flight
- Canberra PR.3 WE146 IEE Flight
- Canberra B.6 WH952 and XH568 SME Flight
- Canberra PR.7 WH776 Radio Flight
- Canberra T.4 WH844 SME Flight
- Canberra B(I)6s WT308 and WT309 Weapons Flight
- Devon C.1s VP959, VP975, XG496 and XM223 Transport Flight
- Hastings C.1s TG619 and WJ327 Radio Flight
- Hunter T.12 XE531 IEE Flight
- Javelin FAW.7 XH754 SME Flight
- Meteor T.7 WA714 IEE Flight,
- Meteor T.7 WF780 IEE/Radio Flight
- Meteor T.7 WL375, F.8 tail and FR.9 nose, IEE Flight
- Meteor T.7 WL405 Weapons Flight
- Meteor F.8 VZ438 Weapons Flight
- Victor B.1 XA922 SME/Radio Flight

- Varsity T.1s WL674 and WL679 Radio Flight
- Scimitar F.1s XD218 and XD229 Weapons Flight
- Shackleton MR.3 WR972 SME Flight
- Shackleton T.4 VP293 Weapons Flight
- Sycamore 3 WA576 IEE Flight
- Scout AH.1 XP166 IEE Flight
- Wessex HAS.1s XM327 and XM330 IEE Flight
- Whirlwind HAR.1 XA864 IEE Flight
- Whirlwind HAR.10 XJ412 IEE Flight
- Whirlwind HAR.5 XJ445 IEE Flight

The R.A.F. S.E.5a D7000 was undergoing an overhaul during this year.

The last Black Knight rocket was launched from Woomera, Australia, on 25th November. The first was launched in September 1958 and there followed a total of 23 launches. RAE Guided Weapons Department, and later Space Department, in conjunction with West-

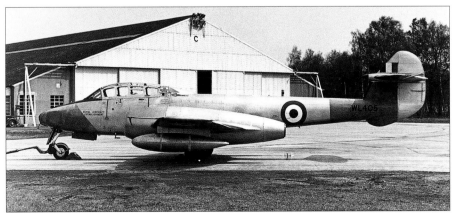

Meteor T.7 WL405 was undertaking low-level flying under closed-circuit TV control during 1966 and is seen here on the parking apron outside 'C' shed. *Author's collection*

lands, had design authority on this project. Black Knight was originally initiated in 1955 to pave the way for the long-range ballistic missile known as Blue Streak. This was cancelled in 1960 but trials continued to investigate hypersonic re-entry into the earth's atmosphere. The Gamma rocket engine was developed by the Rocket Propulsion Establishment at Westcott.

1966

Having arrived from 5MU Kemble on 5th May 1961, Meteor T.7 WF780 was allocated for continuation training, conversion and instrument rating flying with Experimental Flying Department. It continued in this role until February 1966 when it was substantially damaged whilst flying through severe air turbulence causing considerable airframe stress. It was struck off charge on 25th May 1966 and placed on the Farnborough dump, but later that year it was used for aircraft apprentice training, including spares recovery, and was not finally scrapped until the late 1970s. Meteor T.7 WG996 arrived from Boscombe Down on 3rd March 1966, basically as a replacement for WF780, in order that continuation training could still be accomplished by EFD. The Meteor departed back to Boscombe Down on 13th September 1966 and was later spares recovered at Pershore.

On 13th May 1966 the first Mach 2-capable aircraft arrived at Farnborough from Warton, when Lightning T.4 XL629 was delivered (callsign 'Tarnish 6') to the Empire Test Pilots School for fast jet instruction.

Decisions had been made previously to undertake a full environmental fatigue test on a complete Concorde airframe in the Structures Testing facilities at RAE Farnborough. This was to include simulating the heating and cooling of the aircraft in supersonic flight. The purpose of these tests was to simulate all the loads normally experienced by an aircraft flying in different modes of operation and to simulate the effects of external heating, due to the heating of the air at supersonic speeds and the cooling effect of subsonic flight during the descent from cruise altitude of 60,000ft. Over many years Concorde was flexed, pressurised and analysed, and the aerodynamicists, physicists, metallurgists and aircraft designers learnt much from these experiments in reproduction of the long-term cumulative effects of combined thermal and mechanical stress in large complex structures and their effect on the safety of all aircraft. Her Majesty Queen Elizabeth II visited Farnborough on 6th June to officially open this new £3 million Ball Hill laboratory for Structures Department, which housed the Main Test Frame for structural testing of a full-scale Concorde airframe. Her Majesty arrived on board Andover CC.2 XS789 of the Queens Flight, and the Queen also toured some of the workshops and hangars and witnessed a small flying display held in her honour. The flying display included the Handley Page HP.115 XP841 from RAE Bedford, P.1127 XP831 from RAE Bedford, R.A.F. S.E.5a D7000, and Beverley C.1 XB259 performing an ULLA drop.

The last of the Avro 707s, the 707C WZ744, was still in service at this time and was engaged in research with a new Electrical Signalled Manoeuvre Demand System, which was basically an electrically servo power flying control system. The 707 was fitted with a mini-controller, operated by fingertip action, which was a very early version of the side-stick now employed on many commercial and military aircraft today. It left Farnborough by road for the Colerne Museum on 19th April 1967.

The R.A.F. S.E.5a D7000 returned to flying again this year after it had been grounded when metal fatigue had been discovered within the propeller reduction gears.

Extending from Valiant Way in a westerly direction, a 400ft-long gravel bed was dug, parallel to the 07/25 runway, on the southern side at the western extremity of the airfield and filled with ¾-inch Thames Valley gravel. This was to be utilised for trials in arresting aircraft, following overrun from the runway, and this area was given the site designation of T67. Known as the 'Soft Ground Arresting Trials', this gravel-filled bed was first used by a Land Rover, driving into the gravel at 60mph. A P.1B Lightning, XA847, arrived from Warton on 21st April 1966, having been earmarked for these trials. The cockpit canopy was removed, the air intake was covered with a fine mesh guard, and the aircraft was taxied at 90mph into the gravel, in order to test the arresting action. Surprising the scientists undertaking this work, on one of its early runs the Lightning completely overshot the gravel bed – with no retardation whatsoever being noticed! Consequently the bed was dug deeper and the next occasion saw a successful arrest of this aircraft, as indeed was the case on many other occasions at varying speeds up to 100kts. Ex-ETPS Canberra T.4 WH854 was allocated for these trials on 9th December 1966. It was prepared in 'N' shed: minus its canopy and fitted with air intake guards, it was covered with thick sacking over its entire under-fuselage and mainplane surfaces.

P.1B Lightning XA847 enters the soft ground arrester gravel pit at Farnborough on 9th August 1966, creating a shower of stones as it decelerates from 100 knots. It was quite a job digging the aircraft out of the gravel once it had come to rest and then towing it out of the pit. *FAST collection*

Canberra T.4 WH854 also underwent soft ground arrester trials. It is seen here on 17th March 1967, entering the gravel pit, covered in sacking on the under-surfaces to protect the airframe from stone impacts and with the canopy removed. *FAST collection*

Seen here in its cream and red colours during the 1960s, whilst operating with RAE at Farnborough, is Whirlwind HAR.5 XJ445. It came to Farnborough on 17th June 1968 for use by IEE Department and served until it was allotted to the Chemical Defence Establishment at Porton for contamination/decontamination trials on 25th November 1971. *E Fuller collection*

Aerial view of the Army Air Corps hangar (034 Building), as seen during October 1969, with two Scout AH.1s and a Sioux AH.1 of 664 Squadron. This area is now occupied by a brand new office building known as 25 Templar Avenue. *FAST collection*

During 1966/1967, both of these aircraft were dug out of the gravel pit many times but, despite the successful trials conducted, which could have seen runway overruns being installed with this system, the project was abandoned. The Canberra was transferred to A&AEE Boscombe Down on 4th December 1967 and the P.1B Lightning was transported to the RAF Museum on 30th May 1969. A few years later, trials with a foam bed for arresting purposes were conducted at RAE Bedford, again proving successful but not being adopted.

The new Army hangar (O34 building) was now completed. Hitherto, a detachment of Sioux AH.1 helicopters had had their base in North Camp, at Lille Barracks, 7 Royal Horse Artillery, along Lynchford Road where Army Aviation (Interim) Squadron, 16 Parachute Brigade operated in support of the Parachute Regiment. From September 1964 the Scout AH.1s of 21 Flight were based at Elles Barracks, Pinehurst Road, just outside the RAE perimeter fence, and they moved to the new accommodation by 20th July 1966. On 1st May 1969 these two units were merged to become No 664 Army Aviation Squadron, with both Scouts and Sioux moving into this purpose-built hangar. The unit was to be again renumbered as No 656 Sqn in April 1978, by now equipped with Scout AH.1s and Gazelle AH.1s, and remained here until March 1982. There then followed the Royal Armoured Medical Corps and finally the Royal Corps of Transport (Training Wing 27

Regiment). Eventually the building became derelict, although it was used to house the Buccaneer S.2C XV344 for its repainting prior to going on outside display in the DERA/QinetiQ complex. The building was demolished in February 2000 and a new office block stands in its place.

Further helicopters arrived in the 1960s to continue with the research into rotary wing development and equipment. Wessex HAS.1 XM327 arrived from Yeovil on 4th July 1962 for IEE Flight, where it was to undertake flight tests of experimental hover controls and a flight director for all-weather operations until its return to Yeovil on 1st September 1966. Whirlwind HAR.5 XJ445 had arrived from Yeovil for IEE Flight on 17th June 1958 for flight trials in connection with development of an all-weather instrument system for helicopters. During June 1961 the work was extended to encompass auto-approach development and system tests, then re-allotted on 24th September 1964 to

rotorcraft instrument approach, overshoot and guidance problems and from November 1968 this included radio and navigational aids, a portable instrument approach system and aerial development. Its role being taken over by Wessex XL728, the Whirlwind was allotted to the Chemical Defence Establishment at Porton Down for contamination/decontamination trials where it arrived by air on 25th November 1971.

Also arriving for use by RAE was another Whirlwind, this being an HAR.10 XJ396, originally built as an HAR.5, which was delivered from Yeovil on 24th June 1966 for IEE Flight. This helicopter was in use for tests in connection with dissipation of static electricity, being fitted with external aerials. It was later transferred by road on 15th March 1968 to RRE Pershore. Pre-production Scout AH.1 XP166, ex-G-APVL, arrived from Yeovil on 16th August 1965 for development of a Head-Up Display for control of helicopters and a flight director system with IEE Flight.

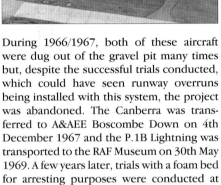

An air-to-ground view showing the Royal Aircraft Establishment in the low winter light of 26th January 1967. A visiting Dragon Rapide, G-AHXW from Fairey's at White Waltham, can be seen outside the black sheds, whilst on the 'A' shed apron are two Devon C.1s, the Hunter T.12, a Met Flight Hastings C.1 and a Varsity T.1. *FAST collection*

Beverley C.1 XB259 is seen through the north doors of 'C' shed during September 1967, whilst the nose of Scimitar F.1 XD248 can be seen on the left. This area is now the TAG Aviation parking apron, and 'C' shed remains in use today. *FAST collection*

Modification work was to be undertaken at the Westland facility at Hayes and the Scout was dispatched there by road on 2nd December 1965, returning to RAE on 23rd March 1966. In May 1969 it was re-allotted for trials with a swivelling pitot head, a stability augmentation system and a Rebecca ranging installation, this work continuing until 1973 when it was re-allotted for research into the effects of the release and trajectory of a standoff flare with Weapons Flight. In August 1974 it was in use for trials on the development of homing aerials for the Gazelle helicopter, making its last flight on 24th April 1975. It remained in use for Aircraft Apprentice Training until 1994 when it was sold to a private buyer.

This year saw the highest number of aircraft movements ever recorded at Farnborough: a total of 34,074, this including SBAC, for the 12-month period. Including the fleets of ETPS, MRF, IAM and RAE there were approximately 80 active aircraft on the airfield.

1967

The SME Flight Beverley C.1 XB259 made a record drop on Salisbury Plain of over 13 tons during trials from Farnborough. Other trials included dummy men being dropped from the rear ramp and dummy tank paradrops over the ranges on Salisbury Plain.

Instruments and Electrical Engineering Department were engaged in aerial recon-naissance trials using a Fairey Aerial Surveys Douglas C-47A Dakota (G-ALWC) from White Waltham. Equipment for control and navigation of aircraft and power supplies were also being researched.

Hunter F.6 XE531 had been converted into a T.12 flying testbed and demonstration aircraft by its makers in June 1961, with installation of a Head-Up Display (HUD) system and an FX126 camera system, the latter for TSR.2 research. This distinctive aircraft in its green and white colour scheme had arrived from Dunsfold for trials with IEE Department on 8th February 1963, its HUD system trials proving a great success. From 1967 it was also in use for take-off director trials, reconnaissance research, head-down instrument display, integrated flight control system trials and shock-wave research. On 17th March 1982 it crashed on take-off from Farnborough after engine turbine failure, both crew ejecting safely, with the aircraft coming to rest in the overrun area on Laffan's Plain.

In its all-white anti-flash nuclear scheme with Day-Glo trim, Buccaneer S.1 XN923 arrived from Holme-on-Spalding Moor on 23rd June 1967 for weapon development trials. In October 1968 it was reallocated for research studies on the parameters affecting acquisition visually and by use of TV, this equipment being transferred from Meteor T.7 WL405. These trials studying TV acquisition of targets had some two years later, by January

1970, developed into the study to match the visual presentation of ground objects with TV presentation. For this work the aircraft was fitted with a chin-mounted TV camera. When these trials were completed, this Buccaneer was re-allotted on 23rd October 1971 to continue on various weapons research and development tasks. It now carried wingtip pod-mounted cameras to record the weapon deliveries. It finally completed its Farnborough R&D flying on 30th April 1974. During its years at Farnborough XN923 frequently deployed to West Freugh to undertake weapon release trials, but returned to Farnborough for routine servicing. It departed for A&AEE Boscombe Down by road on 16th May 1974. It is currently on display at Charlwood with the Gatwick Aviation Museum.

The RAE Gliding Club had become a limited company in 1965 and split from the RAE Aero Club on 6th February 1967. At this time they had over 80 members and operated a Slingsby T.21, Olympia 2B, Olympia 403 and the Kranich that was on loan to the gliding Club at Westcott. Gliding continued at Farnborough until at least 1990.

The forward fuselage section of a Concorde arrived at Farnborough on 23rd April 1967 for structural testing in the Structures Department main test frame on the Ball Hill site. Further parts of the structure followed.

Work on construction of the new airfield radar tower, to stand some 70ft high on Ball Hill, was commenced. It was completed the following year and remained in operation until 2002. The initial Plessey AR.1 Surveillance Radar that was attached during August 1968 was replaced by a Watchman Radar in 1989.

UK3, the first British satellite spacecraft, later known as Ariel 3, was launched at Vandenberg AFB, Western Test Range in Cali-

Having served with Rolls-Royce (engine trials) and A&AEE (armament trials) as a single-seat F.6, Hunter XE531 was modified by Hawkers during 1961/62 into a two-seat variant, designated a T.12, for research work with RAE. It made its first flight after modification on 23rd October 1962 and arrived from Dunsfold on 8th February 1963 for service with IEE Department, undertaking head-up display work, camera research and integrated control system trials. It is seen here on 2nd April 1973, resplendent in its green and white livery. This aircraft served with RAE until it was destroyed in a take-off accident at Farnborough on 17th March 1982. *FAST collection*

By mid-1968 all four of the RAE Transport Flight Devon C.1s (VP959, VP975, XG496 and XM223) had been repainted in the white and blue scheme. They are seen here in formation on 15th October 1968. *FAST collection*

A unique formation of RAE Weapons Flight aircraft, seen on 18th July 1967, with Scimitar F.1 XD248, Buccaneer S.2 XN975, Canberra B(I)6 WT308 and Shackleton T.4 VP293. *FAST collection*

fornia on 5th May 1967. Ariel 4 followed in December 1971; Ariel 5 in October 1974, launched off the coast of Kenya; and Ariel 6 during June 1979. RAE had a considerable involvement in these projects.

1968

Prior to the commencement of the 1968 SBAC display at Farnborough there was a period of torrential rain, which had the disastrous effect of causing the Basingstoke Canal to burst its banks, just outside the south-western boundary of the airfield near to Eelmoor Bridge, with water cascading down over the airfield. This was to be the first day of the SBAC flying programme and this was cancelled for the day, as the water varied in depth from 1 to 2 feet, covering some two-thirds of the airfield and containing some large fish! However all was not lost, as the Royal Engineers, along with RAE personnel, set to repairing the breach. It was noticed that a redundant de Havilland Devon C.1 XA879, previously operated by ETPS, was lying derelict on the Farnborough dump. A rapid decision was made and the redundant aircraft was immediately put to good use. Its wings, tailplane and fin were removed and the fuselage was transported by crane and placed within the canal embankment in order to bridge the gap where the breach had occurred. The bank was then built up around the Devon fuselage so the airfield could be drained and flying continue. The area where the breach occurred was further consolidated with the planting of trees and bushes

and, today, there is no outward trace of where the Devon fuselage lies entombed.

Hastings C.1 TG619 had previously transferred to RAE from the Meteorological Research Flight on 20th April 1955. It made its last flight on 15th March 1968, having accrued 3050 flying hours. During its thirteen years flying with RAE Radio Flight it had been engaged in a variety of tasks including flight trials of 'Indigo Bracket 2' (1955-1961), X-band repeater and jammers, J-band equipment, warning receivers (1961-1963), and a VLF homing system (1963-1967). After a period of storage and spares recovery, it ended its days on the airfield fire dump.

In January the Empire Test Pilots School moved back to their birthplace at Boscombe Down, after nearly 21 years at Farnborough. Not all aircraft departed at the end of January, as some were undergoing deep servicing and they relocated to Boscombe Down over the following months. With the departure of ETPS, the Farnborough circuit became somewhat quieter, with the release of some two dozen aircraft.

The last Meteor to serve at Farnborough was Meteor T.7 XF274, which arrived from Boscombe Down on 29th February 1968 for continuation training and instrument rating flying by Experimental Flying Department pilots, basically replacing WA714. Originally the aircraft was in the standard silver colours with Day-Glo markings but during 1968 it was repainted in the now standard grey/white/blue RAE scheme. This Meteor was flown by most of the RAE test pilots of

the time, for training or instrument rating renewals or just a 'hack' aircraft right up until its unfortunate crash on the airfield on 14th February 1975, close to the Army hangar on Jersey Brow. It had accrued a total of 3123.5 flying hours.

The first Comet 4 for the Royal Aircraft Establishment arrived at Farnborough during 1968. Formerly G-APDF with BOAC, XV814 was delivered from Hawarden on 7th October for use as a flying laboratory by Radio Department. Installation of trials equipment and laboratory observation stations in the cabin meant that the Comet did not enter service with RAE Radio Flight until 2nd February 1971. A dorsal modification was added to the fin to enhance stability after the under-fuselage pannier had been fitted. During 1986 further modifications included the installation of a Nimrod fin from prototype XV147, complete with its fintop-mounted radome, to house state-of-the-art SHF Satcom equipment. Long-range communications trials and Beyond Line of Sight (BLOS) research work were extensively accomplished with this aircraft in its latter years.

During its 22 years of service, XV814 undertook sterling work for RAE and DRA and made many flights around the world on numerous research trials before retirement in December 1992. The last round-the-world trials flight was undertaken between 29th July and 17th August 1992, with the Comet visiting such exotic places as Crete, Bahrain, Sri Lanka, Singapore, Australia, Fiji, American Samoa, Hawaii and the USA.

Seen here on 5th November 1970, in this air-to-air view for the RAE photographer, is the prototype Lightning T.5 XM967 of SME Flight. It was used for boundary layer research and load and temperature measurements, as well as measuring fatigue on the fin, which is fitted with strain gauges and tufts. It arrived at RAE from Warton on 22nd May 1968 and continued in operation until February 1974, undergoing spares recovery during May. It was allocated to Honington for fire practice but was not delivered. On 9th January 1975 it was transported to Colerne, allocated 8433M, and upon closure of this museum it was transferred to Kemble where it was dumped during June 1976 and subsequently burnt. *FAST collection*

The last Meteor to join the RAE fleet was T.7 XF274, which arrived from Boscombe Down on 29th February 1968. Originally in a silver and Day-Glo finish, it was repainted white/grey/blue later in 1968 and generally served in the continuation flying and instrument rating role with Experimental Flying Department, being used by all the RAE Flights. It is seen here on the Southern Squadron apron during October 1973, but unfortunately it was destroyed in an accident on Farnborough airfield on 14th February 1975. *FAST collection*

Farnborough had seen Comet operations and structural testing of the type continuously since 1954 and the final association with the type came to an end on 28th January 1993, when the sound of its Rolls-Royce Avon RA29 turbojets were heard for the last time as XV814 was flown to Boscombe Down to act as a spares source for their own Comet 4C XS235.

1969

A NASA C-141A Starlifter 61-2779 arrived from Mildenhall on 15th July 1969 to undertake runway braking friction trials. Different runway surfaces throughout Europe were being tested to try to reach a conclusion on which surface had the best friction for application in the USA. These trials included both wet and dry surfaces and utilised four water tankers, each carrying 2,500 gallons. The main runway 25/07 and part of the cross-runway 36/18 were used for these trials. The C-141A departed back to Mildenhall on 18th July, a brief visit by the largest aircraft to date to have carried out trials at Farnborough.

The RAE Aviation Society was formed late this year, and continued for some 37 years until March 2006, although latterly it was known by the name of the DRA Aviation Society, it not having quite caught up with the modern name changes. Their first exhibition, celebrating their first anniversary, was held in the RAE Assembly Hall in 1970 which saw a 664 Sqn Army Air Corps Sioux AH.1 displayed in the car park. With decreasing membership numbers, and diffi-

culty in finding a meeting place, a decision was taken during February to disband the Society as from March 2006. Nevertheless there is today still a small band of mainly ex-RAE aircraft enthusiasts who keep the aviation scene alive at this famous airfield.

The RAE outstation at Ambarrow Court was closed on 12th September. Part of Radio Department had deployed there in 1941 after the bombing in 1940 and had remained for the next 27 years undertaking electronic countermeasures research including developing the 'window' that was to prove a success during the latter war years.

1970

HS.748 G-ASJT arrived from Staverton on 13th January 1970 for Instrument Landing System trials with Radio Department. This aircraft had been built at Woodford in 1963 as a flying laboratory for Smiths Industries. It was sold to the MoD for use at RAE and arrived at Farnborough still registered as G-ASJT but the military serial XW750 was allocated the same day. The aircraft flew 534 hours whilst at Farnborough and was dispatched to RAE Bedford on 6th December 1971 using RAE callsign 'Nugget 24'.

Originally it had been proposed that Varsity T.1 WJ887 was to join Radio Flight from Met Flight, but the HS.748 was chosen

Seen lifting off from the Farnborough runway is C-141A Starlifter 61-2779, the fifth built, that had been present undertaking runway surface friction trials during July 1969. *FAST collection*

instead and the Varsity was dispatched to 5MU Kemble on 19th February 1970.

Co-incident with the ILS trials, Visual Approach Slope Indicator (VASI) lights were installed at Farnborough during this year.

During March a Black Arrow rocket launched the R.1 satellite from the Woomera test range, RAE Space Department having an involvement in this project. The Black Arrow was based on the earlier Black Knight ballistic test vehicle that had achieved some 221 launches between 1958 and 1965 without a failure.

Engineering Physics Department continued their Soft Ground Arresting trials with a test rig built in Q153 building where a scaled undercarriage of a VC-10 was propelled into the sintered fuel ash arresting particles. As a result of the earlier trials a complete gravel arresting overrun system was installed at Southend Airport and Jersey Airport, the latter being put to good use in 1977 when it successfully arrested a Viscount during an overrun incident. EP Department were also undertaking rain clearance effectiveness and windscreen wiper trials with a Concorde nose utilising the Blower Tunnel installed on the airfield.

The RAE Museum opened on 27th August in the old theatre building at the top of Theatre Road. The brainchild of Wing Commander N H F (John) Unwin in the mid-1960s, he persuaded the then Director, Sir Morien Morgan, that RAE history should be preserved and it was agreed that a museum should be established. Arguably it could be said that the current FAST Museum has tenuous roots back in the RAE Museum.

Percival Proctor IV G-ANYP, belonging to the Brooklands Technical College, Weybridge, arrived by road at Farnborough for restoration by the Aircraft Engineering Apprentice Department. After completion it was returned to Brooklands in March 1971. It is now reported as being in a museum in Australia wearing its previous RAF identity as NP184.

As the old ETPS hangar (E1 building) was now vacant, various helicopters and aircraft moved to the south side of the airfield to form Southern Squadron.

1971

Tyre wear tests had previously been carried out by Engineering Physics Department using a Meteor where a special course was laid on the surface where runways 18 and 25 crossed. However maximum braking conditions were found to be less than that of the grooved runway surface. These trials led to further research where acceleration and braking trials were accomplished over a flooded test section of the main Farnborough 07/25 runway, laid with a high-friction runway surface to simulate heavy rain conditions. These trials utilised a Scimitar F.1 XD219, which had arrived from Brawdy on 16th December 1968. The aircraft underwent modification for its new role including the cropping of its outer wings, and having one fuel tank full of water. During 1971 trials commenced, in which the aircraft would taxi at high speed along the water-soaked runway, which also had specially prepared surfaces, to record the friction data. These trials continued for a couple of years until, on 9th January 1973, this aircraft overshot the runway and was badly damaged. It was transferred to the PEE at Shoeburyness during July 1975 for projectile research.

A British-built scientific satellite, known as Ariel 4, was launched in an American Scout rocket from Vandenburg AFB, California during December. Britain's first technological satellite, known as Prospero, was launched by a Black Arrow rocket from Woomera on 26th October 1971 and put into orbit. RAE Space Department had design authority and it was controlled and monitored by them from their satellite control centre in Q134 building and from Lasham.

Construction started by Whessoe Ltd on the new £4 million low-speed 5m wind tunnel, being built in a large pressure vessel on the Ball Hill site. This is still in use with Qinetiq today for aerodynamic research by various manufacturers using scale models of their aircraft products.

Pre-production Wessex Mk.5 Hybrid XL728 arrived from Yeovil on 25th March 1971 for use by Radio Department. It replaced a Whirlwind and was initially used for low-altitude hover trials. It was fitted

with an armament platform in the early 1970s for armament trials, and camera pods and various aerials for use by Radio & Navigation Department. It had also been in use by R&N for testing of the receiver mast at Cobbett Hill, having a long line with equipment suspended beneath the fuselage. 'Blue Parrot' was trialled with this helicopter and it was also fitted with a camera pod (previously on Auster AOP.9 XP277) on the port side of the fuselage. At one time it was fitted with a sensing and guidance system that included a 'hele-tele' TICM sensor ball. It made its last flight on 25th July 1985 and was delivered by road to PEE Pendine on 9th December 1985 for vulnerability projectile trials on the range.

The Radio Department Hastings C.1 WD480 had originally arrived from Radlett on 1st April 1953 for sonobuoy tests, along with trials of 'Red Shrimp' radio countermeasures and aerial measurement. The sonobuoys would be released from a bomb carrier within the under-fuselage pannier and were capable of surviving impact with the sea. They would then be automatically lowered to a pre-determined depth to listen for underwater contacts such as submarines, with the aerial attached to a floating buoy to transmit data back to the aircraft.

During 1971 WD480 undertook air pollution trials, flying from 500ft to 5,000ft taking various air samples for analysis. This aircraft had also been installed with a phased array L-band antenna to relay signals and communications by satellite for eventual use by commercial airliners. It made its last flight on 31st August 1974, whereupon it was allocated for EMC ground trials.

Comet 2E XV144 arrived from Bedford on 16th June 1971 to be used as a spares source to keep Farnborough's own Comet 2E, XN453, flying. Besides being robbed for spares it became a training aid for the RAE Aircraft Apprentice Training Department. It was placed on the dump during 1973 and was scrapped during 1976.

Arriving from Kemble on 21st July 1971, Hunter T.7 WV383 was destined to serve with RAE/DRA and DERA for the next 27 years. Arriving in a light grey and Day-Glo

This development batch Wessex XL728, the second of three pre-production examples, underwent a refit by Westlands in 1970/1971 and was brought up to an almost Mk.5 standard and was known as a Mk.5 (hybrid) for service with RAE Farnborough. It is seen here outside 'C' shed on 3rd June 1974, resplendent in its blue/white/grey colour scheme. This helicopter was used for various trials and research with Radio & Navigation Department and is fitted with a modified 'weapons' platform on the starboard undercarriage mount for aerial and equipment installation. It remained in service until 1985 when it was dispatched to Pendine for vulnerability tests. *FAST collection*

With its large under-fuselage pannier, housing special experimental radio equipment and a sonobuoy launcher, Hastings C.2 WD480 is seen in this air-to-air view on 15th October 1973. It spent most of its life at Farnborough with Radio Flight, undertaking numerous research duties, coming to RAE on 1st April 1953 after modifications and a refit with Handley Page where it had the sonobuoy launcher fitted. During June 1966 it returned to Radlett for fitment of a pannier and partial re-skinning with a lighter gauge aluminium to counteract the extra weight of the pannier. It returned to RAE on 28th February 1968 to continue its research duties and was retired on 31st August 1974, ending its days as a Ground Experimental Vehicle for EMC work, being finally scrapped during the late 1970s. *FAST collection*

scheme, it soon adopted a light grey and blue scheme in the same style as other Farnborough aircraft at that time. A standard RAF-configured two-seat aircraft, it went to the Cranfield Institute of Technology on 10th October 1972 to be fitted with twin Head-Up Displays (HUD), raster (TV scan) symbol generator, television camera system and associated equipment and returned on 13th September 1973 for operation by Flight Systems Department. The first actual TV sortie was not undertaken until November 1974, the system being evaluated to investigate the feasibility of the pilot using a TV image of the external view from the cockpit. This evolved with the development of Low Light TV that enabled near-daylight operation with minimum ambient lighting in the night sky, the LLTV system being installed during a scheduled aircraft servicing downtime. The first evaluation sortie for the system was on 4th July 1975 with the first actual night sortie being flown during January 1976. As sorties continued the aircraft altitude gradually reduced to 250ft, which then became the norm … even at night!

The Hunter's side-by-side seating arrangement allowed for close monitoring and cross-checking of crew activity. With the safety pilot in the left hand seat, LLTV trials continued through the mid- to late-1970s with many hours of night flying particularly through the Welsh valleys and the West Country, with flying scheduled around the phases of the moon and dependent on weather conditions. Initially these trials displayed the information on the head-down display TV monitors which progressed to information being projected into the HUD giving real and enhanced image parity and cursive flight information overlay. During this period, due to the large amount of night flying undertaken, the trials team were tagged 'Minions of the Moon'.

The paint scheme also changed during this time, when on 31st August 1976 it flew to Kemble, returning on 5th October in the famous red, white and blue raspberry ripple colour scheme.

In 1978 further upgrades and modifications were undertaken to the aircrafts' systems with the installation of a Ferranti Inertial Navigation System derived from the type fitted in the Tornado with a serial digital data stream output, which was state of the art at the time. Also installed were a digital air data computer, a digital data recording system, and a new symbol generator for the aircraft displays as well as cockpit modifications to control the systems. As part of the installation the entire data transmission system in the aircraft was converted from analogue signalling to digital, giving the aircraft a very flexible systems equipment fit.

As sensor and optical technology was progressing the aircraft became Night Vision Goggle (NVG) equipped, which gave the pilot the ability to see the external view through the goggles mounted on his helmet and, with special cockpit lighting, the cockpit instruments. The first NVG sortie was undertaken in July 1980. The LLTV system was also replaced in the early 1980s with a Forward Looking Infra Red (FLIR) mounted in the nose behind the modified nose cone.

Trials on FLIR, NVG and HUD technology continued, including a large amount of low-level night flying, and in the mid-1980s the aircraft adopted the name 'HECATE – Lady of the Night' which was applied to both sides of the aircraft's nose. Further development continued for 'HECATE' to demonstrate technology to enhance pilot vision systems to aid low-level day and night covert ingress, at high speed, in poor weather conditions that culminated in the PENETRATE programme. This system utilised mid-1980s computer technology and digital databases developed for terrain-referenced navigation to generate synthetic imagery of the terrain ahead of the aircraft. The image was fused with the FLIR picture of the real world and displayed to the pilot on his HUD.

The PENETRATE pod was built by Ferranti at Edinburgh, and housed the avionic systems to generate the synthetic imagery and also a terrain-referenced navigation system, a digital map generator and an optical

disk drive to store terrain data. The pod was fitted to the port inboard pylon of the aircraft, with a balance pod on the starboard inboard pylon, with flight trials commencing in mid-1988. During early trials of the system it was found that improved aircraft position awareness was essential to the accurate registration of the synthetic imagery of the real world. Therefore further upgrades/modifications were undertaken to install an integrated navigation processor and third-generation navigation systems. 'HECATE' was also used to demonstrate these systems as well as Ring Laser Gyros and a Global Positioning System (GPS), and to evaluate their successful integration using the integrated navigation processor into one combined and highly accurate three-dimensional position reference for use by other onboard avionics systems.

The PENETRATE program continued, although the pod was leased for a short period of trials by the US Navy at NATC Patuxent River, with further development including providing passive obstacle avoidance, automatic FLIR target cueing and an Intelligent Ground Proximity Warning System (IGPWS). This work continued through the 1990s and carried on when the aircraft moved to Boscombe Down on 24th March 1994 when experimental flying transferred from Farnborough.

'HECATE' had a long and pioneering experimental career evaluating technologies that are now commonplace, with the aircraft eventually having over 20 years of covert mission research. During this time a large amount of flying was undertaken at low level, a mere 250ft above ground level, at night, sometimes in adverse weather which must have generated some 'interesting' moments. In addition several smaller trials were undertaken throughout HECATE's career including the evaluation of early terrain referenced navigation systems, the evaluation of a proposed replacement of the Tornado moving map known as Remote Map Generator (ROMAG), assessment of an optical disc drive for the Tornado

Digital Map Generator introduced into the Tornado GR.4, the appraisal of other digital map generator products and the evaluation and comparison of NVGs.

After her last flight, with a total time since new of 3,670.30 hours, 'HECATE' was placed in storage at Boscombe Down and then negotiations began to return the aircraft to Farnborough for display at the FAST Museum. During April 2000 'HECATE' was carefully dismantled and was road-transported up the A303 to Farnborough on 13th April 2000. Upon arrival at its old 'stomping ground' it was placed in 'M' shed, in a dismantled state, for a further period of storage, before being moved to the FAST Museum on 14th June 2002.

1972

By now the Devon C.1s of the RAE Transport Flight (VP959, VP975, XG496 and XM223) had collectively achieved 25,000 flying hours. The four aircraft were operating ferry services to the RAE outstations as well as general communications duties to other airfields within the UK and Europe.

Further Buccaneer arrivals at Farnborough were S.1s XN965 and XN960, flown in from Lossiemouth for cockpit noise investigation trials, the latter on 18th April 1972. They were struck off charge during 1973 and 1974 respectively, both were eventually placed on the Farnborough dump by April 1980.

Sikorsky-built development batch Sea King HAS.1 XV371 was transferred to RAE Farnborough from Filton on 22nd May 1972 to begin a long career in research flying with Avionics Department, later becoming Flight Systems Department. Still in its midnight blue colour scheme, and eventually wearing Royal Aircraft Establishment titles, the Sea King was put to immediate use on trials with an approach guidance radar, followed by research into a Helicopter Engine Rotor Management Electronic System (HERMES), then Doppler trials followed by Defect Survival Auto-Stabilisation trials (DSAS). In 1977 trials began with a low-light TV camera mounted on the starboard side giving a head-down display to the pilot, this work including night flying and instrument night approaches to ships. At this stage the helicopter had received Day-Glo stripes around the fuselage to make it more visible, and it also wore the adopted duck badge (actually a Peking Duck

motif, suitably copied, that was liberated from a local Chinese restaurant) that became standard, albeit unofficial, with RAE Farnborough Rotary Wing Squadron helicopters.

As night vision systems advanced so the work of XV371 intensified and this helicopter was used for Night Vision Goggle trials in 1978, and in 1980 much night flying was accomplished for trials of a stabilised hand-held night surveillance aid, all this work being put to eventual good use in the Falklands campaign of 1982. By now the Sea King had changed to the standard 'Raspberry Ripple' colour scheme and was fitted with a nose-mounted Forward Looking Infra-Red (FLIR) system. For a short time, around 1982, this Sea King had its starboard side painted grey with an anti-laser reflective paint for detection trials.

In 1983 the Sea King was transferred to Weapons Department at RAE and underwent another nose profile change to incorporate a NATO flange that could carry a number of different sensors and the like. Missile seeker heads were carried and in 1985 trials were commenced on an early version of the High-Speed Anti-Radiation Missile (HARM), and later the Sea Eagle, with the helicopter being deployed to locations away from Farnborough. There then followed Millimetric wave and Infra-Red Test Head (MIRTH) trials, with sensors carried in a Heli-Tele ball mounted on the nose.

Various other trials were flown from RAE (later DRA), until flying was transferred and XV371 moved to Boscombe Down on 3rd March 1994.

1973

De Havilland Comet 2E XN453, an RAE veteran engaged in navigation and communications systems development since 1959, made its last flight on 9th February 1973, having flown c.4,600 hours. It was stored for a period and in 1977 its wings were removed and sent to BAC at Woodford for tests while the fuselage was placed on the Farnborough dump and during 1985 it was burnt during practice exercises by the RAE Fire Service. A further arrival, on 19th July 1973 from Lasham, was Comet 4 XX944, ex-G-APDP

with Dan-Air. On 5th October 1973 the Comet was dispatched to Boscombe Down where it was to undergo an instrument installation. After the installation work was completed it continued to operate from Boscombe Down on a temporary basis whilst the Farnborough main runway was undergoing resurfacing work and it returned to RAE on 14th August 1974 for use by Radio Department. It then made an overseas trip undertaking radio and navigation research to the USA and the Azores during August/September 1974, callsign 'MPDXC'. Further work included Microwave Landing System (MLS) trials at RAE Bedford in January 1975 followed by two more trips to the Azores in February/March and probably what was its final trial, a further MLS round-trip to RAE Bedford on 16th April 1975. Thereafter the aircraft required maintenance and, during the course of inspection at Farnborough, severe corrosion was found that resulted in the aircraft being withdrawn from service. In 1977 the Comet underwent a partial spares recovery by the Aircraft Apprentice Department before it went on to be used for smoke trials up to 1978/1979. It was then placed on the Farnborough dump and was eventually scrapped in August 1984.

Andover C.1 XS646, an ex-RAF Middle East Air Force example, was delivered from 5MU Kemble, via Bedford, on 26th January 1973, to be used to investigate the operational problems likely to be encountered in making automatic approaches to runways in low visibility. This aircraft continued to serve at Farnborough for many years and could be fitted with a variety of nose profiles for different sensor trials, housing infra-red cameras for research into electro-optic sensors, being affectionately known as 'Miss Piggy'. There was also an under-fuselage pylon that carried a Vinten camera pod and it had a FLIR installation undertaken at Farnborough during 1994 that was integrated with a navigation system. The aircraft relocated to Boscombe Down on 11th July 1994 and is still in operation with QinetiQ today. Already in use at Farnborough was Andover C.1 XS606, an ex-RAF Far East Air Force example, that had arrived from 5MU Kemble

Shortly after Hunter T.7 WV383 was delivered to Farnborough in its grey/Day-Glo scheme, a colourful 4-ship formation was staged for photographic purposes on 27th July 1971. Seen here are Hunter T.7 WV383 (Flight Systems Department); green/white T.12 XE531 (IEE Department); camouflaged T.7 WV372, wearing the markings of 'R' of II (AC) Squadron (on loan to RAE); and white/red T.7 XL563 of the Institute of Aviation Medicine.
FAST collection

on 2nd August 1972. It was based with Western Sqn and was operated by SME Flight and
Engineering Physics Dept and was engaged
in parachute drop trials. Its stay was relatively short as it departed for Boscombe
Down on 24th September 1975 as 'Tester
63' to join the ETPS fleet with whom it still
operates as a flying classroom today. Other
than XS790, mentioned later, there was one
more Andover that served at Farnborough,
this being C.1 XS607 that arrived at RAE for
'B' Flight on 16th September 1976 from
Boscombe Down. Undertaking various trials
with onboard equipment this Andover was
frequently deployed to West Freugh for
sonobuoy research among other tasks.
Towards the latter days of Farnborough
operations this aircraft was fitted with an
Anti-Radar Missile Airborne Data Analysis
System (ARMADAS) that underwent trials to
analyse the electro-magnetic signatures
emanating from radar equipment to enable
more effective anti-radar techniques to be
developed to improve the protection
against airborne attacks of friendly air
defence radar units. It was also fitted with
equipment for towed decoy trials. It
departed for Boscombe Down on 15th
August 1994 to continue its research.

Meteor F.4 EE531 was sold to the Midland
Aircraft Preservation Society on 26th June
and was transported from Lasham to Coventry by road. It is still at Coventry, resplen-

dent in its former camouflage markings,
with the Midland Air Museum. Although an
RAE airframe it had been moved by road
from Farnborough to Lasham on 24th
August 1953 for use by Radio Department
for trials of various mock-up radio aerial
installations and spent the next twenty years
at Lasham, mostly inside the RAE hangar
there but occasionally glimpsed outside.
The Meteor was 'replaced' at Lasham by the
centre fuselage of Comet 1 G-ALYX, which
was moved from Farnborough by road in
1963, and continued the aerial research up
until closure of the site in 1996.

A Skylark rocket carrying an Ariel IV satellite was successfully launched from the
Andoya rocket range in Norway on 16th
October. This was of RAE design and produced by the British Aircraft Corporation
and further launches followed. RAE Space
Department were involved with research
into the Aurora Borealis (Northern Lights)
and magnetic sub-storms, to investigate the
structure of the ionosphere during particular auroral disturbances.

Three large piston-engined aircraft were
retired from RAE service during this year.
These were Shackleton MR.3 WR972, Hastings C.1 WJ327 and Beverley C.1 XB259.
The Shackleton had come to RAE on 13th
April 1961 from Boscombe Down and was
used by SME Flight for a variety of trials,
including towing and drop testing of para-

chutes and dropping of bomblets. It was
retired on 31st January 1973, having made
its last flight on 19th January, and was subsequently handed over to the RAE fire service for training.

Hastings C.1 WJ327 had arrived on 6th
November 1967 from Colerne for use by
Radio Flight for a variety of trials in its role
as a flying radio laboratory, including
Doppler and ILS research, ECM, air pollution and improved satellite communications systems. It had achieved some 8,300
flying hours when it was retired, having
made its last flight on 30th March 1973, to
become a spares source for WD480,
although it was eventually scrapped.

The Beverley had arrived way back on
16th September 1959 from Brough and
operated with SME Flight for its entire life at
Farnborough until its retirement in 1973. It
was then purchased by Court Line, as a
freighter to transport RB.211 engines for the
airline's L-1011 TriStars, and was flown to
Luton on 14th March 1973. This aircraft, the
sole example of the type extant, can still be
seen at the Fort Paull Museum, Hull.

The RRE at Pershore had now completed
their work with Varsity T.1 WL679 and it
came back to RAE Farnborough on 18th July
1973, at the time in an aluminium finish with
a white roof and broad blue cheat-line. It had
previously been with Radio Flight at RAE for
various trials from 18th January 1954 until its
departure for Pershore on 29th August 1968.
On 7th August 1973, as 'Bluebell 1', it was
flown to Short Brothers at West Malling,
Kent, where Low-Light Television (LLTV)
equipment from WJ893 was installed along
with the new FLIR both housed in the bomb
aimer's position in the ventral pannier. It did
not return until 28th March 1977. The cock-

pit was now redesigned and rebuilt with extensive modifications undertaken at Cranfield with new instrumentation and cockpit TV monitor. From this time various FLIR trials continued with initial trials for evaluating infra-red television when used in starlight and subject to the effects of headlights and the like. FLIR technology was now increasing in importance and in 1979 the aircraft undertook the first of several trials during army exercises in Germany to identify and obtain data on armour on the ground. By the end of the decade the aircraft had received the standard red, white and blue 'Raspberry Ripple' colour scheme.

Various other trials were subsequently undertaken as the use of FLIR was expanded, including researching the effects of radiation from the airframe of a fast jet, this being conducted from Aberporth where a Jaguar was flown across the sight-line and head-on towards the aircraft. Battlefield dust interfering with thermal imagery was examined with the aircraft flying towards armour obscured by controlled explosions on the ground. Other data gathering and identifying exercises were undertaken including shipping, industrial areas and refineries, with trials flown both day and night in different weather conditions contributing to form a comprehensive data base. Another 'interesting' trial was flying the aircraft low-level at night over defined routes then landing without runway lights using only the FLIR and cockpit monitor.

During the 1980s, as FLIR technology evolved, GEC Avionics built two new FLIR systems: a High Spatial Bandwidth (HSB) with wide and narrow field of view lenses, and a space stabilised system being developed for the narrow field of view system. The FLIRs were fitted in the nose and bomb aimer's position of the aircraft.

Service continued through the decade with Missile Technology and Counter Measures Department including, during 1989, trials in conjunction with the US Wright Research and Development Centre with a month-long trial in Germany to obtain data on American armour.

In the latter days the aircraft flew an average of two sorties a week, each of two hours duration, all carried out at low level (250ft) over particular targets. Trials continued into the 1990s and on 17th July 1991, as the

world's last flying Varsity, it made three low passes over Brooklands to commemorate the first flight of the Varsity (VX828), from Wisley on 17th July 1949. By this time a decision had been made to retire the Varsity and replace it with Andover CC.2 XS790. The last operational flight, which involved ADAPS (an airborne transponder ranging system), was undertaken on 2nd August 1991. During this flight a number of passes were flown over its birthplace at Hurn Airport with a low pass along the runway at Boscombe Down. When it finally touched down at Farnborough the aircraft had accrued some 4,350 flying hours. The Varsity was placed in storage at Farnborough and during this period the trials equipment was removed and the aircraft maintained in a 'flying condition' with engine ground-runs regularly undertaken.

Then on 27th July 1992 the Varsity was to make its final flight as it was delivered to the Aerospace Museum at Cosford.

1974

The eventually familiar shape of 'Snoopy', the unique Hercules W.2, arrived at Farnborough on 3rd January for the Meteorological Research Flight (MRF). Details of its career at Farnborough appear in chapter 9.

Three specially-built new Buccaneer S.2Bs (XW986, XW987 and XW988) were delivered to RAE during this year from Holme-on-Spalding Moor. Originally there were four ordered, but XW989 was cancelled and not built. These aircraft were delivered in a yellow and green scheme, with two of them eventually succumbing to the overall 'raspberry ripple' house colours, whilst XW988 retained its original scheme. All three were initially delivered to RAE West Freugh: XW986 on 25th January 1974, XW987 on 15th March 1974 and XW988 on 16th May 1974. Their 'home' base was still RAE Farnborough as this is where the major servicing took place. The aircraft were engaged on bombing trials and other weapon research operating from West Freugh over the nearby Luce Bay range. During 1988 XW986 was fitted with a dummy TIALD pod beneath its port wing as a proof-of-concept aerodynamic demonstrator for airworthiness clearance trials. The full development trials were conducted with XV344. All three of these new-

build aircraft eventually saw service at Boscombe Down, all being retired in 1994. All three now operate from Thunder City at Cape Town, South Africa, either as air display performers or giving the paying public the ride of their life!

The SBAC display heralded the appearance of the sinister Lockheed SR-71A Blackbird 64-17972, callsign 'Aspen 01', after its record-breaking flight from New York to London.

The small blister hangar adjacent to the Southern Squadron apron, once in use by the RAE Aero Club, was removed to make way for further SBAC development.

The main runway 07/25 underwent resurfacing work, including the laying of a special friction course to assist with aircraft braking, between February and July 1974. The larger RAE aircraft, including the fast jets, were temporarily relocated to RAE Bedford and A&AEE Boscombe Down, while smaller aircraft and helicopters still operated using the other operational runways.

BAC 1-11 Srs 402AP XX919 (ex-PI-C1121) was purchased from BAC during April 1973 as a research aircraft. It was delivered to RAE on 16th May 1974 but flew from Hurn to Bedford, via a fly-by at Farnborough en route, due to the resurfacing work. It eventually arrived at Farnborough on 14th August for operations with Radio Flight on satellite communications research, long-range navigation aids, sonobuoy research, aerials and high frequency communications trials.

A Miranda X4 was launched from California in March, this being the first three-axis attitude stabilised spacecraft built in the UK. The gyro-processing and switching technology, and the solar cell arrays were RAE-designed. This spacecraft was tracked and controlled from Q134 building and Lasham and the data received was processed at Farnborough. This year also saw the cancellation of the Black Arrow project.

In May the College of Arms issued a badge for the Royal Air Force Element of the Royal Aircraft Establishment, with the inscription *Scientiae Auxilium* – Service to Science. The full description states: *'Issuant from the Astral Crown a Pterodactyl is displayed supporting in the beak a key bendwise wards downwards'*.

Seen making a low-level fly-by down runway 29 at Farnborough is BAC 1-11 Srs 402AP XX919, en route from Hurn on its delivery flight to Bedford on 16th May 1974. The main runway, vector 25, was closed for resurfacing work and the aircraft was flown direct to Bedford, where it joined the Radio Flight fleet, which had temporarily detached to Bedford during this period. The 1-11 relocated to Farnborough permanently on 14th August 1974. *FAST collection*

1975 to 1984

Sensors, Night Vision, FLIR, and Target Systems

For over 70 years, important research work had been accomplished at Farnborough and, during the latter years, this had included many UK and overseas trials detachments. During the past two decades, although numbers of aircraft and personnel had progressively decreased, there was still an extraordinary amount of data accumulated from all these trials, which led on to even further development.

By now the RAE motto, '*Alis Apta Scientia – Winged Knowledge*', was truly merited and the RAE was at the forefront of aviation research and development worldwide.

Development work continued at Farnborough, and much research and testing was directed towards Head-Up Displays, Low-Light TV Systems, Radar and Sensor technology, Weapons, Night Vision Goggles, Forward-Looking Infra-Red, Laser Ranging Marked Target Seeker (LRMTS), Thermal Imaging, Airborne Laser Designators and other projects.

1975

Avro Shackleton T.4 VP293 was retired on 23rd May 1975. It had been delivered to Farnborough on 6th January 1964 from Aldergrove and latterly used by Weapons Flight for low-level flying in conjunction with closed circuit TV control, which included weapons applications. It was sold to the Strathallan Museum, being flown to Auchterarder from Farnborough on 3rd May 1976. It was scrapped in 1990 although the nose and cockpit section has been restored by the Shackleton Association to its original white livery and is extant today.

Aircraft now in use by RAE at Farnborough included Andover C.1s XS606 and XS646 'B' Flight; BAC 1-11 XX919 Radio Flight; Buccaneer S.2Bs XW986, XW987 and XW988 Weapons Flight, Western Sqn; Canberra T.4 WH844 'C' Flight, PR.7 WH793 'C' Flight, B(I)6s WT308 and WT309 Weapons Flight, Western Sqn; Comet Mk.4s XV814 and XX944 Radio Flight; Devon C.2s VP959, VP975, XG496 and XM223 Transport Flight; Hunter T.7s WV383 and XF321 Western Sqn; Meteor T.7 XF274 Radio Flight and NF.11 WM167 stored; Varsity T.1s WL635, Cranfield-based, and WL679, West Malling-based, were operating from Farnborough on trials work; Sea King HAS.1 XV371 Avionics Flight; Wessex HAS.1 XM330 Avionics Flight/'A' Flight, HU.5s XL728, XS241 and XS484 Avionics Flight/'A' Flight; Scout AH.1 XP166 made its last flight on 24th April 1975, Avionics Flight/'A' Flight and Gazelle AH.1 XW849 'A' Flight.

The Waghorn Eagle was unveiled at the No 1 Officers Mess on 6th December 1975 to commemorate Flt Lt H R D Waghorn who was the Schneider Trophy winner in 1931. Flt Lt Waghorn was killed on the Farnborough airfield on 5th May 1931 when Hawker Horsley J8932 of ER Flight, which he was flying, crashed during a radiator test of the prototype Rolls-Royce Buzzard engine. The Eagle was transferred to Boscombe Down when the Mess closed.

This classic RAE buildings back-drop, for an aircraft about to land on runway 25, has been seen in many SBAC views over the years. Day-Glo orange and grey Shackleton T.4 VP293, ex-Weapons Flight, is seen here about to land on 5th November 1975 after undertaking a test flight. Most of the buildings seen here are now history, having been demolished in 2000/2001. The nose of this aircraft is still extant with the Shackleton Association. *FAST collection*

Andover C.1 XS606, now with ETPS at Boscombe Down, had spent three years at Farnborough, having been transferred from the RAF. It had been used for a variety of trials with SME Flight and is seen here on the western apron at Farnborough on 17th April 1975 in the grey/white/blue colour scheme applied in 1972. It left Farnborough for Boscombe Down on 24th September 1975 and still serves with ETPS under the QinetiQ fleet. *FAST collection*

BAC 1-11 Srs 402AP XX919 is seen here in its original RAE scheme on 22nd April 1978. It was repainted 'raspberry ripple' in the 1980s and served with Radio & Navigation Flight on many trials. It remained in service to the end and was relocated to Boscombe Down on 23rd March 1994, being eventually withdrawn from use and broken up at Boscombe Down on 6th July 2000. *FAST collection*

A classic air-to-air study of RAE Farnborough Radio Flight Comet 4 XV814, as seen on 10th March 1977. Having arrived in October 1968, this aircraft went on to spend nearly 25 years with Radio & Navigation Department, undertaking much valuable research work. It left Farnborough for Boscombe Down on 28th January 1993 and was scrapped on 12th August 1997. *FAST collection*

1976

The Aircraft Apprentice Training Department moved to 'E' Shed, this hangar being locally known as the 'Secret' hangar during the 1950s and 1960s and latterly the temporary home for many stored Sea Vixens. It was demolished in the late 1980s, this area now being part of the BAE Systems Headquarters complex.

In conjunction with RAE Bedford and Plessey Radar, Radio and Navigation Department were evaluating the Doppler MLS (Microwave Landing System) on the ground and in the air, with a view to installation at commercial airports.

This work had commenced in the 1960s using a HS Trident airliner for auto-land and trials at Bedford. In the mid-1970s, BAC 1-11 XX919, Comet Mk.4 XX944 and Andover C.1 XS646 aircraft flew these trials from Bedford, with all the data being analysed at Farnborough. The 1-11 and Andover visited various other airports including Manchester, Berne, Switzerland and Kjevik, Norway, where many approaches were flown and data obtained. Unfortunately, under great competition, this system eventually lost out to the competition from USA/Australia in April

The second development Sea King/SH-3D XV371, known as a Sea King HAS.1 (DB), came to RAE Farnborough on 22nd May 1972 as a trials helicopter with Avionics Department/Flight Systems. It is seen here on 8th August 1977, in its original midnight-blue scheme, but with Day-Glo trimmings and RAE titles, a scheme it retained for five years until it was repainted in the standard 'raspberry ripple' house colours. This helicopter underwent various modifications, including a profile change, when a NATO flange was housed in the nose to carry various sensing equipment. It is still extant with the School of Flight Deck Operations at RNAS Culdrose. *FAST collection*

The Aircraft Apprentice Training Department trained many aircraft engineers throughout its 30 years of instruction. Seen here in June 1976, outside 'E' shed, are the then current aircraft apprentice trainees, with supervisor Reg Weeding, posing in front of their four instructional airframes: Meteor T.7 WL405 (now at Yatesbury); Scout AH.1 XP166 (now at East Dereham); Provost T.1 XF844, still in its original No 6 FTS scheme (now at Bruntingthorpe); and Canberra B.2 WJ728 (ex-100 Squadron), which arrived in 1976 was broken up in 1984. This important training department moved back to 'A' shed and then to 'Q' shed, where it was disbanded in 1994. *FAST collection*

Devon C.1 VP959, the oldest of the four in RAE Transport Flight service, is seen here outside 'Q' shed on 14th October 1975, having recently been repainted in the blue/white scheme. This aircraft arrived at Farnborough on 9th March 1949 and departed on 3rd November 1986, having spent over 37 years undertaking ferry transport duties and other communications flight tasks. *FAST collection*

1978 when the TRSB (Time Reference Scanning Beam)/Interscan landing guidance system was adopted for worldwide use.

1977

The oldest of the RAE Transport Flight Devon C.1s, VP959, clocked up 10,000 flying hours (20,563 landings) on 18th May whilst operating a routine ferry service to RAE Bedford.

The Goodyear Airship N2A flew overhead Farnborough on a few occasions during June, this being the first airship seen in the Farnborough circuit since the R-100 in 1930.

Three Lightning F.2As arrived from Gutersloh, Germany for eventual scrapping at Farnborough. These were XN727 (allocated 8547M), XN726 (allocated 8545M) and XN771, using callsigns 'MSUYA/B/C', all previously being operated by No 92 Sqn; and coded 'W', 'N' and 'S' respectively. These were all disassembled during 1978 with parts going to the PEE at Shoeburyness although the cockpit section of XN726 was saved and is with a private collector at the Boscombe Down museum.

Following on from previous unmanned/pilotless aircraft projects, there was consideration given during the early 1970s to the possibility of Sea Vixen FAW.2s being converted to drone aircraft, to be known as the D.3 variant. Consequently a number of ex-Squadron aircraft arrived at RAE Llanbedr and Farnborough during the 1970s, initially for storage, but ostensibly for refurbishment, removal of equipment and to make airworthy prior to conversion to drones at Flight Refuelling Ltd, once the decision had been made. The aircraft that originally went to Llanbedr came to Farnborough and between 1972 and 1977 some 26 Sea Vixens passed through Farnborough, many of these being stored in 'E' shed, whilst others were parked in open storage on the airfield. Four drone conversions were undertaken by FRL, (XN657, XP924, XS577 and the partial conversion of XN652), along with two FAW.2(TT) variants (XJ524 and XS587), but during 1982 the project was abandoned and the aircraft were either scrapped, sold or used as instructional airframes. Indeed the only airworthy Sea Vixen today, XP924/

G-CVIX, was the second D.3 variant converted. The 26 aircraft that passed through Farnborough, some arriving by road, were as follows: XJ494 (1976-83); XJ524 (1972-1977); XJ560 (1977-79); XJ572 (1975-84); XJ579 (1975-84); XJ580 (1972-80); XJ604 (1977-86); XJ608 (1977-79); XN649 (1973-84); XN652 (1972-74 and 1979-80); XN653 (1978-84); XN658 (1976-83); XN688 (1977-84); XN696 (1976-82); XN699 (1977-88); XN700 (1977-83); XN705 (1977-84); XN706 (1976-83); XN707 (1977-79); XP920 (1976-83); XP924 (1976-77); XP925 (1976-83); XP956 (1976-83); XS577 (1972-76 and 1978); XS580 (1976-80); and XS587 (1976-78).

An RAE outpost at Oakhanger, near Bordon, was brought into use for the first time for satellite remote sensing operations. It was used to track the Seasat satellite, the data being processed at Farnborough. The NAVSTAR satellite navigation system receivers were designed by Radio and Navigation Department.

1978

On 1st April the resident Army Air Corps unit, No 664 Squadron, was renumbered 656 Squadron, with their Scout AH.1 and Gazelle AH.1 helicopters based on Jersey Brow. This Squadron was now tasked to provide aircraft support for 6 Field Force.

The northernmost part of the 'Black Sheds' was demolished early this year, having been built in 1913/14. The remaining part has 'listed building' status and remains in use as a store for the TAG Aviation airfield equipment.

Following on from the drone conversions of the Meteors (the last Meteor D.16, WH286, was converted in 1974), there was planned to be a number of Sea Vixen FAW.2 conversions to D.3 variants. Most of these Vixens were gathered at Farnborough, to bring them up to a fully serviceable condition, and some were then flown to Flight Refuelling Limited at Tarrant Rushton and Hurn for conversion. Seen here in the early 1980s are a group of Sea Vixen FAW.2s (including XJ529, XN696 and XP925) stored in 'E' shed, with RAE BAC 1-11 XX919 undergoing servicing beyond. The Sea Vixen conversion project was later abandoned with only four being converted to drone status. *Author's collection*

Three Buccaneer S2Bs (XW986, 987, 988) were specially built for RAE. All three were initially delivered to West Freugh as weapons trials aircraft, but maintenance was still carried out at Farnborough. Seen here on 24th December 1974, at low speed with everything down, is XW988 in the yellow/green scheme that all three were delivered in, which it wore to the end, being delivered from Boscombe Down to Exeter on 19th April 1996 and on to South Africa on 2nd May 1996. *FAST collection*

The 5-metre wind tunnel (5m wide x 4.2m high) on the Ball Hill site was first used during this year when a 1/13th scale model of the Airbus A300B was tested. This new wind tunnel, a unique facility in the UK, was opened for research into low-speed aerodynamics of modern aircraft and their complex lift systems. Able to simulate full-scale landings and take-off conditions for combat aircraft and light transport types, a number of models were initially tested within this facility, not only from the UK but overseas too. High incidence research models (HIRM), including some interesting shapes and designs, were also used to investigate the drag on various aircraft weapons stores.

The famous RAE Dakota C.3, KG661, arrived from Exeter on 9th June 1978, making its first operational sortie with Transport Flight on 6th July 1978; a return support flight to Kinloss, where the RAE Varsity T.1 WL635 was on a trials detachment. The Dakota had initially been delivered to RAE West Freugh for sonobuoy trials where it had then received the name 'Portpatrick Princess'. Evidence later came to light that indicated the original KG661 was destroyed in an accident in December 1944 while in Royal Canadian Air Force service, therefore this elderly Dakota was re-serialled as ZA947 in June 1979, later acquiring the 'Raspberry Ripple' colour scheme. It operated from Farnborough as a support aircraft for Radio and Navigation Department and for general passenger and cargo use by Transport Flight also undertaking trials with sonobuoys, unmanned aircraft (UMA) development of payload systems and parachute dropping. However it suffered an accident at Farnborough on 8th September 1989 that required a substantial repair including fitment at Farnborough of a donor wing from Dakota N9050T, stored in Malta. It was retired from the DRA Transport Flight on 30th March

1993 but still flies with the Battle of Britain Memorial Flight at Coningsby.

Buccaneer S.2 XV344, one of the last of the type to operate with No 809 NAS from HMS *Ark Royal*, arrived on 12th December 1978 from St Athan. This aircraft was destined to become no ordinary Buccaneer, indeed it became the most modified aircraft of the entire fleet. It made its first flight under RAE charge on 13th March 1979 being initially involved in Radar Navigation trials, a role it took over from Canberra B.2/6 WJ643. Further modifications then ensued, including a second-stick installation by the Cranfield Institute of Technology during 1981/1982. Upon return during March 1982, installation work continued which included compatible lighting in both cockpits for Night Vision Goggle (NVG) equipment, first flown as such on 26th April 1982. Repaint at Kemble in the by now standard RAE 'raspberry ripple' house colours and fitment of a Thermal Imager Common Module Mk.II/Forward Looking Infra-Red System (TICM II FLIR), housed within a re-shaped nose profile, followed.

A Ferranti FIN1064B Inertial Navigation System (INS) had been fitted, within the rear Doppler bay forward of the rear hold, with control and display in the front cockpit, along with moving map displays and TV monitors. A comprehensive MIL Std 1553B data-bus system was installed, the first fitted to an aircraft, which enabled a fully integrated experimental system with flexibility in both control and display formats to be achieved utilising a Modular Data Acquisition System (MODAS). The early FLIR trials were successful and were a marked improvement at night and in poor weather over the earlier Low Level TV (LLTV) systems.

Thus 'Nightbird' (<u>Night By Infra-Red Detec</u>tor) was born, making its first flight after complete installation of the above equipment on 12th January 1984, although further enhancements and modifications followed. During its second flight in this mode on 19th January the Buccaneer suffered a bird strike that resulted in a port wing change.

During the mid-1980s trials were continued by Flight Systems/Avionic and Sensors Department concentrating upon enhanced

In its original scheme, as delivered to RAE on 9th June 1978, Dakota C.3 KG661 'Portpatrick Princess' is about to touch down on the Farnborough runway during September 1978. It was re-serialled as ZA947 in June 1979 and repainted in the 'raspberry ripple' scheme during the mid-1980s. It was eventually retired on 3rd March 1993 and now flies with the Battle of Britain Memorial Flight from RAF Coningsby. *FAST collection*

medium to low-level navigation at night and in poor weather. A further re-fit saw the introduction of a Ferranti (GEC) re-programmable Head-Up Display (HUD) with a mode controller to give greater pilot safety at high speed and low level. At this time the original FLIR was replaced by the GEC SR(A) 1010 FLIR, which incorporated integral detector cooling, utilising the already modified distinctive chisel nose profile housing the Germanium window and FLIR system, XV344 first flying in this guise on 26th January 1987. At this stage, the 'Nightbird' nose art emblem was applied to the forward fuselage, this being devised by the engineers and scientists working on this project. Work had also been undertaken on a Harrier T.4 XW267, similarly known as 'Nightbird' and wearing the appropriate nose art emblem.

A Passive Night Bombing System (PNBS), was installed during May 1988, this later being upgraded to an Enhanced Passive Night Bombing System (EPNBS), which enabled the 1010 FLIR Data to give thermal cueing and weapon release formats, directly onto the HUD. This FLIR system, developed as an Infra-Red Weapons delivery system, was eventually installed within the Harrier GR.7 and was incorporated into the Tornado GR.4 update programme. It also appeared on the DERA 'Nightfox' programme during the late 1990s, which utilised SAOEU's Tornado GR.1A ZG706.

Laser ranging and marked target seeking (LRMTS) for accurate weapon delivery was still being researched during this period and the combination of a laser seeker with an IR detector looking through a common stabilised path was developed by RAE/DRA and

GEC. Therefore, and in parallel with the FLIR research work, extensive rewiring of the inboard pylon, bomb bay and rear cockpit was undertaken, to prepare the aircraft for trials of the miniaturised podded system, which became the Ferranti (GEC), SR(A) 1015 Thermal Imaging Airborne Laser Designator (TIALD) pod. The TIALD pod was mounted on the port wing inner pylon, which was modified by the RAE, and the aircraft made its first flight on these trials on 20th June 1988. These trials, along with subsequent updates and enhancements, were heralded a complete success and led to successful development of a TIALD System for Tornado GR.1s during the 1991 Gulf War. Indeed the pod trialled on XV344 actually saw service in the Gulf War.

Other subsequent work undertaken by 'Nightbird' has included 'Hardnight' which comprised an Airborne Image Processing System (AIPS), data recorder and multi-purpose colour display unit; high-definition Electro Optic Sensor trials, known as 'Midnight'; a dual wave-band FLIR sensor called 'Twilight'; and a Staring Array, with a FLIR database, coupled to the AIPS, which was called 'Farsight', the latter continuing until the aircraft retired. The successor to this aircraft is Tornado F.2A TIARA (Tornado Integrated Avionics Research Aircraft), ZD902, which continues to be operated by QinetiQ at Boscombe Down for Electro Optics and Sensor data fusion research.

Having relocated from Farnborough to Boscombe Down on 13th July 1994, XV344 made its last flight on 28th September 1994 having accrued a total time of 2894.30 hours. It was loaded on board a road transportation vehicle on 26th January 1998 and

Coming alive at night is Hunter T.7 WV383, of Flight Systems Department, seen about to depart on another night sortie on 27th April 1979. This aircraft trialled NVGs and covert night systems, and later the Penetrate pod. It was given the title 'Hecate-Lady of the Night', after the Greek goddess. Having flown with RAE, DRA and DERA for over 27 years, this aircraft was retired in 1998 and is now in the FAST Museum. *FAST collection*

returned to Farnborough to be mounted on its display pad adjacent to A5 Building on 31st March, where Signals and Processing Sector (its predecessor being Flight Systems and Avionics and Systems Department) have their offices and laboratories.

Whilst operating from Farnborough, 'Nightbird' had flown 909 hours, undertaking extremely valuable and demanding research and trials work that had included some notable 'firsts': the first digital data bus (1553B) fitted to an aircraft; first to use Infra-Red for weapons aiming; first TIALD pod fitment and operation; first dual waveband FLIR; first Airborne Image Processing System; and first large Infra-Red staring arrays.

A new main gate to RAE was opened during June providing access off of Elles Road at Pinehurst. At this point South Gate was no longer the main entrance to RAE and was later closed. The new Pinehurst Gate remained in use until 2000.

1979

The next delivery of a Buccaneer to Farnborough occurred on 16th July 1979 when S2A XN982 arrived from St Athan by road.

The RAE Aero Club sold its Tiger Moth G-AJHS in 1979 and replaced it with another de Havilland type, Chipmunk Mk.22 G-BDDD. Both are seen here banking over the Farnborough airfield on 26th April 1979, just prior to the departure of the Tiger Moth. *Rawlings Family collection*

This aircraft had been damaged whilst it was in the USA and having spent some time in storage at St Athan it was transported to RAE for repair and allocated for eventual flight trials with a Helmet-Mounted Display and an Inertial Navigation System for strike and combat aircraft (SCAINS). However this work was not accomplished and the aircraft was transported by road to Brough on 15th June 1982 where it was put to use as a fatigue test airframe.

De Havilland DH.82A Tiger Moth G-AJHS, long-term resident of the RAE Aero Club since 30th June 1953, finally departed for a new home during the summer. It had been replaced by de Havilland Chipmunk 22 G-BDDD, which arrived from Netheravon on 10th January 1979, making its first club flight on 20th March, and is still on strength with the Aero Club today.

Another DH.82A Tiger Moth, G-ANNG, was a long term resident, albeit privately owned by Mr P Walter. This aircraft had been loaned to the club whilst G-AJHS was undergoing a rebuild during October 1963 and it was agreed that the club would rebuild G-ANNG at Farnborough on behalf of the owner once G-AJHS had returned. This took many years, being worked on only in the members' spare time, and was not completed until 1995, the aircraft having been dismantled in O14 building, adjacent to 'Q' shed, for many of those years. Still owned by Peter Walter it was flown by RAE Aero Club members until 2003, but as there was no longer any suitable grass strip for operating from the airfield it departed on 14th July 2004, taking off from Stirling Way, an old taxiway.

For a few years there was also an Auster J/1N Alpha, G-AHHT, with the club that arrived on 23rd February 1982 from a farm strip near Bristol. There have been other aircraft operating with the club but privately owned, namely a Nord NC.858S G-BDJR owned by Roger Marson, and still stored in the Aero Club hangar having had its C of A expire in May 1992, a DH.87B Hornet Moth G-AESE, a Tipsy Trainer, Piper PA-22 Caribbean G-ARCC, Pitts S-1S Special G-AZPH, CAP.10 G-BECZ the latter types owned by Aerobatics International, then based at Farnborough in the late 1960s and 1970s and the Zlin Z.526 G-AWAR that was previously operated by the late Neil Williams during the 1960s and Zlin Z.526s G-AWJX and G-AWSH in the 1970s.

Defence Weapons Department were studying aircraft camouflage and in con-junction with the RAF Central Tactics and Trials Organisation (CTTO) they were engaged in looking at a counter-shaded grey colour for combat aircraft. Trials were flown in conjunction with the RAF and the new colour was applied to some Phantom FGR.2s for evaluation. Just after these trials the UK Government found itself embroiled in the Falklands War and the Royal Navy Task Force dispatched south in April 1982 included a large number of BAe Sea Harrier FRS.1s painted with dark sea grey upper surfaces and white lower surfaces. These aircraft clearly had to be toned down and they were painted an overall extra dark sea grey, followed by others in a medium sea grey. However the later Sea Harrier detachments south were painted in the counter-shaded grey, a scheme commonly known as 'Barley Grey' named after RAE's Philip Barley, the man who originally devised the colour for the new camouflage.

Avro Vulcan B.1 XA903, which had previously been in use for Blue Steel trials at Edinburgh Field, Australia and as Bristol Siddeley Engines' Olympus 593 testbed, had now finished its flying days as the Turbo-Union RB.199 testbed and arrived at Farnborough for ground training purposes on 22nd February 1979. It was struck off charge as a Ground Experimental Vehicle for fire-fighting purposes on 19th July 1979, and subsequently moved to the RAE aircraft dump area, near Ively Gate, and was eventually broken up. The nose passed to a private collector and is now on display at Wellesbourne Mountford.

1980

Wessex HU.5 XL728 was temporarily released from Radio and Navigation Department for Aero-Acoustic research in conjunction with Aero Flight at RAE Bedford. The Wessex would hover at 2,600ft for about 90 minutes whilst a British Airways Lockheed L-1011 TriStar G-BEAM flew below at 1,500ft. The noise-measuring equipment was suspended in a sphere dangling 500ft below the helicopter.

The No 1 11ft x 8ft low-speed wind tunnel was by now redundant and it was sold to the Southampton University where it became operational in 1981, being named the Glauert Tunnel after the distinguished RAE aerodynamicist

Instrumentation and Trials Department, based at the Bramshot outstation were engaged in various research tasks with equipment installed in many of the Farnborough aircraft to record and measure stresses, pressures, acceleration and so on.

As far back as 1969, a Forward Looking Infra-red (FLIR) system had been developed, but this was too large and heavy for general aircraft usage. However ground evaluation had shown a great potential for this new system. In 1975, EMI built a new version for airborne usage and Attack Weapons Department initially used this system in Shackleton T.4 VP293, but later a dedicated aircraft, Varsity T.1 WL679, was allocated for this task. The LLTV and FLIR were installed at the forward end of the bomb bay, along with two video recorders and two observer stations within the fuselage. A Decca Navigator system, cinerecorder, radio altimeter, and full cockpit display for the co-pilot were also installed. Trials to evaluate the FLIR as a night-flying aid were conducted during this period, whilst the FLIR trials also included infra-red camouflage, detection and recognition of submarines and surface vessels, use in air-to-air situations, detection and recognition of battlefield targets and surveillance.

By late 1980 the RAE aircraft of Experimental Flying Squadron had been allocated to two 'Flights': Southern Squadron in the old ETPS hangar, building E1, and Western Squadron in 'C' and 'L' sheds. However, Transport Flight at 'A' shed was a 'Flight' in its own right and was loosely known as Northern Squadron.

Wearing the unofficial RAE Rotary Wing Squadron duck motive and Royal Aircraft Establishment titles, is Puma HC.1 ZA941. It joined the Farnborough fleet on 21st September 1981 and is seen here during November 1983, fitted with a spherical 'heli-tele' TICM (Thermal Imaging Common Module) ball on the port side, for various sensor trials. It was later written off in an accident on 8th August 1991. *FAST collection*

By now there were rumblings at Government level in respect of the future of Farnborough. A Steering Group was set up to look at the future of Research and Development Establishments and their respective airfields, and it was recommended that the closure of Farnborough airfield was the preferred option that would have the least disadvantage, although it would involve severe problems. No firm decision was made at that time to close Farnborough, but further examination and consultation would take place to look at the options for general aviation usage. A working party was set up in 1982 to look at the future of flying at Farnborough, especially for business/general aviation usage.

1981

Puma HC.1 ZA941, the last British Puma built, arrived at Farnborough on 21st September 1981 for use by Flight Systems Department and Defensive Weapons Department. This helicopter, affectionately known as 'Erica', was used for various sensor trials, including a sensing and guidance system for helicopters and was later fitted with a spherical 'hele-tele' TICM (Thermal Imaging Common Module) ball. By 1986 it had adopted an overall drab green colour scheme and was detached to Germany for a NATO exercise, and later for various sensing trials during 1989/1990. At this stage the Puma was installed with special equipment for the Trigat anti-tank missile being devel-

oped at the time, but unfortunately it crashed during a trials deployment to Conjuers in southern France on 8th August 1991 and was written off.

Air Traffic Control at Farnborough had utilised a runway caravan for many years but in February 1981, at the time of its operator's retirement, the decision was made that this was also to cease. So the familiar orange and white chequered vehicle to be seen alongside the threshold of the duty runway was withdrawn.

1982

By now there were some 36 aircraft based at Farnborough, a far cry from previous years. This was to fall further as, after 13 years on the airfield at Jersey Brow, the Army Air Corps moved from Farnborough. No 656 Squadron, with their eight Scout AH.1s (XP903, XR628, XT626, XT642, XT645, XT649, XV130, and XV139), and six Gazelle AH.1s (XW912, XX381, XZ329, XZ332, XZ340 and XZ346), were relocated to Netheravon on 12th March. Their hangar remained in Army use until 1996 for storage purposes and it was eventually demolished during February 2000, as part of the redevelopment of the 'Factory' site by Slough Estates. Upon this site where this hangar once stood, is a modern four-storey office block, known as 'No 25 Templar Avenue', with at present two companies, Agusta-Westland and Imagine Homes, occupying offices therein.

Buccaneer S.2A XT272 arrived from RAE Bedford on 21st January 1982. This aircraft had a modified nose for trials with the Tornado GR.1 radar that had been undertaken at RAE Bedford and BAe Warton. It was repainted in the 'raspberry ripple' scheme

Three of Farnborough's large flying laboratories are seen here in formation during January 1981. Andover C.1 XS646 is seen in its earlier RAE scheme and was undergoing various trials, including Electro-Optic sensors. BAC 1-11 Srs 402AP XX919 was in use by Radio Flight for various communications and navigation trials and Comet Mk.4 XV814 in use for radio communications, navigation and avionic trials. All three of these aircraft were generically operated by 'B' Flight, although it was Radio and Navigation Department that was undertaking the relevant trials work. *FAST collection*

Resplendent in its newly-applied 'raspberry ripple' paint scheme is Buccaneer S.2A XT272, seen parked on the western apron at Farnborough during October 1982. This aircraft has a modified nose profile, akin to the Tornado GR.1, having undertaken radar trials for the type. It continued to operate from Farnborough and Bedford until 1987, whereupon it was placed on the Farnborough dump and later transferred to the Pendine, then Shoeburyness ranges. *FAST collection*

at St Athan from 27th August to 29th September 1982 and returned to operate from Farnborough. It returned to Bedford on 29th January 1987, but was to arrive back at Farnborough one more time, only now rather ignominiously by road, to be placed in the dump compound on 1st December 1987. It remained there, a forlorn sight right to the end, until it was transported by road to Pendine range on 27th February 1997.

The Accidents Investigation Branch moved from London to Bramshot, this RAE outstation had recently been relinquished, but only as a temporary measure until their new headquarters complex on the airfield at Berkshire Copse had been completed

During the SBAC display in September a Skyship 500 airship, G-BIHN, was seen at Farnborough, this being both the first airship at an SBAC show and a poignant reminder of what had gone on here some 75 years previously.

On 6th July the de Havilland Moth Club used Farnborough as a staging point for their 'Famous Grouse' DH100 Rally, celebrating the centenary of the birth of Geoffrey de Havilland. Some fifty Moths – Cirrus, Gypsy, Puss, Hornet and Tiger – as well as a Dragon Rapide and Dragonfly descended on the airfield for fuel and a break in their journey around the country. Indeed the 'A' shed apron looked as if it was back in the 1930s era!

Varsity T.1 WL635, which had come to RAE from the Cranfield Institute of Technology (CIT) on 15th August 1977 for FLIR turret trials, made its last flight on 28th June 1982 when it flew from Farnborough to Macrihanish for ground instruction purposes with the RAF Police School.

Jaguar B-08 XW566, the eighth and final prototype Jaguar, arrived at RAE Farnborough on 3rd February 1982 in a camouflage colour scheme with a white fin and outer mainplanes and an LLTV pod mounted on the fuselage centre pylon. The aircraft arrived in need of much work to bring it up

to the then standard modification state, having acquired various non-standard systems including a large wiring loom as a result of trials undertaken by the manufacturer on the Agave radar, LLTV and a helmet mounted display. The essential modifications were undertaken and the aircraft repainted at Kemble before Flight Systems Department commenced trials of a Smiths-supplied enhanced diffractive optics Head-Up Display (HUD) and LLTV, as well as vibration measurement trials for Southampton University. XW566 made its last flight on 17th June 1985 due to extensive servicing and updates required, and was then allocated to ground trials. It was used for Electro-Magnetic Compatibility (EMC) trials by Avionics and Sensors Department, including research into external radio frequency field penetration and lightning strikes until 2004, and is now on loan to FAST from QinetiQ, being moved across the airfield to the Museum on 8th June 2004.

The very last UK Jaguar built, T.2 ZB615, arrived on 17th December 1982 from RAF Kemble, where it had been painted. It had a

NAVWASS installed and was NVG-compatible and upon arrival at RAE it was allocated for use mainly by Experimental Flying Department for continuation training, instrument flying and type proficiency work along with some minor research trials which included some NVG work and cockpit noise research. It was modified to a T.2A variant in the late 1980s and transferred to Boscombe Down on 24th March 1994.

The RAE Museum was moved to G1 building and re-opened during this year with a display of artefacts in the old Royal Engineers balloon store. The museum was to remain here until its closure in 1994.

Flight Systems Department were requested to evaluate low-light level piloting aids. Research and trials with passive night vision goggles were ongoing, and experiments were conducted into cockpit lighting and modifications to accommodate the Night Vision Goggle system. These trials were a great success and led to the system being adopted throughout the services and seeing action during 'Operation Corporate' – the Falklands campaign.

Jaguar B XW566 is seen here in the old Structures Building during May 1993, fitted with a special wooden frame and copper piping rig for lightning strike investigation. The aircraft would be jacked and current injected along the pipes to simulate the effect of lightning whilst the aircraft is airborne. *FAST collection*

Seen here outside 'L' shed, a few days after its arrival in February 1982, is Jaguar B.08 XW566. It has a white fin and outer mainplanes, whilst the remainder is in standard camouflage for the time. The aircraft carries an under-fuselage low-light TV pod, which had been in use by the manufacturer. Flight Systems Department used this aircraft for head-up display and LLTV work until it was retired during 1985. It is now part of the FAST Museum collection. *FAST collection*

Sea King HAS.1 (DB) XV371, of Flight Systems Department, was undergoing flight trials of RED OWL (Remote Eyes in the Dark Operating Without Light), which allowed a helicopter pilot to fly very low by night in light levels below that of clear starlight. The uses of this system were considered to be in the operation of helicopters in the take-off, landing and flight modes, where piloting, navigation, reconnaissance and SAR operations would all benefit. This system gives the pilot an image of the outside world on a miniature TV set mounted on his helmet, called a Heli-Mounted Display. A camera is mounted in the helicopter nose, moving with the pilot's head movement, in the line of sight.

Wessex HAS.1 (DB) XM330 made its last flight on 26th June 1982; during engine start on 29th June an explosion within the Avpin injector in the starboard side of the nose left it substantially damaged. Damage occurred to the fuselage structure as well as the intake and compressor of the engine and it was decided that repairs would be uneconomic. It was struck off charge on 16th June 1983. The heli-

copter had arrived at Farnborough from Yeovil on 24th June 1964 initially for WE177 weapon proving trials with Weapons Flight, which included deployments to West Freugh. Its overall midnite-blue colour scheme had slightly changed with the addition of titles and a white 'lightning flash' cheatline by early 1973, then it became 'raspberry ripple' in August 1976. It was also engaged in development of armament for helicopters and investigation of target acquisition and recognition, having previously undertaken some of this work with the manufacturer and at A&AEE. On 1st December 1970 the Wessex was re-allotted for continuation training, as the weapons tasks had been taken over by XS241, and further tasks such as instrument flying, proficiency flying training and checks, engine-off landings and fireball rescue duties were undertaken. Between April and July 1975 it was temporarily detached for short periods to Culdrose for parachute trials, where dummies were dropped from the helicopter to determine the parachute trajectory into the sea. It maintained its continuation flying train-

ing role right to the end, but was used for a brief period by Avionics and Sensors Department for EMC trials work, including placement on the wooden platform, away from any metallic clutter. It was transported to Weston-Super-Mare on 16th May 1994 where it is now part of the International Helicopter Museum.

The RAE helicopter flight moved to 'A' shed during this year, having been operating from Southern Squadron since around 1970. It was to move again in March 1993, this time to 'L' shed where it stayed until the aircraft departed for Boscombe Down in 1994.

1983

The National Gas Turbine Establishment at nearby Pyestock became integrated into RAE.

Aircraft Apprentice Department moved to 'Q' shed, along with the RAE Gliding Club. The Aircraft Apprentices made a further move to 'A' shed during the late 1980s, but returned to 'Q' shed and remained there until the demise of the department and the RAE Apprentice Training Scheme in 1994. The RAE Gliding Club eventually moved to RAF Odiham as the influx of business aircraft from the late-1980s prevented glider flying from what had previously been a closed airfield during weekends.

By now the RAE Transport Flight aircraft were becoming rather elderly, the Douglas Dakota being 41 years of age, and the four Devon C.2s being 35 years, 34 years, 29 years and 25 years of age. On 17th January a Cessna 404 Titan, G-PATT, and on 24th January a Piper PA-31-350 Navajo Chieftain, G-BASU, were evaluated at Farnborough as potential Devon replacements. It was eventually decided that the Chieftain would be the type to replace the Devons, three for Farnborough and one for Boscombe Down.

One of two specially-built Sea King Mk.4Xs, ZB507 arrived at Farnborough on 4th February 1983. This helicopter was used

The total complement of RAE Transport Flight can be seen in this view from the Farnborough control tower during May 1983. The four Devons in the foreground, VP975/M, VP959/L, XG496/K and XM223/J, were the stalwarts of the RAE fleet for many years. Dakota C.3 ZA947 can be seen beyond, in its original colour scheme, carrying a UMA pod under the centre fuselage. The fifth Devon is a visitor, XA880 from Llanbedr. *FAST collection*

Canberra B(I)6 WT308 was the last Canberra to serve with RAE Farnborough, arriving on 23rd September 1955 and eventually departing on 10th June 1983. It is seen here on the western parking apron during June 1981, operated by Weapons Flight, as this aircraft was used for numerous weapons trials on the West Freugh range. It is still extant at Predannack airfield, used for fire and rescue training by the School of Flight Deck Operations. *FAST collection*

for a variety of trials with Radio and Navigation Department and Attack Weapons/ Defensive Weapons Departments, including a detachment to Norway in 1984. Amongst the onboard equipment was a downward-looking radar sensor, known as ADADS, fitted in the starboard side doorway for detection of vessels above and below the sea surface as well as airfield radar targets – for these trials the Sea King was deployed to Plockton, Isle of Skye. It was modified to carry the DRA Magnetometer, an all-plastic aero-body that is deployed beneath the helicopter for overwater magnetic anomaly trials. This, and various other trials including the 'Dodge' radar trials in early 1994 in conjunction with DRA Malvern, continued at Farnborough and, from 9th May 1994, Boscombe Down. Since October 1998 it has served with 848 NAS as a standard HC.4.

The other Sea King Mk.4X, ZB506, was initially part of the RAE Bedford fleet, specifically modified to take the Ferranti 'Blue Kestrel' radar that was to be fitted to the Merlin HM.1s. However, with the radar now removed, this helicopter came to Farnborough on 4th June 1992 and had the attachment beams for the radar removed and reverted to a normal nose profile. It continued in service with RAE and DRA, being deployed to Farnborough from Bedford on various occasions before re-positioning to Boscombe Down where it is still operational as part of the QinetiQ fleet.

A long-time resident, Canberra B(I)6 WT309, was transferred to A&AEE Boscombe Down on 16th May 1983. It had arrived on 11th July 1957 from Marshall's Flying School Cambridge, although the 'official' transfer from the RAF to RAE was on 28th February 1958. The aircraft arrived with a Total Time of just 29.50 hours and was painted in an overall white and Day-Glo scheme until it departed for Kemble on 2nd November 1981 for painting in the famous red, white and blue 'raspberry ripple' scheme, arriving back on 16th December. This Canberra operated from both Farnborough and West Freugh on various weapons trials over the years. After providing a useful training aid to the apprentices at Boscombe Down it was scrapped in January 1998. The author of this book, the majority shareholder, and a group of other FAST members, purchased the nose from

the scrap dealer and moved it back to Farnborough where it was stored in 'M' shed, re-painted, and subsequently moved to FAST Museum for display on 14th June 2002.

Sister-ship B(I)6 WT308 was also a long-term Farnborough resident having arrived on 23rd September 1955 from Samlesbury, and was also used for trials of various weapons, including bombs and rocket projectiles, by Armament (later Weapons) Flight, operating from Farnborough and West Freugh. Also wearing the overall white and Day-Glo scheme it too was subsequently painted in the 'raspberry ripple' scheme. Eventually departing for Boscombe Down on 10th June 1983 it briefly continued its weapons trials but returned to Farnborough for storage on 24th July 1984, ending its flying days with a total of 2,736 flying hours. It remained derelict until it was removed by road, in two loads, departing on 24th September and 7th October 1992 to Predannack for fire and rescue training by the School of Aircraft Handling.

Panavia Tornado GR.1 ZA326 arrived at RAE Bedford from Warton on 26th May. Although Bedford-based, this aircraft was used for various trials by RAE Farnborough Attack Weapons Department, Materials and Structures and Radio and Navigation Departments. This aircraft relocated to DRA Boscombe Down on 23rd March 1994 and continued with its research flying until retired by QinetiQ, making its last flight on 13th December 2005.

1984

The RAE Douglas Dakota 3 (this time as ZA947) again visited Berlin-Tempelhof on 9th May where it took part in a flypast to commemorate the 36th reunion of the Berlin Airlift operations.

Work commenced in 1982 on building Q108 for housing the main RAE computer system, known as the central computing facility – at the time the most powerful computer in the country. It was opened in September 1984 and remained in use until 1998, being demolished in 2002.

The third spinning tower, built in 1938 for propeller testing, was still in use at this time with rain erosion trials being conducted, but this facility was soon to be withdrawn and subsequently demolished during 1985. The first spinning tower was operating until the late 1960s and the second was demolished in 1960.

The AIB moved into their new headquarters at Berkshire Copse on the southwestern corner of the Farnborough airfield. HRH Prince of Wales officially opened the facility on 19th June 1984.

A brand new Lynx AH.5, ZD285, arrived from Yeovil on 10th December 1984 for Flight Systems Department where it was to be used in support of research programmes on the development and integration of sensors, displays and management systems for future military helicopters. During the late 1980s this helicopter underwent considerable modifications at Farnborough, with a new nose housing a steerable sensor platform fitted with a thermal imaging camera. It departed to Fleetlands for conversion to an AH.7 variant during June 1990. There was also a facility for a port-side mounted steerable sphere, known as a GEC Sunfish, where this could be used for radar signature experiments on a variety of ground targets. This Lynx was used for flight research into Visually Coupled Systems (VCS) where this programme was part of the UK Rotorcraft Day/Night All-Weather (D/NAW) research project. A helmet-mounted display (HMD) and head tracking system (HTS) are coupled together to form the basis of the system with the mixed imagery and flight symbology being presented through the visor. This was all part of the overall programme for COvert Night/Day Operations Rotorcraft, (known as CONDOR), where the HMD was being developed, and this helicopter was the technical demonstrator. Consequently this versatile helicopter was often engaged in flying very low on high-speed/low-level, nap-of-the-earth operations. The Lynx relocated to Boscombe Down on 13th April 1994 and continued this research for a number of years.

AIR ACCIDENTS INVESTIGATION BRANCH

The Ultimate Jigsaw

Farnborough can rightly lay claim to being the birthplace of powered flight in the UK, thanks to that epic foray into the skies by Samuel F Cody on 16th October 1908. This flight from the then-Farnborough Common ended in a crash when his aircraft, Army Aeroplane No 1, struck the ground as the intrepid pilot tried to avoid some trees. This, and subsequent accidents in those pioneering years, were all part of the learning curve. Sadly for Cody it would later end in

disaster when his 'Waterplane' crashed on Ball Hill, killing him and his passenger on 7th August 1913.

Thus aircraft accidents have been occurring ever since flying commenced and it therefore is rather fitting that Farnborough should today be heralded as a centre of excellence for aircraft accident investigation. From the early days of the flimsy string and fabric biplanes through the development of metal aircraft construction, to the

years of World War Two and the jet era, right up to the high technology of today's civil and military aircraft, Farnborough has remained at the cutting edge of the world's aviation industry. Accident investigation remains one of the most visible aspects of Farnborough's world leadership today.

The southwestern corner of the airfield has always been somewhat shrouded in secrecy. From the 1940s through to the 1990s, it was here that the Airfield Radio Laboratory (ARL) and Weapons Department were housed, in an area that was known as 'T' Site. It was also within this area, and secure compound, that the initial trials of the new jet-engined types and the later V-Bombers took place. Just across Barracuda Road, away from prying eyes, lies Berkshire Copse in the southwestern corner of the now Farnborough Airport. This area is defined as part of the original Laffan's Plain, close to where balloons, airships and those defining powered flights by Cody were first conducted. A T2-series hangar (known as T49 Building) was erected on the site in the late 1950s for accident investigation work to be undertaken by the Royal Aircraft Establishment Structures Department. This sector was responsible for handling important accident investigations within the RAE, assisting the Air Ministry and Ministry of Civil Aviation in this role. This relationship continues with today's modern incarnations, with QinetiQ and its specialist laboratories on the northwestern side of the airfield assisting the UK Air Accidents Investigation Branch (AAIB) when requested.

Indeed, Berkshire Copse has hosted the AAIB's Headquarters since 1983. Now outside the airfield boundary and benefiting

Attempting to get airborne on its first flight from Farnborough, the giant Tarrant Tabor, F1765, crashed onto its nose on 26th May 1919. Both pilots were killed, although other crewmembers escaped. This view shows the aircraft a few minutes after the accident, with the ambulance in attendance and one of the crew being helped from the wreckage. Note the triple tyre tracks in the grass. *Author's collection*

The wreckage is seen here, now cordoned off to preserve the crash scene whilst investigation takes place. *FAST collection*

Many accidents were investigated by the AIB during World War Two and this Halifax II, R9384, was one such investigation, after it lost power on take-off from Topcliffe and crashed close to the airfield on 23rd April 1944. *via AAIB*

from its own secure compound since March 2000, this area consists of purpose-built accommodation, laboratory and hangar facilities, where the remains of crashed aircraft are pieced together for detailed investigations to take place in an endeavour to establish the cause of the accident.

Early Investigations

'The Branch', as it is known colloquially within the AAIB, does in fact have a much deeper-rooted history that goes back to its foundation days of 1915.

Capt C B Cockburn was a founder member of the Royal Aero Club and held Pilot Certificate No 5. He was commonly known as 'the famous instructor' and was appointed to the independent post of 'Inspector of Accidents' of the Accident Investigation Unit of the Royal Flying Corps, as a considerable number of flying accidents were befalling the flimsy biplanes of that era. A Public Safety and Accident Investigation Committee had been founded by the Royal Aero Club in 1912, which had safety officers strategically placed at the newly formed aerodromes at Brooklands, Eastchurch, Hendon and Salisbury, tasked to investigate and report on aeroplane accidents. Capt Cockburn had, by this time, already become a leading aviation expert in his role as the Safety Officer for the Salisbury area, where much of the early flying was undertaken and inevitable accidents occurred.

The early accidents were all investigated by inspectors reporting to the Director General of Military Aeronautics in the War Office. The resultant reports were disseminated in an endeavour to make flying safer for all, as this activity was now becoming more popular with civilians as well as the Royal Flying Corps (RFC) and rapidly increasing numbers of aeroplanes were taking to the air. Indeed the learning curve was steep during these days and early accidents

at Farnborough, suffered by prototype and production aircraft of the Royal Aircraft Factory, were independently investigated. The findings would often directly lead to various types being modified in order to improve safety or airworthiness.

Many accidents were investigated during World War One, as about half of the aviators killed at the time were as a result of non-combat accidents. At the cessation of hostilities, the first Department of Civil Aviation (DCA) within the Air Ministry was established, as there were by now a growing number of aircraft being used for limited passenger and recreational flying. Therefore the early AIB, with its (by now) considerable expertise, became part of the new DCA and was tasked with investigating both civil and military accidents within the United Kingdom.

With the introduction of the Air Navigation Act of 1920, the Secretary of State for Air was empowered to make statutory regulations for the investigation of civil air accidents. These were implemented under the Air Navigation (Investigation of Accidents) Regulations 1922, which resulted in the AIB

actually becoming part of the Air Ministry.

Many civil accidents were investigated during these early pioneering days of civil air transport and the RAE itself had been asked to assist in many cases, particularly where structural failures to airframes had occurred. In most instances the Farnborough scientists were able to assist in establishing the prime causes from within their respective laboratories – the two organisations complemented each other well at the start of a mutually beneficial relationship.

Peak Years

With the clouds of war gathering again in 1939, and the dramatic reduction of civilian flying, full attention was being directed towards military aircraft accidents. Large numbers of differing aircraft types were being developed and built in the UK during the World War Two years, which inevitably led to many accidents and incidents being recorded. This was confounded by the steepening of the learning curve, as the manufacturers and the test establishments tried to achieve more from their aircraft and systems

Whilst operating an Air Ministry charter flight from Idris, Tripoli carrying servicemen's families, Britavia Hermes IVA G-ALDJ crashed on approach to Blackbushe Airport on 5th November 1956. The aircraft had descended too low in poor visibility at night and undershot the runway impacting with trees at Star Hill, Hartfordbridge, at the Hartley Wintney end of the airport. The Hermes was destroyed by impact and fire. During the 1940s/50s there were a number of airliner accidents that required investigation by the AIB, the lessons learned paving the way for safer aircraft and air travel in general. *E Fuller collection*

Seen here in the AAIB hangar at Farnborough, on 1st April 1966, is Canberra B.16 WJ771 of No 6 Squadron. The aircraft broke up in the air at 5,000ft, 15 miles south of Khartoum, Sudan on 16th July 1964. The remains of a Lightning can be seen at lower left, Auster J/1 Autocrat G-AGYG at centre and, beyond, BEA Vanguard G-APEE. The latter crashed onto the runway at Heathrow on 27th October 1965 after an attempted overshoot, in fog, at night. *FAST collection*

in order to gain an edge over the adversary. It was therefore hardly surprising that the AIB was at its peak during this wartime period, with 80 inspectors having the task of piecing together a multitude of accidents throughout the UK – one accident never being quite the same as the next. This was a period of high demand and change, which saw much learning and improvements in the methods of investigation (and aircraft design) that paved the way for safer operation of civilian aircraft after the war years.

The Mechanical Test Department had been established at Farnborough during 1918. This later evolved into Structural and Mechanical Engineering Department, and then simply Structures Department in 1947. These all played a key role in aircraft accident investi-gation along with the Metallurgical Department, similarly established during 1917, and the Airworthiness Department, which came into being during 1922. These early days of accident investigation, and subsequent assistance by the RAE, led to firm foundations being laid for the AIB to have the use of laboratory space at Farnborough, although it was a civilian lodger unit at the time.

The AIB was incorporated into the newly formed Ministry of Civil Aviation (MCA) in 1946, structured and empowered to have full control of investigating all accidents and incidents to aircraft within the United Kingdom. As stated earlier, much of the AIB's early work was spent in investigation of military aircraft accidents and there was by now some concern within the military circles that this valuable service would be lost and the AIB would only investigate civil accidents. However, the military role was to carry on, with 'the Branch' continuing to assist RAF Boards of Inquiry (BOI) with their accident investigations. It is the responsibility of the BOI to conduct the investigation and issue the relevant report and comments, but valuable assistance is given to them by the AIB.

Restructuring Process
Due to changes in government structures throughout the years, various Ministries had parented the AIB. This changed when it became firmly rooted within the Department of Transport (DoT) in 1983, followed by a subtle title change during November 1987 to that of the Air Accidents Investigation Branch (AAIB) in order to distinguish it from the newly created Marine Accidents Investigation Branch. A minor change, due to government re-organisation in 2002, saw the AAIB report to the Department for Transport (DfT).

The main hangar (T49), situated on the southern boundary of the Farnborough aerodrome, was originally part of the RAE Structures Department and it was in this area that the AIB first established their work-

Photography of an accident can play a big part in the investigation. Seen here on 20th September 1958 is the Vulcan B.1 prototype VX770, suffering from structural disintegration and about to crash on the airfield at Syerston during a Battle of Britain flying display. The four crew on board were all killed. *FAST collection*

On 18th June 1972, Trident 1C G-ARPI, of British European Airways, stalled and crashed at Staines shortly after take-off from Heathrow. In what was a considerable removal and recovery exercise, the wreckage was taken to Farnborough, where it was installed in the AIB hangar for partial reconstruction. The wreckage is seen here on 2nd April 1973, laid out for investigation purposes. *FAST collection*

shops, as a lodger unit, working in close liaison with the various RAE departments. Many aircraft that had suffered accidents had their wreckage entirely removed to Farnborough for analysis and it was in this hangar that the early investigative rebuilds of wreckage occurred. Notwithstanding the military accidents of World War Two, the jet age brought its own set of challenging accidents. Aircraft were now suffering high-speed impacts with the ground and were fragmented over wide areas, sometimes into many thousands of parts, thus giving the investigators an even further daunting task of analysing and establishing the cause. Early post-war airliners also had their fair share of accidents, including Hermes, Bristol Freighters, Tudors and Vikings, with these often being brought to Farnborough for investigation.

The infamous BOAC de Havilland Comet 1 disasters, with G-ALYP crashing into the Mediterranean Sea off Elba, Italy, on 10th January 1954 and G-ALYY into the Mediterranean Sea off Naples, Italy, on 8th April 1954, resulted in recovery and return of wreckage to Farnborough for intense analysis and investigation. This eventually led to a structural pressure test water tank being installed in order to determine the integrity of the Comet structure; from this the failure mode of the fuselage was eventually determined and thus modifications were implemented in the new-build aircraft.

The hangars T9/T10 and T49 were ceded to the AAIB by the MoD in 1977 and at that stage the initial planning for a new Headquarters building was being considered. In 1982, the AIB relocated its Headquarters from Kingsgate House, London, to the RAE outstation at Bramshot before moving in 1983 to the new purpose-built HQ on the Farnborough site, which was opened by HRH The Prince of Wales on 19th June 1984. The smaller hangar (T10) was demolished during October 1991 and a new small but modern hangar facility (a new T10), was

built in its place, which affords a further element of security. An extension to the HQ building, which will cover two storeys with an area of 1,050m², was started in late August 2005 for completion during the late summer of 2006. This new building will enable the FDR/CVR data analysis section to move into more modern facilities, whilst more offices, meeting and conference rooms, and a new reception area will also be accommodated.

Despite not being part of QinetiQ or its antecedents, (Royal Aircraft Factory, Royal Aircraft Establishment, Royal Aerospace Establishment, Defence Research Agency and Defence Evaluation and Research Agency), the AAIB continued to receive much valuable assistance from the 'Establishment' over the years, particularly in respect of scientific and investigation expertise in the area of materials and structural failures. By far the most notable of these were the aforementioned Comet 1 accidents of the 1950s as well as the 1988 Lockerbie Pan Am Boeing 747 tragedy, where

the RAE, and latterly DERA, departments were directly involved in the research that came out in the AAIB Report Safety Recommendations.

The Investigation Process
All accidents are advised via a 'reporting hotline' that is connected direct to the AAIB Headquarters at Farnborough. An on-call duty officer, provided by the Department for Transport outside of normal hours, would receive notification and immediately transfer this to the AAIB Duty Co-ordinator. A plan of action would then be implemented, dependent upon the circumstances of the situation. If it is deemed necessary, engineering, operations and flight recorder teams will travel to the site as soon as possible. Where relatively minor accidents occur, the inspectors may not travel to the site, but will monitor the situation from Farnborough and request a standard reporting form and questionnaire to be completed and returned forthwith.

Phantom FGR.2 XV463, 'R' of 41 Squadron, dived into the Solway Firth after loss of control on 17th December 1975. As much of the wreckage as possible was recovered from the sea and it was taken back to the AIB facility at Farnborough for investigation. It is seen here in the hangar on 25th March 1976. *FAST collection*

Seen making a big impact during its STOL landing at the SBAC show on 4th September 1984, is DHC-5E Buffalo C-GCTC, which is still sliding along the runway with both wings broken and debris still flying off. Luckily it is not very often that the AAIB have to investigate an accident on their doorstep but, in this case, the wreckage could be recovered directly to the compound on the southwestern side of the airfield for investigation. *FAST collection*

There are 34 Inspectors of Air Accidents – 21 from an engineering background, drawn from within the UK Armed Forces or from manufacturers, and 13 classified as Inspectors of Air Accidents (Operations). The latter are qualified pilots, to Air Transport Pilots Licence standard, and have had considerable experience of being in command of large commercial jet aircraft. In some cases, they will also have been manufacturer or military test pilots. The Operations Inspectors maintain their currency on a number of commercial aircraft types and it is not uncommon to have an AAIB Inspector flying a commercial airliner from the UK to European or holiday destinations. The Engineering Inspectors are highly qualified to chartered aeronautical engineering (CEng) levels within their disciplines, and retain currency on aircraft types and systems through regular attendance at manufacturers' courses. They too are pilots, trained to Private Pilots Licence (PPL) level, to give them more than a basic insight into piloting and airmanship. This, it goes without saying, increases the understanding and interfaces with the engineering and operational aspects.

The Inspectors of Air Accidents travel throughout the UK and the world when a British-registered or British-built aircraft is involved in an accident. A foreign government can request the AAIB to participate in an investigation involving British aircraft or

Seen here *in situ* on the following day, are the remains of British Midland Boeing 737-4YO G-OBME, which had departed from Heathrow bound for Belfast on 8th January 1989. Whilst en route engine vibration was experienced and it was elected to divert to East Midlands Airport with the starboard engine shut down. During the final approach, at night, to runway 27 the port engine failed and the aircraft descended and struck the M1 motorway embankment, some 800 yards short of the runway threshold. The initial bounce impact can be seen on the ground in the foreground, with the aircraft coming to rest up the embankment beyond. The approach lights and the runway can be seen beyond, indicating just how close the aircraft was to touchdown. The AAIB conducted an intensive investigation into this accident, initially on site, with later removal of the wreckage to Farnborough for detailed analysis. *R Carter/AAIB*

Seen here, still dominating the AAIB investigation hangar during early 2006, is the partial wreckage from the Pan Am 747-121 N739PA that was blown up by a terrorist bomb over Lockerbie on 21st December 1988. The debris in the foreground is that from a Reims Cessna F.406 that impacted the ground near Inverness during October 2004, whilst beyond can be seen two Robinson R44 helicopters and an assortment of general aviation types, all undergoing investigation. *Falcon*

subjects, and these arrangements come under Annex 13 to the Chicago Convention of the International Civil Aviation Organization (ICAO), which provides for representation of all interested parties. The AAIB has signed a European Union Council Directive 94/56/EC that requires member states to assist one another, as required. There is also a Memorandum of Agreement in place with the UK dependent territories for assistance if necessary. It is not just UK-registered civil aircraft that get the attention of the AAIB however. One of the more horrific, but nevertheless in-depth, investigations of recent times concerned the Pan Am Boeing 747 that was blown up by a terrorist bomb over Lockerbie in Dumfriesshire, Scotland on 21st December 1988. This was one of the largest wreckage trails that the AAIB had ever seen, as it covered an area of some 840 square miles to the east of the actual incident site. The wreckage had drifted, due to high-altitude winds, over a distance of more than 100 miles. The forward cabin section of this Boeing 747, with the explosive structural failure prominently displayed, is still within the AAIB hangar at Farnborough, but this will be sent to the USA in the future.

Some military aircraft wreckage is also returned to Farnborough for analysis, though a number of the more recent accidents have been investigated at RAF airfields where wreckage has been laid out within RAF hangars or Hardened Aircraft Shelters.

Nuts and Bolts

So how does an investigation take place? Once an accident has been reported and it is deemed necessary to send a team to the site, the inspectors will initially liaise with the local police or airport authorities, who are usually in attendance shortly after the accident has occurred. The inspectors could be faced with anything upon their arrival. There could a substantially intact aircraft or fragmented wreckage debris strewn over a hillside or, in some cases, a large hole in the ground that may for example contain the remains of a military jet that had made a high-speed impact and left a crater some 20m in diameter, and similar in depth, with no large pieces visible. Alternatively, it could be an air-

craft lying at the bottom of a seabed in deep water. Each location is different, the variables being dependent upon the type of impact, the size of the aircraft, the speed of impact and the prevailing weather conditions.

Picking up the pieces is the easy part. The reality strikes with the realisation that this is just the beginning of what could be a long and detailed analysis. A debris trail can be spread over a wide area – as stated earlier, the Lockerbie Boeing 747 trail was in fact 100 miles in length, to the east of the actual impact site. Engines and other components may only be found from excavation of the crater, which could contain the compressed forward fuselage and part of the wings. The remaining parts of the aircraft could be scattered down-wind from the extensive compressive explosive force.

Naturally, the preservation of any wreckage is of a high priority at the early stage because so much can be determined from the wreckage trail and components in their 'as found' state. Instruments normally freeze at the moment of impact and other items such as engine throttles, positions of screw jacks and flying control actuators, all have their part to play. Integrity of flying controls and systems will be basically checked at the site, as far as possible, whilst the condition of the engines and the positions of propeller blades would also be noted. The actual position and the subsequent deformation of the blades of a pro-

Boeing-Vertol 234LR (Commercial) Chinook G-BWFC, of British International Helicopters, crashed into the sea after a catastrophic failure of the forward transmission resulted in desynchronisation of the forward and aft rotors, on approach to Sumburgh, Shetland Islands on 6th November 1986, whilst inbound from the Brent Oil field in the East Shetland Basin. The wreckage was recovered from the seabed and an intensive investigation commenced at Farnborough, resulting in the cause being established as a failure of a modified spiral bevel ring gear in the forward transmission system. The wreckage is seen here, laid out in the AAIB hangar on 13th April 1987. *FAST collection*

peller driven aircraft, can give a good indi-
cation as to whether the engine was developing power at the time of impact. Similarly
the condition of a turbine engine would
indicate whether power was present, or
parts had separated in flight, all giving valuable evidence to assist in piecing together
the seemingly impossible jigsaw. In the case
of helicopters, with their intricate systems
and considerable number of rotating and
dynamic components, the investigation task
may be somewhat more onerous. Nevertheless, all the relevant systems, controls and
drive-shafts would be closely scrutinised for
indicative signs of failure or malfunction
during the early stage of investigation.

An aircraft's wreckage, which in some
cases can consist of hundreds of bags of fragmented parts, will then be laid out within the
AAIB hangar and 'rebuilt' as far as possible in
order to replicate the whole aircraft. This
will assist the inspectors in determining the
integrity of such parts as control runs, fuel
and hydraulic systems or airframe structures,
covering even the minutest detail that may
yield that all-important clue to the disaster.

In the event of an accident involving a civil
passenger aircraft, much early information
could be gained from the playback of the
Cockpit Voice Recorder or Flight Data
Recorder (CVR and FDR – known as the
'Black Box'), for which the AAIB have a
sophisticated laboratory full of equipment
for playback and analysis. This can indicate
what was happening at the time of the accident, and can even be used to reconstruct the
crash as a computer simulation. Similarly, the
CVR read-outs can be edited with 'highlights'
on specific channels, whilst the elimination
of background noise gives clearer audible
data to the investigators. Although commonly known as 'Black Boxes', these
recorders are in fact bright orange in colour
to aid their location after a crash, and are
capable of withstanding high impacts up to
1,000 'G' and heat up to 1,100∞C. Valuable
data has been secured from many damaged
FDRs, including some that have been

immersed in seawater for lengthy periods yet
have still produced enough detailed information to lead to a successful conclusion of
the accident investigation. The AAIB Farnborough facility is a world leader in this field
with considerable expertise and equipment
on hand within its specialised laboratory.

Minor Investigations

Contrary to some beliefs, all accidents and
serious incidents must be reported to the
AAIB in accordance with the Civil Aviation
(Investigation of Air Accidents & Incidents)
Regulations 1996, which came into force on
21st November of that year. It is from these
regulations that all aircraft accidents and
incidents are investigated by the AAIB on
behalf of The Secretary of State for Transport. The regulations are harmonised with
the UK's international obligations under the
provisions of the ICAO Annex 13 and the EU
Directive. The Chief Inspector of Air Accidents, currently Mr David King, is appointed
by the Secretary of State to carry out investigations into accidents and incidents, in
respect of the applicable regulations.

Not all civilian accidents will undergo a
'Field' investigation by the AAIB, as these will
largely depend upon the nature of the accident or incident, and on whether there have
been any casualties. Where no 'Field' investigation is accomplished, the AAIB will investigate an incident from the information received
from the pilot and operator, who will have
been furnished with their standard Aircraft
Accident Report Form (AARF) that is required
to be returned to the AAIB within 14 days.

When finalised, the Chief Inspector of Air
Accidents will submit the report direct to
the Secretary of State, and the Chief Inspector will arrange for its publication. The all-
too-familiar yellow Aircraft Accident Report
will then be published and will be available
for general release throughout the world of
aviation to all parties that have an interest.

The lesser accidents are covered in a
monthly Bulletin produced by the AAIB,
where a description covering the accident

and any analysis and findings are reported.
All the AAIB Reports, monthly Bulletins and
the occasional Special Bulletins are available on the website at www.aaib.gov.uk.

Military investigations take a slightly different avenue, in that the AAIB report will be
presented to a service Board of Inquiry, and
any flight safety recommendations are circu-
lated widely within the MoD, as well as to the
manufacturers. The BOI findings are published in the form of Military Aircraft Accident
Summaries, or Aircraft Accident Reports, and
are classed as 'Restricted' documents (that is,
not for general circulation) where information is provided on the circumstances leading
up to the accident and its proximate cause.

Vital Work

The AAIB handles approximately 360
reportable civil aviation air accidents and
incidents within the UK each year, whilst
there are approximately eight to ten military
accidents where AAIB assistance would be
requested by the RAF/MoD. The Royal Navy
and Army Air Corps have their own accident
investigation personnel.

This dedicated band of AAIB Inspectors of
Air Accidents all play a vital part within this
onerous but rewarding task of establishing
the cause of the accident. Their findings can
result in the overall improvement of flight
safety, which is of utmost importance to the
furtherance and development at the cutting
edge of technology in this ever-changing
world of military and commercial aviation.

Farnborough has been synonymous with
aircraft accident investigation for as long as
flight has been conducted on these shores
and, contrary to some belief, the AAIB
remains separate from QinetiQ and indeed
the Civil Aviation Authority. Neither was it
ever part of the RAE structure, having its roots
instead firmly within the Royal Aero Club. As
stated throughout, however, the RAE, DRA
and DERA lent vital assistance over the years
and this still rings true today with various
QinetiQ departments actively assisting in aircraft accident investigations into material and
structural failures, lightning strikes, explosive force and other forensic evidence. The
teamwork between the experts of the AAIB
and the scientists of QinetiQ has been instru-
mental in countless firm conclusions drawn
over causation factors, which, in some cases,
appear to be the ultimate jigsaw.

1985 to 1994

The End of Research Flying is Nigh

Throughout the 1970s, considerable advances had been achieved in enhancing airborne optical systems to improve aircrew situational awareness at night and in poor weather conditions. During the 1980s this research was consolidated and saw the introduction of probably the greatest advancement in sensor technology since radar – that of the electro-optic sensor system. Systems integration was developing in these fields and it was not long before the sensor technology was being adapted to a variety of uses.

Head-Up Displays (HUD) had been undergoing research since the early 1960s and, along with various improvements to cockpit instrumentation and moving map displays, Flight Systems Department continued to move ahead with improvements to existing systems and formulating new technology.

Sadly this decade saw the demise of the title Royal Aircraft Establishment and also the cessation of research flying at Farnborough, thus bringing to an end a tradition that had lasted for nearly 90 years.

1985

During January a division of the Carroll Group formed a company called Stase Flight Limited, however its name was changed during April to the Farnborough Aerospace Development Corporation Limited, under its Chairman, Air Marshal Sir Ivor Broom KCB, CBE, DSO, DFC, AFC. The Farnborough Aerospace Development Corporation was formed

as the lessee to promote the proposed integrated aerospace business park, Britain's first, on the south side of the airfield where some 23 acres were available for the Aerospace Business Park and a further 27 acres for Business Aviation usage as a civilian enclave within the airfield boundary.

The MoD invited tenders for the site on a 125-year lease on 6th March, stating that the maximum numbers of aircraft based at Farnborough could not exceed 40 and annual movements were to be capped at 25,000 maximum.

Q109 building was finished in 1985 and the RAE printing branch and photographic

section moved in. This building then housed the valuable negative collection until the photographic section moved out in 1997 to the new DERA site and the negatives were moved to 415 building at Pyestock. Q109 building was demolished in 2003.

In June/July three Piper PA-31-350 Navajo Chieftains replaced the RAE Devon C.2 Transport Flight fleet with ZF520 (N35823) arriving on 5th June; ZF521 (N27509) on 22nd July; and ZF522 (N27728/G-RNAV/N4261A) on 21st June. ZF520 operated with a civil registration G-BLZK also applied for a couple of days during June whilst the aircraft was undertaking crew-training sorties.

The cocooned fuselage of Comet 1A G-AOJT/F-BGNX is seen here on the Farnborough fire dump (Laffan's Plain area) on 11th March 1985, whilst the partially burnt fuselage of ex-RAE Comet Mk.2E XN453 can be seen beyond. The cocooned fuselage was removed on 17th March 1985 and was transported to the Mosquito Museum at London Colney, now the de Havilland Aircraft Heritage Centre. It is extant there today, still in its previous Air France markings. *FAST collection*

Piper PA-31 Navajo Chieftain ZF522 is seen here on the 'A' shed apron on a snowy February day in 1986, with the famous landmark Farnborough control tower (N1 building) beyond. The Navajos took over from the Devons in 1985. *FAST collection*

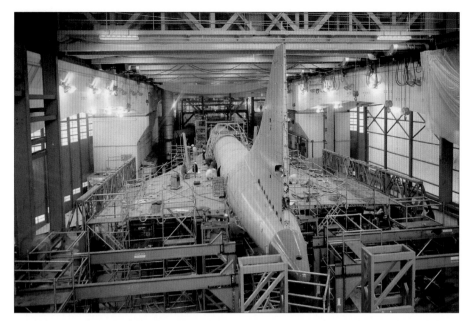

Fatigue testing on a Concorde airframe was completed during 1985. Seen here in the mid-1970s is the test airframe installed within the Ball Hill Structures Department main test frame. Upon completion of tests the airframe was scrapped. *FAST collection*

The Dakota C.3 ZA947 had 50th anniversary markings applied, the type having been first flown on 17th December 1935, and appeared as such at the International Air Tattoo at RAF Fairford.

The Concorde structural test airframe had completed 15 years of tests and was cut up on site. The Main Test Frame of the Structures building (X31) had opened on 6th June 1966 and RAE and BAC (later BAe) engineers had worked closely together throughout the intensive test programme. By 1984 the airframe had achieved the equivalent of some 33,000 flying hours since full-scale testing started in 1973, although initial tests had begun in 1970.

1986

During September the Dakota C.3 ZA947 flew a commemorative trip to Arnhem, dropping eight paratroopers from the Parachute Regiment over Ginkel Heide. This flight also encompassed a routine trial where a control and navigation system was tested for use in an unmanned aircraft (UMA) under development for reconnaissance work.

A GAF Jindivik Mk.103B A92-729 had arrived from Llanbedr by road and Instrument and Trials Department fitted some experimental equipment with solid state television cameras installed in the wingtip pods, facing rearwards, to enable the ground station to have some direct visual footage of the towed-target behaviour and any damage sustained. This resulted in the Jindivik fleet being modified with this equipment. Interestingly, the last Jindivik operation was conducted from the QinetiQ facility at Llanbedr on 26th October 2004, bringing to an end a long era of RAE involvement in pilotless and drone aircraft flying from the Welsh base.

Now surplus to requirements, the ex-RAE Transport Flight Devon C.2s all found new homes and departed as follows: VP959 to Hurn for servicing on 3rd November 1986; VP975 to Wroughton (Science Museum store) on 24th January 1986; XG496 to Salvair at Newcastle as G-ANDX on 5th March

1986; and XM223 to Hurn for servicing on 3rd November 1986. Two of these Devons, VP959 and XM223, still had some service left as they were subsequently allocated for communications duties at West Freugh, where VP959 also undertook sonobuoy research and remained in service until at least July 1990. XM223, having firstly positioned to Llanbedr on 22nd April 1986 for communications duties, then passed to West Freugh where it operated until at least July 1993.

1987

The Accident Investigation Branch underwent a subtle name change during November, when it became the Air Accidents Investigation Branch (AAIB) and continues as such today.

Westland Wessex HU.5 XS241, the RAE's last serving example, was retired on 27th November 1987, the type having been operating with RAE since 1962 undertaking various roles and being engaged in numerous trials programmes. This year was also the 30th anniversary of the type's first flight in the UK (17th May 1957) and to mark these occasions a formation of RAE helicopters comprising Sea King HAS.1 (DB) XV371; Wessex HU.5 XS241; Puma HC.1 ZA941; Lynx AH.5 ZD285 and Gazelle HT.2 ZB648 was flown, and photographed, over the airfield on 27th November. Wessex HU.5 XS241 had been delivered from Fleetlands on 24th September 1968, in a 'sand and spinach' colour scheme, for IEE (later Avionics) Flight, but it was also used by Weapons Flight. During its nineteen years at RAE it was used for many different trials and was deployed to Culdrose, Portland, Thorney Island, Larkhill and West Freugh on many occasions. It was fitted with an armament platform where dummy missiles were trialled and it also undertook torpedo trials, these being 'flown' beneath the helicopter suspended on the hook. Also, during the late 1970s, the Stingray was attached to the port side weapons platform. These trials

Buccaneer S.2B XW986 is seen on the western apron at Farnborough during September 1985, with an AN/ALQ-123 Infra-red Countermeasures system pod (being developed by the US Navy for use on the A-4M, A-6, A-7 and F-4) that was undergoing trials with Defence Weapons Department on the starboard wing pylon. This aircraft is now operated by Classic Jets based at Thunder City, Cape Town, South Africa. *FAST collection*

View of the Rotary Wing Flight of RAE in 'A' shed during March 1987; showing Gazelle HT.2 ZB648, Puma HC.1 ZA941, Wessex HU.5 XS241 and Sea King Mk.4X ZB507. The Flight moved to 'L' shed in 1993. *FAST collection*

Wessex HU.5 XS241 was used by Avionics Flight and Weapons Flight. It is seen here outside 'A' shed during February 1985, with a MIRTH (<u>M</u>illimetric wave and <u>I</u>nfra-<u>R</u>ed <u>T</u>est <u>H</u>ead) ball on its starboard undercarriage attachment. The Wessex was retired in 1987 and was eventually scrapped. *FAST collection*

were flown from Culdrose in connection with the ATDU. This Wessex was repainted in the 'raspberry ripple' scheme in 1976 having previously had a white cheat line and RAE titles added during the early 1970s. It left Farnborough by road to RNAY Wroughton for storage on 19th May 1988.

A Gloster Meteor T.7, WA662, arrived by road from Shoeburyness for trials with Instrumentation and Trials Department. It was taken into the Structures Department Ball Hill facility where it was inverted and secured to a series of trestles. These trials during January 1988 were in conjunction with the development of a short-range radar, known as a Radar Vector Miss Distance Indicator, for fitment to the drone Meteor D.16s to measure the trajectory of an incoming missile. The same trial was applied to Meteor D.16 WK800, which arrived at Farnborough from Llanbedr on 24th February 1987 and was placed within the Structures Department hall, returning to Llanbedr on 11th March.

Royal Air Force and Royal Navy personnel moved into Q111 building during early 1987, this being designated as the Joint Acoustic Analysis Centre (JAAC). It continued as such until 2003 and was demolished in January/February 2004.

1988

The most modern jet to join the RAE fleet arrived on 24th February 1988 when Tornado F.2 ZD902 positioned from RAF Coningsby where it had previously served with No 229 OCU. This aircraft departed for St Athan by road on 17th March 1989 but returned by air on 14th August 1992 after some maintenance upgrade work had been accomplished. It was to undergo various other modifications, and

Just prior to the retirement of Wessex HU.5 XS241 from the RAE fleet, a unique five-helicopter formation was staged and it is seen here crossing the threshold of runway 25, in front of the 'black sheds', during late November 1987. The helicopters are, from top to bottom: Sea King HAS.1 (DB) XV371; Wessex HU.5 XS241; Puma HC.1 ZA941; Lynx AH.5 ZD285 and Gazelle HT.2 ZB648. *FAST collection*

Seen inverted on a special rig in the Ball Hill Structures Department in January 1988 is Meteor T.7 WA662. Its modified nose houses a Miss Distance Indicator (MDI). The Meteor arrived at Farnborough to undergo tests of a radar vector MDI for fitment to the drone Meteor D.16. The dummy missile, its trajectory indicating a near miss, is seen hanging from suspended cables at the top of the photograph. *FAST collection*

Parked on the western apron, having just arrived from Coningsby on 24th February 1988, is Tornado F.2 ZD902, still wearing its 229 OCU markings. This aircraft underwent some major installation and modification work, becoming known as TIARA (Tornado Integrated Avionic Research Aircraft). It still operates with QinetiQ from Boscombe Down today. *FAST collection*

Jaguar T.2A XX835 is seen here in June 1987 carrying the under-fuselage LLTV pod. This aircraft was later used for other trials work, including HMS, NVG and Jobtac, before being returned to the RAF. *FAST collection*

installations, and was to be devoted to advanced air-to-air equipment trials with various sensors and enhanced systems. It was modified to an F.2A variant and became known as 'TIARA – Tornado Integrated Avionic Research Aircraft'. It featured a glass cockpit with holographic HUD, full colour Head-Down CRT displays on three screens, Helmet-mounted sights and Hands-On Throttle And Stick (HOTAS) control system. By the time it left for Boscombe Down on 8th October 1994, the last of the DERA aircraft to depart, the installation of the new systems had only partially been completed, but this was finished at Boscombe Down and the aircraft remains part of the active QinetiQ fleet today undertaking valuable sensor, including FLIR and IRST, research.

Buccaneer S.2C XV344, 'Nightbird', is seen here on the western apron at Farnborough during July 1988, carrying an experimental TIALD pod under the port wing pylon. This aircraft underwent many modifications and served at Farnborough for sixteen years before transferring to Boscombe Down, where it was eventually retired during September 1994. It is now preserved as a centrepiece within the QinetiQ headquarters at Farnborough. The 'Nightbird' motif can be seen on the nose, just forward of the roundel. *FAST collection*

Jaguar T.2A XX833 arrived on 8th August 1988 on loan from the SAOEU. This Jaguar, in its standard camouflage scheme and wearing code letter 'N', was classed as a project support aircraft and shared between RAE/DRA and the SAOEU. Initially it was fitted with a podded FLIR and used for development of the GEC Atlantic pod, which basically gave an image in the HUD of the pilot's view of the outside world. In this guise it became known as 'Nightcat', giving an enhanced forward view at night. During 1991 the aircraft was tasked with the development of the Thermal Imaging Airborne Laser Designator (TIALD) pod for single-seat strike aircraft operations, initially carried beneath the mainplane. Another Jaguar from Boscombe Down, the ETPS T.2 XX145, was deployed to Farnborough between 19th November and 7th December 1992 for clearance to carry the TIALD pod beneath the fuselage on the centreline pylon. At this time XX833 was continually passing between Farnborough and Boscombe Down and was fitted with a CRT Head-down display, a GPWS, rear cockpit hand controller, video processor and a computer symbology generator. It now carried the TIALD pod on the under-fuselage pylon and continued with this work after its re-location to Boscombe Down on 20th June 1994, these trials proving the system to be a success. The Jaguar was also utilised for other trials, including a Helmet-Mounted Sight (HMS) and ASRAAM. It was repainted in the overall grey scheme in 1996 and is still operational with QinetiQ today.

Jaguar T.2 XX835 had arrived at Farnborough on 6th August 1984 and after a short trial period it underwent installation and servicing. It was then converted to a T.2A variant and was fitted with a Diffractive Optics Z-HUD and NVG-compatible lighting and commenced research flying on 16th May 1986 for LLTV and HUD trials. Various improved installations were undertaken,

including a new Data Acquisition System and Multi-Function Displays in the rear cockpit, although the LLTV system was still in use. During 1989 it was fitted with a Jobtac (Jaguar Off-Boresight Target Acquisition) system with HMS, NVG and an AIM-9L Sidewinder acquisition round as part of an air-to-air and air-to-ground system for target cueing. This aircraft retained its standard RAF camouflage markings although it received a Jaguar cat motif on the nose, and it returned to the RAF, departing for St Athan on 23rd March 1994.

The first of two Powerchute Raiders (Mk.1 ZG879) arrived at RAE in August for a series of trials over the next three years with Mission Management Department for research into the characteristics of advanced ram-air

gliding parachutes and handling tasks. The Powerchute operated from 'A' Flight, where taxying, take-off, general handling, landing, performance and climb trials with data measurement were undertaken. A second example, Mk.2 ZG927, arrived in 1989 and the research was completed in 1991.

During May there was a subtle name change when RAE became the Royal Aerospace Establishment: retaining its initials but reflecting its growing importance within the spacecraft technology field. However this name change did not last for long, as the UK Government's controversial decision to split the Civil Service into commercial organisations took its toll and the name again changed, to the Defence Research Agency, in 1991.

Powerchute Raider Mk.1 ZG879 is seen here outside 'D' shed in August 1988, shortly after arrival but without its ram air parachute. It undertook research into flight characteristics along with another example, ZG927. *FAST collection*

Wearing the short-lived Royal Aerospace Establishment titles is Lynx AH.7 ZD285, seen on the tarmac outside 'A' shed during September 1991. This view is prior to the extensive nose modifications undertaken by Aircraft Engineering Servicing Department during 1992. *FAST collection*

1989

British International Helicopters, which became known as Brintel, arrived on the scene and a facility was built during 1989 on the side of Q153 building to house their Chinook simulator. This was relocated from the company's Aberdeen base to be nearer to RAF Odiham, whose RAF aircrew became the prime user of this valuable training aid. It remained in use until 17th January 2000 and, upon closure of the BIH operations at Farnborough, the simulator was moved back to Longside, Peterhead.

Flight Systems leased 'D' shed and positioned their North American F-100F Super Sabres to Farnborough from Germany, the first arrivals being N414FS and N417FS on 15th November 1989, followed by N416FS on 16th November. The first operations of these were on 2nd February 1990 when N416FS and N417FS deployed to Germany for target work. A further example, N419FS, arrived on 6th August 1990. However the Farnborough operations were short-lived; the last aircraft, N417FS, departing on 28th February 1991.

The Unmanned Aircraft Section of Defence Systems Department were actively engaged in researching an Unmanned Aircraft (UMA) system to provide the Army with information in seeing-over-the-hill scenarios and providing data to direct effective fire. The evolution of UMA systems to operate in the surveillance and reconnaissance roles has resulted in accurate data being available in a real-time basis, proving that these unmanned aerial vehicles and aerial reconnaissance platforms are an important asset in the battlefield. RAE were undertaking studies into UMA craft and their systems including airframe design, engines, launchers, recovery systems, avionics, flight controls, navigation, payloads, sensors and ground control stations. During the mid-1980s RAE had produced their own indigenous fly-by-wire, 18kg UMA known as the XRAE-1. After successful flight trials the UMA was further developed into the XRAE-2, weighing 40kg, to evaluate the UMA technology and payload assessments. RAE did not progress with the XRAE types, which were further developed by FR Aviation. The Raven surveillance drone

evolved from this earlier work and went into production. UMA work is still undertaken by QinetiQ today.

Originally built in 1965 on the Ball Hill site, the 70ft-high radar tower came into operation circa 1967. It was upgraded with a Plessey Watchman radar in February 1989 and became operational on 24th July 1989, this continuing until 2002 when the new Raytheon Airfield Surveillance Radar tower installed on the airfield commenced operations. The Watchman tower, a familiar landmark on the airfield, was demolished by a controlled explosion on 1st March 2003 and reduced to rubble during the next couple of weeks.

Lord Trefgarne, the Minister of State for Defence Procurement, officially opened the civil enclave, on the south side of Farnborough Airfield, on 25th January 1989. The Farnborough Business Aviation Centre commenced operations with Carroll Aircraft Corporation operating the fixed-base operator (FBO) business.

1990

Aerospatiale SA.330E Puma XW241 arrived from Bedford on 9th February 1990 for eventual use as a ground experimental vehicle. This early Puma was French-built, having ended its rotor blade trials it was passed to Avionics and Sensors Department for use as an EMC test airframe, a role in which it is still engaged today.

A Hunter F.4 WV276 (7847M) arrived by road from No 1 STT Halton during December 1990 for EMC ground trials work with Avionics and Sensors Department. It passed to Duxford where it arrived by road from Farnborough on 14th January 1997 for the Old Flying Machine Company, then to Sandown, IoW, on 5th August 1998, by road, and then on to Scampton where it still exists with Hawker Hunter Aviation Ltd, and is currently for sale.

A series of Portakabin buildings were erected on the former site of Q2/Q3 Buildings, for use by British Aerospace to accommodate the influx of personnel transferred to Farnborough as a result of the closure of the Weybridge facility. Work started in

This internal view of 'L' shed during March 1987 shows Buccaneer S.2B XW986 with S.2C XV344 at right, while Andover C.1 XS646 and Varsity T.1 WL679 are beyond. This hangar, built circa 1952, is now in use by Gama Aviation Support Services. *FAST collection*

Sea King Mk.4X ZB506 is seen outside 'D' shed in March 1990, fitted with a 'heli-tele' sphere at the front of the original beams fitted for installation of the Blue Kestrel Radar. This helicopter had served with RAE Bedford, was transferred to Farnborough and then relocated to Boscombe Down.

Ex-British Airways BAC 1-11 Srs 539GL G-BGKE arrived on 24th June 1991 for a public relations visit, prior to its being dispatched to DRA Bedford for trials work. It is seen here taxying past 'A' shed, which still had the RAE initials, although the aircraft has the inscription 'Aerospace Division DRA'. This aircraft later became ZH763 and came back on 7th February 1994, prior to relocation to Boscombe Down, where it continues in service today.

Seen here on 2nd August 1991, during its last operational flight, is Varsity T.1 WL679, banking over Brookwood to make its final approach to land at Farnborough. Having spent many years with RAE on FLIR research, it can still be seen with the RAF Museum at Cosford. *All FAST collection*

Andover CC.2 XS790 is seen during a test flight from Farnborough in March 1994, having had the modifications to the nose completed. Various sensors were fitted in the nose, whilst the weather radar was positioned above the cockpit and an antenna assembly on the starboard lower fuselage. The aircraft repositioned to Boscombe Down in September 1994 and was eventually scrapped during 23/24th November 1998. *FAST collection*

November 1989 and was basically completed during January 1990, these continuing in use until the new British Aerospace headquarters buildings were finished on the south side of the airfield.

Mission Management Department installed a tail-mounted miniature TV camera and video system on board BAC 1-11 XX919. This installation was born out of work undertaken on a Jaguar, where a mini-CCTV camera system was installed to give a wide-angle view of the pilot and his movements, as he performed various high-speed and 'G' manoeuvres. The installation in the One-Eleven was a proof of concept to research this application as a means of flight safety recording and of providing the crew with a view outside the aircraft. This basically stemmed from AAIB investigation of accidents where an external view of the aircraft would have been beneficial to the crew. XX919 made its first flight with this installation on 21st March, with good views of the aircraft from the rear

being available to the crew. Having also been engaged in high frequency (HF) communications research and sonobuoy launching through the rear stairwell, it relocated to Boscombe Down on 24th March 1994.

A full-scale wooden mock-up of a MiG-25 *Foxbat* was produced in the RAE carpentry shop on behalf of Attack Weapons Department, for ground trials in presenting a realistic aircraft image to a range of optical sensors. The mock-up was installed on the southern side of the airfield and could be seen there on various occasions, looking very much like the type it depicted, albeit supported on fifty ground trestles and jacks.

1991

On 1st April the Defence Research Agency came into being, which resulted in the much-lamented demise of the Royal Aircraft Establishment and the famous RAE abbreviation. This, of course, also resulted in the loss of the Royal status within the title,

bestowed back in April 1912. However, for a short while, the title was known as Defence Research Agency – Aerospace Division, which, interestingly also contained a suffix, 'RAE Farnborough', but the divisional structure of the DRA was abandoned by 1st April 1992.

The Ministry of Defence announced that Farnborough Airfield was to be disposed of and that flying would eventually be rationalised at Boscombe Down. This also had the effect of closing the airfield at DRA Bedford. Meanwhile the Air Fleet had diminished somewhat, with only eighteen active research aircraft at Farnborough.

As a replacement for the long-serving Varsity T.1 WL679, an ex-Queens Flight Andover CC.2, XS790, was allocated for conversion to a flying laboratory. Its primary task was to be for research, testing and development of experimental equipment designed by the RAE and the Defence Research Agency (DRA). These included trials to evaluate thermal imaging with electro-optical sensors for development of an autonomous weapons system by the Missile Technology and Countermeasures section, part of the Weapons Department, at RAE Farnborough. Usage of the Andover was also to be shared with DRA Malvern (formerly the Royal Signals and Radar Establishment RSRE). The colour scheme at this time was also slightly changed to that of 'raspberry ripple', being partially re-painted by Fields at East Midlands during March 1991, although much of the previous colour scheme, basically as per Queens Flight, still existed, with RAE crests added and wearing Royal Aerospace Establishment titles.

Looking immaculate in its new paint scheme, XS790 arrived at Farnborough on 26th March 1991 for its new life with the Defence Research Agency (DRA), which came into being a few days later on 1st April 1991. Whilst design work for the extensive modifi-

Transport Flight Dakota C.3 ZA947 and Piper PA-31 Navajo Chieftains ZF520, ZF521 and ZF522 are seen here in formation over the former ETPS hangar and dispersal used by Southern Squadron. In this view, the area has already been cordoned off for operation as a civilian enclave. Transport Flight was disbanded in March 1993, although this view was taken during the late 1980s. *FAST collection*

cations had already been undertaken at RAE/DRA Bedford, the task of accomplishing this work was undertaken at Farnborough. After the nose and cockpit had been stripped, a modified nose structure was incorporated, including a large internal structural frame fitted to the forward nose bulkhead to house various sensors and camera equipment.

This resulted in a distinctive looking bulbous nose, with optical panels on the forward upper and lower positions. There was also the capability for a later fitment of an infra-red sensor housed in a steerable turret utilising a further modified bulbous nose. The lower platform was designed to carry various FLIR sensors plus a video and still camera, and the upper platform contained a three-axis stabilised platform for the GEC HSB (High Spatial Bandwith) FLIR sensor, whilst both the germanium windows had remotely controlled shutters to protect the surface when not in use. Accordingly the NARCO KWX58 weather radar was repositioned and housed in a pod above the cockpit, whilst a flat plate antenna assembly was fitted to the starboard side of the rear fuselage for the short-range centrimetric Synthetic Aperture Radar. Other equipment fitted included two Inertial Navigation Systems (FIN 1064 and a Litton 93), a Doppler radar as removed from the Varsity, a Sonar locator beacon, TACAN, two HF and three UHF/VHF comms, various recorders, a cockpit installation which was NVG-capable and more recently a Trimble TNL2000 GPS. Internal stations for operation/observation of the equipment were also added, eventually totalling six, two for radar operators and four for observers of the equipment, whilst the cockpit was also modified for two-crew operation.

Having undergone a major servicing the Andover was first flown from Farnborough on 13th February 1992 basically as an air test for systems functioning, followed by further modifications and systems installation work. It finally emerged with its new nose profile, and the other appendages, for its initial post-modification test flight on 1st September 1993. However, due to handling difficulties, the pitot-static system required modification and the Andover went back into the hangars for the addition of pitot-probes to be positioned on the wingtips. Once completed, a few weeks later, the aircraft underwent further handling trials which proved successful. The Andover then commenced its research flying, with its turret-mounted electro-optic sensors, but relocated briefly to A&AEE Boscombe Down on 21st March 1994 when the DRA research flying was relocated to this Wiltshire airfield, although it did return for further modifications and installations by Aircraft Engineering Services Department at Farnborough. This was duly completed and the Andover finally departed from Farnborough on 2nd September 1994, for its further flying laboratory research duties at Boscombe Down.

1992

RAE Bedford HS.125 Srs1B XW930, previously G-ATPC, that had been operating with Aero Flight since 1971, arrived at Farnborough for storage on 21st May 1992. It remained in 'D' shed until it was stripped for spares. The airframe then passed to Osprey and, in 1995, was transported to Dunsfold by road where it was scrapped during June 1997.

August saw the last apprentice entry at Farnborough, with only four apprentices being accepted for training within the Aircraft Apprentice Training Department. With the intended relocation of flying, there was no further requirement for apprentice aircraft engineers at Farnborough. Also 1992 was the

Seen here in storage during August 1994, is ex-DRA Bedford BAe (HS) 125 XW930. Beyond are three former Bedford Canberras: B.6 (mod) WT333, B.2/6 WK163 and B.6 (mod) WH953. All these aircraft were disposed of and cleared by January 1995. *Falcon*

Internal view of 'N' shed at Farnborough, seen during March 1994, with Tornado F.2A 'Tiara' ZD902 undergoing servicing and installation work. GR.1 ZA449, on loan to DRA from British Aerospace for evaluating systems for the standard GR.1 variant, is seen beyond. Today 'N' shed is in use by TAG Farnborough Engineering Ltd. *FAST collection*

Two Canberras, B.6 (mod) WH953 and B.2/6 (mod) WK163, are seen here over the Farnborough airfield on 24th March 1994 making a break for landing having relocated from DRA Bedford for disposal. They both remained stored on the airfield until January 1995. *R A Cooper*

Hunter T.7 WV383, 'Hecate', is seen on the Western Squadron flight line, just prior to departure for Boscombe Down on 24th March 1994 having been at Farnborough since 1971. It later returned to Farnborough by road and is now in the FAST Museum. *Falcon*

On 24th March 1994, DRA Jaguar T.2A ZB615 leads the departing aircraft, taxiing from the Western Squadron apron for take-off on runway 25. The two Canberras beyond, B.6 (mod) WH953 and B.2/6 (mod) WK163, have just arrived from RAE Bedford. This area is where the TAG Aviation hangar has now been built. *Falcon*

With crews being strapped in the IAM Hawk T.1 XX327, DRA Hunter T.7 WV383, DRA Tornado GR.1 ZA449 and Jaguar T.2 ZB615 the aircraft are being prepared for departure from Farnborough on 24th March 1994 bound for Boscombe Down. *FAST collection*

last entry at Farnborough for general engineering apprentices. At this time airframes with the Aircraft Apprentice Training Department were as follows: Canberra PR.7 WH774 fuselage, ex-RAE; Canberra T.4 WJ865 ex-ETPS and A&AEE, in open storage, and later to be scrapped; Hunter F.6 XE587 ex-ETPS; Provost T.1 XF844 ex-RAE Structures Department; Scout AH.1 XP166 ex-RAE; Wessex HU.5 XS482 ex-A&AEE; Jet Provost T.5A XW428 ex-RAF College, Cranwell. MS.880B Rallye Club G-BIOR underwent rebuild by the apprentices using parts from a donor aircraft (G-AZGJ) and was used for air experi-

Andover C.1 XS646, with its distinctively shaped sensor nose, is seen outside 'D' shed on 24th March 1994. This aircraft was still undergoing work at this time and eventually departed to Boscombe Down on 11th July 1994. It is still operational with QinetiQ. *Falcon*

The final flypast. BAC One-Eleven XX919 leads the Hunter T.7 WV383, Tornado GR.1 ZA449, Jaguar T.2 ZB615 and IAM Hawk T.1 XX327 on the final flypast over Farnborough on 24th March 1994. *R A Cooper*

ence flights. It was eventually sold to a private buyer, departing on 17th October 1994.

Towards the end of its life Farnborough's Comet Mk.4, XV814, was engaged in some further overseas trials. It departed for Alaska on 23rd November and returned via Keflavik on 28th November. Then came its very last overseas flight, departing from Farnborough on 14th December to Bahrain and Akrotiri, returning to Farnborough on 18th December, its usefulness as a flying laboratory at an end. Prior to this it had also undertaken a round-the-world trials flight departing from Farnborough on 29th July operating a Beyond Line of Sight (BLOS) radio trial, with secure communications, as far as Australia. It returned on 17th August, this epic journey being heralded a success.

1993

The last Comet flight from Farnborough was made on 28th January, when XV814 relocated to Boscombe Down to be a source of spares for their own Comet 4 XS235. Comets had been in continual service with RAE since April 1959, with various marks of the type serving as flying laboratories for radio / navigation systems. Even the remains of the Nimrod XV147, which had been at Farnborough since arrival from Woodford on 24th September 1981, departed for Warton by road on 11th November 1993.

The DRA Transport Flight was disbanded, the last operation being a round trip to Bedford by ZF521 on 31st March 1993. All three Navajo Chieftains were flown out, ZF520 to Manchester for servicing on 23rd March 1993, then on to Boscombe Down; ZF521 to Boscombe Down on 6th April 1993 and ZF522 to Boscombe Down on 1st April 1993.

On loan from British Aerospace to DRA Farnborough was Tornado GR.1 ZA449 and this aircraft arrived from Bedford on 6th December 1993. It was classed as a fast-jet

project support aircraft and was engaged in evaluating systems for the in-service GR.1s including Skyshadow Electronic Warfare (EW) pod and Radar Homing and Warning Receiver (RHWR) updates. This aircraft relocated to Boscombe Down on 24th March 1994.

Lynx AH.5 ZD285 underwent extensive modifications to its nose during this year at Farnborough, with the fitment of a unique steerable FLIR sensor visually coupled to the pilot's helmet-mounted display. These were the last aircraft modifications carried out by Experimental Aircraft Servicing Department at Farnborough.

During November of this year, Farnborough Air Sciences Trust (FAST) was formed as an organisation to promote and endeavour to safeguard the unique historic structures and aerospace-related facilities situated on the original Factory site of the former RAE. As the years progressed, FAST was to play a very important part in this, in conjunction with the preservation of many aircraft and artefacts.

The Rotary Wing Flight moved from 'A' shed into 'L' shed on 8th April 1993. This, coupled with the demise of the Transport Flight, left 'A' shed without any aircraft for the first time since it was built in 1934.

Andover C.1 XS607 is seen waiting to depart for Boscombe Down on 20th July 1994, whilst parked in the western 'diamonds' area. The ARMADAS chin-mounted turret can be seen in this view. This aircraft was subsequently withdrawn from use and sold by tender for operation in Zaïre as 9Q-CPW. *Falcon*

BAC One-Eleven Srs 201AC XX105 relocated from Bedford to Farnborough on 23rd March 1994 and is seen here parked on the western dispersal the following day. It, too, relocated to Boscombe Down, departing from Farnborough on 23rd August 1994. *Falcon*

Seen on the western apron on 19th June 1994, just prior to departure for Boscombe Down, is Jaguar T.2A XX833 still wearing its SAOEU markings. This aircraft had undertaken a number of different research trials, but here it is seen carrying a TIALD pod on its centre-line pylon. This aircraft continues to operate with QinetiQ today. *Falcon*

Seen in the low hover on 9th May 1994, having just lifted off for relocation to Boscombe Down, is Sea King Mk.4X ZB507. This aircraft was transferred to the Royal Navy from Boscombe Down and currently serves with No 848 NAS at RNAS Yeovilton. *Falcon*

1994

With the rundown of DRA Bedford three of their Canberras arrived for storage: B.6 (mod) WT333 on 9th February and B.6 (mod) WH953 with B.2/6 (mod) WK163 on 24th March – this being the last day of flying at Bedford. All three of these aircraft were eventually housed in 'D' shed, along with HS.125 XW930, to await disposal.

The most poignant and significant event that occurred during this year was the relocation of the DRA aircraft, and engineering facilities, from Farnborough to Boscombe Down. Amidst much sadness an *en masse* departure occurred on 24th March. This saw One-Eleven XX919, Hunter T.7 WV383, Hawk T.1 XX327 (IAM), Tornado GR.1 ZA449, Jaguar T.2 ZB615 and Hercules W.2 XV208 (MRF) leave Farnborough for the last time. Two One-Elevens, Srs 201AC XX105 and Srs 539GL ZH763 had arrived from Bedford, on 23rd March 1994 and 9th February 1994 respectively, but these repositioned to Boscombe Down on 23rd August 1994 and 15th July 1994 respectively to continue with their trials programmes. The last official day of research flying was Friday 25th March; this seeing the return to Farnborough, from West Freugh, of Buccaneer S.2C XV344 … and then it was all over.

Further aircraft of the Air Fleet Department were undergoing varying degrees of maintenance at this time and these progressively were relocated to Boscombe Down as follows: Andover C.1 XS607 on 15th August; Andover C.1 XS646 on 11th July; Andover CC.2 XS790 on 2nd September; HS.748 Srs 107 XW750 relocated from Bedford on 24th March then on to Boscombe Down on 1st June; Buccaneer S.2C XV344 on 13th July; Canberra B(I)8 (mod) WT327 relocated from Bedford to Boscombe Down on 24th March, but required some installation work and was flown to Farnborough on 11th

April, departing back to Boscombe Down on 30th September; Hawk T.1 XX162 (IAM) on 13th May; Jaguar T.2A XX833 on 9th August; Lynx AH.7 ZD285 on 28th July; Sea King HAS.1 (DB) XV371 on 3rd March; Sea King HC.4X ZB507 on 9th May; Tornado F.2A ZD902 on 18th October (the very last aircraft to depart) and Wessex HC.2 XR503, arriving from Bedford on 14th March and relocating to Boscombe Down on 18th April.

And so it was that the final departure occurred at 13.10 hours on 18th October, when Tornado F.2A (TIARA) ZD902, flown by Flt Lt Tim Price and Sqn Ldr Dave Southwood lifted off from runway 07 at Farnborough, thus bringing to close the research flying at this famous airfield that had been ongoing for nearly 90 years.

The RAE Museum closed, and the artefacts were taken by the Science Museum and placed in storage. The RAE Museum was housed in the Balloon Store of the original RFC Building, which is now the FAST Museum and headquarters building, with its artefacts displayed in the same area.

The Institute of Aviation Medicine became the RAF School of Aviation Medicine during this year and, although their Hawk T.1 aircraft relocated to Boscombe Down, their headquarters remained on the airfield site, on what was originally called Danger Hill.

Apprentice training ceased at Farnborough and those apprentices that were in midterm of their training period were relocated to Boscombe Down. 'Q' hangar, which housed the Aircraft Apprentice Training Department, was now cleared out, with the airframes being dispersed and the RAE Aero Club aircraft being relocated to 'M' shed. Apprentice training, then known as the Trade Lads Scheme, had been started at Farnborough in 1918 and had continued ever since, with over 400 aircraft apprentices successfully completing their training at Farnborough during the 30 years that the Aircraft Apprentice Training Scheme had actually been in existence. Disposed of by tender, the remaining instructional airframes departed as follows: Canberra T.4 WJ865 was broken up for scrap during January 1995; Canberra PR.7 fuselage WH776 was scrapped in 1994; Scout AH.1 XP166 departed for a private owner, Russell Dagless, on 30th September 1994 and is currently registered as G-APVL; Provost T.1 XF844 departed on 31st March 1995 and is current at Bruntingthorpe with Phoenix Aviation; Jet Provost T.5A XW428 departed for the USA in 1994 where it was registered as N4311M in North Carolina; Wessex HU.5 XS482 departed in 1994 for a private buyer in Sussex but is now with the RAF Manston History Museum.Since 2003 it has been painted in the standard yellow RAF Rescue scheme; and PA-28-140 Cherokee G-ATJG (transferred from DRA Bedford during March 1994) left for Germany later in 1994 for a private buyer.

The very last research aircraft to depart from Farnborough was Tornado F.2A 'Tiara' ZD902, which is seen in full afterburner departing from Farnborough's runway 07 on 18th October 1994. In the background can be seen the British Aerospace (now BAE Systems) headquarters building. *Falcon*

Standing amidst various models and artefacts of the RAE/DRA Museum is its last curator, Brian Kervell, shortly before the museum closed in 1994. This building, the former Royal Flying Corps headquarters, is now the FAST Museum. *Falcon*

The Aircraft Apprentice Training Department was disbanded during August 1994, as there was no longer a requirement to train aircraft engineers at Farnborough, and the apprentices were relocated. Seen in this late 1993 view of the Apprentice Training area in 'Q' shed are Jet Provost T.5A XW428, Wessex HU.5 XS482, the fuselage of Canberra PR.7 WH774, and Scout AH.1 XP166. All these airframes were disposed of by tender during 1994. *Falcon*

THE CHANGING LANDSCAPE

Out with the Old...in with the New

Throughout the 100 years' operation of this airfield there have been many stages of development, expansion and progression; but not to the same degree that occurred in the new millennium, which saw this military airfield transformed into a modern airport structure.

Much research and development work on aircraft, engines, systems, weapons, spacecraft, materials and the like has been conducted on this famous site, which has seen the airfield grow from the original Farnborough Common, later stretching away towards Long Valley in the west, encompassing Laffan's Plain, and taking over Cove Common and the reservoir on the northern side. Paved runways were laid, and lengthened over the years, with the current site now encompassing some 450 acres.

Slough Estates purchased the old 'Factory' site, an area of 125 acres, from the Ministry of Defence in March 1999 with the purpose of re-developing the area into a modern high-tech business park, independent from the airfield. Most of the old RAE buildings and laboratories, some dating back to the Royal Aircraft Factory days and familiar landmarks for many years, had by now been fenced off from the airfield. Most of these buildings have now been demolished, the site having lain derelict since 1996, until the first buildings were demolished in 2000. The 24ft wind tunnel, the last facility in use, finally ceased 'blowing' in December 1998, having undertaken trials of an air-conditioning filtering system for the then under-construction Bluewater shopping centre in Kent during November 1997. The very last trial was that of a scale rotor head with blades. The site remained derelict and, until the demolition team moved in, it was an eerie feeling walking amongst those abandoned buildings, where an uncanny silence hung over the area except for the wind blowing open doors and windows and the occasional pigeon in the rafters. So much had gone on here over such a long period of time and what a hive of activity it

once was, but it had now all come to a standstill – unthinkable as it may seem! The vast machine shops, foundry, laboratories, test rigs, wind tunnels, power station, apprentice training department, workshops, stores, numerous offices and the once active railway yard and depot, all were now devoid of activity and consigned to a bygone era, as if it were all in the imagination! Not so, as thousands of workers, industrial and clerical, have passed through the 'Factory' site and even now many still have lasting memories of what once was. However time inevitably marches on, and so does development and technology, and what was originally built as a large industrial area to house the various RAE Departments is no more, the DRA having moved their facilities into a smaller, more concentrated, and purpose-built modern complex on the north-western corner of the airfield.

Once the buildings had been demolished much ground work ensued with new facilities laid where some of the original pipe work, ducts and cabling dated back many years and no longer met modern-day criteria. New roads were laid, tons of rubble was crushed, and new foundations were put down. The first two new buildings were finished early in 2002. The first is 1 Meadow Gate Avenue, a 37,000ft^2 two-storey office building, partly occupied by Autodesk, built on the former 'Q' shed (O 15 building) dispersal beside what used to be RAE Meadow Gate in the 1950s. The second is known as

A new dawn breaks over Farnborough Airport on 6th February 2003, with this dramatic 'skyscape' over the new Farnborough control tower. *Falcon*

25 Templar Avenue, an 80,000ft^2 four-storey multi-occupancy modern office building, built where the wooden Army hangar (O34 building) used to be, and partly occupied by Agusta-Westland and Imagine Homes.

P67 building, previously known as F1E, is seen here in the advanced process of being demolished during June 2000. This building of circa 1912, although modified over the years, was originally used as an aircraft production workshop in the Royal Aircraft Factory days. *Falcon*

The old RAE administration building was built circa 1910 and extended over the years. It remained in use until 1997 and was demolished during December 2000. Here, only part of the southern wing is still standing, the remainder being a heap of rubble. The airfield control tower (N1) and the earlier tower/Meteorological office (N2) can be seen beyond. *Falcon*

Further demolition work occurred during 2004/2005 and more new buildings are in the process of being built, the next two being known as 200 and 250 Fowler Avenue, to be completed during the summer of 2006, in the area known as The Hub on the Slough plans, to the southwest of Q134, to enable Slough Estates to progress their business park concept. This will ultimately see some 1.75m ft² of office space for future use at a value of £500 million, under the banner 'Vision to Reality', which in 2004 changed to a new promotional slogan, 'Success is in the air' – after all that is what Farnborough is all about! When completed the business park should see an enormous growth in terms of personnel, somewhere between 6,000 and 10,000 could be employed, with all that means for the area's economy. A new through access road has been built, although not open to the public as a thoroughfare as yet, linking Meadow Gate Roundabout with the junction on the Farnborough Road and Boundary Road, where the old RAE North Gate used to be. There will also be a new road constructed, external to the airfield, linking Hall Road to Queens Gate and the roundabout on the Farnborough Road by the Holiday Inn hotel.

During 2002/3, there had been a recession in the marketing of office accommodation and Slough held off from any further building work, but much planning was still ongoing for the Listed buildings on the site. During this period, and in conjunction with SAVE Britain's Heritage, the Farnborough Air Sciences Trust and Rushmoor Council, the significance of the historic buildings was brought to a high-profile awareness with a firm set of proposals drawn up by Slough Estates International for future use of these important Listed buildings. During April 2004 it was agreed that the construction plan would be split into four zones – The Square; The Hub; The Historic Quarter; and

The Residential District. This in itself is a massive overall £50 million-plus project but the end product of the transformation will not only contain the historic buildings but will considerably enhance the whole area in a modernistic feature that still retains the character and architectural charm of some of Britain's important historical buildings.

Q121 building, the 24ft wind tunnel, is Grade I listed along with R133, the transonic tunnel. Four other buildings are Grade II listed, including the two buildings that contained the original girders of the old portable airship shed, Q65 and R51. These were demolished over the period between November 2004 and February 2005 but the girder sections (the reason why they were listed) have been retained in their entirety and is being reassembled to reform part of the original airship shed of 1912 vintage as a centrepiece on the site. The remaining listed buildings are G29, the famous Black Sheds of RFC vintage; R52, the original wind tunnel building; and G1, the old RFC Lord Trenchard HQ which started life as a balloon store with the Royal Engineers – the latter has been upgraded to Grade II*. Thus the five remaining listed buildings will not be destroyed and four will form part of the

proposed heritage area, over which the Farnborough Air Sciences Trust Association have been campaigning for the past twelve years. Indeed R52, the former FAST headquarters and museum building with the internal wooden wind tunnel, will not be demolished, although some of its annexes have been removed during the spring of 2005. This circa-1910 building will become part of the proposed heritage site.

The former weapons/space four-storey building, Q134, is having the top storey (an early 1950s addition) removed and the main entrance will be repositioned on the south-facing side. The building has been entirely gutted and is being renovated as a modern office block, but retaining its original external appearance. Due for completion by September 2006, this will become the centrepiece of the site and will incorporate management offices and facilities, a Heritage Centre (working in conjunction with FAST), a café and general modern office space. Q120, the old seaplane tank building, was essentially demolished in the spring of 2005, except for a 20ft-long section at the eastern extremity that is to be retained. The tank below ground level will be opened up to a length of 150ft to show the original

Built around 1907, Q27 building, as it became known, was originally in use for airship gondola construction and aircraft production. It then became the RAE machine shop and inspection department, amongst other uses. Unfortunately this building was not Listed and it succumbed to the demolition teams during August 2001, with the annexes seen being partially demolished in this view, which was taken from the top of a huge pile of rubble from Q1 and surrounding buildings. *Falcon*

This view, seen from the 24ft wind tunnel on 22nd March 2006, shows the new car park buildings at left, and the new office accommodation, known as 200 and 250 Fowler Avenue, whilst, at extreme right, is 'Q134' building, which is also well advanced with refurbishment. This area will become known as The Hub. In the distance can be seen the TAG Aviation hangar complex. *Falcon*

structure and will incorporate a carriage and aircraft model placed on the water. Q170, the old RAE telephone exchange building, is set to become a children's nursery and play building bordered by a small park area, whilst nearby Q153, the old structures building, will also be retained and converted into studio flats as part of the Residential District although the large hall area where the test frames used to be housed is to be demolished in due course. R136, the 'rolling road' wind tunnel, is not listed but is to be retained and refurbished. Nearby the Grade I listed Transonic Wind Tunnel, R133, is undergoing external and internal refurbishment, although some annexe buildings have now been demolished. This will feature a see-through area to show the tunnel chamber capsule to good effect within the actual complex. The brine tanks will be retained as an art feature as will the two large transformers that will also be incorporated within a landscaped area. Nearby the old Chemical building, R178, is also to be retained. It will have all its external pipes and appendages removed and will be transformed into studio flats for use in the Residential District, this area extending

around the back of the Transonic Wind Tunnel, where residential homes will be built, to join up with Q153 building.

The 24ft wind tunnel building, Q121, has now had some of its external appendages removed. As Stage 1 of the restoration project, the initial external renovation, has commenced, this being due to continue until late 2006. There is much work to be done here as all-new cabling, ducting and services will be installed, but the old generator plant room will be retained as a showpiece. Stage 2 will see the internal restoration, which again will be time-consuming, but this will include the probability of retaining the 24ft fan in an operational working condition. The precise use of the building has not yet been fully decided but options include a restaurant facility with corporate entertaining facilities; art gallery/library usage; venue for conferences/exhibitions with a stage arena; or to bring the tunnel back to full operational order for use as a working tunnel once again. All these options are being considered at present and decisions will eventually be made in the interests of all concerned with this ambitious and exciting project. Some £20 million is being spent on

the renovation of the listed wind tunnel buildings, this work is currently well under way and progressing on schedule.

A National Aerospace Library is being planned by the Royal Aeronautical Society to possibly be housed in the preparation area within the historic 24ft wind tunnel and a working group has been formed to co-ordinate the necessary fund-raising and to oversee the project from development to finalisation, which is envisaged for 2008.

After the last DRA aircraft left in October 1994, the airfield was retained for MoD usage but there was very little military traffic and more emphasis had been put into business usage since the civilian enclave was defined in the early 1980s and opened in 1989. Initially the business traffic was managed by Carroll Aircraft, operating from the old ETPS, later RAE Southern Squadron, hangar complex on the south side of the airfield. This was taken over by British Aerospace in 1995 and then by TAG Aviation in September 2000 and development of business traffic forged further ahead. By the mid-1990s British Aerospace, now BAE Systems, had their corporate headquarters on the southern edge, where the Comet water test-tanks used to be, and Farnborough began to take on a much different profile.

The Royal Air Force Institute of Aviation Medicine (IAM), for so long resident on Danger Hill behind where SBAC have their exhibition halls, moved to RAF Henlow in 1998, except for the centrifuge, which is still currently operational until a planned new facility is built at Henlow. The Army Personnel Research Establishment (APRE) was moved from the site as was the Centre for Human Sciences (CHS), the latter being part

This aerial view of the old 'Factory' site at Farnborough, as seen during June 2005, shows the extent of the demolition. The key buildings are the 24ft wind tunnel (Q121) in centre, R52 to the right and the Transonic wind tunnel (R133) at centre-right. The seaplane tank building (Q120) has been shortened and is just discernible below the 24ft wind tunnel. The long building at centre-left is R134, which has started undergoing refurbishment. Two new buildings, and an adjacent car park, have been built at the extreme left of R134. The neat row of Pinehurst Cottages, dating from World War One, can also be seen beyond. *Falcon*

of QinetiQ. Both were relocated to new buildings on the old NGTE Pyestock site, now part of QinetiQ, in what is now called the Cody Technology Park. The No 1 RAF Officers Mess, on the eastern edge of the airfield adjacent to the A325 Farnborough Road, had its final closure dinner on 27th November 1998. It was decommissioned on 31st March 1999 and handed back to MoD Estates. The entire Mess complex has now been demolished, commencing in late November 2004 and finally completed by the end of January 2005. This area of land, now owned by TAG, is currently undergoing a local planning policy approval for the construction of a modern hotel on site to enhance the airport facilities even more.

The Ministry of Defence ceased to have a requirement for Farnborough Airfield from the mid-1990s. Government policy was to retain the airfield for business aviation to relieve the pressure on London Heathrow and Gatwick Airports. When the airfield was put on the market TAG Aviation was selected by the MoD as the preferred airport operator.

For the airfield to function as a business airport it was necessary to obtain a CAA Licence to operate. Even though Farnborough had been operating as a military airfield, occasionally catering for the world's largest aircraft during the SBAC Air Shows, the CAA required that the airport be brought up to its stringent full regulations and standards before a licence would be granted. TAG Aviation obtained a CAA Licence in January 2003, having taken over the airfield from 1st January 2001, and having implemented many improvements to the airfield equipment, systems and layout.

The type of aircraft that were envisaged for Farnborough were the most modern of business jets, up to Boeing 737BBJ and Airbus A319CJ size. For aircraft of this size to operate under the strict CAA safety regulations from Farnborough, and fly without refuelling to the west coast of the United States, it was essential to maximise the potential of the Farnborough site. This process required see-sawing the configuration of the runway approaches and take-offs between the irremovable constraints of Farnborough Road to the east and the Fleet road to the west and applying the CAA's obstacle limitation surfaces to the proposed runway. Additionally it was necessary to consider the protection of the 'listed' buildings at the east end of the site and the anticipated Public Safety Zones. Eventually it was found that a runway having 1,800m landing distance in each direction,

2,200m take-off towards the west and 2,000m towards the east, was possible. This was just sufficient to satisfy the business need and was therefore set as the design requirement but represented enormous challenges to achieve because for each landing or take-off criteria it was essential to clear the obstacles that penetrated the particular surface.

To achieve landing distances of 1,800m, the threshold for Runway 25 was moved 300m further west, away from Farnborough town, and a 40m length of runway was added to the western end. Runway 07 threshold, on the old Laffan's Plain, was moved 175m east, which left the required 1,800m of existing runway for landing. To achieve the required take-off distance for runway 25 it was necessary to cut the cap off Miles Hill within the Army Training Ground at Long Valley to the west and to remove much of the intruding forestry. The 2,000m take-off for runway 07 was achieved by adding a 150m starter strip and turning head at its western end.

Reshaping Miles Hill to reduce its height by 6 metres required the moving of 35,000m³ of earth. All of this work was carried out in close co-operation with the Army Training Authority and English Nature due to Miles Hill being a Site of Special Scientific Interest (SSSI). English Nature required that the work be carried out in a manner that maintained the value of the site's SSSI status by restoring the site to heathland and kept its value as a Special Protection Area (SPA) for its population of protected woodlark and nightjar birds.

Part of the forestry work included a project-sharing objective with the Basingstoke Canal Authority, which was endeavouring to open up the canal and allow more light in for the development of rare canalside plants. The removal of trees from the canal bank was therefore mutually beneficial. A

small blast fence has been erected along the airport boundary fence at the 07 end to protect the canal and towpath area.

The only significant 'hard' obstacle that had to be removed was the existing Control Tower, Building N1, which was constructed in 1946. This became the most critical item in the whole raft of other essential work to achieve CAA Licensing. The location of the new Control Tower was determined by the CAA requirements for Air Traffic Controllers to have the best vision of the whole aircraft manoeuvring area and was determined to be at the north of the runway approximately halfway along its length. (Visibility from the old Control Tower had not extended to the Western apron and taxiway area.) In this location it was necessary to elevate the tower in order to see over the trees of the adjacent copse, requiring a height of 34 metres from ground level to the top of the visual control room. In spite of this elevation some trees still had to be removed and some to have arboreal treatment to achieve full vision for Air Traffic Control. Therefore, having been operational for 56 years, the old Control Tower closed to operations at 21.18 hours on 25th November 2002. The new Control Tower, a landmark item of architecture representing the future of Farnborough Airport as Britain's only dedicated Business Airport, became fully operational on 26th November 2002 at 07.00 hours. Air Traffic and Airport management have their offices at the base of the tower complex. The old tower building was reduced to piles of rubble by 23rd January 2003 and had been totally cleared by the end of February.

As the airfield had been part of the old RAE 'Factory' complex, all of the primary services were fed from that source or led to it. To become self-sufficient the Airport had to lay in independent new surface water drainage, foul drainage, electricity, gas and water.

The new Farnborough Airport air traffic control tower is seen here during September 2004, with some of the parked business aircraft reflected in its glass frontage. This futuristic tower was first used operationally on 26th November 2002. *Falcon*

Seen here during January 2003 is the partially demolished control tower, N1 building, which had been originally built in 1946 and had become operational in 1948 and continued until November 2002. *Falcon*

The existing airfield ground lighting was to a military specification and too old to be dependable for the new era. An entirely new system of runway and taxiway edge lights, approach lights, stop-bars and extensive signage to CAA standards therefore had to be installed.

Farnborough's runway had last been re-surfaced in 1974, and was one of the oldest surfaces of its type still in service. To restore the runway to the CAA's required operational characteristics of friction and surface profile, it was necessary to re-surface the entire runway. This entailed building up the low areas and planing off some high spots, and finally surfacing with the optimum material for runway surfaces, a Porous Friction Course. To maintain the current TAG operation whilst this work was carried out the majority of the re-surfacing and other work adjacent to the runway was done at night with the airport only closing for a few weekends to complete the most critical of the works.

To satisfy the demands of potential users, and ensure that aircraft had the ability to land at Farnborough in all but the worst of weather conditions, a full Instrument Landing System (ILS) has been installed comprising Localiser and Glidepath aerials and Distance Measuring Equipment (DME). Additional air traffic control equipment and navigation aids that have been installed are illuminated wind sleeves, anemometers, automated runway visual range indicators and a complete new Raytheon Airfield Surveillance Radar (ASR) system.

The airport had two remote radio stations on the high ground of Beacon Hill and Odiham Road. As part of the centralisation of airport facilities these have been replaced with an 'on site' tower and connected to new radio transmitters and receivers positioned on the airfield.

One of the CAA requirements is for 'delethalisation' ramps to be installed in the ground within the area known as the 'cleared and graded strip' that extends 105 metres either side of the runway centre line. These ramps are required at every point where an aircraft that has run off of the runway might come up against a vertical buried surface and thus sustain more damage than would have

been expected from running over the airfield grassland. To limit the amount of this work all of the disused tracks and experimental installations that were within the area subject to this requirement were removed. This included the 1940 'Direction Controlled Take-Off' (DCTO) track that for many years had remained buried under the grassed area to the north of the main runway; the Harrier Ski-Jump pad, built in the late 1970s; some of the experimental 'arrester' gear; and the recently de-commissioned Precision Approach Radar (PAR), Rotary Hydraulic Arrester Gear (RHAG) and 'Safeland' barriers.

As Farnborough Airport is located in a shallow hollow it collects surface water from a large surrounding area including the Army Golf Course, BAE Systems centre, Basingstoke Canal overflow and parts of Farnborough Town to add to its own surface water drainage. This situation required a major redevelopment of the system to avoid flooding on the airfield and avoid exacerbating the flooding problems of Elles Road and Cove Brook beyond the airfield. Balancing ponds were constructed on the airfield to receive the floodwater and control its rate of discharge into the Cove Brook system. The balancing ponds are constructed with oil interceptors and reed beds to purify the water before discharge into the open Brook.

Owners of business aircraft generally prefer to have their aircraft stored inside, hence there was a requirement to construct new hangars. This has been done in the form of a triple-bay hangar of modern curved architecture to reflect the new image of the Airport, each bay being capable of housing two B737BBJs. A second hangar of the same type will be constructed in the mid-term future although outline planning permission is under way. Until then the existing hangars – 'A' (taken over by BAE Systems), 'C', 'D' & 'N', and 'L' will remain in use, with 'L' hangar being replaced by the second new hangar in due course. 'C' hangar will stay even when the new hangars are constructed. 'Q' shed, latterly in use by the RAE/DRA Aircraft Apprentice Department, was demolished in February/March 2004 and a new simulator building, operated by Flight Safety International, has now been built in its place.

The RAE / DERA / QinetiQ / Farnborough Aero Club continue to operate from the Airport but from a 'new' hangar (a second-

The new Flight Safety International Building is seen here during December 2005. This was built on the former site of 'Q' shed, and will eventually house some 15 business aircraft simulators. *Falcon*

The futuristic landmark TAG Aviation Terminal building was operational during January 2006 and is situated on the northwestern corner of the airport complex, close to the airport entrance off the Ively Road roundabout. *Falcon*

Aerial view of the TAG Aviation operations, parking and hangarage facility at Farnborough, as seen on 8th June 2005. Aircraft in this view range from a Citation to a Boeing BBJ2. The new terminal building is under construction and was completed in December 2005. The massive north apron parking area can be seen to good effect, being extensively modified from the previous RAE taxiways, parking area and runways 11 and 18 thresholds. *Falcon*

hand construction brought to the site) constructed adjacent to the airfield but within the QinetiQ site along Victor Way. 'M' Shed, latterly occupied by the Aero Club, was demolished during December 2002 and January 2003.

Also reflecting the modern image is the new terminal building, which is in the general form of an aircraft wing. It was designed by Geoffrey Reid (as was the TAG Aviation hangar complex), project managed by TAG Aviation and constructed by various contractors. The style and finish of this building is to the very high standards expected by the 'Captains of Industry', Royalty and VVIPs that will be using it. It has been built between the hangar and the new Airport main entrance off the A327, in the northern corner with easy access to junction 4A of the M3. Completed in January and opened on 2nd May 2006, this Terminal building has become the TAG Aviation operations centre at Farnborough having moved to this modern complex from the temporary accommodation that served as their offices and their ground operations centre previously. The civil enclave on the south side of the airfield closed to aircraft operations on 12th May 2003, with all aircraft, staff and operations transferred to the north side complex on the same day. At that time the temporary buildings were erected on the north side, followed by careful dismantling of the old operations building and its re-erection on the north side to provide extra office accommodation. New aircraft parking aprons, and associated taxiways, have been constructed and these were completed in mid-2002. The move from the south side of the airfield released this complex back to BAE Systems who own the area. At present the old ETPS hangar ('E1' shed) and late-1940s built offices are still extant but redevelopment of this area has commenced. The area was purchased by Terrace Hill Properties during April 2005 and will be shortly developed for light industry, although part of the old parking apron has already been torn up.

TAG Farnborough Airport Ltd now run

the airport using mainly their own staff for all airport functions and employing contract staff for security services. The Airport Fire and Rescue Service is run by TAG (it was previously operated by Amey) and Air Traffic Control is handled by the National Air Traffic Services (NATS). On-site ambulance services had been active for many years, being undertaken by the St John Ambulance Service, fulfilling the requirement for military operations, but these too ceased on 31st December 2003 and were transferred to the external local Ambulance Service.

As the modern aircraft that will use Farnborough can tolerate considerable crosswind effects, it is only necessary to have one runway. For this reason Runway 11/29 was decommissioned in February 2000 to allow the new development to proceed; the old north/south runway, 18/36, having been closed for different reasons back in 1996. Other losses that have taken place with the changes at Farnborough are Cody's Tree, which was moved to the new DERA (now QinetiQ) site on 23rd July 1996; all of the old RAE taxiway names like Wellington Way, Vampire Way, Meteor Way, which have been changed to letter titles to comply with CAA requirements; and many of the old MoD

buildings demolished as they had no further use and were beyond safe economic maintenance. The new Raytheon radar head, situated near the old 18 runway, meant that the previous local landmark of the Plessey Watchman Radar Tower, within the QinetiQ site on Ball Hill, was redundant and accordingly the radar scanner was removed on 21st January 2003 with the tower being demolished by a controlled explosion on 1st March. One Farnborough feature that will remain is the 'Black Sheds', of 1914 vintage, situated at the eastern end of the airfield, although one part of this building was demolished in the late 1970s, this now being a Grade II listed building due to its history as one of the first hangars of the Royal Flying Corps. This building remains in use today as the airfield equipment store.

The boundaries of Farnborough Airport have changed several times since it was part of 'RAE'. The Airport is now separated from the old RAE Factory site at the northeast corner, which is being developed into a new business park by Slough Estates; DERA moved to new quarters at the northwest of the site encompassing the area of the old Concorde Structural test building and at that time including 'N' & 'D' Hangars (X1 and X4 buildings).

These hangars have been partially refurbished and have subsequently been brought back into the Airport boundary. Indeed they are both in use today for aircraft accommodation although TAG Aviation Engineering now use 'D' shed for their aircraft servicing facility. This was officially opened by the local MP, Gerald Howarth, on 17th September 2004.

At the southwest corner of the Airport the Air Accidents Investigation Branch (AAIB) and the old RAE Weapons Department 'T' area (including ARL) were sectioned off, with the 'T' area being owned by Slough Estates. The 'T' area was brought back into the Airport boundary and the Weapons Building (T70) and the old historic ARL complex were demolished throughout March/April/May 2004, although 'H' hangar (T1) still stands. The High Speed track, running from east to west along Victoria Track, was partly demolished in 1988 but was dissected further in 2000 by the new airfield boundary fence. The majority of the track still remains today, albeit in a derelict condition. A length of this track, and the powered maintenance trolley, has been saved and is in store with FAST. Owned by MoD Estates the

'Queens Site', at the southeast corner of the Airport where IAM and CHS were based, is currently up for sale for future development. The vast majority of these buildings are still standing at present but development is planned for 2006. The former RAE Apprentice Hostel buildings, and the former ETPS Mess, on the 'F' site, are still extant albeit disused, and until 2005 were still in use as student accommodation by the Farnborough College of Technology, but these too are planned to be demolished in 2006. The area occupied by SBAC will remain as part of the Airport and will continue to be sub-leased to SBAC for the foreseeable future.

SBAC will continue to run the biennial Air Show at Farnborough. There have already been some changes in the presentation due to TAG Aviation operations continuing at all times other than during the Flying Display periods: hence denying SBAC the opportunity to place display aircraft on the main runway during the mornings. TAG Aviation made alternative areas to the south of the runway available to SBAC for the static display aircraft during the past two displays but part of this area is now under redevelopment.

During the extensive excavations for all of the new works, several items of munitions were to be uncovered – two 500 lb bombs, numerous 40mm rocket heads and other devices, all of which were found to be either practice or dummy bombs, were dealt with by the Bomb Disposal Squad.

During the course of the airport development the earth's magnetic variation has crossed the point that Farnborough's runway heading was closer to 240 degrees than that of 250. The newly resurfaced runway was therefore re-designated from 07/25 to 06/24 during October 2001.

After a century of fame for its flying and development, Farnborough's future prestige will come through the association with the rich and famous as they grace the airport with their presence. Aircraft types now frequenting the airport include Boeing B737BBJs, Airbus A319CJs, Bombardier Global Expresses, Regional Jets, Challengers, Gulfstreams, Citations, Lear Jets, BAE/Hawker 125s, Embraers and Beech Jets, plus various turboprop, rotary and piston-engined executive types. The location of the country's premier Business Airport on this historic site, with its modern facilities, has set Farnborough apart from all the other towns throughout the area.

Fast jets, piston and rotary types going about their research duties will be seen and heard no more from this famous airfield, but to move ahead into the 21st Century, this Airport has become a showcase, high-technology business jet operation, now with a limitation of 28,000 movements per annum. The movements for 2001 amounted to 14,640, a far cry from the busy days of RAE/ETPS flying in the 1960s where over 30,000 per annum was quite common, whilst figures released for 2005 give a total of 20,506 movements. Farnborough is not set to become a commercial airport in the full sense of the word, where flights to holiday destinations are the norm, but it has become a second-to-none, user-friendly, state-of-the-art Business Aviation centre, probably the best in the world.

The new welcome sign, seen beside taxiway 'A' (the old 11/29 runway), with part of the new airport buildings and parking apron seen beyond. At left is the new radar tower with the triple bay hangar beyond and, at right, can be seen the brand new airport terminal. *Falcon*

Gerald Howarth, MP for Aldershot and Farnborough and Shadow Defence Minister, performs the honours by unveiling a plaque at the opening of the TAG Farnborough Engineering facility within the refurbished 'D' hangar. Les Batty, Director of TAG Farnborough Engineering, looks on at left, and Roger McMullen, a member of the Executive Board of TAG Aviation, helps with the curtain. *Falcon*

1995 to 2004
The Dawning of a New Era

With research flying from Farnborough coming to an untimely end on 25th March 1994, after nearly 90 years of aviation development that had seen so many changes and innovations, what next?

Name changes were paramount with the demise of the Defence Research Agency and the establishment of the Defence Evaluation and Research Agency, which would not last long as QinetiQ came into being in July 2001 and continues today with its headquarters firmly rooted on the Ball Hill site. Defence Science and Technology Laboratory (DSTL) also came into being at this time.

A change of ownership of the airfield would also occur, and with it the establishment of a business aviation operation, which would make such types as the BAe 125, Boeing BBJ, Global Express, Challenger, Citation, Falcon and Gulfstream IV/V commonplace here.

Farnborough airfield had now become firmly established in the business aviation sector, but more was to come.

1995

1st April heralded another name change, this time to the Defence Evaluation and Research Agency (DERA).

Over on the northwest corner of the airfield, building work was by now rapidly progressing for the new £71 million research complex for the DERA. When, during 1993/1994, it was elected to demolish the Structures Building where the Concorde test airframe was housed, it was decided that the massive robust concrete floor of the Laboratory should remain. This was utilised as the base foundations for the flooring of the new DERA Central Administration Building.

The frontage of the QinetiQ headquarters buildings, known as the Cody Technology Park, is seen here. Cody's tree, positioned outside the main front entrance, was moved here on 23rd July 1996. *Falcon*

This aerial view, seen during July 1996, shows the extent of the civil enclave, with the sliding gates at the northern and western exits. The hangar and adjacent buildings are from the ETPS days, being built in 1949/1950. The British Aerospace, now BAE Systems, headquarters complex can be seen beyond. *Falcon*

As part of the DRA's (this was before the advent of DERA) £230 million rationalisation project, which also extends to eight other sites, the new DRA laboratory workshops and administration buildings were required as the old Farnborough 'Factory' site was too large and inefficient to remain in full-scale operation. The contract for the new £71 million research complex was awarded to Shepherd Design and Build Project with work commencing during August 1994. Some 180,000m³ of earth had to be moved to level the site, eventually some 15 different buildings will be erected, all purpose-designed and -built, covering an area of some 97,000m². A glazed concourse, a quarter-mile long, connects the various business centres. These buildings now all house different departments within the DERA, with some 5,000 pieces of scientific equipment that are positioned within the laboratories for Structural Materials, Flight Systems, Weapons, Imagery and Space, Site Services and Operational Studies, all with their own tailored individual designs. Some 48,000 m³ of concrete have been poured, with approximately 1.25 million bricks being laid. The completed site also included a new road system, car parks, wildlife area and water features.

Now operated by Air Atlantique Classic Flight at Coventry, Canberra B.2/6 WK163 recorded a height record of 70,310ft on 28th August 1957, while fitted with a double Napier Scorpion rocket motor in its bomb bay. This aircraft became a long-term resident with the Royal Radar Establishment at Pershore. It then relocated to Bedford on 1st July 1976 and continued operating with RAE/DRA until flown to Farnborough for storage on 24th March 1994. It is seen here at Farnborough on 28th January 1995 prior to departure for Classic Aviation Projects at Bruntingthorpe, still as WK163 although its civil registration G-BVWC had been allocated on 2nd December 1994. *Falcon*

The third Canberra to relocate to Farnborough from DRA Bedford was B.6 (mod) WH953. This had operated initially with the Royal Radar Establishment from February 1955, at Defford and later Pershore, before relocating to RAE Bedford on 16th December 1976. It arrived at Farnborough on 24th March 1994 and was placed in storage, surplus to requirements. It was broken up on 31st January 1995 and is seen here outside 'D' shed, the day before the breakers' torch struck. The nose has been preserved and is with the Blyth Valley Aviation Collection at Walpole, whilst the author retained the fin assembly. *Falcon*

The 'Topping Out' ceremony, to mark the moment when a building is structurally 'roofed in', took place at the new site on 15th September 1995, when the final bucket of cement was poured in on top of the Central Administration Building. Defence Evaluation and Research Agency Chief Executive, John Chisholm, with MoD Chief Scientific Adviser, Professor Sir David Davies, performed the ceremony, accompanied by the Managing Director of Shepherd Construction, Paul Shepherd, the new building also being dedicated by the DRA Chaplain, Rev. David Welbourn. John

Chisholm said he was delighted with the current progress and 'this new complex will be among the most modern in Europe and our commitment to the project is a mark of our confidence in a strong future for both defence research and DERA'. He then thanked Shepherd for their dedicated hard work and with the project currently on schedule they all looked forward to occupying the finished buildings on the site during August/September 1996.

Another historic event also took place, again with John Chisholm and Professor Sir David Davies performing the honours,

when a time capsule was buried alongside the foundations of the Administration building. This capsule, made of Zeron 100, a super-duplex stainless steel with new anti-corrosion materials currently being developed by the DRA for marine usage, contained a number of items relating to the Farnborough (RAE) DRA site including samples both of the first development of carbon fibres and a recently produced example. The foreplane of a wind tunnel model tested in the Farnborough transonic wind tunnel during the 1980s was also included, as was a sensor from an infra-red missile seeker, Transputer Processor chip as applied to the infra-red missile for target recognition, a GPS processor of the type to be fitted to the Eurofighter 2000 aircraft, radar-absorbent materials, a space image of Farnborough as seen from a Russian satellite on 19th June 1989, an artist's impression of two space technology vehicles built by Space Department and launched by Ariane on 17th June 1994, plus a compact disk

Canberra B.6 (mod) WT333 arrived from DRA Bedford on 9th February 1994. It had been a long-term resident with the Royal Radar Establishment at Pershore, before relocating to Bedford on 18th May 1977. After arrival at Farnborough, it was placed in storage and was then sold to Classic Aviation and was later registered as G-BVXC on 9th January 1995, although it is now de-registered. It is seen here outside 'D' shed on 28th January 1995, just prior to its departure for Bruntingthorpe where it is still located. *Falcon*

Richard Noble's ThrustSSC, is seen here on 30th August 1997 undergoing final preparation work in P8 building at Farnborough. A few days later, it was shipped to the USA for the land speed record attempt. *Falcon*

This view of the old RAE 'Factory' site was taken in November 1996, from the Virgin Lightship. It shows the extent of the site, as it was just before it was vacated by DERA. Most of these buildings have now been demolished. *Falcon*

containing various current data and images showing pictures of earth and a hurricane over America and Japan, along with issues of the in-house DRA news magazine. All these items are designed to give details of the type of activities being undertaken at Farnborough during the years leading up to the 21st Century, and should remain entombed for at least 100 years.

Richard Noble and his team moved to Farnborough for final assembly and preparations of the ThrustSSC. The team initially took over 'Q' shed (O15 building) where final assembly of the vehicle was accomplished and test runs were eventually made along the Farnborough runway during 1996 followed by two 'detachments' to Jordan in November 1996 and May 1997 for proving runs. By this time the Supporters Club was gaining momentum both with interest and financial support.

Sqn Ldr Andy Green, the driver of the SSC, was by now seconded to DERA for work on the Joust air combat simulator so he was on site with the rest of the team. DERA had an involvement with the project and assisted where they could, notwithstanding the use of their airfield facilities, and they were a part of the co-sponsors for the event. Having moved out of 'Q' shed the team re-positioned in P8 building where further open days for the ThrustSSC Mach 1 Supporters Club were held, these being a huge success.

During the summer months of 1997 the ThrustSSC team left for the Nevada desert to prepare for the land speed record attempts. During September, with build-

up for the record attempt and tension increasing, Andy Green made a series of high-speed runs over the desert that resulted in the land speed record being broken on a number of occasions. However on 15th October 1997 the stage was set at Black Rock, under perfect conditions, when during run number 65 a speed of 759.333mph (Mach 1.015) was achieved and on the return run a speed of 771mph (Mach 1.03) to give an average speed of 763.035mph (Mach 1.0175). The Land Speed Record, at supersonic speed, was theirs and a remarkable achievement had been accomplished.

ThrustSSC returned to Farnborough, to be positioned in 'D' shed where Richard Noble began the design work on the Farnborough F1 aircraft. The ThrustSSC's engines were run for the last time in December 1997, although the vehicle was transported around the country for display and presentation purposes. It was presented to Coventry's Museum of British Road Transport in August 2001.

1996

The old 'RAE Factory' site closes, with the DERA element moving to the new ultramodern purpose-built headquarters buildings on the northwestern side of the airfield, just beyond Ball Hill, the move being basically complete by the autumn.

Cody's Tree was removed from its site outside of the Black Sheds on 23rd July 1996, to become the frontispiece of the new DERA headquarters Cody Building, now known as the Cody Technology Park. The unveiling ceremony to mark its relocation took place on 26th November 1996 with the Mayor of Rushmoor, Cllr Maurice Banner, undertaking the honours.

1997

During this year the DRA Aero Club celebrated its 75th anniversary, culminating in a small fly-in with the visiting aircraft parked on the western apron. The lineage of this small, but very active, aero club goes back to October 1922 when recreational flying was being considered and the then RAE Light

The sun sets beyond the famous RAE 24ft wind tunnel building, as seen on 23rd September 1997. This was towards the end of operation of this historic landmark building, although restoration of the building continues today. Note the many birds resting on the top structure and aerials. *Falcon*

The Virgin Lightship, an American Blimp Corp A-60+ registered N2017A, is seen here moored to its securing mast on Jersey Brow on 26th November 1996. The Lightship was based on the airfield for a few days and performed many local flights, being probably the first airship to be based and actually fly from the airfield since 1914, although the SBAC shows have seen airships fly overhead on some occasions. The fire station can be seen in the left background, whilst 'A' shed can be seen at centre and the control tower at right of centre. *Falcon*

Hurricane XII 'BE417' (G-HURR and ex-RCAF 5589), in 402 Squadron markings as 'AE-K', heads the line-up on the western apron on 28th September 1997 to celebrate the DRA Aero Club's 75th anniversary. Beyond can be seen the Aero Club aircraft (Cherokee Challenger G-BBKX, Chipmunk 22 G-BDDD and Tiger Moth G-ANNG), together with a few visiting aircraft. The Hurricane was at Farnborough undergoing some minor work, prior to its sale to the Real Aeroplane Company. It is now based at Breighton, albeit now repainted in the marks of 87 Squadron. *Falcon*

Chipmunk 22 G-BDDD is seen here outside the Club hangar during June 2004. This aircraft has served with the RAE/DRA/Farnborough Aero Club since 1979. *Falcon*

Piper PA-28-180 Cherokee Challenger G-BBKX, of the Farnborough Aero Club, was repainted during 2004 and is seen here on the parking area outside their hangar. *Falcon*

Aeroplane Club was formed to design, build and fly light aircraft and gliders.

With the cessation of private flying during World War Two, the Aero Club became dormant until 1950, when it became recognised as a benefit to the scientists and engineers of the RAE for air experience flying. Accordingly it was reformed in 1950, with its first DH.82A Tiger Moth, G-AMCM on strength in 1951, and was granted a licence to operate and use the facilities at Farnborough, which it has continued to do ever since.

Small though it may be, the DRA Aero Club, now known as the Farnborough Aero Club although the registered company name is still the RAE Aero Club, is a particularly active organisation. It currently has some 65 members, of varying ages, who benefit from private and recreational flying from the Farnborough site. The club has two aircraft available: the PA-28-180 Cherokee Challenger G-BBKX and Chipmunk 22 G-BDDD. Indeed Chris Kelleher, one of the club's directors and a check pilot, is three times British Advanced Level Aerobatic Champion and he demonstrated his skills at Farnborough International 2000, flying the club Chipmunk. The Club is fully CAA M3 Maintenance approved and is self-funded by its club members. Its small hangar (X101 building) is on the QinetiQ site and the aircraft are wheeled out to the apron through the security gates.

The fuselage hulk of Buccaneer S.2A XT272 is seen here languishing on the Farnborough dump during September 1996. This was the last airframe to leave the dump, when it was transported to Pendine on 27th February 1997. It later went to Shoeburyness in March 1998 and was removed for disposal and scrapping in November 2003. *Falcon*

Retired on 28th September 1994, Buccaneer S.2C XV344 was placed in storage at Boscombe Down as negotiations were under way to retain the aircraft as a 'gate guard' at the new DERA, now QinetiQ, headquarters complex at Farnborough. After much preparation, the aircraft was road-transported to Farnborough on 26th January 1998 and, after further work that included a respray, was lifted onto its specially prepared display area on 31st March 1998. It is seen here shortly after installation, in immaculate condition. This aircraft is maintained by FAST personnel. *Falcon*

'Nightfox' TIALD-carrying Tornado GR.1A ZG706 is wearing its markings as 'E' of SAOEU (Strike Attack Operational Evaluation Unit). It is seen parked on Victor Way, near the junction with Range Road, in the DERA complex at Farnborough, for the official opening day on 20th May 1998. This aircraft was undergoing trials with DERA, but was operating from the SAOEU at Boscombe Down. It is now in storage, still as a GR.1A, at St Athan. *Falcon*

The very last aircraft to languish on the famous Farnborough dump, graveyard of many an ex-RAE aircraft, was Buccaneer S.2 XT272, which had been withdrawn since 1987. It was transported by road to PEE Pendine on 27th February 1997, thus leaving the area near to Ively Gate, where the TAG Aviation hangar complex is now situated, devoid of dumped aircraft for probably the first time in over fifty years. The fuselage wreck of Hawk T.1 XX344, which had crashed at Bedford on 7th January 1982, was also finally removed from the dump and scrapped.

1998

Just prior to closure of the No 1 RAF Officers Mess there was a special dinner held on 16th October 1998 to commemorate the 90th anniversary of Cody's first flight. This was followed by the final closure dinner on 27th November 1998, when Air Commodore A N Nicholson, Air Officer Farnborough, returned to the Mayor of Rushmoor the sword that had been received in 1988 to mark the granting of the 'Honorary Freedom of the Borough'.

Thus the Royal Air Force No 1 Officers Mess finally closed at the end of December 1998, being finally de-commissioned on 31st March 1999, having been fully functional for at least 83 years, with the Mess memorabilia, artefacts and fittings being auctioned off,

leaving this fine array of buildings and gardens in an uninhabited state.

The new Farnborough DERA Headquarters complex, near Ball Hill, was officially opened by the Secretary of State for Defence the Rt Hon George Robertson MP on 20th May 1998. During the opening ceremony held around the Piazza water feature outside the Cody building, and after the official speeches, a formation of four fast jet research aircraft (Hunter T.7 WV383,

Hunter FGA.9 XE601, a Jaguar T.2 and Tornado F.2A ZD902) from DERA Boscombe Down, flew overhead the proceedings.

A small static aircraft display was also present, comprising the 'NightFox' Tornado GR.1A ZG706 (DERA/SAOEU); Jaguar B XW566 (Avionics and Sensors Dept); Harrier T.4 XW934 (Avionics and Sensors Dept); a Eurofighter replica; One-Eleven ZE432 (ETPS/DERA Boscombe Down); Andover C.1 XS596 (Open Skies, Boscombe Down);

Seen here is the mock-up of the Farnborough F.1 fuselage, in storage at Pyestock during 2004. It has since been destroyed. *Falcon*

Jetstream T.1 XX475 (DERA West Freugh); PBN-2T Islander Astor ZG989/G-DLRA (PBN); SA.330E Puma XW241 (Avionics and Sensors Dept); Gazelle AH.1 XW897 (658 Sqn); Piper PA-28-180 Cherokee Challenger G-BBKX (DERA Aero Club); and DH.82A Tiger Moth G-ANNG (DERA Aero Club). Farnborough Business Aviation also had a couple of the based executive aircraft parked outside of 'N' shed. Many of the DERA scientific laboratories were also open to visitors, to show some of the current projects under research and development.

Besides the official opening, the occasion also celebrated Ninety Years of Flight from this famous airfield. To celebrate this there was a low-key cavalcade flypast of various aircraft types that have seen service with the DERA, or previously with its antecedents. How aviation has developed in that period was perhaps summed up by the arrival, during late afternoon, of a British Airways Concorde (G-BOAE) from Heathrow with 90 schoolchildren on board, landing across the very area where Cody made his epic flight nearly ninety years previously.

The cavalcade flypast commenced with Tiger Moth G-ANNG (DERA Aero Club) running through in stately fashion, followed by Harvard T.2B KF183 (DERA, Boscombe Down); Spitfire HF.IXe MJ730/G-HFIX; Meteor T.7 Mod WL419 (Martin-Baker); Canberra B.2TT WH734 (DERA Llanbedr); Hunter T.7 WV383 (DERA Boscombe Down); Lynx AH.7 (Army Air Corps); Cherokee Challenger G-BBKX (DERA Aero Club); Andover C.1 XS606 (ETPS/DERA Boscombe Down); One-Eleven XX105 (DERA, Boscombe Down); Jaguar GR.1A (DERA, Boscombe Down); Tornado F.2A TIARA ZD902 (DERA, Boscombe Down); and a Harrier GR.7 (DERA, Boscombe Down). Concorde G-BOAE arrived, flown by President-elect of the RAeS, Captain Jack Lowe.

Richard Noble's ThrustSSC was on display in 'D' shed (X1 building) alongside, with a good selection of artefacts, photographs and display boards from the Farnborough Air Sciences Trust, along with the Canberra B(I)6 nose (WT309), displayed on a trolley.

During late November and early December 1998, the 5ft wind tunnel that was housed in the northern part of R52 building was carefully dismantled and moved across the road to R153 building, where it was laid out like a giant jigsaw puzzle before being road transported to Lisbon. Originally built in 1929/30, constructed predominately of wood, this open-section tunnel was initially used as a working model for the mighty 24-foot tunnel, and at the height of its operations was used for various scale aircraft model tests, armament airflow tests and more recently noise measurement tests on propellers, and tests on UAV aerodynamics and propellers.

The tunnel was modified in the 1970s: the fan was re-located to the downstream leg for instance, with splitters being added within the circuit, and with an enclosed working section noise measurements of propellers could be achieved. Speeds of approximately 140mph could be reached; the power source being a 200hp DC electric motor.

However during 1998 it was finally sold to the Instituto Superior Technico (IST), of the Lisbon Technical University, the sale taking over two years to materialise, the 5ft tunnel is to be used for aerodynamic studies by the Aeroacoustic Group at post-graduate level.

1999

Richard Noble of ThrustSSC fame, with a small design team, had been working for the past 18 months in utmost secrecy to design and produce a revolutionary new light business aircraft. This was known simply as the Farnborough F1. It had been designed to set new standards in executive travel, and would be of carbon composite construction. Intended to operate with a single pilot, and seating up to five passengers, the F1 was to be powered by a reliable and mature engine, a Pratt & Whitney Canada PT6A-60A of 850shp designed for a short field performance.

Utilising high-technology computer-optimised design and computational fluid dynamics (CFD), the F1 was designed with an advanced laminar flow, high-lift, low-drag wing and the aircraft was to be built in large sections, the fuselage being finally bonded within an autoclave. Scale model wind-tunnel tests were accomplished at Cranfield and these proved successful. Designed for a low workload by the pilot, the cockpit included integrated graphical multi-functional displays and, perhaps more surprisingly, a side-stick controller.

The design and mock-up build initially started in 'D' shed, where the ThrustSSC was kept. As development of the airfield occurred and the hangars became part of the TAG Aviation site, the Farnborough F1 team moved to X96 building on the DERA site as a temporary measure. A more permanent move occurred in September 1999 when they moved to the old stores building on the Slough Estates site, a hangar originally known as 'B' shed (P71 building), where the autoclave was eventually assembled for full-scale aircraft production. When this building was destined for demolition in 2001, Noble and his team moved to Pyestock (405 building) where work continued.

During 1999 the programme was running to schedule, with initial design and aerodynamic models being tested; detailed design and build of three prototypes was scheduled for 1999-2001; first flight and establishment of the production line projected for 2002; certification was foreseen for 2003; followed by projected first deliveries from the No 1 plant in 2004 and, by 2005, a cloned production line would also have been commenced. Noble's preliminary studies indicated that there could be a requirement for some 13,000 aircraft of this nature, to achieve only a 5% share of the USA and European Business travel market.

With a projected cost of US$ 1.9 million per unit and a required US$ 11 million spend on the initial investment programme by 2003, this was a very ambitious project. Spurred on by the enormous success of the ThrustSSC Mach I Club, and the generous donations, sponsorships and investments that enabled the SSC project to succeed, the Farnborough Airforce Supporters Club was launched to recruit members and investors to support the F1. This saw some 500+ signed up, but was envisaged to build up to 20,000 members.

The TAG Aviation hangar complex and parking apron is seen under construction in this view taken during June 2002. There was a considerable amount of ground work required here, to remove the old taxiways and runway thresholds prior to establishing a new large parking apron, hangar and operations complex. *Falcon*

Consequently, on 14th October 1999, the company's Internet website, www.farnborough-aircraft.com, was launched and the web became a central focus of the project, as the Farnborough F1 was to be built live on the Internet, thus creating better understanding in aircraft design and development, and also enabling the project followers and Farnborough Airforce Supporters to take an active part in this fascinating venture by being able to closely monitor the situation as the aircraft develops. This follows the amazing success of the ThrustSSC Internet site, which as Noble said at the time, has had some 58 million hits!

However Noble and his team required considerable funding and regrettably this was not forthcoming in the way that was required. Slowly his team was dissolved and the Farnborough F1 mock-up, jigs, parts and equipment were put into storage, moved from Pyestock by the end of March 2005 and subsequently destroyed. The shareholders of the original farnborough-aircraft.com voted to wind the company up in February 2003 as a result of the lack of funding but in September 2003, after interest and funding from Epic Aircraft in the USA, the Farnborough Aircraft Corporation Ltd (FACL) was formed and entered into an agreement with Epic to build two aircraft. These would have some 70% commonality, although the Epic LT would be slightly smaller than the F1. Although a design and development agreement was made and the Epic prototype was finished in 2004, FACL says that Epic failed to honour their agreement and a legal battle commenced in 2005. The Farnborough F1C3 was registered in the USA as N352F during September 2005. In November FACL signed a Memorandum of Understanding with the Gulf Aircraft Maintenance Company (GAMCO) to develop the F1 under the guise of the Kestrel JP100, with FACL predicting a first flight in the summer of 2006. Although production of the F1 will not be at Farnborough, there is still a connection to this ambitious project as FACL still have their design office on the QinetiQ site in X92 building.

Interestingly, on 2nd and 17th March 1999, runway 25 was in use for a trial. Airbus A.320 F-WWIF had positioned from Toulouse

to undertake wet runway braking trials as a precursor to the use of the airfield by the A319CJ/A320 types.

2000
Redevelopment of the old 'RAE Factory' site commenced, with Slough Estates having prepared a redevelopment plan to transform the site into a high-tech business park. Consequently many of the old Factory buildings were demolished during this year and others followed in 2001/2002.

2001
Farnborough Airfield underwent a major upgrading programme to conform with Civil Aviation Authority regulations in passing from military to civilian use.

QinetiQ, with its headquarters offices and laboratories at Farnborough, was born out of DERA on 2nd July 2001 and was set up as a Private Public Partnership (PPP), with a workforce of 11,000. A quarter of the old DERA was retained by the UK MoD and renamed as the Defence Science and Technology Laboratory (DSTL) on 2nd July 2001, with some offices at Farnborough, to man-

age various sensitive research programmes. DSTL, an integral part of the UK MoD, is the centre of scientific excellence to the UK Government, with a workforce of around 3,000 personnel. DSTL gives specialist knowledge in defence research and technical services, to the Armed Forces and the UK Government. QinetiQ continued in much the same research and development fields as DERA had previously.

2002
A futuristic new three-bay hangar complex was constructed for TAG Aviation, in the northwestern corner of the airfield, close to Ively Gate, on the area that the Farnborough aircraft dump, weapons compound and aircraft parking 'diamonds' used to be.

'M' shed (W2 building), once the servicing bay for the aircraft department ground equipment and latterly occupied by the DERA Aero Club from 1994 to 2002, was finally demolished, work having commenced during December 2002 and being completed during January 2003. This was one of the final obstacles on the airfield that required removal for the modernisation process.

TAG Aviation Global Express HB-ITG is seen here making a low fly-by across Farnborough airfield on 5th February 2003 to signify the commissioning and opening of the new Farnborough control tower. *Falcon*

The replica Gloster E28/39 Whittle is seen
here placed on the Ively Road roundabout,
outside the main entrance to Farnborough
Airport, commemorating Sir Frank Whittle
and the work undertaken on the aircraft
and engine at Farnborough and Pyestock.
The TAG hangar complex can be seen
beyond, although the terminal has not yet
been built in this view, seen during August
2004. *Falcon*

2003

The various improvements required to the
airfield, equipment and systems having been
completed, the UK Civil Aviation Authority
granted the airfield a licence in January.

5th February saw the official opening of
Farnborough Airport, including commis-
sioning and opening of the new Air Traffic
Control Tower. The Rt Hon John Spellar
MP, Minister of State for Transport, did the
honours and TAG Aviation Global Express
HB-ITG made a low flypast along the run-
way to honour the occasion.

The Watchman Radar Tower on Ball Hill
was demolished on 1st March, with the
assistance of an explosive charge. The concrete structure was cut up over the period of
the next two weeks.

On 21st August the replica Gloster E28/39
Whittle was assembled and installed on the
Ively Road roundabout, outside the TAG
Aviation/QinetiQ entrance, off of Ively Road.
The official opening ceremony occurred on
28th August, which saw a flypast by Martin-
Baker's Meteor T.7½ WA638, a former Farn-
borough resident.

Made from 5 tonnes of polyethylene and
with an envelope volume of 40 million ft³,
QinetiQ 1 was the largest manned helium
balloon ever built. It was due to be launched
during the summer from the QinetiQ tri-
maran vessel RV *Triton*. This was to be an
attempt to ascend to a record-breaking
height of 132,000ft and obtain the world altitude record for a manned balloon. *Zephyr*, a
QinetiQ-built experimental solar-powered
unmanned aircraft, with five electric motor
engines driving propellers at 5,000rpm, a
12m wingspan, and weighing only 14.7kg,
would be attached to *QinetiQ 1*. When at altitude *Zephyr* would be launched, still tethered, to circle the balloon and send back live
images to the control centre. However after
much careful planning the ascent was
thwarted in September 2003 as the balloon
split during inflation on board the vessel and
no further attempts have yet been made.

2004

Further buildings demolished included 'Q'
shed (O15 building) on the airfield; R51 and
R177 in the Factory site; and Q111, on the
Pinehurst site, latterly part of the DSTL.

Farnborough Aircraft Services Engineering Technology (FASET) became part of
TAG Aviation and the new TAG Engineering
complex, re-sited from 'L' shed (Y1 building) to a renovated 'D' shed (X1 building),
was officially opened by Gerald Howarth MP
on 17th September 2004.

Further ex-RAE / DERA / QinetiQ aircraft
were delivered to the Farnborough Air Sciences Trust Museum on 8th June, when
Gnat T.1 XP516 and Jaguar B XW566 were
transported across the airfield from the
QinetiQ site to the FAST headquarters to be
put on external display.

'Q' shed was demolished during
January/February 2004 and this view on
17th February shows the large sliding
doors, having collapsed in a heap as the
structure beyond was torn down. This is
now the site of the new Flight Safety
International simulator building. *Falcon*

BAE Systems operate a shuttle service
between Warton and Farnborough, utilising
their BAe 146 Srs 200 G-TBAE. The aircraft
is seen here on the south apron, ready for
departure back to Warton during August
2003. The new control tower can be seen
beyond. *Falcon*

2005 to 2006

Modernisation Continues

Improvements to the airport facilities are still being implemented, whilst the erection of new buildings and renovation of others on the old 'Factory' site is forging ahead.

2005

The new TAG Aviation terminal was basically completed during December 2005.

Flight Safety International moved into the new 92,000ft² building on the former site of 'Q' shed on 1st April 2005. Six simulators have been installed and are now operational, these being the Citation Bravo, CitationJet2, Gulfstream IV, King Air 200, Beech 1900D, and Saab 340. The first course commenced in June 2005. More are to follow during 2006, including the Dash 8Q-400, Hawker 800 and Hawker 400XP toward a planned total of fifteen simulators.

Demolition of the No 1 RAF Officers Mess (Buildings G37/38/39 and annexes) was completed during January/February 2005, in order to make way for a proposed new hotel complex for the airport. A new road, to link with the Slough Estates Business Park and the entrance at Queens Gate, is also planned for the future.

The upright portable airship shed stanchions were removed from Q65 building as this was demolished during January/February. (R51 building, which housed the upper structure of the portable airship shed, was demolished during November/December 2004 with the structures being carefully removed.) All sections of the portable air-

The former, and classic, No 1 RAF Officers' Mess, built as the No 1 RFC Mess during 1914-1915, was demolished between December 2004 and February 2005. This view shows one of the demolition machines tearing off the roof structure during January 2005. *Falcon*

The former RAE Foundry, R51 building, was constructed by using the top section girders from the portable airship shed that was dismantled in 1915. R51 was a listed building because of the importance of these girders, and a top section is seen here being dismantled from the structure of the building during December 2004. These girders have been reconstructed during 2006 to form a feature depicting the portable airship shed, within the Business Park complex. *Falcon*

ship shed structure were laid out in Q153 building, the former structural testing laboratory, for initial inspection prior to being sent for further inspection, cleaning and re-protection.

During March 2005 the former seaplane tank, Q120 building, was demolished except for some 20ft or so at the eastern end.

2006

The new TAG Aviation terminal building was fully occupied by the end of January 2006 and therefore this led to the former temporary buildings being removed and the apron area extended on the northern extremity for further parking slots for the business aircraft. The terminal building was

SA.330E Puma XW241 is still in use by QinetiQ for Electro-Magnetic Compatibility work with the EMC Business Group, part of the Spectrum Solutions Division of the Defence Technology Sector. It is seen here, still wearing Royal Aircraft Establishment titles, in June 2004. *Falcon*

Still wearing its faded No 20 (R) Squadron markings and coded 'Y', Harrier T.4 XW934 arrived from Wittering on 21st August 1995 for use as a ground experimental vehicle, undertaking Electro-Magnetic Compatibility trials. It is still in use with the EMC Business Group, part of the Spectrum Solutions Division of the Defence Technology Sector. It is seen here within the QinetiQ facility during June 2004. *Falcon*

Some airframes in use as Ground Experimental Vehicles with QinetiQ are still extant, these being Buccaneer S.2C XV344, as the 'gate guard' feature close to A5 building on the QinetiQ site; SA.330E Puma XW241 and Harrier T.4 XW934, both still in use for EMC work with the EMC Business Group during early 2006; Lynx AH.7 (composite airframe XZ646/649) is due to return to Farnborough from Bristol University, where it has been temporarily on loan for various research studies; Lynx HAS.2 XZ166 fuselage, previously used for acoustics research, is currently stored; Wasp HAS.1 XV631 is still in use for vibration studies, mounted on a special rig.

So, with Farnborough having entered its second century of aviation, although it will undoubtedly never reach the heights and achievements that it saw during the first century, nevertheless flying is a way of life here and long may it continue onwards and upwards.

QinetiQ is to be floated on the Stock Exchange in 2006 and the UK Government is to sell a major part of the organisation to the private sector. The shareholders, at the beginning of 2006, were MoD at 56%, US private equity firm The Carlyle Group at 31% and QinetiQ management staff at 13%.

Although no flying is conducted from Farnborough, QinetiQ is still very active in the aviation sector, with much background development and research undertaken in the Farnborough laboratories. Flying continues from Boscombe Down, with Test and Evaluation of aircraft systems and new technology programmes for modifying and upgrading existing aircraft. QinetiQ's Air Systems work includes: Airborne Mission Systems (management of the airborne environment); From Concept to Develop-

officially opened on 2nd May 2006 by HRH The Duke of York.

Re-erection of the old portable airship shed structure commenced in April 2006, and thus adding a unique focal point within the Farnborough Business Park site. Work on the listed wind tunnel buildings still pro-

gresses and their renovation will be complete later in 2006.

Disposal of the former IAM buildings on Danger Hill should also take place during the latter part of 2006. Plans for the National Aviation Archive move ahead and this should meet its establishment goal of 2008.

Lynx AH.7 composite airframe XZ646/649 is seen here in the dynamic testbed in the QinetiQ A9 building during January 2004, undergoing research studies into the reduction of helicopter vibration. *Falcon*

The forward fuselage of Wasp HAS.1 XV631 is still in use by QinetiQ with the Air Division of Air Vehicle Integration Department, investigating human responses to vibration. The Wasp arrived by road from Wroughton on 6th March 1984 and was dismantled by the aircraft apprentices. Since that time it has been used for experiments on the vibration rig that was originally housed in R132 building. It continues to be used in this role, as it has been for the past 20 years, and is seen here outside its A6 QinetiQ laboratory during March 2006 as maintenance was being conducted on the vibration rig. It is marked 'HMS Endurance', but this is a panel from a different helicopter as this example was originally allocated to HMS *Eskimo* Flight as '453' of 829 NAS and was then Portland-based as '617' of 829 NAS. *Falcon*

ment (the Integrated Flight and Propulsion Control System, IFPCS, for the Lockheed Martin F-35 Joint Strike Fighter), this technology helping to reduce pilot workload, increase safety margins and ease of operation; Unmanned Aerial Vehicles, flying for this is undertaken at Aberporth, with the test and evaluation of civil and military UAVs (includes sharing technology with the US for the UAVs, new concepts, beyond-line-of-sight communications, sensors, thermal imaging, dual field of view detectors, and technical data link development); Integrating Avionic Systems (designing systems and software); Rotorcraft Services (manufacture and test of prototype model rotor blades and specialising in performance, systems, acoustics and icing of blades and equipment), and test and evaluation of aircraft and equipment.

Air-to-ground view of the QinetiQ headquarters site, as seen on 8th June 2005. DERA moved to this new site during 1997, with its official opening on 20th May 1998, and became QinetiQ in July 2001. This area is now known as the Cody Technology Park and extends into part of the former NGTE area, with new buildings constructed in the area at right upper centre. The Buccaneer S.2C 'gate guard' can be seen at centre left. *Falcon*

FARNBOROUGH AIR SCIENCES TRUST
The Vision Becomes Reality

A Brief History

With the end of research flying at Farnborough approaching, the Ministry of Defence prepared for the closure of the main Factory Site of the former Royal Aircraft Establishment (RAE). The proud title RAE had already been dropped in 1991, to be replaced by the Defence Research Agency (DRA). This was a new organisation, moving towards privatisation and planning a smart headquarters on the other side of the airfield. The MoD would fund the £90 million new centre on condition that the old Factory Site, the oldest and most historically significant of all the RAE sites, was totally vacated for sale as a prime brownfield site for commercial development, the most valuable of all the MoD disposals currently under way.

By 1993, the ex-RAE departments occupying over 250 buildings on the Factory Site were under strict orders to clear out everything down to the last office chair and decommission all machinery, ready for hand-over to MoD Disposals and Lands. Many people would lose their jobs. Specialist skills and the highest craftsmanship, often handed down through families, would no longer be required. A very special community was being deliberately broken up. In the middle of this unhappy scene, a former RAF pilot (and non-DRA employee) became curious at the noise of heavy machinery in a

huge, shabby concrete building nearby. Putting his head round the door and fully expecting to be ejected from what was clearly a 'secret' facility, he was instead invited in to watch the last test running of the famous 8 x 6ft Transonic wind tunnel before decommissioning.

What he saw was a massive steel machine, built to the highest order of engineering capability in 1942 but about to become history. He had little difficulty persuading a friend specialising in architectural conservation to accompany him on a visitor's pass to look at the Transonic and other wind tunnels on the site. Their guide was the engineer who ran the most visually impressive of them all: the 24-foot wind tunnel with its 30-foot diameter mahogany fan and lofty superstructure famous for its public clock. The visitors realised that a site of immense historical importance was threatened, and they sensed, with some apprehension, that if *they* did not speak for these extraordinary buildings, who would?

Receiving some encouragement from the borough architect of Rushmoor Borough Council (RBC), they decided to write a report on the wind tunnels, both to understand what they had seen and as a tool for gaining support. But the planners were not impressed. Nothing had been submitted about historic buildings to the first public

consultation on the future of the airfield; the main concerns being the continuation of flying and the Special Sites of Scientific Interest (SSSI) at the far end of the airfield. The borough had been re-surveyed by English Heritage in the 1980s, resulting in three Grade II listings on the site (buildings G1, G29 and R51) and therefore it was assumed that other buildings, such as the wind tunnels, were not considered sufficiently important. A provisional list of buildings of some importance did exist, but no effort had been made to do the necessary research. The two 'would-be conservationists' (as they were called by RBC's then chief executive) suspected that the secrecy of the site, by intention or default, had prevented entry by the English Heritage inspectors.

Letters were written to potential supporters in high places. The replies commended the idea of conservation, but were deeply pessimistic about any chance of success. One influential person had directly appealed to MoD for the retention of the existing private RAE/DRA Museum on site if nothing else could be saved, only to be told that due to new flight safety constraints, building G1, which housed the museum, and G29 (the 'Black Sheds') would probably have to be knocked down, together with the majority of Q121, the 24-foot wind tunnel. This was alarming! If true, it would leave R51, the old foundry, as the only listed building on the whole site.

The DRA claimed to have no 'scorched earth' policy; their role was simply to hand over empty buildings. They gave assurances that the museum collection was in good hands with the Science Museum and indeed seemed guardedly supportive of the idea of conserving the best of the RAE legacy. More letters were written in a final attempt to save the museum on site, but to no avail. The curator retired, and the collection was moved intact to a reserve store in London

R52 building was the initial home of FAST and a considerable number of artefacts were collected and put on eventual display. This view shows the main area in this building during October 2001 and includes photographs, wind tunnel models, a test-model rotor system, parts of engines and a suspended XRAE-1 UMA, along with a scale model of an S.E.5a. *Falcon*

Aerial view of G1 building during June 2005, with eight complete airframes and five noses on display. Other than the RAE/DERA/QinetiQ aircraft, these are all privately owned. Not much has changed with the external appearance of this building since it was built in 1910. *Falcon*

for safekeeping, where it remains. However, it did look as if MoD really meant business. When it was rumoured that an application had been filed for R51 to be de-listed, not much hope was left for the Factory Site.

No-one in Whitehall, within the aviation industry or at local level, seemed able or willing to support the case for conserving the buildings. One exception was the Aldershot Member of Parliament. Another was the local Cody Society, and at a meeting at the house of the founder, the two 'would-be conservationists' received welcome encouragement and met a local councillor who soon joined them. In November 1993, they formed a charitable trust, called the Farnborough Air Sciences Trust (FAST). The main aim of the three founders was to protect the historic buildings, but they rapidly took on the dual role of unofficial guardians of a huge quantity of archive material and artefacts being thrown out of the various RAE departments – hiding it in the 24-foot wind tunnel! A supporting Association was formed on which the Trust soon became totally reliant (and has been ever since) for the task of moving, sorting, cataloguing and storing the growing collection. The DRA declared the embryonic FAST to be the 'official' guardians of the material, and ultimately helped them secure a temporary lease with MoD in building R52 for storage, whereupon FAST moved into R52 on 30th April 1996.

Although the archive was now relatively secure, the site itself certainly was not. It emerged that the two superb wooden wind tunnels in R52 (the 5ft and the 4 x 3ft) had been sold to Portugal. The Transonic had been decommissioned and was rusting in spilt brine coolant. Its neighbour, the 11½-foot wind tunnel in R136, would test Benetton Formula 1 cars for a year or two more, but was suffering serious decay of its wartime concrete structure. The 24-foot wind tunnel, also still working, was threatened with having its superstructure removed in the interests of airfield safety. And there were dozens of important buildings that had barely been visited, let alone surveyed. What was to be done?

Seen in this view of 22nd March 2006, is the remainder of the Sea Plane tank building (Q120) in the foreground, which is being retained, overshadowed by the 24ft wind tunnel beyond (Q121 building), which is covered over with protective sheeting whilst restoration of the external structure is being undertaken. *Falcon*

The trustees of FAST decided that the best option was to come up with firm creative proposals for the site, to attract positive publicity, and to try to build a professional rather than confrontational relationship with the many people responsible for the site's disposal. Thus was born the hugely ambitious FAST Plan for regenerating 12 large buildings on 25 acres at the east end of the site into a unique visitor centre and industrial showcase, its focus being the magnificent restored wind tunnels fortuitously grouped at the centre, and to display their efforts, what better opportunity than the Farnborough International Airshow 1994? With the support of SBAC and many others, the stand was built. Many visitors were sceptical, but a few people began to share the FAST vision, including one who is now FAST's chairman.

The trustees realised, however, that no real funding or progress could be made until the key buildings were listed. Hamp-

shire County Council supported this initiative. English Heritage were given a tour of the site by FAST in the autumn of 1994, but nothing tangible happened until a letter written by FAST directly to the Minister of Defence Procurement caught the attention of the chairman of English Heritage in early 1995. A long round of consultations ensued. Progress was nearly halted in 1996 when an influential, but erroneous, objection was made that the listings would jeopardise the future of flying at Farnborough. FAST in fact fully supported flying and had carried out a study showing how, if absolutely necessary, the 24-foot wind tunnel could be reduced in height without destroying its function.

Hopes and Dreams

The listings were not officially confirmed until December 1996. The Minister agreed with the retention of the three existing listed buildings at Grade II: G1, the original Bal-

The FAST Museum model room in G1 building contains a collection entitled 'British Experimental Aircraft', loaned to FAST by Peter Lockhart, who made the models. This is an excellent collection, some of which are seen here, and a large number of these aircraft either served, or were displayed, at Farnborough. The model collection also includes 'The History of Airpower', some of which can be seen beyond. This was a vast collection made by R L Ward, D Cook and A W Hall during the 1960s/1970s, the remainder of these being donated to FAST and some exhibited in the model room. *Falcon*

loon School and Trenchard's HQ; G29, the historic Black Sheds; and R51, the Forge and Foundry (built from the upper components of a portable airship shed of 1912). To these were added Q65, the Fabric Shop (built, as proved by FAST, from the lower components of the airship shed) at Grade II; Q121, the 24-foot wind tunnel, at Grade II* (although recommended by English Heritage at Grade I); and R133, the Transonic wind tunnel complex, at Grade II (although recommended at Grade II*). Although hugely relieved by these listings, FAST were disappointed that their recommendations for Q120, the seaplane-testing tank; R52, the original wind tunnel building at Farnborough; and Q27, the balloon gondola shop and earliest workshop on the site, had not been accepted. It was also worrying that only one building had II* listing, as it meant that the fate of all the others could be settled at local level without reference back to English Heritage. Clearly much work still had to be done, but at least while the buildings remained standing, there was hope.

The FAST Plan was developed into a Millennium Lottery bid in 1995, which not unexpectedly did not pass beyond the second stage. Without ownership of the site or backing from MoD, it had little chance. There was also a setback at the local level when the Plan was seen as serious competition for the Aldershot Challenge project. A hopeful lead for FAST to combine with a proposed National Science Centre at Farnborough, came to nothing when the Centre moved to Leicester. And RBC, in their Issues Papers about the future of the airfield, still did not recognise the full historical significance and potential of the Factory Site. Fortunately, the chief executive of RBC did

Seen here in the FAST Museum display area is a compressor assembly, sectioned by former RAE apprentices, of the Metropolitan-Vickers F2/4 Beryl engine. The development of this engine was in collaboration with RAE and it powered the SRA.1 jet flying boat. Beyond, at left, can be seen a Power Jets W2/700 engine, which powered the Gloster B28/39 Whittle. Suspended from the ceiling is an XRAE-1 UMA, No 35. *Falcon*

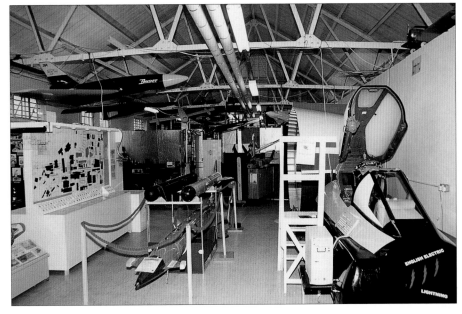

Seen during early 2006, in the exhibition hall at the FAST Museum, is a combat flight simulator at right, depicting a Lightning cockpit; a Comet fuselage section behind; a Beech Stiletto supersonic target drone on the floor, at centre, with Ruston tow targets above; and a privately owned TTL Banshee, No 384, suspended from the ceiling; with other artefacts beyond. *Falcon*

appreciate the idea of the industrial showcase, and encouraged FAST to make a new study in early 1996 of a joint FAST/FNTC (Farnborough New Technology Centre) project on the Factory Site. This brought enthusiastic response from a sector of DRA (by now DERA) for 'combining the best of the old with the best of the new' – exactly what FAST was trying to promote. The constructive support of SAVE Britain's Heritage became increasingly important as the vision began to turn into a possibility.

RBC encouraged FAST to apply for KONVER funding: a European fund they had themselves used aimed at the regeneration of redundant MoD land. The starting point for FAST successfully raising over £60,000 for a proper feasibility study into their proposals, however, was obtaining the Architectural Heritage Fund's maximum grant of £7,500, applicable only to listed buildings. Private sponsors soon followed. Arup Economics were appointed as lead consultants, and architects and a museum specialist engaged. The study looked at three possible schemes ranging from a minimal visitor centre utilising only the Transonic and re-erected Airship Shed, through to the 'grand plan' with a permanent showcase for the aviation industry as the dominant element. The study was very well received, and certainly vindicated the original FAST vision.

FAST were recommended to develop a version of the intermediate scheme into a

Concept Development Plan, which they did just in time for the formal disposal of the site by MoD when key boundaries were established. MoD were inviting tenders for the sale of the Factory Site by January 1997, but announced that the selection of a developer would have to follow a public inquiry into the Local Plan. Until then, planning permission for either the proposed business park or the new civil airport could not be properly granted.

The FAST trustees knew they had made real progress when the MoD sales particulars recommended the shortlisted developers to talk to FAST. All were duly escorted around the wind tunnels. Two of the developers became quite excited about FAST's plan, and opened confidential discussions, but they came to nothing. One developer said very little except to refer to the Transonic as old scrap iron. By the time the public inquiry

took place in July 1998, it was clear that Slough Estates plc were the preferred developer. They gave a broad account of their proposals, which, apart from saying there would be 'provision of a heritage centre', said nothing about the historic buildings. This was not encouraging. FAST had had time to brief a planning consultant and, now with several years of research behind them, were able to make a strong written case – but were not called on to speak. The inquiry was a foretaste of what was to come: the FAST vision would clearly have to be defended at every twist and turn of the planning process. At one crucial point, as the developer's plans were being debated by RBC, FAST intervened to stop the so-called heritage site being shrunk to just a few acres. The Factory Site was finally sold to Slough Estates in 2000, for a sum very much less than MoD had originally hoped.

FAST initiated an approach to congratulate the new owners, only to be told that plans for the historic buildings included possible de-listing, and to be given a weighty report concluding that a major visitor centre on the site would not work. Any idea that the wind tunnels might continue to work could be forgotten: they were totally obsolete. A ray of hope was that the Airship Shed frame might be re-erected as a symbol of the lost RAE, but this would be as an uncovered skeleton on a public open space away from the other historic buildings. All the rest of the buildings would start to go – soon. And for good measure, the lease would be ter-

Hunter T.7 WV383, 'Hecate', served with RAE/DRA/DERA for 27 years. It came back to Farnborough by road from Boscombe Down on 13th April 2000 and was moved to the FAST Museum at G1 building on 14th June 2002. It is seen here on display during May 2004. *Falcon*

Gnat T.1 XP516, still wearing its former 4 FTS markings, is seen here outside of the FAST Museum at G1 building on 21st August 2004. Beyond can be seen a Lightning F.6 nose (XS932), Canberra B(I)6 nose (WT309), Buccaneer S.2B nose (XV165), MiG-21PF (503) and Hunter F.51 (E-402). The Gnat arrived from QinetiQ on 8th June 2004, where it had previously been in use as a ground experimental vehicle for many years. *Falcon*

minated on R52 and all FAST's huge collection would have to be removed or scrapped. These were dark days for FAST.

In 2000 the demolition teams moved in and most of the buildings came tumbling down. Some were of historic interest, such as P67 (the old F1E production/repair shed), P68 (the Apprentice Training shop) and Q1 (the RAE administration building). It was agonising to watch a huge mechanical claw tug at the roof trusses of Q27 and shake them to the ground in a minute or two each. The power station (Q6), which had supplied steam heat and electric power to the whole site originally from coal brought in by train, went next and thus cut off power to the wind tunnels. This was far, far worse than the Luftwaffe's work in 1940.

FAST's main task was to look beyond the destruction and to try to constructively criticise the developer's emerging plans. After all, any regeneration plan would depend first and foremost on financial benefits flowing from the commercial success of the whole business park. Encouragingly, Slough Estates appointed first class consultants to record and research the listed buildings and prepare a Conservation Plan. RBC worked hard to ensure that other buildings would also be retained, in particular Q134 (the former Weapons building) and R52, which by good fortune still contained one of the wind tunnels (the 4 x 3ft) left behind by Portugal. The design of the airfield runway had been modified and the revised safety constraints allowed G29, G1 and Q121 to remain unscathed, though subject to strict planning controls. Slough Estates were persuaded to refurbish the majority of G1 and make it available to FAST for their headquarters and a small museum. The great move to G1 and a reserve store in the old fire station at Pyestock began in November 2002. Leaving R52 was difficult emotionally

for the FAST team: it was the last foothold on the original RAE site, now reduced to an island of shabby, vulnerable buildings in the middle of acres of landscaped roads and empty plots.

For the trustees of FAST, the most unexpected good news came in early 2002 when the Department of Culture, Media and Sport announced that as a result of new work by English Heritage, the listings were revised – upwards! R52 was listed Grade II for the first time; G1 was be upgraded to II*; and, beyond wildest hopes, both the main wind tunnels Q121 and R133 were upgraded to Grade I, thus bringing them into the same fold as Britain's most important historic buildings. Only a few buildings of similar, relatively youthful, age have reached this status, for example the Jodrell Bank radio telescope and Coventry Cathedral. Now, at last, the 24-foot and Transonic wind tunnels had been recognised for their true importance, and should be safe from the acetylene torch.

The government's endorsement of the historic importance of the wind tunnels coincided with Slough Estates speaking publicly about the prolonged downturn internationally in the business park field. The whole attitude began to shift to seeing the group of retained historic buildings not as a burden but as a creative asset, unique to Farnborough, alongside a thriving commercial airfield. At around the same time, SAVE came forward with a plan for housing and live/work units on part of the Factory Site, further enriching the mix of new uses. FAST and SAVE pressed for a review of the wind tunnels to be used for their original purpose, since research suggested there was a market for testing work. This led to commissions for FAST and their consultants to assess the machinery, and resulted in Slough Estates making provision for 11,000-volt power supplies to be laid on to three of the wind tunnels. Meanwhile, FAST helped with mothballing heavy and sensitive equipment ready for the building restoration, and raised funds for its own independent study

Having arrived at the FAST Museum from QinetiQ on 8th June, Jaguar B XW566 is seen here in its display position a few days later. Beyond can be seen the remnants of the old RAE main gate and 'A' shed in the distance. *Falcon*

Seen from the Trenchard Room within the FAST Museum (G1 building) in June 2005 are Hunter T.7 WV383 'Hecate' and Gnat T.1 XP516, whilst the two noses in the foreground are Lightning F.6 XS932 and Canberra B(I)6 WT309; the latter being owned by the author and a number of FAST members. *Falcon*

into the re-use of R52. A mixed educational/commercial use is proposed around the 4 x 3ft wind tunnel, supported by QinetiQ, with an arts or similar use of the rest of the building. But without doubt the most striking and rewarding sight for the public at present (early 2006) is the massive, sheeted scaffolding which completely encloses the listed buildings, and the activity everywhere, as Slough Estates begin in earnest their £20 million restoration project.

Onwards and Upwards

With artefacts now prepared for display in G1, the FAST Museum flourished after its formal opening in October 2003. The main archive was consolidated in G1 and alternative buildings and containers found for the reserve. It was a great morale-boost when, in April 2005, G1 hosted a ceremony conducted by the American Institute of Aeronautics and Astronautics, the Royal Aeronautical Society and FAST to designate Farnborough as an Historic Aerospace Site of world importance.

There are now three ex-RAE Farnborough aircraft on the Museum site: Hunter T.7 WV383, Jaguar B XW566 and Gnat T1 XP516, plus the nose of Canberra B(I)6 WT309 and an X-RAE1 unmanned aircraft (UMA), within the museum; and from Llanbedr a Jindivik Mk.104A, ZJ496, that is currently held in storage. There are other aircraft on display that are privately owned, but more ex-RAE/DERA/QinetiQ aircraft will follow. The grounds at G1 are now cared for, the building has received a new coat of paint, the rooms have been renovated, the area is secure within its own compound, and the museum is open at weekends with free admission. Last summer an air raid shelter of brick construction, and in remarkable condition, was unearthed from beneath a thicket of brambles and undergrowth. This is also to be fully refurbished.

Many of the artefacts from R52 building had been stored within 405 building in the old NGTE site at Pyestock. However, this too was being redeveloped, and FAST were instructed by the site developers to remove them by the end of March 2005. This was no mean feat, as a small dedicated band of helpers managed to move all of the items from the store building and a piece of land was leased from QinetiQ, within a secure site, with the artefacts in containers, until such time as they can go on permanent display.

Vision to Reality

What of the future? As the 'new look' Factory Site begins to take shape, it is very encouraging that Slough Estates and everyone involved welcomes the prospect of the wind tunnels contributing positively to the cultural, commercial and social mix of uses at the Park. At the moment, it seems likely the archive library of the Royal Aeronautical Society will find a home on the site, and

FAST will do all it can to ensure that the best possible mix of uses is found for each building as well as for the Historic Area as a whole.

Much has happened with FAST over the past 13 years, and much more is to follow. There are over 600 members supporting FAST's goal to preserve the rich RAE heritage for all to see in years to come, and to tell the story of what went on behind the scenes at RAE, whose lineage now goes back over 100 years. Plans are under way, and talks have opened between FAST and Slough Estates, TAG Aviation, BAE Systems, QinetiQ, SBAC, Hampshire County Council, Rushmoor Borough Council and the Farnborough Aerospace Consortium to stage a memorable centennial event in October 2008 to commemorate the first powered flight in the UK.

FAST should be congratulated on their achievement and the small band of key people that caught the vision those 13 years ago can now see this becoming a reality.

If any reader wishes to know more about FAST, then visit www.airsciences.org.uk.

One of the Llanbedr's last operational Jindiviks, Mk.104A ZJ496/A92-901, was acquired from QinetiQ immediately after the type had been withdrawn from service. Having spent a short time in storage at Boscombe Down, it arrived at Farnborough on 10th May 2005 and it is seen here, prior to removal from its transportation vehicle, within the FAST storage area. *Falcon*

RAE FLIGHTS

There were great variations over the years in the size and composition of the RAE aircraft fleet, likewise in the purpose and scope of the research being conducted. This series of snapshots of activities at the beginning of each decade of Farnborough's long history effectively shows the colossal contribution made to the development of British aviation over the years.

1920

It had only been twelve years since powered flight was achieved in the UK but so much had happened during this time and Farnborough had been at the forefront of it all. The Royal Aircraft Factory, with their design and build of so many prototypes and production aircraft, and their ongoing testing and development of same, had by now given way to the formation of the Royal Aircraft Establishment in 1918, as well as the Royal Air Force – evolved from the Royal Flying Corps that was earlier formed at Farnborough in 1912. Of course the World War One period saw, as a necessity, considerable growth in the aircraft industry along with the trials and tribulations that befell many of the early types as well as the sad loss of some of the test pilots of the era. At the end of hostilities many service aircraft were disposed of and future projects cancelled, but there were still many different types being produced, or in prototype form, and accordingly the RAE was still actively engaged in aircraft, engines, systems and equipment testing of the types of the day. Perhaps not as busy as during the World War One years, there had by now been a slump in industry that was also affecting the RAE, nevertheless a varied assortment of biplanes were still undergoing research, development and testing, as this listing shows:

A Flight

Bristol F.2B Fighter	B1201	Aspect ratio
DH.9A	E746	Engine and heating, ceiling tests and test of Meteorological Instruments
Bristol F.2B Fighter	A7260	Aspect ratio
Bristol F.2B Fighter	D7860	Aspect ratio
Martinsyde Buzzard IA	H6541	Petrol system, and propeller tests.
Handley Page O/400	C9773	Silencer tests, 'tank-dropping' experiments (probably a cover for bombing experiments) and slipstream tests
Sopwith Cuckoo I	N6920	Rudder tests
Avro 504K	H2402	Steel wings, accelerometer tests and test of clear-view windscreen
B.E.2c	4550	Tail load
B.E.2e	2029	Stalling tests, speed test and thrust meters, elevator angle indicator
S.E.5b	A8947	Flow through radiator and forces on joy stick
S.E.5a	D7019	Auxiliary ground indicators
S.E.5a	C1091	Variable pitch propeller tests
DH.10	E6042	Thermo-static indicator and rudder forces and trim
S.E.5a	D203	Control recorder and spinning
DH.9A	E746	RAE sextant, smoke puff tests, gyro rudder tests
Bristol F.2B Fighter	H6055	Investigation of nose heaviness
Avro 504K	E3269	All-steel propeller test
S.E.5a	C1148	Variable pitch propeller test
Sopwith Pup	B7565	Tests of gauze windscreen

B Flight

Sopwith Salamander	F6660	Engine tests, camouflage tests
B.E.2e	E4120	RAF.19 Section wings
Sopwith Camel	D1965	Longitudinal stability
Sopwith Salamander	F6608	Undercarriage tests and camouflage tests
S.E.5a	B600	Propeller tests, undercarriage tests.
Bristol F.2B Fighter	F4675	Incidence meter and angle of attack, and dropping gliders
Sopwith Camel	F6456	Inverted flying and camouflage tests
S.E.5a	C1063	Engine and undercarriage tests
Sopwith Dolphin	C8194	Speed tests
S.E.5a	E5923	Engine tests
Sopwith Camel	F6456	Balloon experiments, Sutton safety belt tests, and inverted flying.
Bristol F.2B Fighter	H1560	Rotary deviation, and test of Baud brakes
Vickers Vimy	F3151	Turning incidence tendency
Sopwith Camel	D1965	Modified version, handling tests
Avro 504K	E3269	Steel wings
S.E.5a	E5923	Spinning and oscillation tests
DH.9	D5755	Engine power at height
Bristol F.2B Fighter	F4329	Propeller test
S.E.5a	B600	Propeller test, gravity flow indicator
Bristol F.2B Fighter	F4329	Reduced dihedral
S.E.5a	D7020	Reduced dihedral
Sopwith Dolphin	C8194	Speed course factor
Bristol F.2B Fighter	F4329	Aerial target
Bristol F.2B Fighter	F4675	Aerial target
R.E.9	A3542	Variable gear aileron and flap control
DH.9	H9140	Handley Page section wing
Bristol F.2B Fighter	F1561	Endurance and petrol joints test

C Flight

Bulldog	X4	Altitude test and cylinder temperatures
DH.9	D5748	Experimental water system
S.E.5a	D314	Engine and petrol tests, turn indicator test
Bristol F.2B Fighter	H1559	Engine test
Sopwith Snipe	E8137	Parachute test
Nieuport Nighthawk	J2405	Engine test, endurance test
BAT Bantam	F1656	Engine test, petrol cock test, balloon tests, and experimental rudder and elevators
Bristol F.2B Fighter	C4655	Douglas starter test
Avro 504K	F8857	Turn indicator test
Sopwith Dragon	J3809	Engine test, climb and slow running test, throttling down tests, climb on oxygen test and magneto test.
DH.9	D5748	Experimental water system test
DH.9A	F1630	Supercharger test
Nieuport Nighthawk	J2414 & J2415	Endurance tests
Avro 504K	D9068	Engine climb tests
Nieuport Nighthawk	J2413	Test on 21TD engine
Bristol F.2B Fighter	F1561	Vacuum test on air intake, all-metal petrol joints and Persian spirit (petrol) tests
Sopwith Dragon	F7003	(Converted from Snipe) Endurance tests
Avro 504K	E3269	Steel wing test
Austin Greyhound	H4318	Endurance, cylinder head, and slipstream tests
BAT Bantam	F1653	Looping test and engine tests
DH.9A	E755	Petrol flows and oil temperature tests
Bristol F.2B Fighter	F4776	Radiator, petrol joint and flow experiments
Bristol F.2B Fighter	A7260	Inclinometer test
DH.9	C1393	Radiator tests
DH.9A	E917	Undercarriage tests
Bristol F.2B Fighter	F6235	Aerial target
Bristol F.2B Fighter	C4654	Silencer test

U Flight

Bristol F1	B3990	Engine test
S.E.5a	D7018	Engine test, rudder forces and balloon barrage test
Vickers Vimy	H651	Engine tests, Reid apparatus, propeller tests, cable lock tests and camouflage research.
DH.9A	J597	Parachute test
Sopwith Salamander	J5941	Camouflage test
S.E.5a	D7020	Oscillation test
DH.9A	E775	Propeller tip speeds
DH.9A	E746	Smoke bombs
S.E.5a	D7022	Aerial target

1930

The years between the wars saw perhaps a reduced activity at Farnborough but nonetheless there were still plenty of aircraft of many different types, undergoing various trials all with a purpose to develop and perfect ongoing and new systems. In these days there was still a reasonably steep learning curve, in what was a biplane-dominated scene, but, with the technological advancements of the time and new aircraft, there was still much to do. Many of the new aircraft being built at the time came to RAE for handling experiments – some being successful, others not. Autogiros had now appeared on the scene and early handling tests were being undertaken. Examples of aircraft that were undergoing various trials and research during this year included:

Aerodynamics Flight

Gloster Gorcock	J7502	Airscrew test
Bristol F.2B Fighter	A7260	Control at low speed, vibrograph & spinning tests.
Bristol F.2B Fighter IIIA	J8264	Forces in control wires, floating ailerons, force recorders, towed target.
AW Siskin IIIA	J8391	Automatic slots and aileron controls.
Cierva C.8 Rotaplane	J8930	Handling and investigation.
Bristol F.2B Fighter	F6235	Stability and flight path recorders.
Fairey Fox	J8427	Radiator drag
Bristol F.2B Fighter	F4360	34 section wings.
Hawker Hornbill	J7782	Directional stability
Bristol F.2B Fighter	F4886	Control beyond the stall.
Boulton & Paul Partridge (F9/26)	J8459	Stability
Bristol F.2B Fighter	F4587	Interceptor on spinning and lateral control.
HP.33 Hinaidi	J9035	Servo rudder
Bristol F.2B Fighter	C4776	Spinning
Cierva C.19 Autogiro Mk.II	G-AALA	Handling experiments
Westland Wapiti IIA	J9498	Towed target
Bristol Bulldog II	J9580	Townend ring
AW Siskin IIIA	J9881	Interceptor slots
Armstrong Whitworth Atlas	J9477	Elevator angles to fin at large incidence.
Boulton & Paul Sidestrand I	J7938	Silencers and pitot head
Westland Pterodactyl Mk.IA	J9251	Controllability and display
Westland Pterodactyl Mk.IA	J8067	Controllability and display
Hawker Harrier	J8325	Airscrew test
Cierva C.19 Autogiro Mk.III	K1696	
	(G-AAYO)	Investigation and handling
Parnall Parasol	K1229	Flight path recorder
Parnall Parasol	K1228	Test of wing section
Bristol F.2B Fighter	F4360	Pressure plotting on slats
HP.36 Hinaidi	K1064	Wing deflection

Engine Research Flight

DH.9A	E867	Super-chargers
Bristol F.2B Fighter Mk.II	J6721	Evaporative cooling
Gloster Gamecock I	J8091	Development
AW Siskin IIIA	J7000	Development, boost control & carburation development
Westland Wapiti (Prototype)	J8495	Development
Fairey IIIF Mk.I	S1207	Petrol flow meter
Fairey IIIF Mk.IV	J9154	Development
Bristol Bloodhound	J7237	Development and silencers
Hawker Harrier	J8325	Cylinder temperature
DH.56 Hyena	J7781	Auto AC development
Avro 504N	J8726	Carburettor tests
DH.9A	E755	Super-charger tests

Avro Avian IIIA	J9182	Engine tests
Avro Antelope	J9183	High-altitude tests
Avro 504N	E9261	Non-swirl air intake

Wireless and Electrical Flight

Fokker F.VIIA/3m	J7986	Directive beacon, WT transmission & reception
Bristol F.2B Fighter	H1450	Engine tests, voltage regulator, W/T reception and night flying lights
DH.9A	E746	General W/T
Armstrong Whitworth Atlas I (2nd prototype)	J8777	General W/T, sound experiments, direction finding, illumination, camera sight and photographic apparatus
Fairey IIIF Mk.III	S1317	General W/T, RX35 receiver, transmission tests, catapult launching
Bristol F.2B Fighter	F4967	Generator test, navigation lamps, formation lights, & heated clothing
Armstrong Whitworth Starling I	J8027	General W/T
Armstrong Whitworth Siskin IIIA	J8428	Electrical interferences
Bristol Bulldog	K1084	General W/T tests and heated clothing
Vickers Venture	J7278	General W/T, direction finding and sound experiments
Hawker Hornet (no serial allocated)		General W/T tests (drop-in for tests)
Armstrong Whitworth Atlas	J9516	General W/T tests, and, lighting interference
Vickers Valentia	K1314	W/T installation and automatic controls

Instrument & Photographic Flight

Bristol F.2B Fighter Mk.IIIA	J8251	Film tests, night photography, neon landing lights, camera gun, accelerometer, presentation of revolution indicator, turn indicator and pitch incidence, pitch & azimuth indicator and oxygen tests.
DH.9A	J6968	Anemometer, thermometer, oil-pressure gauges, triple recorder, compass, oxygen regulator and endurance for steel wings.
DH.60X Moth	J9115	Fog landing, pitch and azimuth indicators, pneumatic revolution indicator.
Vickers Venture	J7277	Gyro azimuth, drift sight, compass and turn indicator, vacuum altimeter and aerial refuelling.
DH.9	D2825	Pitch and azimuth indicator and aerial refuelling
HP.24 Hyderabad	J7748	Automatic controls
Blackburn Dart	N9694	Smokescreen
DH.9A	J6957	Mail drop, oxygen and tyre tests
Vickers Virginia VIII	J7275	Automatic controls, artificial horizon
DH.9A	H3588	Lens test, RAM and aerial refuelling
Avro 504N	E9261	Fog landing
Bristol F.2B Fighter Mk.II	J6689	RAM
Nieuport Nighthawk	J2405	General tests, camera gun and turn indicator
Kite Balloon		Fog landing
Vickers Virginia VII	J7432	Experimental night photography
HP.36 Hinaidi II	J9478	Automatic controls
Avro Antelope	J9183	General tests
Fairey IIIF Mk.IIIB	S1490	Target
Vickers Virginia IX	J8236	Night landings

Equipment Flight

AW Siskin IIIA	J8391	General test
Blackburn Dart	N9551	General test
Avro 504N	E9261	Fog landing
Vickers Virginia X	J8238	General test
Blackburn Ripon II	S1270 &	
	S1271	Periscope tests
Bristol Bulldog II	J9580	General test
HP.24 Hyderabad	J8815	Heated clothing
Hawker Horsley III	J8606	Smoke screen
Vickers Virginia IX	J8326	Catapult launch, generator, windmill tests, and aerial refuelling
Westland Pterodactyl Mk.1A	J8067	Display practice for Hendon
Cierva C.19 Autogiro Mk.IIA	G-AAUA	Display practice for Hendon
HP.39 Gugnunc	G-AACN	Display practice for Hendon
Hawker Hart I	K1102	Display practice for Hendon
Hawker Hornet (serial not allocated)		Launched from catapult (drop-in for tests)

Bristol 109	R2/G-EBZK	General test, endurance tests
Hawker Hart (Prototype)	J9052	Launched from catapult
Fairey Fleetwing	N235	General tests
Fairey IIIF Mk.III	S1351	Deck landing arresting gear
Fairey Fox	J8427	Tow target
Hawker Horsley I	J7999	Height finding trial
Fairey IIIF Mk.III	S1317	Launched from catapult, reception and Galitti beam tests
Fairey IIIF Mk.IV	J9056	Test of Goodyear wheels
Bristol F.2B Fighter	F4697	Tests on a No 4 Sqn aircraft

1940

World War Two was a busy time for the various RAE Flights with many trials and much research being undertaken for the war effort. Also by this time, 1940, the first captured German aircraft had arrived at RAE and assessments and handling trials were well in hand. The RAE was also bombed during this year and this action led to the formation of a Defence Flight. It is worth mentioning here that the Pilots assigned to Experimental Flying Department were allocated to the respective Flights for periods of short postings before moving on in the services. They were expected to perform numerous duties and fly many different types of aircraft as the requirement arose. Indeed on some occasions a pilot could fly four or five different aircraft types in a day's work. Some Flights, such as W&E (later Radio) and Armament Flight, had a bigger contingent of pilots and aircrew as they were involved with some larger aircraft types and were involved in some overseas detachments. Examples of aircraft that were undergoing various trials and research during 1940 included:

Aerodynamics Flight

GAL Cygnet I	G-AEMA	Tricycle undercarriage research
Curtiss 75	No 188	(French Air Force) Research handling
Messerschmitt Bf 108B-1	G-AFRN	Research handling
Fairey Battle I	N2183	Drag research
Waco ZVN	P6330	Tricycle undercarriage research
Bristol Blenheim	L6595	Take-off research
Airspeed Oxford I	N6327	Handling
HP.52 Hampden I	P1183	Stalling
Miles M.3 Falcon	R4071	Fairey wing, spoilers and retractable aileron
Gloster F5/34	K8089	Research handling
Westland Lysander II	N1217	Parachute exit
Miles M.3B Falcon Six	L9705	High-speed wing section
Hawker Hurricane I	L1717	Stalling
Brewster Buffalo	AS430	Research handling
Douglas Boston I	AE461	Research handling
Fairey P4/34 (2nd prototype)	K7555	Research handling and Fairey flap
BA Swallow II	G-AFGC	Swallow tests
Airspeed Oxford II	N6410	Stalling tests
Airspeed Courier	K4047	Spoiler controls
Spitfire I	K9796	Stall warning
Bristol Beaufort I	L4478	Research handling
Hafner Gyroplane II	G-ADMV	Handling tests
Blackburn Botha I	L6185	Diving tests
Flamingo	G-AFUE	Handling tests
Gotha Go 145B		(became BV207) Research handling
Martin Maryland I	AR717	Research handling
HP.50 Heyford III	K6874	Glider tests towing Glider 10/40 (later known as the Hotspur I); and the Swallow (including some flights with two Swallows in tow)
BA Swallow IIs	G-AEHL, G-AELH, G-AFGD & G-AFGE	Glider tests
Avro 504N	G-ADEV	Glider tests towing a Swallow
Hillson Helvellyn	G-AFKT	Stalling
Short Stirling	M4	Undercarriage drag tests
Me Bf 110C-5	AX772	Research handling
Fairey P4/34	K7555	Flap research
Hawker Hurricane II	Z2385	Tailwheel shimmy
Avro Manchester (Prototype)	L7246	Handling
Me Bf 109E-3	AE479	Research handling
Percival Proctor IA	P6000	Tail buffeting
Bristol Blenheim I	L1290	Turret drag
Heinkel He 111H-1	AW177	Research handling
Boulton Paul Defiant I	L7024	Medical research
Douglas Boston I	AX926	Research handling

Engine Research Flight

Hawker Henley	K7554	Merlin investigation
Fairey Battle I	K9371	Merlin investigation
Vickers Wellington I	L4212	Cabin heating
Spitfire I	K9944	Merlin investigation
Blackburn Skua	L2872	Fuel pumps
Bristol Blenheim IV	N6241	High boost
Westland Lysander II	P9120	Carburettor investigation
Gloster Gladiator II	N5575	Aircraft recognition
HP.52 Hampden I	P1183	Oil cooling
Fairey Battle I	K9240	Dagger development
Vickers Wellington I	L4298	Exhaust flames
Gloster Gauntlet (Prototype)	J9125	Flexible engine mounting
Spitfire I	N3053	Ice guard
Gloster Gladiator (Prototype)	K5200	Snow guard
Hawker Hurricane I	L1780	Glycol tests

Wireless & Electrical Flight

Bristol Blenheim I	L1186	DF loop
Harvard I	N7013	Radio transmitter handling
Handley Page HP.43/51	J9833	Radio transmitter handling
DH.89 Dominie	R2487	Direction-finding loop
Avro Anson I	N4872	Radio transmitter handling
Fairey Seal	K3576	RX78 receiver
Hawker Hurricane I	L1788	TR1133 transmitter
Bristol 142	K7557	Terrain clearance
Westland Whirlwind (Prototype)	L6844	Radio installation
DH.82B Queen Bee	N1818	RX73 transmitter
Vickers Wellington IC	P9237	Pye transmitter
Avro Anson I	N5154	Blind approach
Avro Anson I	N4874	Cathode Ray tests
Lockheed 12A	R8987	Blind approach

Instrument & Air Defence Flight

Fairey Battle I	K7587	Tow target and food containers
Airspeed Oxford I	N4560	Sextant navigation
Bristol Blenheim I	L1474	Food containers
Vickers Wellesley	K7744	Automatics and camouflage
Blackburn Skua I	L3006	Towed target
Blackburn Roc I	L3060	Handling
DH.60T Tiger Moth I	K2567	Marker flares
Bristol Blenheim I	L1494	Camera heating
Gloster Gladiator (Prototype)	K5200	Undercarriage reaction
Fairey Battle I	K9258	Medical research
HP.52 Hampden I	P1169	Stabilised bomb sight
Bristol Blenheim IV	N3522	Stabilised bomb sight
Fairey Swordfish	P4031	Dive bomb sight
Bristol Blenheim IV	R3601	Armaments
Douglas Havoc I	BJ496	Towed flares
Airspeed Queen Wasp	K8887	Aerial target
Hawker Henley (2nd prototype)	K7554	Electrical tests

Havoc 1 BJ496, Turbinlite-equipped, came to RAE from Odiham on 21st November 1940 for use with IAD Flight on towed flares, armament and fuel jettison trials, before passing to E Flight for camouflage trials. It departed for Aldergrove on 23rd April 1941 and continued in RAF service until it crashed during searchlight practice near Colerne on 23rd October 1941. *FAST collection*

Scientific Technical Training Flight

In January 1950 this Flight was dissolved with the aircraft passing to other RAE Flights. During its final month, it operated the following on training duties:

Harvard IIB	KF427 & FX365
Miles Magister I	L8326 & P2388
Airspeed Oxford I	LX198

RAE Defence Flight

After the German bombing raid on 16th August 1940 defensive action was also established at RAE, using aircraft from the various flights, loosely known as the RAE Defence Flight. These included:

Spitfire I K9796 (A Flight)
Hawker Hurricane I L1788 (WE Flight)
Hawker Hurricane I L1780 (ER Flight)
Gloster Gladiator (Prototype) K5200 (ER Flight)
Spitfire I N3053 (ER Flight)
Gloster Gladiator I K7946 (ER Flight)
Hawker Hurricane I P3864 (A & WE Flight)
Hawker Hurricane I V7541 (ER Flight)

It should be noted that all the aircraft listed still went about their normal research duties but were pressed into service for defence duties as and when required and were armed accordingly.

Equipment Flight

All aircraft were used for general duties although some were also used for specific work by other Flights.

Lockheed Hudson I	N7205 & N3717
Hawker Hart I	K2434
Vickers Wellington I	L4212, L4227
Vickers Wellington IA	N2865
Avro Anson I	N5065
Bristol Blenheim I	L6783
DH.60T Tiger Moth	K2567
HP.52 Hampden I	L4035 & P1169
Miles Magister I	L5965 & L8168
Bristol Blenheim IV	L9389
DH.89M Dragon Rapide (Prototype)	K4772
Waco ZVN	P6330
HP.54 Harrow I	K6943
Gloster Gladiator (Prototype) & Mk.I	K5200 & K7946
Fairey Fulmar I	N1854
AW Whitley V	N1467
Hawker Henley I	L3243
Fairey Battle I	L5496
Hawker Hurricane I	L1696
Spitfire I	N3053
DH.87B Hornet Moth	W5747 & W5778

Medical Research Flight

The aircraft listed below were all engaged in various medical research duties although most were also in use with other Flights and were loaned to MR Flight when required.

Fairey Battle I	K9289
Spitfire I	L1095 and P9448
Gloster Gladiator (Prototype)	K5200
Hawker Hurricane I	P3089 and V7541
Boulton Paul Defiant I	L7024

1950

By now the RAE was back to normal again after the war years. Although there were many wartime types still undergoing research and trials, with only one German aircraft left on strength, it was the jets that were now arriving in force, both production types and experimental types, and the great leap forward in technology had commenced. Examples of aircraft that were undergoing various trials and research during this year, included:

Aerodynamics Flight

Avro Lancaster B.1	PP755	Hydraulic controls
DH Vampire F.1	TG299	Shock waves
DH Vampire F.3	VF343	Wing flow
DH Vampire F.1	TG314	Variable lift control
DH Vampire F.3	VT804 & VT795	Handling, catapult and flexible deck landings
Spitfire PR.XIX	PM501	Handling and gust research

The first DH.108, TG283, arrived on 5th October 1948 to undertake trials with Aero Flight. It is seen here on the airfield during November 1949, some six months before it crashed at Hartley Wintney on 1st May 1950. *FAST collection*

Blackburn YA.7 (GR17/45)	WB781	Handling
Grumman Avenger III	KE436 & KE446	Arresting and catapulting
DH.108 (Prototype)	TG283	Approach and landing
Fieseler Fi 156C Storch	VP546	Handling and glider towing
Sikorsky S-51	VW209	Stability and control
Avro Lancaster B.1	RF131	Power controls
Supermarine Seafire F.XVII	SX342	Handling
Bristol Brigand I	RH748	Handling, catapult and arresting
Fairey Firefly AS.5	VT393	RATOG
Supermarine Attacker (3rd Prot)	TS416	Handling and arresting
DH.108 (3rd Prototype)	VW120	High-speed tests
Short Sturgeon TT.1	TS475	RATOG
DH Vampire F.1	TG299	Handling and windflow
Gloster Meteor F.4	EE476	Snaking
Gloster Meteor F.8	VZ438	Snaking
Supermarine 510	VV106	Maximum lift trials and assessment of suitability for deck landings, carried out at Farnborough and on board HMS *Illustrious*.
Gloster GA2 (E1/44) Prototype	TX145	Handling at high Mach number
Hawker P.1052 (E38/46) Prototype	VX272	Handling
DH Vampire FB.5	VV215	Damped rudder
Gloster Meteor T.7	VW412	Trailing static and auto-dive brakes
Westland Wyvern TF.2 (Prototype)	VP109	Vibrograph tests
Bell 47B-3	G-AKFB	Auto-stabiliser
Boulton Paul Balliol T.2	VR591	Longitudinal stability
Bristol 171 Mk.1 (2nd Prot Sycamore)	VL963	Stability and control
Westland Wyvern TF.2 (3rd Prot)	VP120	Arresting and safety barriers
AW.52 (E9/44 2nd Prototype)	TS368	Boundary layer experiments
Hawker Sea Fury FB.11	VW588	RATOG
Hawker P.1040 (2nd Prot Sea Hawk)	VP413	Boundary layer experiments

Instrument Flight

Avro Lancaster B.VII	NX636	Mk.IX Auto-pilot and development of cameras
Avro Lincoln B.II	SS716	Radar navigation
Avro Anson Mk.X	NK832	General navigation
Gloster Meteor F.4	EE530	Handling and air temperature bulbs
Vickers Viking 1A	VX238	Mk.IX auto-pilot
Avro Lincoln B.2	SX974	Night photography
Gloster Meteor T.7	WA638	General navigation work
DH Mosquito PR.34	RG257	Sperry auto-pilot

Wireless & Electrical Flight

Avro Lincoln B.1	RA637	Radio receiver trials and aerial icing
Fairey Firefly AS.5	WB251	X569
Vickers Viking C.1A	VL227	Radio compass
Vickers Viking 1A	VW215	Radio altimeter
Avro Lancaster B.1	PA343	Suppressed aerials and radio compass
Hawker Sea Fury FB.11	VR920	Communications
DH Sea Hornet F.20	VR851	Altimeters and radio compass
Avro York C.1	MW272	Handling and long-range navigation aids
DH Sea Hornet F.20	TT199	Improved communications
Avro Lancaster B.III	RE171	X569
Westland Welkin NF.2	WE997	Handling and UHF
Gloster GA2 (2nd Prototype E1/44)	TX148	Handling, suppressed aerials and communications

Gloster Meteor T.7	VW478	Handling
Vickers Valetta C.1	VW197	ILS
Avro Athena T.2	VR568	Communications
DH Mosquito PR.34	VL623	Generator brush wear
Vickers Varsity T.1 (Prototype)	VX828	Communications
Avro Shackleton (3rd Prototype)	VW135	Communications
EE Canberra (2nd Prototype B3/45)	VN813	Aerial tests

Structures & Mechanical Engineering Flight

Avro Tudor 2	VZ366	Cabin conditioning and noise levels
Fairey Firefly AS.5	VT427	Vibrograph
Short Sturgeon TT.2 (2nd Prototype)	VR371	Type H winch
Gloster Meteor F.3	EE246	Seat ejection
HP Halifax VII	PP350	Supply dropping
DH Vampire FB.5	VV463	Anti-G
Bristol Brigand B.1	VS854	Nitrogen tank
Boeing Fortress III	HB778	Heaters
Gloster Meteor F.4	VT259	Fuel boiling
Avro Anson C.19	TX210	Crash-proof tanks
Bristol Beaufighter TT.10	RD688	Handling and sleeve targets
DH Mosquito T.III	TV974	Instrument presentation and comparison vibrations

Armament Flight

Avro Lancaster B.III	PB752	Electric fusing
Avro Lancaster B.III	PB284	Supply dropping
DH Vampire FB.5	VZ117	Development of rockets
Avro Lancaster B.1	PD119	Towed targets
DH Mosquito FB.VI	RF892	Rocket projectile trials
DH Mosquito B.35	TK621	Handling, 'Blue Boar' and missile guidance
DH Mosquito NF.38	VT655	AI Mk.IX radar
Avro Lancaster B.III	ED842	Bomb development
Gloster Meteor T.7	VW441	Photo dive trials
Avro Lancaster B.VII	RT690	Flare installation and missile guidance
DH Vampire FB.5	VV218	Multi-rocket launcher

Transport Flight

All aircraft used for various transport and communications duties.

DH Dominie I	X7396, NR721 and NR728
Harvard IIB	FX216 and FX365
DH Devon C.1	VP959
Airspeed Oxford I	LX198
Douglas Dakota IV	KJ836
Avro Athena T.2 (Prototype)	VW890

1960

By now, forty-two years since RAE was established, only a few piston-engined aircraft were amongst the Farnborough fleet. However, with the ever-growing number of jet types and helicopters, the Flights were still operating a varied selection of aircraft: something that RAE had become renowned for over the years. Examples of aircraft that were undergoing various trials and research during this year included:

Armament Flight

EE Canberra B.2	WJ994	Guided weapons trials and guided weapon recovery system
EE Canberra B.2	WD947	General weapons and bombing trials
EE Canberra B(I)6	WT308 & WT309	General weapons and bombing trials
EE Canberra B.2	WH912	Weapons fuse system
Supermarine Scimitar F.1	XD229	Armament development trials, including cluster bombs
Avro Lincoln B.2	SX930	Bomb trials
Avro Lincoln B.2	WD129	Bomb trials
Avro Shackleton MR.2	WG557	Trials and development of fusing systems for nuclear weapons
DH Sea Vixen FAW.1	XJ494	2,000 lb weapons trials
Hawker Hunter F.6	WW592	Rocket firing and air-to-air ballistic trials
Vickers Valiant B.1	WP201	Shared with IAP Department for general research and development of loading armaments, flutter, vibration and equipment development. (V flight)
Avro Vulcan B.1	XA890	Development of ballistic armaments including 'Red Beard' and 'Yellow Sun' and fuse trials. (V flight)

HP Victor B.1	XA922	Armament clearance trials for nuclear weapons (V flight)
Vickers Valiant B(PR)1	WZ383	Ballistic bombing trials (V flight)
Avro Vulcan B.1	XA892	Development and clearance trials of nuclear weapons (V flight)
Avro Vulcan (2nd Prototype)	VX777	Ground vibration trials of installation equipment.

Structures & Mechanical Engineering Flight

EE Canberra B.6	XH568	Air sampling trials
HP Hastings C.1	TG506	Parachutes test and development
Avro Lincoln B.2	RF533	Parachute testing and windscreen development
EE Canberra B.2	WH657	Parachute stability system, using dummies dropped from bomb bay.
Gloster Meteor F.8	VZ438	Test of parachute system, opening at speed
Avro Ashton Mk.2	WB491	Noise tests (also used for engine development by NGTE)
Blackburn Beverley C.1	XB259	Supply parachute dropping trials
Gloster Javelin FAW.7	XH753	(replaced by XH754 11.60) Development of windscreen rain clearance system
Bristol Sycamore 3	WA576	Structural design and airworthiness criteria for helicopters.

Radio Flight

Vickers Varsity T.1	WL679	Radio trials
HP Hastings C.1	TG619	Receivers, jammers and warning receiver trials
EE Canberra PR.3	WH776	Tacan and 'window' trials
Auster AOP.9	XN412	Brief radio trials, in connection with 'Green Salad'
DH Comet 2E	XN453	Trials in respect of navigation aids, 'window', 'Yellow Barley', 'Orange Harvest' and repeater jamming development
Vickers Varsity T.1	WL674	Data transmission system and TACAN
HP Hastings C.1	WD480	Sonobuoy development
Westland Whirlwind HAR.1	XA864	Location and identification of submarines, using magnetic detection.
Gloster Meteor T.7	WA714	This aircraft was generally used by all flights for continuation training purposes.
EE Canberra (2nd Prototype B5/47)	VX169	Radio wave propagation for UHF and VHF high-altitude research.

Instrument and Photographic Flight
(Later became Instruments and Electrical Engineering, IEE Flight)

Westland Whirlwind HAR.5	XJ445	Development of all-weather instrumentation system for helicopters and auto-approach (blind flying) system.
EE Canberra PR.3	WE146	FX89 and FX96 Camera trials
Gloster Meteor T.7½	WL375	Development of integrated instrument system which included an early airborne Head-Up-Display.
Gloster Meteor F.8/FR.9 nose	VZ473	Assessment of standby equipment.
Gloster Javelin FAW.1	XA622	To check use of OR.946 equipment and presentation in high-speed flight.
Avro 707C	WZ744	Electrical signalling system and evaluation of manoeuvre demand system, known as the Electrical Signalled Manoeuvre Demand System

Transport Flight

Devon C.1s		VP959, VP975, VP980, XG496 and XM223. Various transport and communications duties

1970

The number of aircraft based at Farnborough had diminished during the past decade but nevertheless trials and research work were ongoing on a variety of aircraft types and systems. A few piston types were still operational, and by now more rotary types had arrived. Emphasis by now had begun to shift towards more sophisticated weapons, navigation and communications equipment and accordingly some of the Farnborough aircraft were fitted with varied installations and were multi-tasked to fulfil various requirements of the time. Examples of aircraft that were undergoing various trials and research during 1970, included:

Weapons Flight

EE Canberra B(I)6	WT308 & WT309	Various armament trials
Avro Shackleton MR.3	WR972	Various armament trials, para-drops, towing and drop testing of parachutes.
Avro Shackleton T.4	VP293	Low-level flying under closed circuit TV control and research into TV as an aid to navigation and application to the Martel weapon.
Blackburn Buccaneer S.1	XK525	Weapon development
Blackburn Buccaneer S.1	XK530	Armament development trials
Blackburn Buccaneer S.1	XN923	Armament development trials and research studies into parameters affecting target acquisition visually and by use of TV; long-term studies matching visual presentation of ground objects with TV presentation
Blackburn Buccaneer S.2	XN975	Weapon development trials
EE Canberra B.2/8	WJ643	General weapon aiming and navigation attack research and laser range-finding system for Jaguar
Westland Wessex HAS.1	XM330	Development of armament for helicopters under OR.358 and investigation of target acquisition and recognition.

Avionics Flight/IEE Flight

Westland Whirlwind HAR.5	XJ445	Instrument Landing System approach and guidance trials, radio and navigation trials, aerials for helicopters, and research into a portable instrument approach system for VTOL aircraft and helicopters
Westland Wessex HU.5	XS241	Various trials with onboard avionics and sensors
Westland Wessex HU.5	XS517	On loan for a short-term trial
Hawker Hunter T.7A	XL614 & T.7 XL597	Continuation training, instrument ratings and flying practice
Westland Scout AH.1	XP166	Development of Head-Up Display for helicopters and experiments on a helicopter flight director system, a stability augmentation system, and a 'Rebecca' ranging installation
Hawker Hunter T.12	XE531	Integrated flight control system trials and head-up instrument display research
Gloster Meteor T.7	XF274	This aircraft was used by RAE Experimental Flying Department for general continuation training and instrument rating duties.

Radio Flight

HP Hastings C.1	WD480	Long-range development of sonobuoys, aerial measurements, instrument landing system approaches and satellite communication system research
HP Hastings C.1	WJ327	Radio Laboratory and used for a variety of radio and communications trials
DH Comet 2E	XN453	Infra-red countermeasures, navigational studies and satellite communications research
HS.748 Srs 107	XW750	Instrument Landing System trials
Auster AOP.9	XP277	Development of low frequency tactical navigation support equipment and other navigation system experiments

Structures & Mechanical Engineering Flight

EE Canberra B.6	WH952	Research and development on avionics and parachutes
EE Canberra T.4	WH844	Continuation training and instrument rating
Blackburn Beverley C.1	XB259	Various parachute drops, soft ground trials for multi-wheeled aircraft and aquaplaning trials
EE Lightning T.4	XM967	Loaned to BAC for a period as chase aircraft for Jaguar trials at Warton. Development of load and temperature measurement techniques, boundary layer (fitted with wing tufts), and noise studies
Supermarine Scimitar F.1	XD228	Arrived for structural tests as a Ground Experimental Vehicle.

Transport Flight

DH Devon C.1s	VP959, VP975, XG496 & XM223	Various transport and communications duties.

Aircraft Apprentice Training Department

DH Vampire T.11	WZ475	ex ETPS
Gloster Meteor T.7	WL405	ex Weapons Department

1980

Consolidation had now taken a step further and, with a dwindling number of aircraft, more multi-tasking was required. However some important research work was still ongoing, mainly with new systems or enhanced equipment from previous trials, which led to some of the onboard equipment that is in service today on RAF front-line aircraft. Basically the aircraft were now loosely allocated to 'Flights', depending upon which hangar they were based in, but due to multi-tasking they could be shared by different departments rather than being allocated to just one specific end-user. By now only seven piston aircraft were in the fleet. Examples of aircraft that were undergoing various trials and research during this year included:

A Flight

Westland Wessex Mk.5 (Hybrid)	XL728	Radio trials, dunking trials and torpedo drops.
Westland Wessex HAS.1	XM330	Continuation training, instrument flying and trials support
Westland Sea King HAS.1 (DB)	XV371	Helmet-mounted binocular image intensifiers.
Westland Wessex HU.5	XS241	MIRTH trials
Hawker Hunter T.7	WV383	Low-light TV, FLIR and Head-up-Display
Hawker Hunter T.12	XE531	IEE Department. Integrated flight control system, fly-by-wire trials and head-up instrument display research
Hawker Hunter T.7	XF321	Continuation training and Instrument rating

B Flight

BAC 1-11 Srs 402AP	XX919	Sonobuoy and radio and avionics trials
DH Comet 4	XV814	Radio and Navigation trials, infra-red trials, satellite communications research
HS Andover C.1	XS607	Towed decoy trials
HS Andover C.1	XS646	Electro-optic sensors

C Flight

Vickers Varsity T.1	WL679	Weapons Department. High resolution FLIR
Vickers Varsity T.1	WL635	Flight testing of FLIR turret
EE Canberra B.2/8 (Mod)	WJ643	Flight Systems Department. Weapons aiming, Laser Range-finding and Target acquisition System (nav-attack system), and FLIR
EE Canberra B(I)6	WT308	Weapons Department. Torpedoes and other weapons

Buccaneer S.2C XV344 is seen here, about to land on runway 25 at Farnborough on 20th September 1982. Having previously seen service with the Fleet Air Arm, the Buccaneer arrived on 12th September 1978 and continued to operate with Flight Systems Department until its withdrawal from use at Boscombe Down during September 1994. It is now preserved at the QinetiQ headquarters at Farnborough. *FAST collection*

EE Canberra B(I)6	WT309	Weapons Department. Torpedoes and other weapons
HS Buccaneer S.2B	XV350	Deployed to the USA for Skyshadow trials
EE Canberra T.4	WH844	Continuation training and instrument rating
HS Buccaneer S.2C	XV344	Low-level FLIR navigation and weapon aiming techniques
HS Buccaneer S.2Bs XW986, XW987, XW988		Weapons Department. All three aircraft were built for RAE and were engaged on weapons development trials including BL755 Cluster bombs and JP233 airfield denial bomblets

Transport Flight

Douglas Dakota C.3	ZA947	Various transport and communications duties
DH Devon C.2s VP959, VP975, XG496 & XM223		Various transport and communications duties

Aircraft Apprentice Training Department

Gloster Meteor T.7	WL405	ex Weapons Department
EE Canberra B.2	WJ728	ex RAF No 100 Sqn
Hunting-Percival Provost T.1	XF844	ex Structures Department
Westland Scout AH.1	XP166	ex IEE Department
Folland Gnat T.1	XP532	ex RAF No 4 FTS

1990

By now more aircraft had either departed or been withdrawn from the RAE Air Fleet Department and, with even more multi-aircraft tasking being undertaken, further reduction was unavoidable. In April 1991 the Royal Aerospace Establishment name was replaced by the Defence Research Agency and, by now, it was becoming inevitable that research flying was to cease at Farnborough. Indeed this became a reality on 25th March 1994, when research flying officially finished at Farnborough, with the relocation of the remaining aircraft to Boscombe Down.

Due to the multi-tasking of most of the remaining RAE aircraft at this time, it is considered that the easiest way to differentiate the Air Fleet, is to split them into their respective hangar locations, although these were always loosely referred to as 'Squadrons'.

'A' Shed (Northern Squadron)

PA-31 Chieftains	ZF520, ZF521, ZF522	Used by the Transport Flight for general communication duties.
Dakota C.3	ZA947	Under repair, following undercarriage collapse 8.9.89. To Coventry on 6.8.90.
Powerchute Raider Mk.1 & Mk.2	ZG879 & ZG927	Research by Flight Systems, MM Department, into general handling including taxi, take-off, climb, circuits, landing and performance data measurement
Westland Sea King HAS.1 (DB)	XV371	Millimetric wave and Infra-Red Test Head (MIRTH) trials
Westland Sea King Mk.4X	ZB507	Radar, navigation and communications equipment trials
Westland Puma HC.1	ZA941	Research with a port side-mounted sensor turret and TRIGAT anti-tank weapons system
Westland Gazelle HT.2	Various	General communications and support duties
Westland Lynx AH.5	ZD285	Modified with steerable FLIR ball sensor in nose. This sensor was slaved to pilot's helmet-mounted display, known as a Visually Coupled System, to provide thermally enhanced images on screens attached to the helmet at eyelevel. A GEC Sunfish side-mounted sensor was also undergoing research

'C' Shed (Southern Squadron)

SEPECAT Jaguar T.2	ZB615	Head-Up Display, plus Night Vision Goggles compatibility and continuation training.
SEPECAT Jaguar T.2	XX833	'ATLANTIC' pod system. This was an improved GEC-Marconi version of the SR(1010) FLIR System, to assess the system for future Harrier GR.7 application, on behalf of the Central Trials & Tactical Development Organisation
SEPECAT Jaguar T.2	XX835	JOBTAC (Jaguar Off-Boresight Target Acquisition) system

Hawker Hunter T.7	WV383	FLIR and PENETRATE pod trials. Named 'HECATE'.
DH Comet Mk.4	XV814	Satellite communications, radar and navigation research.
BAC 1-11 Srs 402AP	XX919	Radio HF/VHF communication research and Sonobuoy trials
HS.801 Nimrod Prototype	XV147	Ex-Comet 4C airframe. Non-flying airframe, used for ground trials and subsequently broken up.

'L' Shed (Western Squadron)

HS Buccaneer S.2C	XV344	Night Vision Goggles, FLIR sensor development, target identification and weapon aiming techniques, and Thermal Imaging Airborne Laser Designator (TIALD) pod research. Named *Nightbird*
HS Buccaneer S.2B	XW986	Inertial Navigation System trials. In conjunction with the USN Air Warfare Centre off-set targeting research with navigation data transferred to the weapon prior to launch.
HS Andover C.1	XS607	Sonobuoy research
HS Andover C.1	XS646	FLIR, electro-optic sensors and Vinten camera pod
Vickers Varsity T.1	WL679	FLIR and ATRS – Airborne Transponder Ranging System trials
Panavia Tornado F.2A	ZD902	Installation of experimental equipment to become TIARA – Tornado Integrated Avionic Research Aircraft

'Q' Shed Aircraft Apprentice Training Department

Hawker Hunter F.6	XE587	ex A&AEE Boscombe Down, arrived 16.3.82
Westland Scout AH.1	XP166	ex IEE Department
EE Canberra T.4	WJ865	ex A&AEE Boscombe Down, arrived 6.1.82
Hunting-Percival Provost T.1	XF844	ex Structures Department
Westland Wessex HU.5	XS482	ex A&AEE Boscombe Down, arrived 20.3.86
EE Canberra PR.7	WH774	(Fuselage) ex-RAE Bedford, arrived 4.1.84
MS.880B Rallye Club	G-BIOR	Under rebuild utilising components from G-AZGJ

Airframes retained as Ground Experimental Vehicles in various laboratories

Westland Lynx AH.1	XX907	Helicopter vibration reduction, active control of structural response, and noise reduction and path identification techniques with Structures Department from 1.2.82 (to Westland's 14.3.03; now on Yeovil dump)
Westland Lynx HAS.2 (DB)	XX910	Arrived 3.3.78. Helicopter vibration reduction, active control of structural response with Structures Department. (to Helicopter Museum 5.1.00)
Westland Lynx HAS.2 (DB)	XZ166	Arrived 18.2.81. Fitted with large speakers in the cabin, the helicopter fuselage is used for research into acoustics and vibration by the Human Engineering Noise and Vibration Laboratory (currently stored)
Folland Gnat T.1	XP516	(8580M) Arrived 12.2.79 for development of test techniques for validation of airframe vibration and flutter, with Structures Department. (to the FAST Museum 8.6.04)
Hawker Hunter F.4	WV276	(7847M) ex-No 1 STT RAF Halton, arriving December 1990. Electro-magnetic compatibility and protection research, with Avionics & Sensors Department. (to Duxford on 14.1.97)
SEPECAT Jaguar B	XW566	Electro-magnetic compatibility and protection research, with Avionics & Sensors Department. (to the FAST Museum 8.6.04)
Sud SA.330E Puma	XW241	Arrived 9.2.90. Electro-magnetic compatibility and protection research from 6.85, with Avionics & Sensors Department.
Westland Wasp HAS.1	XV631	Arrived 6.3.84. Research into acoustics and vibration, within the Human Engineering Noise & Vibration Laboratory of the Man-Machine Integration (MMI) Department.